CLARENDON LAW SERIES

Edited by

PAUL CRAIG

CLARENDON LAW SERIES

THE CONFLICT OF LAWS

THIRD EDITION

By

ADRIAN BRIGGS

St Edmund Hall,
University of Oxford

OXFORD
UNIVERSITY PRESS

OXFORD
UNIVERSITY PRESS

Great Clarendon Street, Oxford OX2 6DP
United Kingdom

Oxford University Press is a department of the University of Oxford.
It furthers the University's objective of excellence in research, scholarship,
and education by publishing worldwide. Oxford is a registered trade mark of
Oxford University Press in the UK and in certain other countries

© A. Briggs 2013

The moral rights of the author have been asserted

First Edition published in 2002
Second Edition published in 2008
Third Edition published in 2013
Reprinted 2014

Published in the United States of America by Oxford University Press
198 Madison Avenue, New York, NY 10016, United States of America

British Library Cataloguing in Publication Data
Data available

Library of Congress Cataloging in Publication Data
Data available

ISBN 978-0-19-967928-7

PREFACE TO THE THIRD EDITION

The second edition of this book was the last chance to portray this wonderful subject as a common law discipline coming to terms with its new European components. It is now necessary to describe a European legal structure of private international law, if one with a residuum of common law content. If there is a fourth edition, the only certainty is that this residuum will have shrivelled as the project to produce a common European code of private international law moves further in the direction it has set for itself. The core of any course on private international law—civil jurisdiction and judgments, and the entire law of obligations in civil and commercial matters—now exists within a framework devised overseas and legislated in Brussels; the law of ancillary procedure is being quietly but insistently gathered up as well, piece by little piece. If the harmonization of the private international law of property and persons (natural and artificial) has been more uneven, it has all still served to change both the superstructure and infrastructure of the subject, so that the road ahead looks very different from what one can see in the rear-view mirror. The techniques used to make sense of this new European material may reflect concerns which the common law did not have, and may lack some of the instincts which the common law has, but a common lawyer is still happily placed to measure and test it. For whatever one may feel about the new Regulations, which are functional and unelaborated where the common law was elegant but encumbered by history, one takes what one is given and applies the techniques of private international law to it. How could that not be fun?

Yet private international law has not become European law, any more than Europe has become the world. It follows that the relationship between the rules devised for facts and matters which are in every dimension within the domain of the European Union and its law, on the one hand, and those which are not so, remains the challenge it has always been. To be sure, there was much to think about when the project to reform the Brussels I

Regulation got underway. Though the Heidelberg Report promised much, it was not received with the gratitude it deserved. Several tetchy years later the only reforms upon which agreement could be found, and which will take effect on 10 January 2015, really only tinker with the Regulation, *salva rerum substantia*, as we say in Europe. There will be almost as much which will have to be sorted out by debate and litigation as there was before. From the perspective of those who make a modest living from professing it, the subject is still in good health.

This edition paints a picture of the law as the writer saw it at the end of 2012. Insofar as it tries to ask questions which were convenient or inconvenient to ask it is bounded not by date, but only the page count and the writer's imagination, each of which has its limitations. I thank, happily and wholeheartedly, all those with whom I have had need or opportunity to discuss private international law over the years. It is a rare privilege, and it was mine. I valued it at the time; I treasure it now.

Ancient wisdom has it that he who learns but does not think will be bewildered, but that he who thinks but does not learn is in peril. As was said last time, all errors of doctrine and of judgment are mine alone, but if they stimulate the reader to think, they will not have lived in vain. It is therefore hoped that the rest of this book—this little book about a big, big subject—will help the reader avoid peril.

Oxford, New Year's Day, 2013.

CONTENTS

DECISIONS OF NATIONAL COURTS

DECISIONS OF EUROPEAN COURTS

UNITED KINGDOM LEGISLATION

EU LEGISLATION

INTERNATIONAL AGREEMENTS
AND CONVENTIONS

I

INTRODUCTION

A. THE NATURE OF THE SUBJECT

The title of this book suggests that it is concerned with the conflict of laws, but this should not be taken too seriously, for our subject has little to do with conflict, legal or otherwise. Once some very important preliminaries have been dealt with, in the chapters which follow, our fields of inquiry will be three in number. We will first examine the rules which determine whether an English court has jurisdiction to hear a claim where one or more of the parties, or some other aspect of the story, may be foreign to England or to English law: the conflict of jurisdictions.[1] Second, we will examine the effect of a foreign judgment in the English legal order: the conflict of judgments.[2] And third and finally, we will consider the rules and principles which tell an English court hearing a case with a foreign element whether to apply English law or a foreign law or a combination of laws to resolve the dispute: the conflict of laws.[3] But before we do, there is more to be said about the nature of this subject and the aim of this book.

1. THE SUBJECT AND THE WAY IT CHANGES

The common lawyer's label for this entire collection of material was 'the conflict of laws'. This is curious. In the third category just mentioned there may well be a conflict between the answers which would be given by the various potentially applicable systems of law, and a choice between them requiring to be made, but there is more to the subject than that. The traditional title plays down the significance of the law of jurisdiction and judgments. Some prefer to think of our subject as 'private international law', for it is concerned almost entirely with private law in cases and matters having

---

[1] See Ch 2 below.
[2] See Ch 3 below.
[3] See Chs 4–9 below.

international elements or points of contact. The only danger is that this title may suggest a relationship with public international law, which describes or regulates relations between states, and that would be misleading. For very little public international law infiltrates the subject. For example, when dealing with the confiscation or nationalization of private property by states, there may well be rules of public international law which specify whether the property of a foreign citizen may be seized, whether compensation should be paid, and so forth. But private international law has little concern with this: as long as the property was within the territory of the seizing state, title acquired by seizure will usually be effective in private international law, whatever public international law may say about the steps taken to acquire it. Nor is there a private international law of crime, an archetypal matter of public law: the international aspect of criminal law is dealt with by specific local legislation, or by extradition.

The nomenclature of 'conflict of laws' made sense when the subject confined its attention to the question of choice of law: whether a claim for damages for breach of contract was governed by English or French law; whether an alleged tort was governed by English or German law; whether the succession to an estate was governed by English or Spanish law; whether the validity of a marriage or effect of a divorce was governed by English or Italian law, and so on: such questions dominated the subject in the period of its calm and classical development, from the 19th to the middle of the 20th centuries. All this changed, in England at least, when the House of Lords opened a door which allowed, or even encouraged, much closer attention to whether English courts had and would exercise jurisdiction in a given case. At a stroke the law reports were filled with cases fighting the issue of jurisdiction, at the expense of trials which paid attention to choice of law. And though judges occasionally rail at being called upon to decide such questions, even aspersing the parties for having the audacity to 'litigate about where to litigate', they might do well to keep their breath to cool their porridge. Not only is the question where a trial takes place often of critical importance to its outcome, but also parties who have skirmished on the question of jurisdiction may well decide to settle, with considerable saving of resources.

This new concentration on the law of jurisdiction in England (and in that part of the common law world which takes its lead from English law) coincided with developments in Europe. The original Treaty of Rome, establishing the European Economic Community, called upon Contracting States to bring forward legislation to secure the free movement of judgments across the Community. The Contracting States implemented the instruction they had given themselves by enacting a scheme to lay down uniform rules of jurisdiction, it being expected that such foundations would be strong enough to ensure that full faith and credit be given to judgments from the courts of any contracting state. And so it proved. As the Community expanded, and then became a Union, this Convention, which then became a Regulation, on jurisdiction and judgments in civil and commercial matters, was updated and improved; and as it expanded its scope, the common law shrank back.

Not for nothing are the French said to observe that *ce n'est que le premier pas qui coûte*. The organs of the European Union looked at the new law on jurisdiction and judgments and saw that it was good. In no time at all they deduced that if the law on civil jurisdiction and the enforcement of judgments could be directed towards uniformity, so could the rest of private international law. The result was an increasing number of legislative instruments aimed at bringing uniformity to choice of law rules as applied in courts all across Europe. These now cover the whole of the law of obligations, large parts of family law, parts of the law of property, including succession to property, cross-border insolvency and corporate activity, and a host of smaller and more specialist topics. Originally this was said to be necessary to bring about the completion of the internal market, but this justification is now less commonly heard. The harmonization of private international law across Europe is an end in itself, and England is well on the way to arriving at it. The question of whether it is a Good or a Bad Thing does not need to be answered, so it will not be addressed.

What does need to be addressed, however, is how to describe this hybrid corpus of private international law. For it would be a serious error to approach this European legislation in the same way as one might if it had been legislation made at Westminster. It is a mistake, because this legislation is not designed to amend the common law rules of private international law; it is not designed to fit within the framework evolved by the common law. Just as an imperial spanner will not work with a metric bolt, the underlying techniques of the common law will not provide a basis for the proper understanding of this new European material. European legislation is made with the open and important aim of putting in place common, pan-European, rules for the matters which it governs. This requires that it be given, wherever possible, a common interpretation, and be applied to the same effect and in the same circumstances, across the Member States. It would be self-defeating to produce a single legislative text but which was subject to 20-odd different interpretations or modes of application. Where the European Union has legislated rules for choice of law, therefore, there is a threshold question whose importance is not always noticed: does the statutory rule apply within the framework of, or independently of, the common law structure for choice of law? For example, do the statutory rules for choice of law in contract and tort apply only to issues which the common law rules of characterization regard as issues of contract or tort, or does it apply despite, and without regard to, them? The answer is the latter. The European choice of law rules for contracts apply to whatever the European instrument defines as a contractual issue, and without regard to whether the common law rules for choice of law would have regarded the issue as a contractual one. If this is right, as it must be, the common law principles of characterization, which form the point of departure for the application of the common law principles of choice of law, are inapplicable to an issue covered by direct legislation of rules of pan-European choice of law. Not only the superstructure, but also the infrastructure, of the subject is now made in Brussels rather than in London or even in Oxford. The advice that the more things change the more they stay the same certainly does not apply in this subject at this point in its history.

Having said all that, the common law methodology of private international law is still a sensible starting point for the analysis of issues, and in many cases it will not mislead. But where it becomes entangled with European statutory rules for choice of law, it is necessary to ask whether a particular aspect of that common law methodology would, if applied insensitively, damage the legislative aim of the particular provision. If the answer is that it would, the rule of the common law may be expected to yield to the contrary or contradictory statutory rule. In the end, this is the solution most faithful to the intention of Parliament as conveyed in the European Communities Act 1972; for the exercise of Parliamentary sovereignty is the end of every legal debate.

2. THIS BOOK AND ITS APPROACH

There are several ways in which a writer may try to render an account of this subject. One would be to consider the principles of private international law as a matter of legal theory: asking what the proper purpose of private international law is, and seeking to derive answers which accord with a broader philosophy of the nature and purpose of law, or as part of the economic or behavioural organization of society. This would tend to see the law as practised in courts as having illustrative, but not any obviously greater, value. The subject has never lacked theoreticians, of course, though it is fair to say that the place of theory in the world of English private international law has tended to be at the margins, for the common law was supremely pragmatic: the view that 'the lifeblood of the law is not logic but common sense'[4] was nowhere truer than in common law of private international law. Those who hope for a developed or delocalized theory of private international law should look away now.

Another would be to assert, and perhaps to acknowledge, that the pedagogic convenience which segregated private international law from the rest of the law now does more harm than good, and that to continue to treat the subject studied in this book in semi-isolation from the rest of the law is less a virtue, more a form of intellectual glaucoma. There is something in this. Whether it is the relationship with public international law, or human rights, or European law (and especially European law as it regulates its 'four freedoms',[5] the notion of European citizenship,

---

[4] Lord Reid, in *Haughton v Smith* [1975] AC 476, 500.

[5] This is not a reference to President Roosevelt's magisterial State of the Union address in January 1941, where they were identified as the freedom of speech, freedom of worship, freedom from want, and freedom from fear, but to the infinitely less inspiring free movement of goods, money, services, and people.

to say nothing of its seeping into company and competition laws at the domestic level, and elsewhere), it is wrong that private international lawyers sometimes pretend that all this is someone else's business. The French approach to the subject, for example, has always taken the law of nationality or citizenship as the starting point; the common lawyer, for whom citizenship has little importance and less interest, tended to view it as slightly odd; perhaps that ought to be reconsidered. And there is probably a book to be written on private international law as European law, but this is not it. As was said in the preface, the world is not Europe, and Europe is not the world.

A writer must make his or her own choice, and then leave it to the readers to make theirs. The approach taken here is to seek to work with the law as it applies in the English courts, and then to align the coverage of the book with what tends to be found in a university course in private international law. Statutes and judicial decisions therefore supply the framework and the detail of the law. Conclusions derived from this material are certainly open to evaluation and objection, but the concern here is to deal with the law which we have and which lawyers have to deal with, as distinct from the law which we might have had, or may one day have, or which might be encountered in a research institute or other parallel universe. No criticism is made of those writers who take a different point of view, of course; but they are doing a different job from the one taken in hand or enterprised here.

B. PRIVATE INTERNATIONAL LAW AS COMMON LAW

This section will outline the common law's conception of private international law, in order that reference may be made to it when a particular question arises which is not captured by the European legislation on private international law. For though the private international law of obligations (jurisdiction and choice of law) has been mostly removed to the domain of European private international law, the process is not yet complete, and some questions of choice of law in the close vicinity of the law of obligations are still left to the common law. The private international law of family relations and of property is still substantially within the domain of common law private international law: either because there is no European legislation on the subject or because the United Kingdom has exercised its privilege to be not bound by certain acts of such legislation. Moreover, the techniques of the common law are not wholly alien to European private international law, which was built on the foundations of national laws, including English law; and above all, the common law of private international law is how the subject, as practised in the English courts, was made and refined. Its techniques provide a useful point of contrast with the new system of private international law which is being built up by the organs of the European Union; but an appreciation of them makes clear why they have little part to play within the domain private international law which is European law.

1. FOREIGN LAW IN ENGLISH COURTS

The principal characteristic of the conflict of laws is that it will sometimes lead to a judge being asked to apply foreign law to the dispute.[6] In the ordinary course, an English judge will apply English domestic law: common law, equity, and statute law. The judge will apply only English law, and may not apply a foreign law, to an issue unless four conditions are satisfied. First, the choice of law rules which make up English private international law must provide that a foreign law is in principle applicable to the issue in question; second, English legislation must not supervene to forbid the application of foreign law; third, the party who relies on foreign law must plead and establish its applicability; and fourth, the party relying on foreign law must adduce evidence which proves its content to the satisfaction of the court. Meeting these four conditions means that the judge will be enabled and obliged to apply a rule of foreign law.

As regards the first point, we will consider in Chapter 4 and following the rules of choice of law which may mean that the court may be required to apply a foreign law: to the conclusion that the law which governs a contract is French, or that the law applicable to an alleged tort is German, and so forth. As regards the

---

[6] See, generally, Fentiman, *Foreign Law in English Courts* (Oxford University Press, 1998).

second point, however, the rules of choice of law may in certain circumstances be overridden by contradictory English legislation which directs the court not to apply a rule of foreign law. So, for example, a contract admittedly governed by French law may contain a provision limiting the liability of, or even exculpating, the defendant in circumstances where this would not be permitted were the contract governed by English law. In such a case, English legislation may stipulate that the rules of English law on exemption clauses are to be applied even though English law is not otherwise the governing law.[7] This being so, the judge will, to that extent, be precluded from applying foreign law.

As regards the third point, the party or parties seeking to rely on foreign law must plead its applicability. It follows that if neither party does so, the judge will apply English domestic law to the issues in dispute. The judge has neither power nor duty to apply foreign law *ex officio*. So in the example of personal injury or damage to property taking place overseas, a claimant may consider that the law of the place where he was injured affords him a cause of action, whereas English domestic law would not: it will be up to him to plead the applicability of foreign law to the claim. Again, a defendant may consider that the law of the place where the alleged tort happened furnishes her with a defence which would not be available as a matter of English law: it will be for her to plead the applicability of foreign law to the issue raised by way of defence. But neither party is obliged to do this, and a judge will therefore be left to apply English domestic law when the parties do not invoke foreign law. According to the English way of thinking, this is so even when an international convention, or a European Regulation, stipulates that an issue *shall* be governed by a particular law.[8] It is sometimes wondered if the relaxed approach developed by the common law is consistent with a legislative instruction from the European Union that the law indicated by a statutory choice of law rule 'shall be applied'. Not

---

[7] For example, Unfair Contract Terms Act 1977, s 27(2); cf Rome I Regulation (Reg 593/2008: [2008] OJ L177/6), Art 9.

[8] It certainly can be argued that the traditional English approach is part and parcel of the common law, and is in formal conflict with, and inapplicable in relation to, the particular conventions or Regulations, even where these refrain from applying to 'evidence and procedure', as they mostly do.

everyone will consider it correct to understand this as though it actually said 'shall not be applied unless one of the parties chooses to plead and succeeds in proving it'. Yet the point has not really been taken, presumably because it would have a dramatic effect on the way English courts—which try a substantial number of cases with foreign elements—adjudicate. If a change in practice is to take place, it will require a clear and precise direction from a legislator, to say nothing of an impact assessment to explain how it is justified. So far neither such thing has happened.[9]

As a matter of observable fact, contract and tort cases litigated in England will frequently be decided by application of English domestic law, even though choice of law rules might have indicated that a foreign law should be applied.[10] This may reflect the practical truth that the principles of the law of obligations are all very similar, meaning that there is often little point in proving foreign law; and it may also be driven by the practical problem, and expense, of actually proving foreign law, as will be seen below. It means that English courts take a pragmatic, rather than a dogmatic, view of their role: the parties are free to establish a common position on the inapplicability of foreign law, and once they have done that, it is not for a judge to think he knows better. Now this may be fair enough where a court is called on to adjudicate a matter in the law of obligations: the question whether a contract was valid or broken, or whether a defendant was the victim of negligence or *volens* to the risk, is a matter of interest to the two parties alone,[11] and if they agree to the application of English domestic law to their dispute, there is no third party with *locus standi* to object. But in cases where the court is called on to decide an issue which may have an effect *in rem*, such as whether B obtained good title to a car from S, or whether H and W were lawfully married, this relaxed approach to foreign law is less attractive, for a ruling on status may well affect non-parties, such as a subsequent purchaser or an intending spouse. In this context the

---

[9] See further, p 48 below.

[10] This comment is based on cases in which choice of law was or would have been governed by the common law, but there is no compelling reason to believe that the coming into effect of European choice of law rule has brought about any change.

[11] Or, at most, them and their insurers.

decision of the original parties to have their adjudication by reference only to English domestic law affects other interested persons
who were not privy to the agreement. Yet English law has never
taken the view that in questions of status the court is obliged to
enquire into and insist on the application of foreign law contrary
to the wishes of the litigants. Perhaps it should think again.

As regards the fourth point, the content and meaning of an
applicable foreign law is a matter of fact, to be proved as such
by the parties.[12] Every pleaded proposition of fact needs to be
admitted or proved; and as foreign law is a question of fact, evidence will have to be given by experts, usually one for each side
and evaluated by the judge. Expertise in foreign law is, however,
easier to describe than to define. There is no register of individuals who are qualified, still less authorized, to give such evidence
to an English court; there is no reliable way to evaluate the expert
or his evidence; it may not be clear whether an expert's knowledge is practical and up to date, or whether his seeming uncertainty actually reflects the true state of the foreign law itself. An
expert who has written books may have had little or no practical
experience of how the law he has described would be applied
in a court; the fact that a lawyer is in private practice or judicial
office may nevertheless leave her wholly unsuitable to give evidence in an area of law of which she has no direct experience. An
English court may be more impressed by the reported decisions
of a foreign court than a local court would be; it may be less persuaded by the writings of scholars than a foreign court would be.
Nor is it always clear that the content of a foreign law as derived
from statute and code will be consistent in every respect with the
outcome which would result from its application by a foreign
judge; and anyway, is Ruritanian law the law as derived from the
written sources of Ruritanian law, or the outcome which would
be delivered by a Ruritanian judge called upon to apply it?

---

[12] It might be thought to follow that a decision on foreign law is not subject
to reversal on appeal, unless the primary judge's conclusion was so unreasonable
that no judge could properly have reached the conclusion he did. But foreign law
is a fact of a rather peculiar kind, and appeals are more frequent, and the substitution of an appellate court's own conclusion more common, than its status as a
question of fact might suggest.

These are not trivial points, for as English private international law has committed itself to this particular view, it is legitimate to question whether the approach is fit for its purpose. There are many cases in which the judge has had to pick his way through baffling and contradictory evidence of foreign law, with the result that one may applaud the effort yet still lack confidence in the outcome; and the financial cost to the parties can be quite disproportionate to the substance of the claim. But the notion that the judge may go off on a frolic of his own and conduct a personal inquiry into foreign law has no place in an English court. So also is a judge precluded from founding on his own personal recollection of a particular foreign law,[13] even if he was trained and qualified in that system, for the law may have changed, and memory is no less fallible for sporting a wig; and, in any event, for a judge to usurp the privilege of the parties would be to ignore the limits on judicial power: the principle that *curia novit jus*, that the court knows the law, begins and ends with English domestic law.

If the party seeking to rely on foreign law fails to satisfy the judge as to its content, it is sometimes said that the judge will apply the foreign law, but in the sense that foreign law is taken to be the same as English law when the contrary is not proved. This is not very edifying. In default of proof of the content of foreign law, an English judge still has to adjudicate; and although the traditional default position was that English law would be applied, *faute de mieux*, courts have been prepared to dismiss a claim or defence as unproven if foreign law pleaded as its support has not been established by evidence.[14]

It may be thought that the practical difficulties in the English system reveal so many shortcomings that the model of other systems, in which the judge investigates and applies foreign law as well as his own, is to be preferred. Alas, this proposition does not stand up to inspection. A national judge manifestly does not know foreign law; a report on it must be commissioned. Whether it will be possible for a court to locate a competent expert from

---

[13] Examples exist, but are best left unidentified.

[14] *Damberg v Damberg* (2001) 52 NSWLR 492; *Global Multimedia International Ltd v Ara Media Services* [2006] EWHC 3107 (Comm), [2007] 1 All ER (Comm) 1160.

whom to obtain a report must be doubtful, at least where the law in question is specialized or exotic; and in complex cases in which the reporter will require close and detailed knowledge of the entire dispute, in order to be sure that he has seen all the issues which bear on the legal analysis, it is doubtful that a court-commissioned expert will be able to do this. Even if the report is signed off by an authoritative figure, the chances will be that it was researched and written up by someone very much more junior. So despite the claims sometimes heard, that the continental system of establishing and applying foreign law is superior to the English one, the truth is that the application of foreign law by a judge is fraught with difficulty of a general complexity which will not go away unless the trial is made to go away. This in turn may point to the real truth, that a court should have the power to decline to hear certain cases if persuaded that a court elsewhere would be better placed to give the parties the adjudication, together with the prospect of a meaningful appeal, which they deserve.

A final question asks, what, exactly, is the judge asked to do once the law is proved. The common law understanding is that a judge, called upon to apply French or Ruritanian domestic law, should apply it as a French or Ruritanian judge, trying the case, would interpret and apply it. In other words, 'French law' means 'French domestic law as a local judge would apply it'. If the judge would apply this rule to this particular contract, or would not apply that rule to that claim or claimant, then an English judge, in applying foreign law, should do likewise, for this is the truest sense in which foreign law is applied. This technique is particularly helpful when a court is called upon to apply foreign statute law. In deciding whether and how the statute applies, the relevant question is whether, and if so how, a judge trying the case in the foreign court would apply the particular statutory provision. If he would not apply it to the case in question, it is not materially part of the foreign law which an English judge may be invited to apply. So if an Australian judge would not apply a provision of the Competition and Consumer Act 2010 to conduct taking place outside Australia, an English court, if applying Australian law as *lex causae*, should not apply it either. If a New Zealand judge would interpret and apply the Accident Compensation Act 2001 as precluding a civil claim for damages for personal injury, an English court, applying New Zealand law as *lex causae*, should hold that there is no civil liability under the law of New Zealand,[15] and should not be tempted to hold that whilst a New Zealand judge would be required to apply the Act, a non-New Zealand judge need not do so. The other side of the coin is that where a statute is intended by its legislator to be applied, but the *lex causae* is, according to the rules of private international law applied in an English court, the law of another country, it must be ignored by the English court. So, if an English borrower and a Victorian lender enter into a contract of loan governed by English law, Victorian legislation reducing interest rates will be irrelevant to an English court, even if intended by the Victorian legislator to apply to the contract,[16] and even though a Victorian judge would have been required to apply the Act if he had been trying the claim.[17] The simple point is that where a statute is part of the *lex causae*, it should[18] be applied by the English judge, along with all other substantive provisions of the *lex causae*, in the way the foreign judge would have applied it; and if it is not part of the *lex causae* it is to be ignored.

A significant point of principle arises if the foreign judge would not have applied his own domestic law at all, but would instead have used his choice of law rules to point him to a different substantive law which he would then have applied. Whether the parties are entitled to invite an English judge to go down that path depends on the impact of the doctrine of *renvoi*, which is examined below.

2. COMMON LAW CHOICE OF LAW: TECHNIQUES

A judge may therefore be called upon to apply a foreign law in the determination of a dispute. But there is a framework for the

---

[15] *James Hardie & Co Pty Ltd v Hall* (1998) 43 NSWLR 554 (CA); *James Hardie Industries Pty Ltd v Grigor* (1998) 45 NSWLR 20 (CA).

[16] cf *Mount Albert Borough Council v Australasian Temperance and General Mutual Life Assurance Society* [1938] AC 224 (PC) (where the borrower was a New Zealander).

[17] *Akai Pty Ltd v People's Insurance Co Ltd* (1997) 188 CLR 418.

[18] Unless there is some rule of English law which overrides and instructs the English judge to do differently.

analysis, and this framework keeps the exercise under reasonable and reviewable control. We will frequently observe that the basic structure of the common law conflict of laws is built from propositions which connect 'issues' to a particular law. So the common law says that the material validity of a contract is governed by its proper law; liability in tort is governed in part by the law of the place where the person was when injured; the effect of a disposition of movable property is governed by the law of the place where the thing was when transferred; the capacity of an individual to marry another is governed by the law of his or her domicile at the time of the marriage; the ranking of claims and distribution of assets in an insolvency is governed by the law of the court administering the insolvency; and so on.

The simplicity of these propositions is deceptive, for they contain three legal ideas, and suggest a fourth. The first is the concept of an 'issue': how do we know whether to frame our question in terms of the material validity of a contract as opposed to its formal validity, or just its validity? How do we know whether to ask the question in terms of the capacity of persons to marry as opposed to the validity of the marriage? The answer is that we *characterize* an issue, or issues, as arising for decision. The second is the concept of a law: how do we know whether the law we choose means the domestic law of the relevant country, or, if this is different, the national law which would be applied by the judge trying the case in the courts of that country? How do we know whether the law of the domicile means the domestic law of the country in which the person is domiciled or if this is different, the law which would be applied by a judge trying the case in the courts of that country? The answer[19] is that the law relating to *renvoi* tells us whether our rule of decision, our choice of law rule, points to a domestic law only or includes a reference to the private international law rules of that country. The third is this: suppose the facts are characterized as giving rise to two issues, each having a choice of law rule, and for each of which English law and the foreign law would prescribe different solutions. Do we approach them independently, and try to combine

---

[19] Unless the choice of rule is a statutory one, and the statute itself answers the question.

the answers at the end, or does one play a dominant role, applying its rules to the determination of the other issue? This raises the *incidental question*, to which a solution must be found. Fourth and last is the identification of the connection, the 'law of the ...'. These are the *connecting factors*, and once the appropriate one has been found, the process of choice of law is over, and the proof of foreign law may begin. But these four components of the choice of law process, as the common law developed it, need a little elaboration. For though in several areas they have been displaced by statutory rules, they are the very foundation of the conflict of laws.

(a) Characterization: identification of issues to point to a law

If a choice of law rule is formulated by connecting issues to laws, the first step is to think about issues. This requires the facts to be accommodated within one, or perhaps more, legal categories for which a choice of law rule is given. The definition of these categories and the location of facts within them comprise the process of characterization.[20]

Both aspects of characterization are undertaken by reference to English law: the available categories are those created by English private international law; and the placing of the facts within one or more of them is done according to English private international law: for those who find analogies helpful, English law designs the pigeonholes, and an English sorter decides which facts belong in which pigeonhole. This exercise has to be undertaken by reference to English law, for at this stage we are far from having explained whether, still less which, foreign law is going to be relevant.

The definitional list of the available categories or characterizations is established in part by authority, and in part by principle.[21] As we look at different substantive areas of law we will identify them: the capacity to contract, the proprietary effect of a transfer,

---

[20] Dicey, Morris, and Collins, *The Conflict of Laws* (15th edn Sweet & Maxwell, 2012) Ch 2.

[21] *Raiffeisen Zentralbank Österreich AG v Five Star Trading LLC* [2001] EWCA Civ 68, [2001] QB 825.

the formal validity of marriage, the capacity of a corporation to do an act, and so on. Although the categories are established, there is no reason of principle why the law may not develop a new one, and sometimes reason why it should. So, for example, it has been proposed that the category of essential validity of marriage should be broken down into capacity to marry and the quintessential validity of marriage, for which separate choice of laws rules would be prescribed;[22] it has been proposed that the category of capacity to marry should be broken down into the capacity to contract a polygamous marriage and the remainder of capacity to marry.[23] And again, the choice of law rules for the transfer of intangible movables may yet be refined so that certain complex cases, such as arise in the system for indirect holding of financial instruments, are dealt with separately from other intangibles. The process of change in this context will be slow and measured: the certainty of the law would be lost if new categories were created willy-nilly; an alternative response might be to make exceptions in individual cases, rather than new categories for general application. For all that, it is clear that the creation of new characterization categories is not impossible, but is sometimes overdue. For example, there might have been a characterization category for equitable claims, for which the choice of law rule is the *lex fori*, the law of the court hearing the claim.[24] Quite apart from the point that this might not be a desirable choice of law rule, it is doubtful that 'equitable claims' represents a coherent characterization category in the first place. Similar doubts have been expressed whether the law needed a characterization category for 'receipt-based restitutionary claims'.[25] Though these ideas may be indispensable as a matter of domestic English law, it does not follow that there is any use for them in the conflict of laws.

As regards whether a particular issue raised for decision in a case should be fitted into one or another of these categories, the conventional explanation is that this is done by using English

---

[22] *Vervaeke v Smith* [1983] 1 AC 145.
[23] *Radwan v Radwan (No 2)* [1973] Fam 35.
[24] There is some support for this in Australian law.
[25] *Macmillan Inc v Bishopsgate Investment Trust plc (No 3)* [1996] 1 WLR 387 (CA).

law as the point of departure, and treating an issue as one might treat its nearest English equivalent: the exercise is undertaken 'in a broad internationalist spirit in accordance with the principles of the conflict of laws of the forum'.[26] So, for example, whether a contract is unenforceable if not notarized will concern the formal validity of contracts, even though English law does not generally require contracts to be notarized; whether a promise is enforceable as a contract even though not given for consideration will raise a question of the material validity of a contract, even though English law would not see a gratuitous promise as a contract at all;[27] an action claiming damages for insult or for breach of confidence will be treated as tortious even though English domestic law knows no such tort of insult and regards the breach of confidence as an equitable wrong; and a polygamous marriage will be treated as a marriage, even though English domestic law does not allow for polygamy. Occasionally this will lead to a result which appears odd. After a marriage had been celebrated in England between a French man and an English woman it was alleged[28] that it was invalid because the parents of the man had not given their consent. One[29] analysis adopted by the court was that the need for third party consent raised a question of the formal validity of a marriage, which was governed by the law of the place (England) of celebration, under which law the lack of parental consent was immaterial. Some argue, by contrast, that the issue should have been treated as one of capacity to marry and as such governed by the domestic law of the person (French) alleged to lack marital capacity.[30] There is some force in the alternative view, especially if the court really did

---

[26] *Raiffeisen Zentralbank Österreich AG v Five Star Trading LLC* [2001] EWCA Civ 68, [2001] QB 825 at [27].

[27] *Re Bonacina* [1912] 2 Ch 394. These examples are taken from the common law. For contracts made after 1991, however, European legislation, rather than the common law, would determine the choice of law, and the process by which it did so would not be one of characterization properly so called.

[28] *Ogden v Ogden* [1908] P 46 (CA).

[29] The other was that if the facts raised an issue of capacity, it was still governed by English law, under the principle in *Sottomayor v De Barros (No 2)* (1879) 5 PD 94.

[30] Although under the rule in *Sottomayor v De Barros (No 2)*, this would not in fact have been the outcome.

reason that as third party consent is a matter of formal validity in domestic English law it must be the same in the conflict of laws. Quite apart from the fact that the divisions of the two (domestic, private international) systems of law are not bound to be congruent, it is sensible that the allocation of an issue to a characterization category be done with some flexibility. Even so, it is hard to see why the capacity solution, which would mean the marriage was void, is intrinsically better than the formality alternative, which leads to its validity; and the truth may be that some cases are inescapably hard ones. More novel cases can be expected as domestic laws are refashioned and reshaped to meet changing social conditions. Within family law, laws which provide for marriage between persons of the same sex, and regimes which permit the registration of a civil partnership of persons of the same sex or otherwise, might have required the courts to decide whether such unions were to be characterized as marriage, or as contracts, or as *sui generis* and requiring an entirely new characterization category, in order to provide a framework for litigation about their validity and consequences.[31]

As for what represents the object of characterization, the 'thing' characterized, the usual understanding is that issues, rather than rules of law, are characterized.[32] The justification for this is that the very language of the subject is written in terms which connect categories of legal issue with a choice of law. It also has the immense practical advantage that a single law is identified to provide the solution to the single issue. If, by contrast, one were to adopt the approach of characterizing the individual rules of law found in the legal systems having potential connection to the dispute, aiming to apply whichever was formulated so as to apply in the given context, one could end up with two contradictory solutions or none at all. Take the case of marriage without parental consent, discussed above. Suppose it had been held that the English rule that parental consent was not

---

[31] But for the time being, Civil Partnership Act 2004, Sch 20, provides a statutory answer.

[32] However, as will be seen in Ch 4 below, the rule of private international law that an English court will not enforce a foreign penal or revenue law will require characterization of the particular law, and not of an issue.

required was a rule about the formal validity of marriage, and hence applicable when a marriage took place in England; and the French rule requiring parental consent was held to be a rule about capacity to marry, and hence applicable to the marriage of a French domiciliary. Both rules would have been 'characterized' as applicable; the result of their combined application is an impossible contradiction. Or, taking the opposite possibility in each case, each rule might have been characterized as being inapplicable. This does not seem sensible; the ends condemn the means. Accordingly, the judge is required to identify an issue and apply the rule found in the system of law which governs that issue, and to close his ears to objection. In the only case to have confronted the issue directly,[33] a mother and daughter, domiciled in Germany but taking refuge in England, perished in an air raid. The court had to decide who succeeded to the estate of the mother. When it is unknown which of two people died first, both English law and German law solve the problem by applying a presumption: English law presuming that the older died first, German law that they died simultaneously. The judge deduced that he had to decide an issue of inheritance or succession, which was governed by German law, rather than a question of evidence governed by English law. He therefore applied the German rule. But whether he was right or wrong about this, his technique of identifying *an* issue raised by the facts is the critical point to notice. Had he simply characterized the respective rules of German and English law, he might have found that both applied or neither applied: this would have been so self-defeating that, whatever may be said in its defence, the solution could not be right.[34]

A final question concerns exactly what happens after characterization has pointed the court to a particular law in which to find the answer. Suppose a marriage has taken place in France, without the parental consent required by the French domiciliary law of one of the parties. An English court will characterize the issue as one of formal validity, and look to French law for

---

[33] *Re Cohn* [1945] Ch 5.

[34] Though it is fair to say that if this would have been the outcome, there is no chance that the judge would have blundered into following such a course.

its answer. But an answer to what question? If the question is 'is this marriage formally valid as a matter of French law despite the absence of parental consent?' the answer may be a rather puzzled 'yes': puzzled because, in the opinion of the French expert, this is not the right question to be asking. If, by contrast, the question is framed as 'is this marriage valid as a matter of French law despite the lack of parental consent?' the reasoning may be more complex, but the answer will be 'no': the French expert will explain that this issue is seen by French law as one of capacity, governed by the national (French) law of the allegedly incapable party, and according to which the marriage is invalid. It will be seen that the outcome of the case may depend on the manner in which the question is formulated: put shortly, is the question, formulated for the expert to answer, expressed in and bounded by the precise terms of the characterization which led there in the first place, or is characterization defunct and forgotten once it has served to make a connection to a law? The answer may well require an understanding of the principles of *renvoi*, and the suggested solution offered by the common law will be found at the end of the next section.

(b) Renvoi: the meaning of law

If an issue is to be governed by the law of a particular country, what do we mean by the word *law*? Does it mean the rules of domestic law, as these would apply to a wholly local case, or might it refer to law in a wider sense, including in particular the private international law rules of that legal system as a local judge might apply them? Is the issue resolved by applying the domestic law, or by permitting a reference on—a *renvoi*—from that law to another, if the private international law rules of the chosen law would have directed it? The common law's answer is that there is no short answer: sometimes it will be the former, othertimes the latter. Which is which is a matter of authority more than anything else; why this represents the approach of English private international law is more controversial.

Let us take an example. Suppose a woman has died without leaving a will, and the question arises concerning succession to her estate.[35] Suppose she died domiciled in Spain, but still a

---

[35] For the rules on intestate succession, see Ch 7 below.

British citizen. As a matter of English private international law, succession to her movable estate would be governed by Spanish law as the law of her domicile at death. Suppose also that according to Spanish domestic law, X would succeed to the estate, but that according to Spanish private international law, succession would be governed by the law of the nationality, which would be taken to be English; and as a matter of English domestic law, Y would succeed. What is the judge to do?

He may have three possibilities. He may interpret his choice of law rule as pointing him to Spanish domestic law, and hold in favour of X. Or he may interpret his choice of law rule as pointing to Spanish law as including its rules of private international law, follow the path by which this points to English law, interpret this as meaning English domestic law, and find for Y. Or he may interpret his choice of law rule as pointing to Spanish law, follow the path by which this points to English law, interpret this as meaning 'English law including its conflicts rules', which point back to Spain, ask what the Spanish judge would do when she was informed that English law would look back to Spanish law, and accept whatever answer she would then give. As a matter of common law authority, the English judge will not, initially at least, take the second of these three possibilities. Sometimes he will take the first, and interpret the 'law' as meaning the domestic rules of the chosen law. But on other occasions, which include issues of succession, he will take the third, and interpret the 'law' as meaning that system of domestic law which the foreign judge, notionally hearing the case in the court whose law has been chosen, would apply:[36] he will, so far as the evidence of the content of foreign law allows him to do so, impersonate the Spanish judge and decide as she would decide. Such an approach to choice of law may be called the 'foreign court theory' of *renvoi*, or 'total *renvoi*'. Is this not all very difficult? Should the judge not simply have applied Spanish domestic law and left it at that?

Judges and writers have suggested so, and legislators usually say so. Before weighing the authority and the arguments, it is well to be reminded that *renvoi* applies only in certain areas of

---

[36] *Re Annesley* [1926] Ch 692; *Re Ross* [1930] 1 Ch 377; *Re Askew* [1930] 2 Ch 259; *Re Duke of Wellington* [1947] Ch 506.

private international law; and that, as the proof of foreign law lies primarily in the hands of the parties, a court will have neither need nor opportunity to examine the principles of *renvoi* unless the parties choose to raise them. One criticism of *renvoi*, that it can make life difficult for the parties and for the judge, may therefore be overstated. Another, that choice of law rules were formulated without any thought for *renvoi* but as pointers to a domestic system of law, is simply a rejection of the principle without separate justification, for even if it were true, the common law was able to improve itself by refining its rules. Another, that *renvoi* subordinates English choice of law rules to those of a foreign system, is misconceived, for it is English law, and English law alone, which decides whether to follow a foreign court's pattern of reasoning. A fourth is that the English 'impersonation' approach works only if the notional judge who is being impersonated would not be found to be trying to do the very thing which the English judge would do, which just goes to show that the very idea is flawed.[37] But this creation of the febrile academic imagination has never arisen for decision.[38] Were it to do so, the rational answer is that if the foreign rules point back to English law, *renvoi* has shot its bolt, and English domestic law would apply.[39]

Some see the arguments in favour of *renvoi* as stronger. Rules of private international law are rules of a foreign legal system: if this foreign law is selected for application, it is odd that material parts of that law—the very parts which explain whether a local judge would actually apply that law to the case!—are sheared off and ignored. It may be possible to imagine the rules of private international law as separate and distinct, but this is a pedagogic

---

[37] It is said that it is hardly a recommendation that the English doctrine of *renvoi* works only if other states reject it. This is tosh: one may as well say that one should never hold a door open for another to pass through, for if the other person is equally polite neither will make any progress at all.

[38] But the worry of it prompted the dissent of McHugh J in *Neilson v Overseas Projects Corpn of Victoria* [2005] HCA 54, (2005) 233 CLR 331, who was frightened by a paper tiger.

[39] *Casdagli v Casdagli* [1918] P 89, Scrutton LJ. Other answers may be imagined, but there is no sense in looking for an answer which is impossible to work with. This though will be the case in which the second of the three options identified above may be selected: as a response to a problem caused by the third.

convenience which risks damaging the coherence and integrity of the law the English court has chosen to apply. If one is to apply foreign law, it seems right to apply all of it; and equally right to apply it in the same way, and to the same effect, so far as this is possible, as the foreign judge would: realism teaches, and common sense understands, that the law is what a judge will say it is, neither more nor less. Moreover, although in our example it may not matter very much whether X or Y succeeds to the movable estate, it would seem very strange that an English court could consider and declare that one person is entitled to foreign land when, as a matter of that foreign law, the register of title will not be amended to reflect that view. If it is ever open to an English court to make a judgment about title to foreign land, it should surely do so in conformity with what it understands to be the law which the local courts would themselves apply; and if this aligns English choice of law rules to those of another system, so much the better for that.

There may be another justification for the general operation of the principle of *renvoi*. When applied by an English court, it seeks to ensure that the case is decided as it would be if the action were brought in the courts which are probably the closest to the dispute. After all, there will be no incentive to forum shop to England if the English court will try to determine the case in the same as a judge of the court whose law is the chosen law. Viewed in this sense, *renvoi* is an antidote to forum shopping which works, when allowed to operate, by refining the rules for choice of law.[40]

Common law rules for choice of law evidently come in two patterns. In one, the choice of law rule is expressed as the choice of a domestic law to determine the issue. So at common law, the material validity of a contract was governed by the domestic law chosen and expressed by the parties or, in default of such expression, by that domestic law with which it was most closely connected: the rule was formulated as a choice of a domestic law, and *renvoi* was irrelevant to it. In other cases, the choice of law rule might be expressed indirectly, or formulaically, as a choice of 'that law which would be applied by a judge holding court at

---

[40] *Neilson v Overseas Projects Corpn of Victoria* [2005] HCA 54, (2005) 233 CLR 331.

the relevant place'. So a question of title to land is governed by the law which would be applied by a judge sitting at the place where the land is; succession to movable property is governed by that law which would be applied by a judge sitting in the country where the defendant died domiciled. That does not seem conceptually challenging.

One must admit, however, that *renvoi* is viewed in some quarters with a distaste which sometimes borders on mania. In European private international law[41] its exclusion is often legislated, but even in the common law it probably played no part in choice of law for contract or tort. It does, in principle and if pleaded and proved by the parties, apply to questions of title to immovable property; and though it ought to apply to questions of movable property, a string of first instance decisions is to contrary effect.[42] It applies to the validity and invalidity of marriage;[43] but not to divorce where the choice of law rule for granting and recognizing divorces is for the law of the forum.[44] In other words, when the court is being asked to give a judgment which will have its effect only on the litigants themselves, *renvoi* will not apply. But when it is asked to give a judgment on status, either the ownership of a thing or the marriageability of an individual, which will have a potential impact on third parties the court will, if invited to do so, be more likely to interpret the law in the *renvoi* sense where this will tend to increase the chance that the view reached by an English court will align with that which might be reached by a potentially-involved other law.

One may now return to the point left open at the end of the examination of characterization: how to formulate the question which is to be referred to and answered by the expert on foreign law. The answer should be along the following lines. In a legal context where the principle of *renvoi* has no application, there is no compelling need to reach the same answer as would be given by the foreign judge. The question may therefore be asked in

---

[41] Which is a very different thing; see below.

[42] From *Iran v Berend* [2007] EWHC 132 (QB), [2007] 2 All ER (Comm) 132 to *Blue Sky One Ltd v Mahan Air* [2009] EWHC 3314 (Comm). For an approving comment the reader must look elsewhere.

[43] *Taczanowska v Taczanowski* [1957] P 301 (CA); *R v Brentwood Superintendent Registrar of Marriages, ex p Arias* [1968] 2 QB 956.

[44] See Ch 8 below.

terms of the English characterization: 'was the contract formally valid?' etc. But in a case where the principle of *renvoi* does apply, and where the broad aim is to reach the same conclusion as would be stated by a judge in the local court, it will impair the chances of success if the law is not interpreted in a *renvoi* sense: only by allowing the expert to use the characterization and choice of law rules of his own system will it be possible for him and for the court to produce an answer of the quality sought. So in the case of the absence of parental consent, the question put should be whether the absence of parental consent makes the marriage invalid, without regard to the way that the issue was earlier characterized by the English judge or would be characterized by the foreign judge. But if the case were one concerning, say the material validity of a contract, the question should be whether the foreign law regards the contract as materially invalid, even if the foreign law would not have regarded the issue as one of material, as opposed to, say, formal validity.

(c) Interlocking issues and incidental questions

Characterization allows us to identify an issue and attach a law to it. But a set of facts may involve more issues than one, and choice of law may point these to separate laws. So, for example, a claim for damages for an alleged tort might have been defended by reference to a contractual promise not to sue; a claim for the delivery up of goods over which a seller has reserved his title may be met by a defence that they were sold to the defendant who bought them in good faith and thereby displaced the title of the claimant; the validity of a marriage may be impugned by the alleged ineffectiveness of a prior divorce. The problem arises wherever there is a conflict between the laws which English private international law chooses for the two issues. To take the first example, characterization would have applied the *lex delicti* to a claim in tort, but the *lex contractus* to the contractual promise; how it combined them can be left for later.[45] But what if the private international law of the *lex delicti* has its own view, which diverges from that of English private international law, of what the *lex contractus* is? If the intrinsic validity of the contractual defence depends on first

---

[45] See Ch 6 below.

identifying its *lex contractus*, is this done by the rules of English private international law or by the conflicts rules of the *lex delicti*? Again, the capacity of a person to marry will be affected by the recognition or otherwise of the earlier divorce: is the law which determines the validity of the divorce chosen by the conflicts rules of English law or by those of the law which governs the person's capacity to marry? Or is the capacity of the party to marry simply a consequence of the conflicts rules which determine the validity of the earlier divorce?

It may seem complicated, but the law reports suggest that it rarely arises for application and decision in practice. In the end, if statute has not imposed a solution of its own the considerations which underpin the doctrines of characterization and *renvoi* allow a sensible result to be reached. The prevailing view of the common law is to regard one of the issues, if possible, as the main one. The conflicts rules of the law chosen for that main question will then select the law which governs the incidental question, so that the overall result is generated by the law (including its conflicts rules) which governs the main question. This assumes that a question can be identified as the main one; in many cases this will be the question which arises or occurs later in time, because in the end this is the decision which counts the most. By this reasoning, the effectiveness of the ultimate sale of the goods is the main question, the incidental issue being that of the validity and effect of the reservation of title; the law governing the later sale will also supply the conflicts rule to identify the law governing the earlier reservation of title. Again, personal capacity to (re)marry is the main question, the validity and effect of the prior divorce being incidental to it;[46] the law governing capacity to marry will supply the conflicts rule to identify the law which governs the earlier divorce. In neither case does English private international law take a simple chronological approach, applying its choice of law rules to the issues individually and sequentially and then seeking to combine the results.

Title to property and personal status are two areas in which the principles of *renvoi* probably apply, and where the court will aim to replicate the result which would be reached by the foreign

---

[46] *Schwebel v Ungar* (1964) 48 DLR (2d) 644 (Ont CA), but only to the extent that statute has not provided otherwise.

judge if he were trying the case. Where the focus is on the final or main question, any prior or incidental questions should be dealt with as the judge in the final court would deal with them. But a different analysis may be called for in a case where the principles of *renvoi* play no part in the choice of law, and where the need to replicate the final judge's perspective is absent. So in the case of a contractual defence to a tort claim, the *lex delicti* would determine whether there was a claim in tort. If a contractual defence were pleaded, the first step would be to decide whether the conflicts rules of the *lex delicti* or of English law select the *lex contractus*. There being no need to decide the overall question as a judge of the *lex delicti* would, there would be no reason to prefer the conflicts rules of the *lex delicti* to those of English law. Accordingly, the law which governs the contract and assesses the intrinsic validity of the defence would be determined by applying English conflicts rules; whether it defeats the claimant would be a matter for the *lex delicti*; but the *lex delicti* will take the validity of the contract as given, rather than making that judgment for itself.

The incidental question therefore integrates into the common law methodology for choice of law. But it can be overridden by statute,[47] for Parliament may have enacted a law in such a way that it precludes the possibility of assessing, say, the validity of a divorce by anything other than English law. To that extent the solution given above will be displaced, and the validity of the divorce conclusively determined, in accordance with Parliamentary intention, by English law.[48]

(d) Connecting factors

The identifier at the end of the 'law of the [something/somewhere]' formula is traditionally known as a 'connecting factor', on the ground that these points of contact are what connect an individual, or an issue, to a system of the law which will, in principle, furnish the answer being looked for. They are almost all defined by English law, not foreign law: this is inevitable, for until the choice of law rules have identified a foreign law to apply to a dispute, there is no sensible basis for using any law

---

[47] For further consideration of statute law, see below.

[48] *Lawrence v Lawrence* [1985] Fam 106; Family Law Act 1986, s 50.

other than English for definitional purposes. For example, if as a matter of English law X is domiciled in France, this attribution of domicile is unaffected by the possibility that French law may not agree but would regard him as being domiciled in England instead.[49] If English law considers the law applicable to an obligation to be Swiss law, it is irrelevant that a Swiss court, applying rules of Swiss private international law, might have come to a different conclusion.

To be useful the connecting factor must identify a territory having *a* system of law, as opposed to a larger political unit which may have many systems of law or none. For example, an individual may be domiciled in England, but not in the United Kingdom: there is English law on his capacity to marry, but no 'United Kingdom law' on the point; and if a statute has been enacted to apply in England, Scotland, and Northern Ireland, and may in some sense be considered as the law of the United Kingdom, it will apply because it is part of English law, rather than for any other reason. An individual may be domiciled in Florida, but not in the United States, with the result that the law of Florida, as distinct from the law of the United States, will be applied; although where the relevant law of Florida is in fact a federal rule of the law of the United States, the federal rule will be applied as part of the law in the state of Florida. But by contrast, in true cases where a federal state has defined itself as a single legal unit for certain purposes, the connecting factor may point to that law. So a person may be regarded as domiciled in Australia for the purpose of capacity to marry, for Australia is constituted by its own legislation a single law district so far as concerns the law of marriage,[50] but in Queensland for the purpose of making a will, for the law of testamentary succession is a matter on which state law is sovereign, and state laws are several. An occasional form of expression for this special sense of a 'country' is a 'law district'.

---

[49] *Re Annesley* [1926] Ch 692. But if choice of law rules refer to French law in a *renvoi* sense, and as a matter of French law he is domiciled in England, this detail will form part of the overall decision, and will not be contradicted.

[50] And, according to *John Pfeiffer Pty Ltd v Rogerson* [2000] HCA 36, (2000) 203 CLR 503, for all matters which fall within the federal jurisdiction.

Connecting factors fall into two broad categories: those which define a law in terms of a personal connection, and those which define the law in terms of a state of affairs. For ease of exposition they need to be examined separately.

Personal connecting factors: domicile, residence, and nationality

The personal connecting factors are domicile, habitual (or ordinary or usual) residence, (simple) residence, and nationality. As far as the common law is concerned, domicile is the most significant, and it is the law of the domicile which, to a greater or lesser extent, determines the status and capacities of an individual. It is therefore worth examination.

According to the common law of domicile, every person has a domicile and, subject to what appears below,[51] no person can have more than one domicile at any time. The domiciliary law—the *lex domicilii*—still has a significant role in family and in property law, but it may also define the capacity of persons, especially companies,[52] to make contracts; and it plays a part in the law of taxation. From this very general introduction two points may emerge: 'domicile' is used in a wide but diverse range of matters, and it may be that its meaning should take its colour from its context. It is also desirable that it represent a rational connection to a particular law. In these two respects the English law of domicile scores rather badly. On the first, although it has been suggested from time to time that domicile should adjust its definition to its context, the courts have demurred. So a case on UK tax liability, in which it was held that a person had not acquired an English domicile despite 40 years' residence,[53] will be authoritative on whether and how a person may acquire an English domicile for the purpose of his or her capacity to marry or make a will, as also will be a decision on whether an illegal immigrant

---

[51] The persistence of the domicile of origin constitutes a general half-exception to the rule; the jurisdictional domicile which forms the backbone of the Civil Jurisdiction and Judgments Act 1982, the Brussels I Regulation, and the Civil Jurisdiction and Judgments Order 2001 (SI 2001/3929) is a completely separate concept, irrelevant to the common law of domicile.

[52] Where it means the law of the place of incorporation: see p 372 below.

[53] *IRC v Bullock* [1976] 1 WLR 1178 (CA).

or overstayer[54] has acquired a domicile in England. One imagines that the policies which underpin the individual decisions in these various legal contexts are not identical and may even be contradictory, but this fact, if it is a fact, is not reflected in the definition of domicile, for domicile has, as a matter of common law, one definition, not several definitions.

A telling difficulty, on which authority is surprisingly sparse, is how to determine the domicile of a person who, in some sense, belonged to a territory whose borders have moved or which has simply ceased to be. A woman formerly domiciled in Czechoslovakia would now face the impossibility of being domiciled in a non-country which is no longer a law district and has no law. At a guess, she will be held to have acquired a domicile of choice in the part in which she was resident on the date on which the country severed itself, but this will be more difficult to defend as a conclusion if she had not, on that date, made up her mind whether to remain, and hence to reside indefinitely, in the part-country. A person who was domiciled in Yugoslavia or the USSR, which disappeared by disintegration, is in much the same position; likewise one who was domiciled in East Germany, which country disappeared by voluntary absorption. It is probable that one can have a domicile in the *soi-disant* and illegal 'Turkish Republic of Northern Cyprus', but what of Palestine? In all these cases there are practical problems in defining domicile in terms which look backward to an earlier set of facts, but there is no easy solution to the problem created by the fact that political history does not respect the conflict of laws.[55]

Domicile, as a common law concept, is a single species, but with three *genera*. The *domicile of origin* is the domicile of one's father (or mother, for one who is born out of wedlock or after the death of the father) at the date of one's birth. It is the first domicile of a child, and it serves as the actual domicile until superseded by the acquisition of another domicile, either of choice or of dependency. But it is only ever suppressed, with the result that if a later-acquired domicile is lost, then unless at the same moment a new domicile is acquired, the domicile of origin reasserts itself as the person's actual domicile. The domicile of

[54] *Mark v Mark* [2005] UKHL 42, [2006] 1 AC 98.
[55] *Re O'Keefe* [1940] Ch 124.

origin can never be shaken off; and if it revives at a point late in a person's life it has the potential to connect him to a legal system which may be remote from the circumstances of his present life.[56] Some regard this potential for the domicile of origin to reassert itself as showing why it should be abolished by legislation, but the truth is less clear-cut. After all, if a refugee is driven to flee from the country in which she has had a domicile of choice, it may be more offensive to hold that this domicile persists than to revive the domicile of origin unless and until a new domicile of choice is established somewhere less awful.

A *domicile of choice* is acquired by becoming resident in a law district, intending to reside there indefinitely: both conditions must be satisfied in relation to the law district in which the domicile is to be established before acquisition is complete. The *intention* must be geographically specific, unconditional, and deliberate in order to meet the somewhat restrictive requirements of the law. So if a person emigrates to the United States with an intention to remain there, but has not yet settled on which state she will, permanently or indefinitely, reside in, she will not have established a domicile of choice in any American state;[57] if she intends to reside in Texas but has not yet taken up residence there she will not have established a domicile in Texas. The intention must be to reside indefinitely. So an intention to reside for a term of years, or until the occurrence of a certain specific event such as retirement or the death of a spouse, is not enough,[58] although if the condition upon which the residence would come to an end is vague and unspecific it may be disregarded.[59] This means that residence for many decades' length may still not establish a domicile of choice: a fact which certain overpaid foreign nationals living and working in London have shamelessly exploited and at which successive governments have shamefully connived.[60] In a number of weirdly bizarre cases, the courts have assessed a person's distasteful intentions as insufficient to establish an English domicile. It is admittedly plausible that a fugitive from justice,

---

[56] *Udny v Udny* (1869) LR 1 Sc & Div 441. See also *Re O'Keefe* [1940] Ch 124.
[57] *Bell v Kennedy* (1868) LR 1 Sc & Div 307 (England and Scotland).
[58] *IRC v Bullock* [1976] 1 WLR 1178 (CA) (unless wife died first).
[59] *Re Fuld's Estate (No 3)* [1968] P 675; *Re Furse* [1980] 3 All ER 838.
[60] *IRC v Bullock* [1976] 1 WLR 1178 (CA).

who intends to remain only until the passing of time has pre-scribed her offence, will not acquire a domicile of choice,[61] but this was extended to a German terrorist who fled to England but whose intention to remain was evidently unconditional, almost certainly because the court looked on her case with distaste.[62] A wastrel who came to England to sponge off his relatives was held to be too useless to have an intention to establish an English domicile;[63] and an American citizen who was advised on medical grounds to remain in Brighton, but who spent his waking hours devising lunatic schemes to bring about the destruction of the British maritime empire, was held not to have the requisite inten-tion either, even though he knew perfectly well that he would remain in England for ever.[64] It is hard to interpret these cartoon cases as instances of conditional intention, but what they add to the requirements for the acquisition of a domicile of choice is difficult to pin down.

What constitutes *residence* is hard to say; and the definition of 'present as a resident' hardly advances matters very much. The view that residence in England originating in unlawful entry was incapable of sustaining an English domicile of choice has now been abandoned.[65] A person may remain resident in a country while overseas, but it is unclear whether he becomes a resident upon the instant of his arrival, or only some time after.[66] In prin-ciple one can be resident in two countries at once, but to avoid the inadmissible result of this leading to there being two domiciles of choice, it is probable that the residence requirement identifies the principal residence if there is more than one contender.[67]

A domicile of choice can be lost by being abandoned, which means ceasing to reside and ceasing to intend to reside indefinitely—both elements must be terminated—or lost by the acquisition of a new domicile of choice on the basis of the rules

---

[61] *Re Martin* [1900] P 211.

[62] *Puttick v AG* [1980] Fam 1.

[63] *Ramsay v Liverpool Royal Infirmary* [1930] AC 588.

[64] *Winans v AG* [1904] AC 287.

[65] *Mark v Mark* [2005] UKHL 42, [2006] 1 AC 98.

[66] In the case of habitual residence, this will not suffice: *Re J (A Minor) (Abduction: Custody Rights)* [1990] 2 AC 562.

[67] *Plummer v IRC* [1988] 1 WLR 292.

set out above. But if the abandonment is not contemporaneous with the acquisition of a new domicile of choice, the domicile of origin will reassert itself to prevent any domiciliary hiatus.[68]

A child's *domicile of dependency* is that, from time to time, of the parent upon whom, until the age of 16 or lawful marriage under this age, the child is dependent.[69] In principle, therefore, a child may suppress its domicile of origin with a domicile of dependency as soon as the cord is cut. When the age of independence is reached, it is debatable whether the domicile of dependency is lost by operation of law, so that the domicile of origin, if different, revives unless a domicile of choice be immediately acquired, or whether the domicile had as dependent continues as an imposed domicile of choice. Statute suggests that the latter is possible,[70] but principle suggests that it is not, and that the domicile of dependence ceases and is defunct on the attaining of majority.[71] The domicile of dependency of married women was abolished in 1974.[72]

It will have become apparent that the common law of domicile, with its peculiar rules and weirder authorities, has the potential to produce a capricious answer in a given case, and all the more so in Europe as political boundaries come and go.[73] But all proposals for reform[74] have been spurned, and the cause is now lost. One particular consequence of this inability to rationalize the common law of domicile was that it was manifestly unsuitable to identify a court in which a person should be liable to be sued in civil or commercial proceedings. For this reason the term 'domicile' in the Civil Jurisdiction and Judgments Act 1982 and the Civil Jurisdiction and Judgments Order 2001[75] is statutorily defined to make it separate and distinct from its common law homonym; it is examined in Chapter 2.

---

[68] *Udny v Udny* (1869) LR 1 Sc & Div 441.

[69] Domicile and Matrimonial Proceedings Act 1973, s 3.

[70] ibid, s 1.

[71] See Wade (1983) 32 ICLQ 1.

[72] Domicile and Matrimonial Proceedings Act 1973, s 1.

[73] cf *Re O'Keefe* [1940] Ch 124.

[74] Most recently in Law Commission Report No 168, *The Law of Domicile* (1987).

[75] SI 2001/3929.

Residence as a connecting factor, both in its own right and in the variants of *habitual, usual,* and *ordinary residence,* is more usually found in laws which derive from international conventions; but its use will increase each time the cause of reform of the law of domicile is defeated. At one time it would indicate a person's usual residence, but with few of the technical complications of the common law of domicile. But its use in areas liable to generate high emotional stress—child abduction being the most notable[76]—has increasingly meant that courts have to be increasingly precise about its meaning. It is probable that it indicates only one place, although regular absences will not, by themselves, deprive a residence of its habitual or usual character.[77] It is not greatly affected by a party's intention, though where it is contended that a new habitual residence has been acquired, there will need to be evidence of a settled intention to remain there on a long-term basis.[78] By contrast, (simple) *residence* may exist in more than one place. Residence and the concept of presence play a significant part in the rules of the common law dealing with jurisdiction and the recognition of judgments, although the relationship between residence and presence in these contexts can sometimes be obscure. Because its relevance is so closely related to these jurisdictional questions, it is examined in Chapter 2.

Nationality, as a connecting factor, plays little part in the English conflict of laws, by contrast with civilian jurisdictions where the *lex patriae* is still a common personal connecting factor. The reasons for its non-use in English private international law are pragmatic, but are also susceptible to English over-statement. First, a person's status as a national of a particular country is determined by the law of the proposed state: no rule of English law can determine whether someone is or is not a national of Russia, for example. Nationality is therefore immune to the judicial refinement which can be brought to bear on other connecting factors. Though it plays a significant part in the law of the

---

[76] See Ch 8 below.

[77] *R v London Borough of Barnet, ex p Shah* [1983] 2 AC 309. But one does not become habitually resident in a single day: *Re J (A Minor) (Abduction: Custody Rights)* [1990] 2 AC 562; *Nessa v Chief Immigration Officer* [1998] 2 All ER 728.

[78] *Re J (A Minor) (Abduction: Custody Rights)* [1990] 2 AC 562; *Re S (A Minor) (Abduction: European Convention)* [1998] AC 750.

European Union, it may be supposed that the Member States are content for this purpose to accept each other's ascription of nationality; it does not follow that it would be a useful tool outside that context. Second, a person may retain a nationality long after losing all practical connection to the state in question, retaining it, perhaps, for emotional or other idiosyncratic reasons, or even forgetfully: in such a case it may not be the most appropriate law to serve as the person's personal law. Third, dual nationality, or nationality in a federal or complex state, such as the United States or the United Kingdom, or statelessness, would cause real difficulty for any person for whom nationality was a personal connecting factor. Yet it seems reasonable to suppose that those many jurisdictions which employ nationality as a personal connecting factor manage to deal with these practical objections, and it may be wrong to see these instances as so significant that the basic rule must be rejected: tails should not generally be allowed to wag dogs. It is also true that a person who wishes to determine his nationality can usually just look inside his passport. By contrast, the person who needs to ascertain her habitual residence, to say nothing of her common law domicile, may be faced with the kind of question most usually encountered in university examinations. Pragmatism is, perhaps, not all one way.

Causal connecting factors

Terms which describe a connection between a fact or an event and a law are also defined by reference to English law; where the meaning is not obvious it will be explained in the particular area of the law where it is utilized. Some of those which will be encountered are mentioned here. Even though latinate expression is considered by some to add to the obscurity of the law, the definitional concepts of the conflict of laws are still rendered, across Europe and the world, in classical forms. Up to this point in this chapter the attempt has been made to express connecting factors in an English language paraphrase, but it is undeniable, except by those with tin ears, that these lack the elegance and the economy of the traditional usages. From this point on, therefore, these connecting factors will generally be referred to in the form in which they appear in the authorities and as they are used internationally in the discourse of the conflict of laws. In addition to the *lex domicilii*, the law of the domicile, and the *lex patriae*, the law of the nationality, they include: the *lex fori*, the law of the court in which the trial is taking place; the *lex contractus*, the law which governs a contract, whether determined under the rules of the common law (for contracts made before 2 April 1991, the 'proper law') or the Rome Convention (for contracts made after 1 April 1991, the 'governing law') or Rome I Regulation (for contracts made after 17 December 2009, the 'applicable law'); the *lex loci contractus*, the law of the place where the contract was made; the *lex delicti*, the law which governs liability in tort, whether determined under the rules of the common law, statute, or Rome II Regulation; the *lex loci delicti commissi*, the law of the place where the tort was committed; the *lex situs*, the law of the place where land, or other thing, is; the *lex loci actus*, the law of the place where a transaction was carried out; the *lex loci celebrationis*, the law of the place of celebration of marriage; the *lex incorporationis*, the law of the place of incorporation; the *lex protectionis*, the law which grants legal protection to an intellectual property right; the *lex concursus*, the law of the court which is administering an insolvent estate; the *lex successionis*, the law which governs the succession to a deceased estate; and the *lex causae*, which is used to refer generically to the law applicable to the issue in dispute.

(e) Statutes, and the expectations of comity

By contrast with its reasonably sophisticated framework for dealing with the application of foreign law, the common law conflict of laws is not at its best when handling English statutes. Although a court will only apply a foreign statutory rule if the foreign law is the *lex causae*, the reverse is not true. An English court may apply an English statute even though the rules for choice of law otherwise point to the application of a foreign law. All depends on the true construction of the statute, on whether Parliament has directed the judges to apply it without regard to or despite foreign components in the overall dispute.[79] Some, such as the Human Rights Act 1998, can be seen to override

---

[79] For example, Unfair Contract Terms Act 1977, s 27.

all contrary rules for choice of foreign law and jurisdiction, but it is rarely as clear as that. It is sometimes said that there is a presumption that laws are made to be territorially limited, for this is what international comity would expect. But even if that is so, it is only a point of departure; and it will depend on the law, and the precise way in which the 'territory' or 'territorial' is defined: is it by reference to the person, or the property, or the transaction, or something else? When Parliament legislates without making any clear statement of the international reach or 'legislative grasp' of its laws, the courts have to do the best they can; and there are no easy answers.[80]

This leads to a broader question, whether 'comity' has any discernible role in private international law. Some writers taking the view that its lack of clear definition renders it unusable or useless. But other writers, and courts,[81] make reference to comity rather more often than this would suggest. If comity is understood as a rather woolly principle of judicial self-restraint, it would not be useful. However, the principle may be formulated as one which asserts positively that the exercise of jurisdiction and legislative power is territorial and that exercises of sovereign power within the sovereign's own territory are entitled to be respected, but which also accepts passively that parties may assume obligations which either may ask a court to enforce against the other without regard to such territoriality. On that basis it is capable of explaining the law on jurisdiction and foreign judgments, the interpretation and application of statutes, and certain elements of choice of law. It has been observed by leading civilian commentators that comity plays a characteristic role in the common

---

[80] On Employment Rights Act 1996, s 94, for example, see *Serco Ltd v Lawson* [2006] UKHL 3, [2006] ICR 250; *Ravat v Halliburton Manufacturing Services Ltd* [2012] UKSC 1, [2012] ICR 389. On Senior Courts Act 1981, s 36 (service of writ of subpoena), see *Masri v Consolidated Contractors International Co SAL* [2009] UKHL 43, [2010] 1 AC 90. On Insolvency Act 1986, s 423 (recovery of property transferred in fraud of creditors) see *Re Paramount Airways Ltd* [1993] Ch 223; and on orders to recover property derived from the commission of crimes, see *Serious Organised Crime Agency v Perry* [2012] UKSC 35, [2012] 3 WLR 379. It is impossible to see any clear picture in that.

[81] For a recent example, see *Joujou v Masri* [2011] EWCA Civ 746, [2011] 2 CLC 566. It should be noted that US courts make much more frequent reference to the principle.

law of private international law, and there would be no reason for an English lawyer to deny it.[82]

A general principle of comity leads also to the specific conclusion that an English court may not be asked to rule on the validity of a foreign sovereign act carried out within its territory, whether the validity is said to be questionable by reference to the internal law of that state or referred to some precept of public international law. The acts of states as states, done within their territory, are not justiciable; they are beyond the purview of municipal courts, not only because there are no judicial or manageable standards by which to judge them, but also because the intervention of the courts at the instance of private parties may contradict the government in its conduct of the international relations of the United Kingdom.[83] Though from time to time an attempt is made to trim this wise principle of abstention, perhaps by taking instruction from resolutions of the competent organs of the United Nations,[84] the general principle is as sound as it is valuable. Of course, foreign legislation may be refused effect in England in an individual case on grounds of public policy, but such a conclusion does not rest on the invalidity of the foreign act or legislation, but on the ordinary rules of the conflict of laws.[85]

3. QUESTIONING THE COMMON LAW APPROACH

It is accurate to describe the traditional approach of the common law as 'jurisdiction-selecting': the choice of law process selects a legal system whose rule will be taken to govern the issue before the court; this legal system, more or less automatically, provides the answer. Little or no attention is paid to the question—which is not asked—whether this actually produces the 'right' answer, or the 'best' answer. Although it has proved remarkably durable in England and much of the common law world, and although

---

[82] See further, Briggs (2012) 354 *Hague Recueil* (Académie de Droit International; Martinus Nijhoff), p 69.

[83] *Buttes Gas & Oil Co v Hammer* [1982] AC 888, 938.

[84] *Kuwait Airways Corpn v Iraq Airways Co (Nos 4 and 5)* [2002] UKHL 19, [2002] 2 AC 883.

[85] See further, p 208 below.

it appears to be found in most civilian systems as well, it is still open to criticism. Several points may be suggested. First, the creation of characterization categories is to some extent an artificial process, an attempt to impose order on a market of conflicting legal rules and tending, unless care is taken, to be rigid and blinkered.[86] Secondly, the idea that within each of these categories—material validity of contract, personal capacity to marry—there is a conceptual unity which justifies subjecting them all to the same choice of law is not always plausible: should the one law really determine the age at which a person may marry, whether a blood or other relative may be married, whether polygamy or same-sex union is permitted, and the effect of inability or refusal to consummate the marriage? Is this really a single, coherent, group of issues? Thirdly, and tellingly, little interest is shown in whether the rule of law actually chosen for application was developed or enacted with the intention that it be applied in the instant case. Fourthly, little or no attempt is made to compare and evaluate the results which would be produced by the rules of law from the various systems which might connect to the facts, still less to choose between them. For these among other reasons American jurists,[87] and some others drawing their inspiration from them, have proposed a variety of alternative approaches. These are varied in their content; have received some, but not substantial, judicial support; are perhaps most prominent in litigation about inter-state torts; and are more complex, and may be more subtle, than the more mechanical traditional approach. Take for example the case of an inter-state traffic accident, involving cars registered in, and drivers and passengers resident in, different states; and suppose that the laws of some, but not all, of these states restrict the type and extent of damages which can be recovered. It is not hard to see the mechanical application of a *lex delicti*, such as the law of the place where the tort occurred, as being too insensitive to the actual and personal facts of the case.[88]

---

[86] cf *Raiffeisen Zentralbank Österreich AG v Five Star Trading LLC* [2001] EWCA Civ 68, [2001] QB 825.

[87] Especially Cavers, *The Choice of Law Process* (1965) and (1970) 131 Hague Recueil 143; Currie, *Selected Essays on the Conflict of Laws* (1963); American Law Institute, *Restatement Second of the Conflict of Laws* (1971).

[88] cf *Babcock v Jackson* 191 NE 2d 279 (1963).

A modest alternative, which is still jurisdiction-selecting, would be to apply the law having the closest and most real connection to the particular claim, and to assess this on a case-by-case basis; a variant would be to look to the law having the closest connection to the particular issue to be adjudicated, rather than to the tort as a whole. A more radical alternative, which may be thought of as 'rule-selecting', would enquire whether each of the various rules contained in the competing systems was intended by its legislator to apply to the case, or issue, currently before the court. If this analysis reveals that only one of the potentially-applicable rules was designed to apply to a case such as this, there will have been a false or illusory conflict of laws, and the one and only concerned law will be applied. But if it is discovered that more than one of these laws was intended to apply to the given facts, the court will have to resolve the conflict of laws, which it may do by applying its own domestic law if it is one of those which was designed to be applied, or by seeking to identify the 'better', or 'best' law. The scientific analysis of these alternatives to traditional choice of law is not susceptible to concise statement, but insofar as the approach involves construing conflicting statutes to discern what they really intend, it taps into an ancient and orthodox tradition. But it also works better in a system where the majority of actual rules from which the selection must be made are contained in codes or statutes. For the common law has no legislator and its purpose is, in this sense, unknown and unknowable. This may be contrasted with statute law, on which *travaux préparatoires* and constitutional theory may illuminate the actual or presumed legislative intention. This process is sometimes called 'governmental interest analysis', which is unfortunate: call it instead 'searching for the intentions of the legislature' and it seems much less alien. Whether it could ever have been made to work in England is open to debate;[89] and as English choice of law rules are increasingly contained in European legislation, there is relatively little scope for an English judge to follow whatever he may take to be the American way ahead.

If private international law is to continue to use connecting factors which select a law to be applied, a greater challenge may

---

[89] Kahn-Freund (1974) 143 Hague Recueil 147; Fawcett (1982) 31 ICLQ 189.

yet come from those new technologies which make a 'law of the place of ...' rule seem inappropriate. The use of electronic systems of communication for publicity, trade, fraud, and defamation, has yet to be properly examined in the context of the conflict of laws. Opinions vary. On one side are those who consider that these new media mean that a rethinking of jurisdiction, foreign judgments, and choice of law cannot be avoided, and the sooner the better; on the other, those who feel that just as the conflict of laws came to terms with the telephone, telex, and fax, it will simply adapt its basic ideas to the facts of this new-fangled technology. It is too early to announce the death of the traditional conflict of laws; but there is always a risk that rules tailor-made for new technology invite their own obsolescence.

If the past is any guide to the future, specific choice of law rules which have reached the end of their shelf life may be superseded by more flexible ones. A couple of examples may illustrate the point. In the private international law of restitution, there was authority for the view that the obligation to make restitution would, in certain cases, be governed by the law of the place of the enrichment.[90] But when claims result from the electronic transfer—except that nothing is actually transferred as banks electronically adjust their records—of funds by banks, the place of enrichment may be so fortuitous or so artificial that it makes no sense as a choice of law rule. In the private international law of intangible property, dealings with negotiable instruments are traditionally governed by the law of the place where the document is. But widely-used, international electronic dealing or settlement systems, and the custodianship of securities, would risk being confounded by the rigid application of this antique rule of law to such novel methods of dealing. In such cases, new choice of law rules may be required if the most appropriate law to the issues raised by this new technology is to be applied; it is no answer to shrug and say that those who enter into the market risk the surprises which traditional conflict of laws may spring on them; and it would be optimistic to assume that sensible rules can be developed without the need for legislation.

---

[90] Though the issue is now generally governed by the Rome II Regulation, its Art 10(3) applies the law of the country in which the unjust enrichment took place, which rule raises questions of a similar kind.

Maybe similar thinking is required for general electronic commerce and communication. When contracts are made over the internet, it may be necessary to decide where a contract was made or was broken,[91] or whether a supplier directed his professional or commercial activities to the place of a consumer's domicile.[92] It is improbable that a technical analysis of the locations of the customer's computer and internet server, or of the server which hosts the supplier's website, the supplier's computer, and of the various ways in which this information is read or downloaded, etc, will yield a solution which is scientifically respectable, comprehensible for the people involved, and jurisprudentially rational. Where it is alleged that a reputation has been defamed by a statement displayed on a web page accessible by computer users from China to Peru, does it really make sense to ask where the tort or torts occurred, or where the damage occurred, or where was the event which gave rise to the damage?[93] For all these points of contact may be multiplied by the number of people who may have had access to the information. When it comes to jurisdiction[94] or the recognition of foreign judgments,[95] it may be necessary to ask whether the defendant was present (or carrying on business) in or at a particular place. The facts of modern business life may make this a surprisingly difficult question to answer. For the purposes of regulation of deposit-takers and investment businesses, it may be necessary to determine whether an individual carried on specified activities or business in the United Kingdom.[96] The conflict of laws must keep abreast of this brave new world.

In the absence of a more radical alternative, a tentative guess may be that the place where the individuals, or their day-to-day[97] office premises, are located will prove to be more significant than where the hardware is, and that both will be more significant than

---

[91]   See CPR Practice Direction 6B, para 3.1(6).

[92]   Council Regulation (EC) 44/2001, [2001] OJ L12/1, Art 15.

[93]   ibid Art 5(3). cf *Gutnick v Dow Jones & Co Inc* [2002] HCA 56, (2002) 210 CLR 375.

[94]   CPR r 6.9(2).

[95]   *Adams v Cape Industries plc* [1990] Ch 433 (CA).

[96]   For example, Financial Services and Markets Act 2000, s 418.

[97]   As distinct from a letterbox address in a tax haven or money laundry, but which pretends to be a central office.

the notional places where links in the chain of communication may be found. After all, domestic law and the conflict of laws deal with communication and contracts made by telephone, and it appears to be assumed that the place of the telephone subscriber is decisive. It appears not to matter that the offeree left a message on an answering machine on the premises, or in a voicemail box maintained by a telephone company; or that either caller used a mobile phone. Rough-and-ready locations can be ascribed to the persons who communicate, and the legal analysis will proceed from there. For defamation, the eye of the reader is significant, rather than the place where or from which his computer receives the information in question.[98] For presence or the carrying on of business, it seems probable that this can indicate only where living, breathing, individuals do what they do, rather than a notional place where information is transferred. This is not to say coming to terms with conflicts issues presented by the new technology will be plain sailing, or that no legislation will be required. But calm creativity from commercial judges will usually bring about rational solutions.

C. LEGISLATION ESTABLISHING PRIVATE INTERNATIONAL LAW AS EUROPEAN LAW

The system of private international law just described was developed to regulate the private international rules of the common law, making law from cases and the absence of cases, and from not much else. When it was required to accommodate statute law,[99] it generally did so by treating it as though they were no different from rules of non-statute law. English legislation would therefore be applied when, but only when, English law was identified by choice of law rules as being the *lex causae*; foreign law would be applied when that foreign law was the *lex causae*, and so on. Although a rare English statute might be applied in a case in which the *lex causae* was not otherwise English, this happened when and because the legislative instruction to the judge was

---

[98] *Gutnick v Dow Jones & Co Inc* [2002] HCA 56, (2002) 210 CLR 375.

[99] That is, rules of domestic law in statutory form. There was very little legislation of rules of choice of law.

understood to be so peremptory as to override the result which would have been derived from the ordinary process of choice of law.[100] There is no doubt that such a direct instruction from the legislator may have this effect on an English judge. But this effect could be attributed only to English legislation, and then only where the terms in which the legislation was drafted made it sufficiently clear that it really was a direct instruction to the judge, by-passing the rules for choice of law. In the great majority of cases, English legislation was simply fitted into the established common law pattern for choice of law.

But today, legislation is not only made in England, and instructions to judges do not come only from Westminster. Increasingly, rules of law, including rules of private international law, are established by the organs of the European Union. To be technical about it, these laws take effect in England under the authority of the European Communities Act 1972.[101] The law on jurisdiction and the recognition of foreign judgments is mostly governed by European, which means pan-European, legislation: this is true for civil and commercial matters,[102] and in some areas of family law[103] and insolvency,[104] but the legislative aim of the European Union is to exercise more widely yet its authority over the field of jurisdiction and judgments, but also civil procedure.[105] The rules for choice of law are also substantially European and legislative: choice of law for contractual[106] and non-contractual[107] obligations is

---

[100] The traditional terminology of private international law was therefore to refer to these as 'overriding' statutes. A more modern usage is to refer to them as 'mandatory' laws.

[101] Which gave a blank cheque to what is now the European Union to make legislation within the scope of the Treaty of Rome, as amended from time to time.

[102] Regulation (EC) 44/2001, [2001] OJ L12/1.

[103] Regulation (EC) 2201/2003, [2003] OJ L338/1; Regulation (EC) 4/2009, [2009] OJ L7/1.

[104] Regulation (EC) 1346/2000, [2000] OJ L160/1.

[105] Regulations also deal with the service of process (Regulation (EC) 1393/2007, [2008] OJ L331/21), the taking of evidence for use in proceedings (Regulation (EC) 1206/2001, [2001] OJ L174/1), and a growing number of small claims and consumer procedures not listed here.

[106] Regulation (EC) 593/2008, [2008] OJ L177/6.

[107] Regulation (EC) 864/2007, [2007] OJ L199/40.

now covered, as also are maintenance[108] and some other aspects of family law;[109] so also is insolvency.[110] To date, the United Kingdom has stood aside from European legislation governing the dissolution of marriage,[111] and that dealing with wills, succession, and the administration of estates,[112] but this did not prevent the legislation being made, and the United Kingdom may yet opt into it. It has also stood aside from proposed legislation to deal with the private international law of matrimonial property, but again, this will neither prevent the legislation being made nor preclude a later decision to opt into it. Still further, other European legislation which is not directly targeted at private international law may still impinge on issues of private international law. For example, the freedom of establishment guaranteed by the European Treaty is bound to have, and has had, a significant impact on the private international law of corporations. And quite apart from all that, the European Convention on Human Rights, made by the Council of Europe but legislated into English law by the Human Rights Act 1998, is also seeping into private international law.

Whatever else may be true, European legislation is not made to work within or amend the common law. It aims instead to override it and the national laws of all Member States, in order to produce uniform rules of private international law across the European Union. This will make it possible to know which courts will and will not have jurisdiction, and which country's law will be applied to the dispute, no matter where proceedings may be brought. It may be helpful to think of these legislative texts as being pasted onto the pages of an album, initially blank but which, when filled up, will stand as the Code of Private International Law for the European Union, and which is, in its present incomplete state, a part of that intended code of private international law.

This code, or these European materials, come with their own instructions for use. Let us take the choice of law rules for

---

[108] Regulation (EC) 4/2009, [2009] OJ L7/1.
[109] Regulation (EC) 2201/2003, [2003] OJ L338/1.
[110] Regulation (EC) 1346/2000, [2000] OJ L160/1.
[111] Regulation (EU) 1259/2010, [2010] OJ L343/10.
[112] Regulation (EU) 650/2012, [2012] OJ L201/107.

non-contractual obligations in civil or commercial matters arising from events giving rise to damage which occur after 11 January 2009. The choice of law rules of the Rome II Regulation apply if (i) the relationship in question is one of 'non-contractual obligation', (ii) the obligation is within the definition of 'civil or commercial matters', and (iii) events giving rise to damage occur after 11 January 2009. To decide (i) whether the relationship in question is a non-contractual obligation, and (ii) whether the matter is a civil or commercial one, the court is called upon to interpret Article 1 of the Regulation. To decide whether the events giving rise to damage occurred after 11 January 2009, the court is called upon to interpret Article 31 of the Regulation. The court does not 'characterize' the issue as being contractual, tortious, equitable, one of unjust enrichment, or otherwise, insofar as these are terms of art of the common law doctrine of characterization. For the doctrine of characterization is the key to the common law rules of private international law, but where the Regulation applies these rules of the common law are *res extincta*. True, the court may be faced with a problem if, for example, the events giving rise to damage appear to have occurred both before and after 11 January 2009, but it has to answer the question posed by Article 31 by focusing on the Article itself, on the recitals to the Regulation, and on more general principles of European private international law, such as legal certainty. It has to put out of its mind any recollection of how common lawyers might once have dealt with analogous problems, at least until it has concluded that Article 31 excludes the case from the domain of the Regulation, at which point the court assumes the power and responsibility of a common law court applying common law rules and techniques of private international law.

In short, this legislation makes up an entirely new system of private international law, conveniently called 'European Private International Law'. It comes with its own manual, which is written in European, not in English. Of course, the transitional phase is bound to be untidy, as transitional phases always are. If each system—common law, European—is designed to be complete, some turbulence can be expected if a case requires a court to work with materials from each system. But things can only get better.

1. PRINCIPLES OF LEGISLATIVE INTERPRETATION

The skills required by the private international lawyer working with this European legislative material form the counterpart to the common law principles of characterization, etc. What is required in the domain of European private international law are those techniques which will lead to a clear and accurate interpretation of the various legislative texts. The applicable canons of European statutory interpretation are general and particular. Consideration of those which are particular to specific pieces of legislation can be postponed to be dealt with in the context in which they arise: they are most developed in the field of jurisdiction and the recognition of judgments.

Prime among the general principles of interpretation is the requirement that terms of art in the legislation will bear a meaning which is autonomous, which is to say, independent of the national law of the court called upon to apply it. There would, as said before, be little point in enacting a single legislative text which meant different things in each of the 27 Member States: it would make no more sense for the Unfair Contract Terms Act 1977 to mean one thing in Yorkshire but another thing in Kent. Ideally these autonomous definitions of legislative terms will have been laid down by the European Court, on references for preliminary rulings made by national courts,[113] but where this has not yet happened, the national court must guide itself by considering how the European Court would have answered if it were to have been asked.

Second, the interpretation adopted should contribute to legal certainty: this principle has been identified with increasing clarity, and it manifests itself in various ways. It will tend to mean that where one piece of legislation has replaced another, the interpretation given to provisions which are common to both should be consistent, so that a litigant may know where he is able to sue or liable to be sued, or know what law will be applied if the case has to be taken to court, without the need for complicated analysis or expensive advice. In principle, legal certainty should

---

[113] Under Art 267 of the Treaty on the Functioning of the European Union.

also argue for consistency of interpretation across the legislation, though at this point the principle may yield to more contextual concerns, considered below.

Third, rules of general application are interpreted broadly; rules of specific application which derogate from these are interpreted as being no wider than is necessary to achieve the specific purpose for which they were made, for fear that the exception swallow up the rule. This does not always mean that a rule which may be regarded as *lex specialis* must be given the most restrictive interpretation imaginable, but the derogation from *lex generalis* should be no wider than the reason for the legislation requires.

Fourth, legislative rules which are made to protect a weaker party from exploitation may not be circumvented. This may be thought to be obvious, but the true position may be subtly complicated. For example, legislation which gives jurisdictional advantages to consumers in litigation against professionals may not have precisely the same scope as legislation which gives consumers preferential treatment in terms of choice of law. The legislative policies may be similar, but they may not be congruent.

Fifth, each piece of legislation, and (in principle, at least) each Article within that piece of legislation, has a natural scope which neither overlaps with others nor leaves unplanned gaps. So, in principle at least, a claim is either within the Brussels I Regulation for jurisdiction in civil and commercial matters, or it is within the scope of the Insolvency Regulation, but it cannot be within both, for the scope of each is defined to prevent their overlapping. A claim based on breach of an obligation should not fall within the scope of the Rome I (contractual obligations) and Rome II (non-contractual obligations) Regulations, even if at first sight it might appear that it naturally does, such as when a contractual duty of care is said to have been broken. In cases in which the legislator realized that this advice might be easier to formulate than to abide by, specific drafting may lead to the conclusion that where legislative provisions overlap, they point to the same eventual conclusion, with the result that there is no conflict of laws.

One might have expected to find a sixth: that when a Regulation directs a court to apply the law of a foreign country, the court should apply that law rather than falling back on the common law principle that foreign law is a matter of provable (or improbable) fact. It is true that this would be far more fundamental a change than was ever brought about by making changes to the rules for choice of law themselves, and so far, English eyes have been averted from the challenge which this might present. But one day someone will decide that the scheme of European private international law is impaired when some, but not other, national courts decline to investigate foreign law for themselves, and as a result fail to apply it. When that day arrives, a really radical change in private international legal methodology will be forced upon the English courts.[114] It may get messy.

These principles help ensure that the legislation will provide legal stability for those established in the European Union, reduce the cost and unpredictability of litigation and, if this is thought to be material, perfect the internal market and bring closer union among the peoples of Europe. This will be achieved at a cost, which will be paid not only by those who need their answers well before the new legislative code is complete, but also by those versed in, and those who see virtue in, the common law principles of private international law. Still, for every one who would sigh and murmur *sic transit gloria Angliae*, there is another who will observe[115] that one cannot make an omelette without breaking eggs.

---

[114] For a proposal for legislation in the form of a Regulation, see Esplugues Mota (2011) 13 YBPIL 273.

[115] Whether this observation is properly attributed to Delia Smith, or to the Great Stalin, or otherwise, is a matter on which opinion remains divided.

2

JURISDICTION

A. JURISDICTION OR JURISDICTIONS?

To say that a court has jurisdiction means that the law regards it as having the power to hear and determine a case against a defendant. It must have jurisdiction over the subject matter of the claim, and personal jurisdiction over the defendant to it: at least, this is how the common law of jurisdiction organizes itself. This chapter therefore embarks by saying a little about the three aspects of jurisdiction as this is understood by the common law.

First, there is a small number of matters in respect of which an English court lacks jurisdiction over subject matter of a claim. Where this is the case it is irrelevant that the parties may be willing, or purport, to submit to the personal jurisdiction of the court: absence of subject matter jurisdiction is something which lies beyond their power or control. As a matter of common law, a court has no jurisdiction to determine title to foreign land, and therefore no jurisdiction to hear claims which require it to determine a question of title.[1] Statute has modified this common law rule, so that a court may now hear a claim in tort which relates to foreign land unless it is principally concerned with title to that land:[2] the result appears to be that if the defence to an allegation of trespass is that the defendant had a licence to enter, or the defence to a claim for nuisance is that the claimant had no title to the land, the court will be unable to adjudicate the claim by virtue of being unable to deal with the defence to it. It is unnecessary to ask whether the exclusionary rule would apply where no question arises of legal title but equitable title is disputed, such as a claim about shares in the beneficial ownership of land subject to a trust.

---

[1] *British South Africa Co v Companhia de Moçambique* [1893] AC 602; *Hesperides Hotels Ltd v Aegean Turkish Holidays Ltd* [1979] AC 508; cf Civil Jurisdiction and Judgments Act 1982, s 30.
[2] ibid.

By way of over-reaction to some rather shrill complaints about 'defamation tourism', it has been proposed that a court have no jurisdiction in defamation proceedings brought against a defendant not domiciled in a Member State unless England is, in the light of all the places in which the offending material was published, clearly the most appropriate place for the proceedings.[3] It would have been preferable for the court to be given a clear and transparent jurisdictional discretion, but a statutory removal of subject-matter jurisdiction will mean that the court has no jurisdiction in such a case, even if the defendant is willing to defend the claim in England, which makes little obvious sense.

Back to sensible law. As a matter of ancient authority, where there was a contract or an equity between the parties, the court had jurisdiction to adjudicate on and enforce the personal obligations arising from it, even though the subject of this personal obligation was foreign land.[4] So a court may determine the shares in a tenancy in common in foreign land arising from the trust of that land and require the parties to behave accordingly, and may order the specific performance of a contract to mortgage or to convey foreign land. Indeed, the statutory reform mentioned above was required because there is no contract or equity between tortfeasors, and this ancient principle could not therefore be used in the context of a tort committed in relation to foreign land. Authority[5] still supports the conclusion that a court lacks jurisdiction at common law to adjudicate the validity of foreign patents, for the grant or extent of such rights was a matter for the foreign sovereign alone. The better view may, however, be that the court does not lack jurisdiction, in the sense that its adjudication would be a nullity, but should accede to an application to decline to exercise its jurisdiction.

Second, so far as concerns the person against whom the claim may be brought, the principles of state and diplomatic immunity

---

[3] Defamation Bill 2012-13, cl 11. It is expected that this Bill will be passed into law in 2013.

[4] *Penn v Baltimore* (1750) 1 Ves Sen 444.

[5] *Lucasfilm Ltd v Ainsworth* [2011] UKSC 29, [2012] 1 AC 208 (excluding copyright from the scope of any exclusionary rule); cf *Potter v Broken Hill Pty Ltd* (1906) 3 CLR 479.

limit the exercise of jurisdiction over non-commercial claims brought against states and diplomats.[6] Indeed, in these cases it may be subject-matter jurisdiction, rather than personal jurisdiction, which is lacking, on the footing that once the immunity is established, scrutiny of the act of a foreign sovereign lies beyond the competence of the English court. In relation to international organizations, the instrument establishing the organization as a juridical person for the purposes of English law will usually also define the extent of any immunity from the processes of the court.[7] If the organization is not accorded personality by English legislation, its personality may still be recognized if this has been conferred under the law of another state, rather as if it were a corporation created under the law of that state.[8] But subject to that exception, a court will as a matter of common law have personal jurisdiction over a defendant when process has been or is deemed to have been served on him, and rules of jurisdiction *in personam* are therefore rules which specify whether and when it is lawful to serve process on the defendant.[9] As a matter of common law, any defendant present within the territorial jurisdiction of the court was and is liable to be served with process by or on behalf of the claimant, who may do so as of right; but no defendant was liable to be served if he was outside England. To overcome this difficulty, rules of court permitted a claimant to apply for permission to serve process on a defendant out of the jurisdiction: the circumstances in which this may be done are currently set out in Part 6 of the Civil Procedure Rules (CPR).[10]

But third, in the common law scheme it does not follow that, just because a court has jurisdiction, it will always exercise it at the behest of the claimant. A characteristic of the common law of jurisdiction, especially in the context of a conflict of potential

---

[6] State Immunity Act 1978; *Holland v Lampen-Wolfe* [2000] 1 WLR 1573 (HL).

[7] International Organisations Act 1968.

[8] *Arab Monetary Fund v Hashim (No 3)* [1991] 2 AC 114. What happens if it is given legal personality under the laws of more than one state is not very clear.

[9] For the procedure for effecting service see Civil Procedure Rules 1998 (CPR) Pt 6. Personal service is still the most common method.

[10] Previously Rules of the Supreme Court, Order 11. Care must be taken to notice alterations to the wording of these provisions from one incarnation to the next.

jurisdictions, is the power of an English court, on application made by the defendant, to decline to exercise the jurisdiction which it admittedly has, with the consequence that the claimant may in practice have to proceed in a foreign court. There is a coherence to all of this, which results from two fundamental truths: first, that as a matter of common law the jurisdiction of the High Court is inherent, which is to say, its power to try claims is, save as mentioned above, unrestricted by the nature of the claim or the identity of the defendant; and second, that as a matter of common law, a court has inherent power to regulate its own procedure, including the procedural power to not exercise a jurisdiction which it has. This results in the common law relating to jurisdiction being flexible, or unpredictable, according to one's vantage point.

All this changed in 1987. From that date a wave of European legislative instruments, culminating in what is now the Brussels I Regulation, Council Regulation (EC) 44/2001,[11] and which will from 10 January 2015 be recast as Regulation (EU) 1215/2012,[12] enacted a scheme of jurisdiction which was juridically separate and distinct from that which the court had as a matter of common law. The fact that this jurisdiction was enacted in Europe, rather than being inherent, is terribly important. This enacted jurisdiction had the characteristics, and only the characteristics, which the legislator intended it to have. To begin with, its statutory language would be subject to the principles of interpretation described in Chapter 1 rather than any such rules taken from the common law. Next, to take an example which has proved to be controversial, according to the dominant view the contention that a court has a discretion to decide whether to exercise jurisdiction will succeed only if it can be shown to have been conferred on the court by this legislation: it cannot be derived from the common law. To take another, where the common law would deny, or would have denied, that the court had jurisdiction over the subject matter of the claim, but the Regulation nevertheless

---

[11] [2001] OJ L12/1. See the following section for details of these jurisdictional instruments.

[12] [2012] OJ L351/1. For convenience, the recast Regulation is discussed in the context of the treatment of Reg 44/2001, but a summary or reprise of its major changes will be found at p 109 below.

confers jurisdiction over the defendant, it is not obvious that this common law jurisdictional objection could properly be applied to a court exercising this legislative jurisdiction.[13] The powers which would be inherent in or associated with common law jurisdiction would be, *ex hypothesi*, inapplicable to this form of non-inherent, enacted, jurisdiction: in short, a court cannot pick and mix.

The immediate consequence is that a claimant, or a court, must first consider whether the jurisdiction invoked is common law jurisdiction, or this enacted jurisdiction. Where the European instruments are wholly inapplicable, the jurisdictional rules of the common law will apply: in this chapter, the expression 'common law jurisdiction' will be used to refer to the set of rules which operate in an English court when these European instruments make no claim to application. Where by contrast the jurisdiction of the court is governed by this European legislation, the court will be exercising 'Regulation jurisdiction'. To complicate matters only slightly, these European instruments occasionally refer to and rely on the jurisdictional rules developed at common law: incorporating them by reference, as it were. When this happens, the jurisdiction is still 'Regulation jurisdiction', a fact which may affect the rules thus incorporated from the common law, but for this particular form of Regulation jurisdiction, the term 'residual Regulation jurisdiction' may be useful to mark the point that, in such cases, the Regulation still applies and the common law does not.

It may be that this means that an English court should be understood as having *jurisdictions* rather than *jurisdiction*. Of course, this would not make English law on jurisdiction unique. Many legal systems draw a distinction between, for example, federal and state jurisdictions, though they tend to do so by providing for separate courts. What is distinctive in England[14] is that the two forms of jurisdiction are exercised by the one court; and it should not surprise anyone to be told that, on occasion, this can lead to blurring of lines which ought to be kept clean. Still, clarity of thought is more easily maintained if 'Regulation jurisdiction' and 'common law jurisdiction' are treated separately, and in that order. This chapter tries to do just that, examining jurisdiction over defendants generally, and

---

[13] See p 101 below.
[14] And in the other Member States.

trying to keep the two systems of jurisdiction as cleanly separated as possible. But as jurisdiction in the specific contexts of family matters, the administration of estates, bankruptcy and insolvency, and so on is more conveniently treated alongside choice of law in the chapters which deal with those substantive topics, jurisdiction in such cases is postponed to be discussed in those chapters.

B. REGULATION JURISDICTION: INTRODUCTION

1. HISTORY

The interest of the European Community in civil jurisdiction stems from Article 220 of the Treaty of Rome, which committed the six original Member States, Belgium, France, Germany, Italy, Luxembourg, and the Netherlands, to develop a system for the mutual recognition and enforcement of judgments in civil and commercial matters. It was decided that the best way to ensure an uncomplicated enforcement of sister-state judgments—creating a free market in judgments, as some call it—was to limit the power of the judge to review the judgment of which enforcement was sought; and that the proper way to achieve that result was to adopt a uniform set of rules for the taking of jurisdiction in the first place. The Brussels Convention of 27 September 1968[15] was adopted to perform this dual function.

States which joined the European Community acceded to the Brussels Convention, which was successively amended on the accession of the United Kingdom,[16] Denmark, and Ireland; Greece; Portugal, and Spain; and Austria, Finland, and Sweden. By the end of 2000, the re-re-re-amended text[17] of the Brussels Convention served as the common jurisdictional statute of the 15 Member States. In addition, a parallel Convention, signed at Lugano on 16 April 1988,[18] bound the states of the European

---

[15] In force in the six states from 1 January 1973.

[16] Enacted as Sch 1 to the Civil Jurisdiction and Judgments Act 1982 (the 1982 Act), which was amended on each subsequent accession.

[17] SI 2000/1824, in force from 1 January 2001.

[18] Civil Jurisdiction and Judgments Act 1982, Sch 3C, as inserted by Civil Jurisdiction and Judgments Act 1991, Sch 1.

Union and of the European Free Trade Area. Of these, Austria, Finland, and Sweden later acceded to membership of the European Union, and thereby ceased to be 'Lugano states', leaving Iceland, Norway, and Switzerland, which remained, and which remain, outside the European Union, as 'Lugano states'.

The process of amending an international convention can be cumbersome, which is not very helpful when adjustments to the law on civil jurisdiction and judgments prove to be necessary. The Member States therefore agreed to let the European Union legislate directly, transforming the Brussels Convention into a European Regulation, which became known, rather predictably, as the Brussels I Regulation.[19] It came into effect on 1 March 2002. It supplanted the Convention in the then Member States, save for Denmark which elected to stand aside. The 10 states which acceded in 2004,[20] and the two which did so in 2007,[21] were bound by the Regulation from the date of their accession; and Denmark came back in from the cold in 2007 as well.[22] The three remaining Lugano states then agreed with the European Union to amend the Lugano Convention to bring it into line with the Brussels I Regulation. The result of all this effort was that, in effect, a single legislative text now governs jurisdiction and the enforcement of judgments in civil and commercial matters in the 27 Member States and the three Lugano states. At the date of writing, the Brussels I Regulation and the revised Lugano Convention are fully in force across almost of the whole territory of the continent of Europe.

By any reckoning, and notwithstanding occasional unease about what these rules actually do, it was a remarkable achievement. In 2007 a project to consider reforms to the Brussels I Regulation was announced, and in 2008 a Report produced by three distinguished German professors laid the basis for what might have been extensive refurbishment. The journey to reform was, however, slower and less consensual than expected, the final

---

[19] Regulation (EC) 44/2001, [2001] OJ L12/1.

[20] Cyprus, Czech Republic, Estonia, Hungary, Latvia, Lithuania, Malta, Poland, Slovakia, and Slovenia.

[21] Bulgaria and Romania.

[22] SI 2007/1655.

version of the legislative text, made as Regulation (EU) 1215/2012, having taken many years to settle. The recast Regulation[23] will take effect from 10 January 2015. Though many of the changes are of minor detail, a few are substantial, addressing issues of principle on points on which the Brussels I Regulation is considered to have fallen short. It is therefore convenient to note these changes where they impinge, but otherwise to maintain the order and numbering of the Brussels I Regulation,[24] which will serve as the base text. References to 'the Court' are to the Court of Justice of the European Union, or European Court. Although many of the reported cases were decided under the provisions of the Brussels and Lugano Conventions, the account which follows has its focus on the Regulation, and terminology, and numbering of Articles, has been adjusted accordingly. It may be unhistorical, but so is life.

2. GENERAL SCHEME

The Regulation deals with jurisdiction in civil or commercial matters. It is the basic jurisdictional statute for the Member States, and national courts may make references to the European Court for a preliminary ruling on its interpretation.[25] It is drafted in many languages, although these versions are not, perhaps, in every nuance and respect, identical, and occasionally parties may try to exploit the differences. As a matter of procedural law, where the Regulation confers jurisdiction on an English court, process may be served on the defendant as of right, whether in England or (with the appropriate certification of the court's jurisdiction under the Regulation) outside it.[26]

Where the Regulation confers international jurisdiction upon the courts of a Member State, as distinct from the courts of a particular place, it confers it on the courts of the United Kingdom, not England, for England is not a state. To deal with this,

[23] Regulation (EU) 1215/2012: [2012] OJ L351/1.

[24] A useful Table of Correlation is printed as Annex III to Reg 1215/2012.

[25] Article 267 of the Treaty on the Functioning of the European Union (TFEU).

[26] CPR r 6.33.

internal rules of national jurisdiction, resembling but sometimes deliberately diverging from the Regulation, sub-allocate jurisdiction as between the courts of England, Scotland, and Northern Ireland.[27] These rules of internal United Kingdom law are not the concern of the European Court.[28]

Most definitional terms used in the Regulation bear 'autonomous' meanings, distinct from those accorded to the same terms in national law. They were mostly developed in the jurisprudence of the Court on references for preliminary rulings on the Brussels Convention, which remain authoritative.[29] The meanings of 'contract' and 'tort', used for the jurisdictional purpose of the Regulation,[30] for example, do not and should not precisely mirror these terms as they are used in English domestic law. It follows that a court which has Regulation jurisdiction on the basis of the 'contract' rule might have proceeded to determine the merits by using its private international law of tort,[31] though as choice of law in the law of obligations is increasingly governed by European legislation, this discrepancy will certainly reduce in scope. In addition, certain other canons of interpretation have emerged over the years. First, as the basic principle is that a defendant shall be sued in the courts of the Member State where he is domiciled, a provision of the Regulation derogating from this rule will tend to receive a restrictive construction.[32] This was established by the

---

[27] 1982 Act, Sch 4, as amended by Civil Jurisdiction and Judgments Order 2001, Sch 2.

[28] Case C-364/93 *Kleinwort Benson Ltd v City of Glasgow DC* [1995] ECR I-415. The extent to which preliminary rulings from the Court are conclusive on the interpretation of the internal UK rules is uncertain, but they must at least be influential: *Kleinwort Benson Ltd v Glasgow City Council* [1999] 1 AC 153; *Agnew v Länsförsäkringsbolagens AB* [2001] 1 AC 223, 245.

[29] So also, save where the provisions have been materially altered, will the expert reports on the various conventions: Jenard Report [1979] OJ C59/1; Schlosser Report [1979] OJ C59/71; Evrigenis Report [1986] OJ C298/1; Cruz Report [1989] OJ C189/35; Jenard and Möller Report [1990] OJ C189/61.

[30] Article 5.

[31] Case C-26/91 *Soc Jakob Handte GmbH v Soc Traitements Mécano-chimiques des Surfaces* [1992] ECR I-3967, 3984.

[32] For example, Case C-220/88 *Dumez France SA v Hessische Landesbank* [1990] ECR I-49; Case C-364/93 *Marinari v Lloyds Bank plc* [1995] ECR I-2719.

Court in its jurisprudence on the Brussels Convention, and it continues to underpin the interpretation of the Regulation.[33] Second, the Regulation is intended to make it possible for litigants to know where proceedings may and may not be brought, so an interpretation which leans in favour of this form of legal certainty will be favoured over one which make less of a contribution; it also follows that the interpretation of the Regulation will be as consistent with the Convention which preceded it wherever the text has been preserved from the one to the other. Third, as the Regulation seeks to make judgments obtained in one Member State freely enforceable in other Member States, rules which provide for the non-recognition of judgments will be given a restrictive construction, whereas those which prevent parallel litigation should be construed amply.[34] Fourth, the courts of the Member States are mutually trusted to be of equal competence, and it is absolutely impermissible to invite the courts of one Member State to conclude that the courts of another Member State erred in considering that they have or had jurisdiction.[35]

Where a claim falls within the domain of the Regulation, the court exercises 'Regulation jurisdiction'; the Regulation determines its jurisdiction. The application of the Regulation does not depend on the claimant being domiciled in a Member State, for not only would it be wrong to consider the Regulation to be a statute available only to the privileged few, but also, a defendant's position should not be worse when sued by a claimant not established in the European Union.[36] If the defendant is out of the jurisdiction, service of process does not require the permission of the court.[37] Whether the jurisdiction of the court is Regulation jurisdiction depends on mapping the limits of the domain of the Regulation, to which we turn.

[33] Now see recitals 10 and 11 to the Regulation.

[34] Recital 15. See also Case 144/86 *Gubisch Machinenfabrik KG v Palumbo* [1987] ECR 4861.

[35] Case C-351/89 *Overseas Union Insurance Ltd v New Hampshire Insurance Co* [1991] ECR I-3317; Case C-116/02 *Erich Gasser GmbH v Misat srl* [2003] ECR I-14693.

[36] Case C-412/98 *Universal General Insurance Co v Groupe Josi Reinsurance Co SA* [2000] ECR I-5925.

[37] CPR r 6.33.

3. THE DOMAIN OF THE REGULATION: ARTS 1, 66–68, 71

The point of departure is to define the domain of the Regulation in its three elements, that is to say, its material, or subject-matter scope; its temporal scope; and its relationship with other legal instruments.

(a) Material scope

Article 1 of the Regulation applies, like its forerunners, in 'civil and commercial matters'. It will often be obvious whether the claim falls within this expression, but where it is not it will be measured against an autonomous interpretation of the terms. It may include claims made by or against public authorities where the obligations which are enforced are of a kind which may be assumed by or imposed on persons generally, no matter who is enforcing them. So proceedings against a town council which has failed to pay a contractor who did work on the town hall will be a civil and commercial matter; proceedings brought to stop a contractor using unfair terms in consumer contracts are brought in a civil or commercial matter, even though the claimant is a public body charged with the enforcement of the law.[38] But if the obligation enforced is one peculiar to public law the matter will not be civil or commercial.[39] So where a claim for repayment of sums advanced by way of financial assistance is founded on the ordinary law of subrogation or restitution, the fact that the claim is brought by a state in relation to its administrative or public law duty of support does not prevent the claim being seen as civil or commercial.[40] This interpretation of Article 1, which pays attention to the specific legal obligation which founds the claim, or more specifically, the defendant's liability, has eclipsed an earlier view, that a matter was identified as civil or commercial if the laws of the Member States would generally regard comparable claims as being civil or commercial.[41] Such an approach would have been

---

[38] Case C-167/00 *VfK v Henkel* [2002] ECR I-8111.
[39] Case C-265/02 *Frahuil SA v Assitalia SpA* [2004] ECR I-1543.
[40] Case C-433/01 *Freistaat Bayern v Blijdenstein* [2004] ECR I-981.
[41] Case 814/79 *Netherlands v Rüffer* [1980] ECR 3807.

particularly difficult where, for example, a claim was brought against a body which has emerged from the denationalization of public utilities. Working out whether a negligence claim against the body which now supplies water, or owns the railway tracks, would be civil or commercial, would be practically impossible if the laws of all 27 Member States had to be surveyed first. Placing the focus of attention on the actual legal obligation which it is sought to enforce will ensure that the answer will be easier to predict and to arrive at, although it will make for greater variation from one law to another. And it is the claim which identifies the matter as civil or commercial; the nature of the defence to it is, apparently, immaterial.[42]

A claim is also outside the domain of the Regulation if it concerns customs, revenue, or administrative matters;[43] likewise status or legal capacity of natural persons, matrimonial property, or succession; bankruptcy and the winding up of insolvent companies or other legal persons; or social security.[44] It is still uncertain whether, if such an issue arises only incidentally, the claim as a whole may be outside the Regulation. English courts have held that the Regulation will apply unless the excluded matter forms the principal component in the dispute,[45] explaining this as following from the need to construe exceptions to the Regulation restrictively. The result is undoubtedly pragmatic, though the justification is dubious: although the perimeter of the Regulation must be well defined, it is not necessary that it be far flung; and there is an apparent distinction between the Regulation 'not applying to X' and 'not applying to a matter principally concerned with X'. The point may be illustrated by examination of 'arbitration' which, as a single and unelucidated word, is also excluded from the material scope of the Regulation.[46] All agree that arbitration as a procedure for dispute resolution, and proceedings for judicial measures which regulate and control it, and the judicial

---

[42] Case C–266/01 *Préservatrice Foncière TIARD v Netherlands* [2003] ECR I-4867.

[43] Article 1(1).

[44] Article 1(2)(a)–(c).

[45] *Ashurst v Pollard* [2001] Ch 595 (CA) (bankruptcy); *The Ivan Zagubanski* [2002] 2 Lloyd's Rep 106 (arbitration).

[46] Article 1(2)(d).

enforcement of arbitral awards, fall outside the Regulation.[47] But
what of the enforcement of judgments obtained in breach of an
agreement to arbitrate, or of proceedings to obtain an injunction
to restrain a party from breaching an arbitration agreement by
suing in a foreign court?[48] On the one hand, the subject matter of
the commercial dispute, and hence of the judgment, falls within
the domain of the Regulation; on the other, for a court to be
required to recognize the judgment might mean it contradicting
its own law on arbitration, a matter untouched by the Regulation.
The cases conflict. In one, it was held that a Dutch court was not
bound to recognize a German order for maintenance (a matter
within the scope of the Regulation) where this would mean it
had to contradict its own law on the marital status of the parties
(a matter excluded from the Regulation).[49] But another supports the contention that if a court in another Member State has
given judgment in a case, having rejected a jurisdictional defence
based on an arbitration clause, its judgment is given in a civil
or commercial matter.[50] The truth is that the subject matter in
such cases is at one and the same time both inside and outside the
Regulation, and whatever the answer may be it will be barely
more persuasive than the alternative. We return to the question
in Chapter 3, in the context of recognition of judgments.

Proceedings concerned with the enforcement of a judgment
from a non-Member State are not within the Regulation, nor
are ancillary or incidental procedures which arise in the course
of such proceedings, such as the trial of an issue whether the
judgment creditor obtained his non-Member State judgment by
fraud.[51] This same reasoning confirms the exclusion of judgments

---

[47] Case C-190/89 *Marc Rich & Co AG v Soc Italiana Impianti PA* [1991] ECR
I-3855. This exclusion will be made even clearer when Reg 1215/2012 takes effect
from 10 January 2015.

[48] Case C-185/07 *West Tankers Inc v Riunione Adriatica di Sicurtà SpA* [2009] ECR
I-663; referred by the House of Lords: [2007] UKHL 4, [2007] 1 Lloyd's Rep 391.

[49] Case 145/86 *Hoffmann v Krieg* [1988] ECR 645.

[50] The question is examined in Ch 3 below. The effect of Case C-391/95 *Van
Uden Maritime BV v Deco Line* [1998] ECR I-7091 is that agreement to arbitrate
means that a state has no jurisdiction to adjudicate, even though the dispute is
within the scope of the Regulation; jurisdictional error is no basis for denying
recognition to a judgment.

[51] Case C-129/92 *Owens Bank plc v Bracco* [1994] ECR I-117.

which make an order in terms of an arbitral award:[52] the exclusion reflects the fact that the adjudication from which enforcement follows was not that of a judge of a Member State.

If the case falls outside the domain of the Regulation the English courts may exercise common law jurisdiction over the defendant, and the Regulation will have no part to play.

(b) Temporal scope

Article 66 provides that the Regulation applies to the taking of jurisdiction by courts in legal proceedings instituted after 1 March 2002. In England, at least, the institution of proceedings means the issue of process rather than its service on a defendant.[53] The transitional provisions made in respect of states which joined the European Union after 2002 are complex, and devoid of human interest. The recast version of the Regulation[54] will take effect from 10 January 2015.

(c) Other conventions

As regards the relationship with other conventions, one might have expected that existing international agreements, especially those which implicate non-Member States, would remain untouched and unaffected by the Regulation. The reality is not quite so straightforward. Although Article 71 provides that the Regulation 'shall not affect any Conventions ... which in relation to particular matters, govern jurisdiction' it goes on, somewhat ineptly, to explain that this means that if a convention allows for the taking of jurisdiction, that provision shall continue to be effective, even though the defendant is domiciled in a Member State which is not party to it. Accordingly, if another convention, such as those in maritime law which deal with the arrest of sea-going ships, and with cargo claims, authorize the taking of jurisdiction, the Regulation should not impede it. But if the particular convention makes no provision to deal with parallel litigation, the provisions of the Regulation[55] will apply 'to fill the

---

[52] Schlosser Report [1979] OJ C59/71.
[53] *Canada Trust Co v Stolzenberg (No 2)* [2002] 1 AC 1.
[54] Regulation 1215/2012, Art 81.
[55] Articles 27–30.

gap', as though the particular convention were absorbed into the Regulation, with the consequence that it may then be modified in its operation.[56] This is hard to reconcile with the proposition that the Regulation does not affect the assumption of jurisdiction under the particular convention. Even so, Article 71 fails to say is that, where a convention precludes the taking of jurisdiction, that provision shall continue to be effective, whatever the Regulation would otherwise have decreed. The international obligations of the United Kingdom in relation to specific matters include obligations to *refuse* to accept jurisdiction, as well as to exercise it, and for this to be ignored by the Regulation is inexcusable; in the context of arbitration, where the New York Convention lays negative jurisdictional obligations on Contracting States, this is crucial.

In relation to community instruments which make provision for jurisdiction in relation to specific matters, Article 67 provides that these are not prejudiced in their application by the Regulation. So Directive 96/71/EC[57] on workers temporarily posted abroad, and Directive 93/13/EC on unfair terms in consumer contracts,[58] will to this extent prevail over the Regulation.

4. DOMICILE

Where the court is dealing with Regulation jurisdiction, many of the individual provisions turn upon whether the defendant is domiciled in the United Kingdom or another Member State. In this regard it is necessary to distinguish natural persons from companies or other legal persons or associations of persons, and from trusts, for the definition of domicile is not uniform. To decide whether an individual is domiciled in the United Kingdom, Article 59(1) of the Regulation[59] tells a court to apply

---

[56] Case C-406/92 *The Tatry* [1994] ECR I-5439.

[57] [1997] OJ L18/1, Art 6 of which deals with jurisdiction.

[58] Unfair Terms in Consumer Contracts Regulations 1999 (SI 1999/2083), applicable to arbitration and jurisdiction agreements: Case C-240/98 *Océano Grupo Editorial SA v Quintero* [2000] ECR I-4941. The Directive can be found at [1993] OJ L95/29.

[59] Article 59 correlates to Art 62 of Reg 1215/2012, which makes no substantial changes.

the law of the United Kingdom. In this context, domicile in the United Kingdom is defined by statute[60] rather than by the common law. According to this, an individual is domiciled in the United Kingdom if he is resident in the United Kingdom and this residence indicates that he has a substantial connection with the United Kingdom: a fact which may be presumed from three months' residence. Similar rules, *mutatis mutandis*, determine whether an individual is domiciled in a part of the United Kingdom. But to determine whether an individual is domiciled in another Member State, Article 59(2) tells a court to apply the law of the Member State of the proposed domicile. So whether she is domiciled in France is a matter of French law; in Italy, a matter of Italian law, and so on. It follows that an individual may have a domicile in more than one Member State. This is unproblematic, for whereas it would be very inconvenient for concurrent domiciliary laws to determine capacity to marry, for example, it is unsurprising that a person's connections with each of two Member States are sufficient for either to be a proper place in which to sue him in matters of general[61] jurisdiction.

There has been pressure to provide a single autonomous definition of domicile, or to abandon it *holus bolus* and move instead to the concept of habitual residence, not least because of divergence between the separate national law definitions of domicile. But in the absence of a public register of status, however defined, it is difficult to see that such a change would accomplish very much of value. There will be occasional difficult cases, typically where a person maintains or has access to a residence in one country, but manages to cast a veil of secrecy over its ownership and his movements.[62] In such a case his domicile would probably be no more difficult to ascertain than his habitual residence, and it is unlikely that the change would have brought much about.

For a *company, other legal person,* or *association of natural persons,* Article 60(1)[63] provides that it has a domicile in any one or more of

---

[60] Civil Jurisdiction and Judgments Order 2001 (SI 2001/3929) Sch 1, para 9.

[61] Chapter II, Section 1 of the Regulation is entitled 'General provisions'.

[62] cf *Canada Trust Co v Stolzenberg (No 2)* [2002] 1 AC 1.

[63] Article 60 correlates to Art 63 of Reg 1215/2012, which makes no substantial changes.

three places: where it has its statutory seat, or its central administration, or its principal place of business. For the purposes of the United Kingdom, 'statutory seat' is defined as the registered office or, where there is none anywhere, the place of incorporation or, where there is none anywhere, the place under the law of which the formation took place. The purpose[64] of Article 60 is to nudge the law towards a more uniform definition of the domicile of a corporation or other legal person. Previously each national law had supplied its own definition of the domicile of a company, etc, and the result was a complexity which served no useful purpose.

By contrast, to ascertain whether a *trust* is domiciled in the United Kingdom, Article 60(3) provides that the court will apply the law of the United Kingdom. Accordingly, a trust is domiciled in England if English law is that with which the trust has its closest and most real connection.[65] It is never necessary to determine whether a trust is domiciled in another Member State, for no jurisdictional rule is formulated on this basis.

C. REGULATION JURISDICTION: THE DETAIL

Where proceedings fall within the domain of the Regulation, and the jurisdiction of the court is therefore Regulation jurisdiction, the structure of the individual rules forms a natural hierarchy which is not apparent from the layout of the Regulation itself. To obtain a reliable determination whether the court has Regulation jurisdiction, it is prudent to examine the provisions of the Regulation in the order in which they are set out below.

1. EXCLUSIVE JURISDICTION: ARTICLE 22

Article 22 of the Regulation[66] gives exclusive jurisdiction, regardless[67] of domicile, to the courts of a Member State, in five areas: in

---

[64] Recital 11.

[65] Civil Jurisdiction and Judgments Order 2001, Sch 1, para 12, re-enacting 1982 Act, s 45.

[66] Section 6 of Chapter II. Article 22 correlates to Art 24 of Reg 1215/2012, which makes no substantial changes.

[67] That is to say, whether the defendant is domiciled in any Member State or none.

the rare case where it confers exclusive jurisdiction on the courts of two Member States, Article 29 provides that the first court seised alone has exclusive jurisdiction. Where Article 22 confers exclusive jurisdiction on a court, no other court has jurisdiction, even if both parties purport to submit to it;[68] and a judgment which conflicts with Article 22 must be refused recognition.[69] For Article 22 to be engaged, the material connection must be to a Member State. If the land, or public register etc, is in a non-Member State, Article 22 has no application; the relevant question is whether the Regulation permits a court with jurisdiction under some other Article to decline it by pointing to a non-Member State. The issue is not straightforward, and is considered below.

Article 22(1) covers proceedings which have as their (principal[70]) object rights *in rem* in, or tenancies of, immovable property in a Member State, giving exclusive jurisdiction to the state where the land is situated. To this two ancillary rules are added. First, where the proceedings have as their object a tenancy of immovable property concluded for temporary private use for no more than six consecutive months, Article 22(1) provides that the courts of the Member State in which the defendant is domiciled also[71] have exclusive jurisdiction, if the tenant is a natural person and landlord and tenant are domiciled in the same Member State, which is useful if the dispute is a small one concerned with a holiday letting in another Member State. Secondly, Article 6(4) allows a contractual action to be combined with the action *in rem* against the same defendant, which is useful in a mortgage action.

It is not enough that the proceedings concern or are even fought over a tenancy, or have legal title to land as their prize; the words 'have as their object' require the proceedings to be concerned with the extent, content, ownership, or possession of land, rather than having a looser or a descriptive connection.[72] Many Member

---

[68] Article 23(5).

[69] Article 35(1).

[70] This word does not appear in the text of the Article, but was read in Case C-280/90 *Hacker v Euro-Relais GmbH* [1992] ECR I-1111; cf *Ashurst v Pollard* [2001] Ch 595 (CA).

[71] Joint exclusive jurisdiction may occasion the use of Art 29 (Art 31(1) in Reg 1215/2012).

[72] Case C-343/04 *ČEZ v Land Oberösterreich* [2006] ECR I-4557.

States treat the determination of title to land as a matter for only the courts of the *situs*; and in any event, land law, and especially tenancy law, tends to be complicated and better applied by a local court. As the Article derogates from the jurisdiction of the defendant's domicile, it will be interpreted restrictively. This last point has been taken to mean that proceedings in which a tenancy forms only part of the background to the dispute, or comprises only a minor part of a more complex contract, such as an all-inclusive holiday,[73] or timeshare club membership,[74] do not come under Article 22(1). Likewise, claims to enforce obligations contained in or associated with leases but which are not themselves peculiar to tenancies, such as a covenant to pay for the business goodwill in a lease of commercial premises[75] or the statutory obligations of the provider of consumer credit after the landlord has defaulted,[76] fall outside it as well. By contrast, a claim in respect of unpaid rent or utility charges,[77] or for the cost of cleaning up behind departing tenants who made a ruin of the premises,[78] are founded on obligations natural to a tenancy, and no matter how narrow the interpretation of Article 22(1), these fall within it.

Proceedings do not 'have as their object rights *in rem*' if the claimant does not assert that he is already legal proprietor who is suing as such but claims, for example as contractual purchaser, to be entitled to become legal owner[79] or claims, for example, as beneficiary under a resulting trust of the land, already to be equitable owner of the land. The conclusion of the Court[80] that a beneficiary under a resulting trust has only an interest *in personam* and not one *in rem* was wrong, at least as a matter of English law, by several centuries;[81] and its further holding that proceedings do

---

[73] Case C-280/90 *Hacker v Euro-Relais GmbH* [1992] ECR I-1111.

[74] Case C-73/04 *Klein v Rhodos Management Ltd* [2005] ECR I-8667.

[75] Case 73/77 *Sanders v Van der Putte* [1977] ECR 2383.

[76] *Jarrett v Barclays Bank plc* [1999] QB 1 (CA).

[77] Case 241/83 *Rösler v Rottwinkel* [1985] ECR 99.

[78] Case C-8/98 *Dansommer A/S v Götz* [2000] ECR I-393.

[79] Or as contractual seller, seeking rescission of unperformed contract of sale: Case C-518/98 *Gaillard v Chekili* [2001] ECR I-2771.

[80] Case C-294/92 *Webb v Webb* [1994] ECR I-1717.

[81] The interest of the beneficiary can be enforced against all the world except the *bona fide* purchaser for value without notice; it is unreal to see this as a mere right *in personam*.

not have a right *in rem* as their object when brought to acquire legal title from a resulting trustee is curious: if an action brought to acquire a conveyance of legal title does not have legal title as its object, what on earth does it have?[82] If, as will be seen, 'the object of proceedings' means 'the end in view':[83] the end in the beneficiary's view is the acquisition of legal title to the land. On the other hand, the outcome, if not the reasoning, can be defended from two very different points of view. Where the substantive law which the court will apply is not specifically land law or tenancy law, there is no pragmatic need to engage Article 22(1), any more than if the same principles under which a right to conveyance were demanded were to be deployed against the owner of a yacht or of a parcel of shares. Moreover, the common law drew an analogous jurisdictional distinction between determining legal title to foreign land, which it had no power to do, and enforcing a contract or other equity between the parties concerning foreign land, which it would.[84] This just goes to illustrate the manner in which the various policies behind Article 22(1), all sensible in themselves, can collide, and that their reconciliation is not always possible.

Article 22(2) covers proceedings which have as their object the validity of the constitution, the dissolution or winding up of companies, or the decisions of their organs. Exclusive jurisdiction is given to the Member State of the seat of the company but, exceptionally, this means the seat as defined by national law, as distinct from that in Article 60(2).[85] But where a company defends a contractual claim by pleading that it lacked capacity to bind itself to the contract, or that a corporate officer acted without proper authority, the article does not apply: it does not apply to the claim, and a defence to liability cannot define the object of the proceedings. Likewise, where the company brings pre-emptive proceedings for a declaration that it is not contractually liable to an opponent who has not yet issued his claim, relying on the absence of corporate capacity to avoid contractual liability, the Article

---

[82] Not least because it is brought on the basis that the claimant beneficiary does have pre-existing (and exclusive) equitable title.

[83] Case C-406/92 *The Tatry* [1994] ECR I-5439.

[84] *Penn v Baltimore* (1750) 1 Ves Sen 444.

[85] Final sentence of Art 22(2); see SI 2001/3929, Sch 1, para 10.

will not apply, for the real dispute is contractual, and the corporate issue merely an incidental issue or a natural defence to it.[86] Where winding up is a hoped-for remedy, perhaps as a response to oppression of a minority shareholder,[87] rather than the legal basis for the proceedings, Article 22(2) is probably inapplicable.[88]

Article 22(3) gives exclusive jurisdiction to the Member State in which a public register is kept if the proceedings have as their object the validity of an entry in that register. An action to rectify an entry on a land register will be covered;[89] and there is no rational[90] reason to exclude any action which seeks the amendment of an entry in such a register. The Article may also apply to a register maintained by a public limited company if it is open for inspection by the public, but the point is debatable.[91]

Article 22(4) is more troublesome. It gives exclusive jurisdiction to the Member State in which a patent or trade mark is registered or deposited if the proceedings have as their object the registration or validity of that right. A simple action for infringement will not fall within the Article,[92] but where, as frequently happens, the validity of the patent is challenged by way of defence to such the action, the court seised with the infringement claim is forbidden to enter upon the question of validity.[93] Rather unhelpfully, though, the Court disdained to say whether the infringement proceedings were to be stayed pending another court's ruling on validity, or could be transferred to the court with exclusive jurisdiction to rule on validity on the basis that the issue of validity was the principal issue in the proceedings.

Article 22(5) gives exclusive jurisdiction to the Member State in which a judgment from a Member State is being enforced if

---

[86] Case C-144/10 *BVG v JP Morgan Chase Bank NA* [2011] ECR I-(May 12), [2011] 1 WLR 2087.

[87] Companies Act 2006, s 994.

[88] cf Case C-294/92 *Webb v Webb* [1994] ECR I-1717.

[89] *Re Hayward* [1997] Ch 45.

[90] The decision in *Ashurst v Pollard* [2001] Ch 595 (CA) that an application to procure amendment to the register of land ownership in Portugal was not within the predecessor of Art 22(3) is challenging.

[91] *Re Fagin's Bookshop plc* [1992] BCLC 118.

[92] Case 288/82 *Duijnstee v Goderbauer* [1983] ECR 3663.

[93] Case C-4/03 *Gesellschaft für Antriebstechnik mbH & Co KG v Lamellen- und Kupplungsbau Beteiligungs KG* [2006] ECR I-6509.

the proceedings are concerned with its enforcement. There must have been a judgment: proceedings which seek to pave the way for enforcing a prospective judgment, such as by obtaining a freezing injunction, are outside the Article.[94] It is possible that applications against a non-party for an order that there be a contribution to payment of the winning party's costs fall within this provision, for these are concerned with the enforcement of the court's original judgment.[95]

2. JURISDICTION BY APPEARANCE: ARTICLE 24

Unless Article 22 applies, the court before which the defendant enters an appearance has jurisdiction according to Article 24;[96] a prior agreement on jurisdiction will be considered to have been waived or varied by consent.[97] But if the appearance was entered[98] to contest the jurisdiction of the court, which in England will mean following the procedure in CPR Part 11, such appearance will not confer jurisdiction under this rule. One of the bedrock principles of the Regulation is that a defendant must be allowed to appear, without prejudice, to argue for its proper application to his case, and that he must do this *in limine litis* rather than by opposing recognition of the judgment after the event. So long as he does what is necessary to contest the jurisdiction at the first opportunity which the procedural law of the court allows him, he will not lose this protection if he is required in practice to plead his defence to the merits of the claim at the same time.[99] But if he takes a step towards defending the claim on the merits,

---

[94] Case C-261/90 *Reichert v Dresdner Bank (No 2)* [1992] ECR I-2149.

[95] cf *The Ikarian Reefer* [2000] 1 WLR 603 (CA) where the point was not taken. But the text does not require it to be a judgment from *another* Member State.

[96] Section 7 of Chapter II. Article 24 correlates to Art 26(1) of Reg 1215/2012, which makes minor changes for certain cases falling within Sections 3, 4, and 5 of Chapter II.

[97] Case 150/80 *Elefanten Schuh GmbH v Jacqmain* [1981] ECR 1671.

[98] The predecessor to Art 24 (Art 18 of the Brussels Convention) required, in the English language at least, that the appearance be solely to contest the jurisdiction. If the law was ever that restrictive, it is not now.

[99] Case 27/81 *Rohr SA v Ossberger* [1981] ECR 2431.

which was not in this sense required of him, he will have thrown away the shield which Article 24 would have given him.[100]

3. PRIVILEGED JURISDICTION: ARTICLES 8–21

Where disputes arise out of insurance contracts,[101] certain consumer contracts,[102] or individual contracts of employment,[103] and where the insurer, supplier, or employer is domiciled in a Member State (or is not, but made the contract by a local branch or agency which is so domiciled[104]), there risks being such inequality between the parties that the insured or policyholder, consumer, and employee need jurisdictional privileges if their contractual rights are to be effectively safeguarded. These three Sections of Chapter II conform to a template which the policyholder,[105] consumer, or employee may insist on being sued in the Member State of his domicile and may, which is the real novelty, also sue in his 'own' Member State: that is where he is domiciled in the case of insureds, etc, and consumers, and where the work is done for employees. In certain cases the policyholder or insured, consumer, or employee may elect to sue in a Member State other than that of his domicile or workplace; but the insurer, supplier, or employer is generally restricted to suing where the defendant is domiciled. Jurisdiction agreements are generally binding only if entered into

---

[100] cf (in a case not governed by the Regulation) *Marc Rich & Co AG v Soc Italiana Impianti PA* [1992] 2 Lloyd's Rep 624 (CA).

[101] Articles 8–14; Section 3 of Chapter II, correlates to Arts 10–16 of Reg 1215/2012, which make only minor changes.

[102] Articles 15–17; Section 4 of Chapter II, correlates to Arts 17–19 of Reg 1215/2012, which make one significant change for claims brought against a professional who is not domiciled in a Member State.

[103] Articles 18–21; Section 5 of Chapter II, correlates to Arts 20–23 of Reg 1215/2012, which do not make significant changes.

[104] For the definition of domicile in the United Kingdom in this context, see Civil Jurisdiction and Judgments Order 2001, Sch 1, para 11.

[105] In addition to those general rules described in the text there is specific provision for co-insurance (Art 9(1)(c)), liability insurance or insurance of immovables (Art 10), direct actions by an injured party against an insurer (Art 11), joinder of parties (Art 11), and counterclaims (Art 12). Jurisdiction agreements are regulated by Arts 13 and 14.

after the dispute arose, or if they widen the choice[106] given to the policyholder,[107] consumer,[108] or employee.[109] By way of reinforcement, a judgment which violates the jurisdictional provisions governing insurance and consumer contracts will be denied recognition, though for no obvious reason this reinforcing safeguard does not extend to employment contracts.[110] Where the insurer, supplier, or employer neither has, nor is deemed by reason of his having a branch or agency to have, a domicile in a Member State, the residual Regulation jurisdiction provided for by Article 4 will apply to claims against it,[111] though under Regulation 1215/2012,[112] a consumer or employee who is domiciled in a Member State will be able to sue in that Member State regardless of the domicile of the supplier or employer. It is to be observed that these rules do not depend on proof of a relationship of actual inequality; this fact may have contributed to the view that they are to be construed restrictively.[113]

More particularly, the *insurance* provisions do not apply to reinsurance, which is not a relationship of inherent inequality,[114] but they do apply to direct actions by the injured party against the insurer.[115] The restrictions on jurisdiction agreements are relaxed in the cases of marine insurance and in the case of large risks.[116]

---

[106] Which means, in effect, that if they are entered into before the dispute arose, they must be non-exclusive.

[107] Article 13.

[108] Article 17; and see Unfair Terms in Consumer Contracts Regulations 1999 (SI 1999/2083), enacting Directive (EC) 93/13 on unfair terms in consumer contracts [1993] OJ L95/29; Case C-240/98 *Océano Grupo Editorial SA v Quintero* [2000] ECR I-4941.

[109] Article 21.

[110] Article 35(1), which omits reference to Section 5 of Chapter II.

[111] Case C-412/98 *Universal General Insurance Co v Groupe Josi Reinsurance Co SA* [2000] ECR I-5925.

[112] Regulation (EU) 1215/2012, in effect from 10 January 2015.

[113] Case C-464/01 *Gruber v BayWa AG* [2005] ECR I-439.

[114] Case C-412/98 *Universal General Insurance Co v Groupe Josi Reinsurance Co SA* [2000] ECR I-5925.

[115] Article 11(2). In England this will most commonly arise under the Third Parties (Rights Against Insurers) Act 2010. But not where the action is brought by an assignee of the injured party: Case C-347/08 *Vorarlberger Getriebskrankenkasse v WGV* [2009] ECR I-8661.

[116] Articles 13(5) and 14.

A *consumer* contract is one in which an individual concludes the contract for a purpose which is wholly[117] outside his trade or profession and is one which in general secures the needs of an individual in terms of private consumption.[118] Cases in which a consumer seeks to enforce the offer of a prize will be within this Section if the prize offer required the offeree to buy goods,[119] but not if no such condition was imposed.[120] There is no exclusion of investment or other middle-class contracts so long as they otherwise satisfy the definition,[121] for any rule which sought to differentiate between vulnerable consumers and powerful consumers would be terribly imprecise. Within that general definition, the types of consumer contracts actually covered by Section 4 of Chapter II are more restrictive than might be expected: Article 15(1) applies only to (a) a contract for the sale of goods on instalment credit terms, or (b) a contract for a loan repayable by instalments, or other credit, made to finance the sale of goods, or (c) a contract concluded with a person who pursues commercial or professional activities in the Member State of the consumer's domicile or, by any means, directs such activities to that Member State or to several states including that Member State, and contracts falling within the scope of such activities (and in any event Article 15(3) excludes contracts of transport except for package holiday contracts). Point (c) will be the most significant. It replaced an earlier version which was focused on targeted invitations or advertising, but which now appears to be too narrow in scope. The current rule is liable to apply to contracts made by computer-literate consumers, though whether it applies in a given case will depend on its being shown that the trader was evidently minded to contract with consumers in the Member State in question, this being demonstrable from the language used on the website, from indications such as the

---

[117] Case C-464/01 *Gruber v BayWa AG* [2005] ECR I-439.
[118] Case C-269/95 *Benincasa v Dentalkit Srl* [1997] ECR I-3767; and see also Case C-99/96 *Mietz v Intership Yachting Sneek BV* [1999] ECR I-2277.
[119] Case C-96/00 *Gabriel v Schlank & Schick GmbH* [2002] ECR I-6367.
[120] Case C-27/02 *Engler v Janus Versand GmbH* [2004] ECR I-481.
[121] Case C-318/93 *Brenner v Dean Witter Reynolds Inc* [1994] ECR I-4275. But if the consumer has assigned his rights to a body which is not itself a consumer, the jurisdictional privilege is lost: Case C-89/91 *Shearson Lehmann Hutton v TVB* [1993] ECR I-139.

domain name, telephone numbers given with an international dialling code, currency of dealing, points of departure (where the contract is a holiday contract, for example) and itinerary, and so forth: in short, the question may be whether a reasonable man, looking at the external appearance of the website, would conclude that the trader was prepared to deal with, *inter alia*, consumers in the Member State in question. The question will be very fact specific, but the bare fact that a website is accessible by the consumer will not be enough to satisfy the rule.[122] It is not, however, a requirement that the contract actually be concluded at a distance, so long as the steps leading up to it satisfy the requirements of Article 15(1)(c).[123]

The *employment* contract provisions of Section 5 represent the culmination of a series of steps, judicial and legislative, to protect workers from some of the inevitable inequalities arising from contracts written by the bosses. Where the proceedings relate to the employment contract, the employee may sue where the employer is domiciled or in the Member State in which the worker habitually carries out his work, so as to secure the benefits of local[124] employment law. Where the employment involves duties in more Member States than one, they are sorted out on a common sense, centre-of-gravity, basis, which works well enough in most cases.[125]

4. JURISDICTION AGREEMENTS: ARTICLE 23

Apart from the cases mentioned above, where their effect is restricted, agreements on jurisdiction for the courts of a Member State are validated by Article 23.[126] A compliant agreement must be

---

[122] Joined Cases C-585/08 *Pammer v Reederei Karl Schluter GmbH & Co KG* and C-144/09 *Hotel Alpenhof GmbH v Heller* [2010] ECR I-12527.

[123] Case C-190/11 *Mühlleitner v Yusufi* [2012] ECR I-(Sept 6) [2012] ILPr 859, on this point departing from a view expressed in the judgment in the case in the previous footnote.

[124] There is little likelihood of this attracting much litigation business to the United Kingdom.

[125] Case C-125/92 *Mulox IBC v Geels* [1993] ECR I-4075; Case C-37/00 *Weber v Universal Ogden Services Ltd* [2002] ECR I-2013.

[126] Section 7 of Chapter II. Article 23 correlates to Art 25 of Reg 1215/2015, which makes changes to the law on assessment of validity of the agreement, and on the effect of *lis alibi pendens* (which is considered further at p 109 below).

respected both by the court designated and by the courts whose jurisdiction is excluded: the agreement serves to prorogate and derogate. Only if no party to the agreement is domiciled in a Member State may it be overridden, and then not before the nominated court has declined jurisdiction. But there is otherwise no discretion to override a valid jurisdiction agreement, say on grounds of overall trial convenience.[127] An agreement to confer jurisdiction on the courts of the United Kingdom is effective so far as the Regulation is concerned, but raises some practical difficulties: it probably gives jurisdiction to the courts in any part of the United Kingdom unless it can be construed as being more particular than first appears.[128] An agreement nominating the courts of two Member States should be effective;[129] one which is construed as giving non-exclusive jurisdiction to a court will do exactly what it says.[130] But an agreement for the courts of a non-Member State is outside Article 23, not least because the Regulation cannot bind such a court to accept jurisdiction. For them, the relevant question is whether a court with jurisdiction under some other provision of the Regulation may decline it in favour of a non-Member State. The issue is considered below.

To ensure that the parties have a proper opportunity to be aware of the effect of the agreement they are making, the agreement must be in writing or evidenced in writing (which includes electronic means which provide a durable record in writing[131]), or in a form which accords with the parties' established practice, or in a form which is well known to accord with international trade usage of which the parties were or should have been aware. So a printed term in standard conditions of business will be ineffective unless the party to be bound has written his agreement to it;[132] but a settled course of dealing or a trade usage will establish a binding

---

[127] *Hough v P&O Containers Ltd* [1999] QB 834.

[128] cf *The Komninos S* [1991] 1 Lloyd's Rep 370 (CA).

[129] Case 23/78 *Meeth v Glacetal Sàrl* [1978] ECR 2133 (but each court had exclusive jurisdiction over particular actions; there was no overlapping of competences).

[130] Article 23(1).

[131] Which certainly includes fax, and presumably includes a printed or printable message by e-mail.

[132] Case 24/76 *Estasis Salotti v RÜWA Polstereimaschinen GmbH* [1976] ECR 1831, a proposition reiterated in Case C-159/97 *Trasporti Castelletti Spedizioni Internazionali SpA v Hugo Trumpy SpA* [1999] ECR I-1517.

form. There is an inevitable tension between the desire to prevent unfair dealing by strict application of the rules on form, and awareness that this may be inappropriate where both parties were perfectly well aware that they were dealing on terms which included a jurisdiction agreement. Though the Court has insisted on strict application of these formalities,[133] it has endorsed a more flexible approach where a party pleading the formal invalidity would be doing so in bad faith.[134] More radically, a shareholder was bound by a jurisdiction agreement contained in the company's constitution on the ground that he knew or should have known of it, and had assented to be bound by his becoming a shareholder:[135] how far this principle may extend remains to be seen. Problems arise where the written consent was provided by the original contracting parties, but the proceedings involve another who has become involved in the legal relationship. If the third party has succeeded to the contractual rights or liabilities of one of the parties, as under a bill of lading,[136] he may be held to the agreement on jurisdiction, even though his own original consent was not separately written.[137] But where a third party acquires rights or obligations under the contract otherwise than by means of substitution into the position of another, he can be bound to the agreement on jurisdiction only by virtue of his own act of agreement.[138]

An agreement which complies with the formalities of Article 23 may not be impeached on the ground that it fails to comply with some provision, whether as to form[139] or substance,[140]

---

[133] Case 24/76 *Estasis Salotti v RÜWA* [1976] ECR 1831, reiterated in Case C-105/95 *MSG v Les Gravières Rhénanes Sàrl* [1997] ECR I-911.

[134] Case 221/84 *Berghofer v ASA SA* [1985] ECR 2699; Case 313/85 *Iveco Fiat v Van Hool* [1986] ECR 3337 (previous course of dealing).

[135] Case C-214/89 *Powell Duffryn plc v Petereit* [1992] ECR I-1745.

[136] Case 71/83 *The Tilly Russ* [1984] ECR 2417.

[137] Case C-387/98 *Coreck Maritime GmbH v Handelsveem BV* [2000] ECR I-9337.

[138] Case C-112/03 *Soc Financière & Industrielle de Peloux v Soc AXA Belgium* [2005] ECR I-3707; Case C-543/10 *Refcomp SpA v Axa Corporate Solutions Assurance SA* [2013] ECR I-(Feb 7).

[139] Case 150/80 *Elefanten Schuh GmbH v Jacqmain* [1981] ECR 1671 (wrong language).

[140] Case 25/79 *Sanicentral GmbH v Collin* [1979] ECR 3423 (ousting the jurisdiction of the local employment tribunal).

of national (as distinct from European[141]) law which would otherwise deprive it of effect.[142] A contention that the contract containing the agreement on jurisdiction is ineffective or void is irrelevant
to the validity of the jurisdiction agreement, not least because the
latter is juridically distinct from the substantive contract to which
it relates.[143] Indeed, it is possible, and may well be correct, to interpret Article 23 as operating where one party tells another that he
accepts[144] the jurisdiction of a court, almost as if this took the form
of a unilateral undertaking extended to the other: if that is correct,
it means that jurisdiction agreements in the context of Regulation
jurisdiction operate quite differently from the way they do within
common law jurisdiction. On this view, an agreement to waive
or renounce the general jurisdictional rule contained in Article 2
need not be made in a contract: there is no requirement to assess
that party's agreement to jurisdiction in contractual terms.[145] This
may be the reason why the European Court has insisted that the
validity or invalidity of the substantive contract is irrelevant to
the application of Article 23, and why compliance with the formality rules set out in Article 23 is all the validation, or confir-
mation, which a defendant's agreement to accept the jurisdiction
of a court requires. However, if a party claims that his writing
was procured by improper means, or that the writing is not his,
a forgery, a court must be allowed to find that he did not agree

---

[141] Article 67; cf the Unfair Terms in Consumer Contracts Regulations 1999
(SI 1999/2083), enacting Directive (EC) 93/13 on unfair terms in consumer contracts [1993] OJ L95/29.

[142] A conclusion regrettably called into question by the French Cour de cassation in *Soc Banque privée Edmond de Rothschild Europe v X* (26 September 2012),
holding void, by apparent reference to a rule of French contract law, a jurisdiction which was one sided in favour of a bank in disputes with its customer.

[143] Case C-269/95 *Benincasa v Dentalkit Srl* [1997] ECR I-3767.

[144] It is not clear whether it is possible to say that he 'agrees' to the jurisdiction
of a court if he is really only agreeing with himself while telling the other.

[145] The alternative, more obviously contractual, view is unattractive. In *Soc
Banque privée Edmond de Rothschild Europe v X* (Cass I civ, 26 Sept 2012), the French
Cour de cassation invalidated a written jurisdiction agreement as being not contractually binding, utilizing a principle of domestic French law to do it. The
court held that the one-sided ('potestative') nature of the 'agreement', which
restricted the customer while allowing the bank to not be bound to sue in the
designated court, did not display the reciprocity essential to a contract.

in writing to jurisdiction of the named court. An autonomous conception of what amounts to a party's agreement will be sufficient for the task.

In this context, it is regrettable that Regulation 1215/2012 will abandon this clear, sensible, and workable rule, and replace it with a rule which refers a contention that an exclusive choice of court agreement is void of legal effect to the law of the designated court, including whatever[146] rules of private international law that court might apply to the issue.[147] This would appear to require a court, trying to determine whether its jurisdiction is affected by an exclusive choice of court agreement, to undertake investigations into foreign law, including rules of the conflict of laws. It is correct to observe that this avoids treating a written agreement to jurisdiction as a contractual matter, for the reference is not made to a 'proper law of the agreement',[148] but this alteration seems bound to make the assessment of the agreement in writing more complex and involved than it was or needs to be.

The jurisdiction given by Article 23 is exclusive unless the agreement stipulated otherwise,[149] but this 'exclusivity' is of a lower degree of potency than that conferred by Article 22. For example, a judgment which violates Article 23 may not be denied recognition.[150] English courts for many years refused to treat jurisdiction agreements so lightly. To that end they would accept jurisdiction even though a court in another Member State had been seised first, and were prepared to restrain by injunction a party to an agreement on jurisdiction who, in breach of that agreement, launched proceedings in a foreign court.[151] But the European Court held each conclusion to be inconsistent with

---

[146] They may not be contractual, for the law of the designated court may not see the issue of jurisdiction as a contractual issue.

[147] Article 25(1) of, and recital 20 to, Reg 1215/2012.

[148] Article 25(5) makes it plain that the invalidity of the substantive contract does not invalidate the jurisdiction agreement.

[149] This should have been sufficient to secure the validity of the clause in *Soc Banque privée Edmond de Rothschild Europe v X*: it was exclusive if the client sued the bank; it was non-exclusive if the bank sued the customer.

[150] Article 35(1) makes no reference to Section 7 of Chapter II.

[151] *Continental Bank NA v Aeakos Compania Naviera SA* [1994] 1 WLR 588 (CA); *The Angelic Grace* [1995] 1 Lloyd's Rep 87 (CA).

the scheme of the Regulation.[152] In doing so it made plain that the principle that each court must decide for itself, and only for itself, whether it has jurisdiction prevailed over any sense that the most important concern was to hold parties to their agreements on jurisdiction and to prevent chicanery. Whatever else one may be tempted to think of it, it is hard to assert that the conclusion of the Court was based on a misreading of the legislative text as it then stood; and whatever its other shortcomings may be, a strict application of a first seised rule does avoid taking sides between two parties who may disagree, reasonably and in good faith, whether there really was a material agreement upon the jurisdiction of a named court. However, the position adopted in Regulation 1215/2012 is different: the designated court will, even if seised second in time, be entitled to pre-empt the court seised first on the question of which court has jurisdiction.[153]

5. GENERAL JURISDICTION: ARTICLE 2

If none of the provisions examined so far operates to confirm or deny the jurisdiction of the court, the rule in Article 2,[154] that general jurisdiction exists where the defendant is domiciled, will apply: 'general jurisdiction' means that it is not limited by reference to its subject matter or by the form of the action. The definition of domicile in the United Kingdom, and in England, has been given above. It is striking that although this is always said to be the fundamental rule on which the Regulation is constructed, its place in the hierarchy of rules is relatively low.

6. SPECIAL JURISDICTION: ARTICLES 5–7

If none of the provisions examined so far serves to confer or deny the jurisdiction of the court, the defendant will be domiciled

---

[152] Case C-116/02 *Erich Gasser GmbH v Misat srl* [2003] ECR I-14693 (exercising jurisdiction although seised second; referred from an Austrian court); Case C-159/02 *Turner v Grovit* [2004] ECR I-3565 (anti-suit injunction).

[153] Article 31(2), (3) of and recital 22 to, Reg 1215/2012. 'Designated' presumably means 'allegedly designated'.

[154] Section 1 of Chapter II, correlates to Art 4 of Reg 1215/2012, which makes no significant change.

somewhere other than the United Kingdom. Articles 5–7[155] confer special jurisdiction over defendants who are domiciled in another Member State. Article 5 responds to a sense of *forum conveniens*, but jurisdiction based on the wording of Article 5 may not be contested by showing that the court is, in the particular case, not a *forum conveniens*: the contribution of *forum conveniens* was exhausted when the Article was drafted. Article 5 may not be used as a hook upon which to hang claims against defendants over whom or which the court would not otherwise have had jurisdiction: such general jurisdiction is conferred only by Article 2, which may limit the attraction of Article 5.[156] Article 6 deals with some forms of multipartite litigation; and Article 7 with proceedings to limit liability in maritime claims. Article 5 gives special jurisdiction to the courts for a place, as distinct from the courts of a Member State: it specifies local as well as international jurisdiction.

(a) Matters relating to a contract: Article 5(1)

In matters relating to a contract, Article 5(1)(a) gives special jurisdiction to the courts for the place of performance[157] of the obligation in question. A matter does not relate to a contract for the purpose of this jurisdictional rule unless it involves obligations freely entered into with regard to another,[158] but if it does it is irrelevant that it might not be regarded as substantively contractual by a court applying its national law. So a claim to enforce the rules of a club,[159] or the obligation of a shareholder to a company,[160] is contractual even if a national law may disagree;

---

[155] Section 2 of Chapter II, correlates to Arts 7–9 of Reg 1215/2012, which makes a small number of changes, the most significant one of which is that Art 5(3) of Reg 44/2001 appears as Art 7(2), rather than 7(3), in Reg 1215/2012.

[156] It has been persuasively argued that where parties to a contract sue on it, all associated claims should be 'channelled' into that one action, in the interests of efficiency and because the contract rule is of a higher order: Case 189/87 *Kalfelis v Bankhaus Schröder Münchmeyer Hengst & Co* [1988] ECR 5565, where this was proposed by the AG, but rejected by the Court.

[157] The French text renders this as the place where the obligation was or should have been performed, and this is the sense in which it must be understood.

[158] Case C-26/91 *Soc Jakob Handte GmbH v Soc Traitements Mécano-chimiques des Surfaces* [1992] ECR I-3967.

[159] Case 34/82 *Peters v ZNAV* [1983] ECR 987.

[160] Case C-214/89 *Powell Duffryn plc v Petereit* [1992] ECR I-1745.

a claim by a sub-buyer against a manufacturer is not contractual, even if it is regarded as contractual under national law;[161] though it is uncertain whether it covers claims by someone who received negligent advice from another who had voluntarily assumed responsibility to the other and whose liability in English law is regarded as tortious.[162] If the validity of the contract is disputed, the Article may still apply,[163] even if the claimant is asserting, contrary to the submission of the defendant, that an alleged contract is ineffective or that it has been rescinded for misrepresentation, non-disclosure, or duress.[164] But it may be otherwise if both parties accept that a supposed contract was actually invalid and are parties to a claim only for restitution of an unjust enrichment.[165] However, once the issue of special jurisdiction has been settled, the national court will apply its own substantive law, including rules for choice of law, to determine the merits of the claim, and these need not be part of its law of contract.[166]

The place of performance of the obligation in question, which pinpoints the court with special jurisdiction, has to be selected from a menu of four items. The first three are stated in Article 5(1)(b); they are new in the sense that they had no predecessor in the Brussels Convention. In a contract for the sale of goods it is where under the contract the goods were or should

---

[161] Case C-26/91 *Soc Jakob Handte GmbH v Soc Traîtements Mécano-chimiques des Surfaces* [1992] ECR I-3967; Case C-543/10 *Refcomp SpA v Axa Corporate Solutions Assurance SA* [2013] ECR I-(Feb 7).

[162] Under the principle in *Hedley Byrne & Co v Heller & Partners* [1964] AC 465. There may be a difference between two- and three-party cases. In *Hedley Byrne* and *Smith v Eric S Bush* [1990] 1 AC 831, reliance is predictable and the identity of the relier is known. In three-party cases, such as *Caparo Industries plc v Dickman* [1990] 2 AC 605, this is not so. Cases founded on misrepresentation by a contracting party are not completely straightforward, and are examined below.

[163] Case 38/81 *Effer SpA v Kantner* [1982] ECR 825.

[164] *Agnew v Länsförsäkringsbolagens AB* [2001] 1 AC 223; *Boss Group Ltd v Boss France SA* [1997] 1 WLR 351 (CA). If the case falls within Art 5(1)(c), the obligation in question will be the one not to misrepresent or to coerce.

[165] *Kleinwort Benson Ltd v Glasgow City Council* [1999] 1 AC 153 (a case on the intra-UK provisions, and a decision whose scope is curtailed by *Agnew*).

[166] Case C-26/91 *Soc Jakob Handte GmbH v Soc Traîtements Mécano-chimiques des Surfaces* [1992] ECR I-3967, 3984. But as choice of law is increasingly governed by European Regulation, the opportunity for such dissonance will reduce.

have been delivered; in a contract for the provision of services it is where under the contract the services were or should have been provided; and in either of these two classes of contract, it will be the place which the parties otherwise agreed upon if this is what they did (though it has been held that while an agreement on place of performance need not be reduced to writing,[167] a wholly artificial stipulation of a place of performance will be treated as if it were a jurisdiction agreement, and will need to comply with Article 23).[168] If the contract is worded clearly enough, the application of these rules is reasonably straightforward; the case where the contract is not so well drafted is examined below.

The fourth choice is given by Article 5(1)(c), which in substance represents and preserves the original version of Article 5(1): in the case of other contracts, the court with special jurisdiction is the one at the place of performance of the primary[169] obligation on the basis of which the claimant brings the claim: that is, the obligation whose non-performance forms the basis of the claim.[170] The obligation referred to by Article 5(1)(c) need not be one created by the contract and required by the terms of the contract to be performed: an obligation not to use misrepresentation or non-disclosure to procure a contract of reinsurance, for example, is not created by the contract but will within the rule.[171] Once again, if the contract specifies the place for performance of the obligation which founds the claim in this sense, the application of Article 5(1)(c) will be straightforward. If, however, the contract does not specify the place of performance of the relevant obligation for the purpose of Article 5(1)(c), it has to be identified by the court first applying its choice of law rules to ascertain the law which governs the contract, and then using this to specify the place of performance.[172]

---

[167] Case 56/79 *Zelger v Salinitri* [1980] ECR 89.

[168] Case C-106/95 *MSG v Les Gravières Rhénanes Sàrl* [1997] ECR I-911 (contract for carriage by barge; place of performance specified as a place not on a waterway).

[169] That is to say, a performance obligation as distinct from a secondary obligation to compensate for breach of a primary obligation.

[170] Case 14/76 *De Bloos Sprl v Bouyer SA* [1976] ECR 1497.

[171] *Agnew v Länsförsäkringsbolagens AB* [2001] 1 AC 223 (HL).

[172] Case 12/76 *Industrie Tessili Italiana Como v Dunlop AG* [1976] ECR 1473; Case C-440/97 *GIE Groupe Concorde v Master of the Vessel 'Suhadiwarno Panjan'* [1999] ECR I-6307.

Though it is sometimes said that this can make the location of special jurisdiction unpredictable, the Member States have a largely uniform choice of law rule for contracts, and it is unlikely that this criticism needs to be taken too seriously. And in any case, if the parties have not troubled to specify the place of performance of an obligation, a fair assumption is that they are content to have the default option provided by the governing law.

All that being said, there were two substantial objections to the approach which has been preserved in but confined to Article 5(1)(c). The first was that it was not always satisfactory to make special jurisdiction depend on the obligation on which the claim was framed. Where the claimant was an unpaid seller, the obligation in question would therefore be the payment of the price, which was not always due somewhere with a close connection to the facts giving rise to the dispute.[173] Worse, an unpaid seller under a contract governed by English law would be able to sue the buyer in the seller's home courts, for under English law a debt is payable where the creditor resides:[174] an outcome which challenged the principle that it was defendants, not claimants, who were intended to litigate with home advantage. The response was to provide a uniform identification of the place of the obligation in question for the contracts falling within Article 5(1)(b), as we have just considered. The second objection was that the process of conducting an exercise in choice of law, in order to determine whether the court had special jurisdiction to determine a claim which might involve asking that same question of choice of law, could be achingly complex, and damaging to legal certainty. The response of the Court was to interpret the new rule of law set out in Article 5(1)(b) in a radical way. In a contract for the sale of goods, the place of delivery will be taken as the place where the contract provided for the physical transfer of the goods to the purchaser who thereby obtains actual power of disposal at the final destination of the transaction of sale: this place is to be identified directly from the provisions of the contract, or by observation, rather than by recourse to the default answer supplied by the

---

[173] Case C-288/92 *Custom Made Commercial Ltd v Stawa Metallbau GmbH* [1994] ECR I-2913.

[174] *The Eider* [1893] P 119.

lex contractus.[175] The aim is clearly to allow the court with special jurisdiction to be identified without the need to first conduct an exercise in choice of law, and this has more than a little to recommend it. Of course there will be cases in which it is not so easy: consider the sale of goods by transfer of documents of title, which may be effected by transferring the documents to the purchaser, as the contract allows, in state A, while the goods themselves are in state B. Nevertheless, the question in principle is to ask where, in reality or according to the contract, the buyer was to be placed in a position to physically dispose of the goods at the end point of the sale.

The law has therefore embarked on the task of classifying contracts, rather than having an omnibus special jurisdictional rule for them all. Article 5(1)(b) includes contracts for the supply of goods, for example on hire or hire purchase, and contracts for the sale of goods yet to be made,[176] as well as the supply of goods and services, as in a contract for work and materials. But there will be others which may not so easily conform to the standard template of a payment of money[177] promised or made in return for a transfer of property or provision of services: a licensing agreement,[178] commission agency,[179] barter, reinsurance, distribution contracts, and many arrangements in the realm of financial services, will probably not all fit within Article 5(1)(b); and it may be expected that some difficulty will be encountered as the law is hammered out.

Whichever provision of Article 5(1) is applicable to the contract in question, the material obligation may be performed, or require performance, at several places in the one Member State,[180] or in more Member States than one, such as delivery to sites in Belgium and the Netherlands, sales representation[181] in the United Kingdom

---

[175] Case C-381/08 *Car Trim GmbH v KeySafety Systems srl* [2010] ECR I-1255.

[176] ibid.

[177] See the definition in Sale of Goods Act 1979, s 61.

[178] Case C-533/07 *Falco Privatstiftung v Weller-Lindhorst* [2009] ECR I-3327 (itself justified on the slightly surprising basis that as Art 5(1)(b) was an exception to the general rule preserved in Art 5(1)(c), it should be construed in a restrictive manner).

[179] Though commercial agency is within Art 5(1)(b): Case C-19/09 *Wood Floor Solutions Andreas Domberger GmbH v Silva Trade SA* [2010] ECR I-2121.

[180] Case C-386/05 *Color Drack GmbH v Lexx International Vertriebs GmbH* [2007] ECR I-3699.

[181] But if this were seen as a contract of employment, it would have fallen under Arts 18–21.

and Ireland, and so on. One asks where this obligation was principally to be performed, and locates special jurisdiction at the courts for that place:[182] this will often yield a workable and predictable answer. Similarly, in a case falling within Article 5(1)(c), if two obligations are relied on, the one which is principal will be the decisive one.[183] Where it is not possible to marshal the place or places of performance in this way, it is unclear what the outcome should be. The proposition that there may be special jurisdiction over only so much of the claim as results from local performance is possible[184] but is so unattractive that a wise judge will avoid it. Alternatively, it has also been held that the claimant may elect as he chooses between the various places in which substantial performance of the obligation in question was due, which may be a preferable outcome for cases which are awkward, and probably rare, by nature.[185]

(b) Matters relating to tort, delict, or quasi-delict: Article 5(3)

Article 5(3)[186] gives special jurisdiction in matter relating to tort to the courts for the place where the harmful event occurred or may occur: the difference is only one of timing.

A 'matter relating to tort' means any action which seeks to establish the liability of a defendant and which is not a matter relating to a contract within Article 5(1).[187] It will therefore extend to equitable wrongs such as dishonest assistance of a breach of trust,[188] or breach of confidence, and to statutory wrongs such as

---

[182] Case C-125/92 *Mulox IBC v Geels* [1993] ECR I-4075; Case C-383/95 *Rutten v Cross Medical Ltd* [1997] ECR I-57; Case C-19/09 *Wood Floor Solutions Andreas Domberger GmbH v Silva Trade SA* [2010] ECR I-2121.

[183] Case 266/85 *Shenavai v Kreischer* [1987] ECR 239.

[184] Case C-420/97 *Leathertex Divisione Sintetici SpA v Bodetex BVBA* [1999] ECR I-6747.

[185] Case C-386/05 *Color Drack GmbH v Lexx International Vertriebs GmbH* [2007] ECR I-3699; Case C-204/08 *Rehder v Air Baltic Corpn* [2009] ECR I-6073 (but cf Case C-19/09 *Wood Floor Solutions Andreas Domberger GmbH v Silva Trade SA* [2010] ECR I-2121).

[186] Correlating to Art 7(2) in Reg 1215/2012.

[187] Case 189/87 *Kalfelis v Bankhaus Schröder, Münchmeyer, Hengst & Co* [1988] ECR 5565.

[188] *Casio Computer Co Ltd v Sayo* [2001] EWCA Civ 661, [2001] ILPr 594.

patent infringement or occupiers' liability.[189] Yet despite the width of this formulation, and despite the fact that there is no clear line which separates it from restitutionary claims,[190] especially in respect of wrongs, it is probably confined to cases where the claim is based on some semblance of wrongdoing and probably does not extend to claims for restitution which simply allege the injustice of retaining a gain made at the expense of another: there would not usually be special jurisdiction over such claims which are only casually connected to a particular place. So a claim for the repayment of money handed over in the mistaken belief that there was a contract according to which it was due would not be within Article 5(3).[191] If this is correct, it proceeds not from a doctrinaire view about the nature of unjust enrichment in English domestic law, but from the fact that other language versions of what in English is rendered as 'liability' connote rather more clearly the sense of liability for doing wrong or inflicting loss.[192] Guidance from the Rome II Regulation[193] is confusing. That Regulation treats torts and unjust enrichment for the purposes of choice of law as non-contractual obligations, but it places unjust enrichment, and cases of pre-contractual fault, outside the provisions which deal with choice of law for tort and delict. It may be that, contrary to what one would have hoped for, that there is a lack of harmony between the two Regulations at this point, and their provisions must be dealt with independently of each other.

Claims founded on pre-contractual misrepresentation are notoriously tricky to deal with. Insofar as they seek the rescission of the contract, authority[194] suggests that they ought to fall within Article 5(1);[195] where the claim is for damages for tortious wrongdoing, it has been held that the matter is within

---

[189] *Mecklermedia Corpn v DC Congress GmbH* [1998] Ch 40.

[190] Indeed, the Advocate General in Case C-89/91 *Shearson Lehmann Hutton Inc v TVB* [1993] ECR I-139 was clear (at 178) that the effect of *Kalfelis* was to bring claims alleging unjust enrichment within Art 5(3).

[191] *Kleinwort Benson Ltd v Glasgow City Council* [1999] 1 AC 153.

[192] In *Kalfelis*, the language of which was German, the term is 'Schadenshaftung', where the sense of loss caused by wrong is more palpable.

[193] Regulation (EC) 864/2007, [2007] OJ L199/40.

[194] cf Rome II Regulation, Art 12.

[195] *Agnew v Länsförsäkringsbolagens AB* [2001] 1 AC 223.

Article 5(3).[196] But as the measure of damages in the latter case is designed to place the parties in the same financial position as if the contract had not been made, it may be seen as the cash equivalent of rescission; and on that basis, Article 5(1) would be its more natural jurisdictional home. A claim based on the proposition that the failure to conclude a contract was actionable as a wrong is not within Article 5(1),[197] but proceedings founded on the disputed validity of a contract would appear to be within Article 5(1). The Rome II Regulation treats pre-contractual liability as a non-contractual obligation, alongside but outside the choice of law rules for tort,[198] which complicates any re-location of claims based on pre-contractual misrepresentation into Article 5(3). Whatever the answer is, it proceeds from the fact that the strict separation of Article 5(1) and 5(3) is easier to state in principle than to apply in practice where the gist of the complaint is that it was a tort that induced the victim to enter into a contract.

The place where the harmful event occurred means the place where the damage occurred, or of the event giving rise to it: the claimant[199] may elect between them if they diverge.[200] So when river water was polluted and used by a horticulturalist downstream, with disastrous consequences, the damage occurred where the crop was ruined; the event giving rise to the damage was the discharge of poison into the river; and the claimant was entitled to elect between them.[201]

Ascribing a place to damage can be an artificial exercise, but the cases offer some guidance. In principle, damage occurs where the damage or loss first materializes, rather than, if it be different,

[196] *Alfred Dunhill Ltd v Diffusion Internationale de Maroquinerie de Prestige Sarl* [2001] CLC 949.

[197] Case C-334/00 *Fonderie Officine Mecchaniche Tacconi SpA v Heinrich Wagner Sinto Maschinenfabrik GmbH* [2002] ECR I-7357.

[198] Regulation (EC) 864/2007, Art 2(1).

[199] Surprising to say, the claimant does not necessarily mean the victim, for the rule applies equally to declarations of non-liability: Case C-133/11 *Folien Fischer AG v Ritrama SpA* [2012] ECR I-(Oct 25), [2013] 2 WLR 373.

[200] Case 21/76 *Handelskwekerij GJ Bier BV v Mines de Potasse d'Alsace* [1976] ECR 1875; Case C-364/93 *Marinari v Lloyds Bank plc* [1995] ECR I-2719; Case C-68/93 *Shevill v Presse Alliance SA* [1995] ECR I-415.

[201] *Handelskwekerij Bier*, ibid.

where it or its consequence is subsequently felt.[202] So if property is wrongfully taken, the damage occurs at the place of the taking, as distinct from where the claimant's financial records of the loss are kept;[203] or—assuming the case does not fall within Article 5(1)— where the negligent advice is acted on and the money parted with in such a way as to make the financial consequence inevitable,[204] as distinct from where the information was initially received and read,[205] and as further distinct from where the adverse financial consequences of acting on it are eventually felt,[206] and as yet further distinct from the place where the worthless products were acquired; where damaged goods were handed over rather than where the damage later eventually came to light;[207] where the malevolent ingredient which had been supplied was incorporated into a manufactured product rather than where liability was incurred as a result of selling that product;[208] where a trademark is registered as distinct from where sales are reduced;[209] where a person would have carried on business and made a profit had he not been refused a licence by a body which flouted the law on competition in refusing to licence him;[210] where people read defamatory material in the press and lowered their opinion of the victim, as distinct from where the victim lives[211] (though by way of exception, where insolent or insulting material is published on the internet, the damage may be taken to occur, in its entirety and if the victim wishes, where the victim lives, for the ubiquity of the internet makes it, in some respects, a law unto itself).[212]

---

[202] Case C-220/88 *Dumez France SA v Hessische Landesbank* [1990] ECR I-49.

[203] Case C-364/93 *Marinari v Lloyds Bank plc* [1995] ECR I-2719. It is probable that this also excludes the jurisdiction of the place where the claimant's shares are traded.

[204] Case C-168/02 *Kronhofer v Maier* [2004] ECR I-6009.

[205] ibid.

[206] *Domicrest Ltd v Swiss Bank Corpn* [1999] QB 548.

[207] Case C-51/97 *Réunion Européenne SA v Spliethoff's Bevrachtingskantoor BV* [1998] ECR I-6511.

[208] Case C-189/08 *Zuid-Chemie BV v Philippo's Mineralenfabriek NV/SA* [2009] ECR I-6917.

[209] Case C-523/10 *Wintersteiger AG v Products 4U Sondermaschinenbau* [2012] ECR I-(Apr 19), [2012] ILPr 503.

[210] *X v FIFA* (Cass I civ, 1 Feb 2012), [2012] ILPr 836.

[211] Case C-68/93 *Shevill v Presse Alliance SA* [1995] ECR I-415.

[212] Joined Cases C-509/09 *eDate Advertising GmbH v X* and C-161/10 *Martinez v MGN Ltd* [2011] ECR I-(Oct 25), [2012] QB 654.

In identifying and locating the damage, in all these cases and in those to come, the template is that of an autonomous interpretation of the cause of action, as distinct from one shaped by the vision or idiosyncrasy of national tort law of the court seised. A similar principle applies to identify the event giving rise to it. So the event giving rise to the damage caused by defamation in the press is the production of the newspaper and not (as it might be seen in English domestic law) the sale of the newspaper to its readership;[213] the compilation of negligent advice and not (as it would be seen in English domestic law) its reception by the person who acts on it.[214] There will still be some uncertainty while it is decided whether, for example, it is the failure properly to test, or the marketing without adequate warning, which gives rise to the damage in product liability cases,[215] as an entire book of tort will need to be written to fill in the blanks created by the preference for autonomous definitions of causes of action.

(c) Other cases of special jurisdiction under Article 5

In relation to *maintenance claims*, Article 5(2) gave special jurisdiction to the maintenance creditor's place of domicile or habitual residence, but this has been superseded by the Maintenance Regulation,[216] which is examined in Chapter 8. For *civil claims in criminal proceedings*, Article 5(4) allows a court hearing a criminal claim to order damages or restitution to a claimant who, in accordance with the procedure of the court, has intervened as a 'civil party'. This has little practical relevance in England where this is not a common form of procedure.

Article 5(5) deals with *liability arising out of the operation of a branch, agency, or other establishment*: such claims may be brought in the place where it is situated. The concept of a branch, agency, or establishment has to occupy a slippery patch of territory between being too dependent to be anything at all, and too independent to be a branch or agency.[217] A useful test is probably to ask whether it

---

[213] ibid.

[214] *Domicrest Ltd v Swiss Bank Corpn* [1999] QB 548.

[215] cf *Distillers & Co Ltd v Thompson* [1971] AC 458 (PC).

[216] Regulation (EC) 4/2009, [2009] OJ L7/1.

[217] Case 218/86 *SAR Schotte GmbH v Parfums Rothschild Sàrl* [1987] ECR 4905.

has power on its own account to make contracts which will bind its principal. If it does, it will probably be a branch.[218] It is worth noting that the special jurisdictional exposure of the defendant is only to the extent that the claim arises out of the operations of the branch, though it is not implicit that the acts of the defendant must have been performed in that place.[219] The equivalent provision in common law jurisdiction would ask whether the defendant was present within the jurisdiction; and, if so, permit the bringing of any claim against him, whether or not connected to activities undertaken in that place. There is much to be said for the more limited rule contained in Article 5(5).

In relation to *trusts*, Article 5(6) gives special jurisdiction over a settlor, trustee, or beneficiary who is sued as such[220] to the courts of the Member State where the trust is domiciled. For this provision to apply, the trust must be created by the operation of a statute, or by a written instrument, or created orally but evidenced in writing. In relation to claims for payment in respect of *salvage of cargo or freight*, Article 5(7) gives special jurisdiction to the place of the court under the authority of which the freight was arrested to secure payment or could have been arrested but for the fact that bail or other security was given.

(d) Multipartite litigation and consolidated claims: Articles 6 and 7

The Regulation does not provide for special jurisdiction over a defendant on the simple basis that the court has jurisdiction over another claim to which the first is connected. If a claimant wishes to join claims against a single defendant in a single proceeding, this has to be done under the general domiciliary jurisdiction of Article 2. Articles 6 and 7[221] go some way towards allowing the consolidation of separate claims in the interest of coordinating

---

[218] Opinion of the AG in Case C-89/91 *Shearson Lehmann Hutton Inc v TVB* [1993] ECR I-139, 169.

[219] Case C-439/93 *Lloyds Register of Shipping v Soc Campenon Bernard* [1995] ECR I-961.

[220] *Gomez v Gomez-Monche Vives* [2008] EWCA Civ 1065, [2009] Ch 245.

[221] Section 2 of Chapter II, correlating to Arts 8–9 of Reg 1215/2012, which makes no substantial changes.

the judicial function and avoiding inconsistent judgments, but the limits on their operation are surprisingly strict, and at this point the Regulation operates less than perfectly. There are five cases to consider.

Where a claim is brought against *several defendants*, Article 6(1) allows them all to be joined in the one action if it is brought where one of them is domiciled and it is necessary to join the defendants so as to avoid the risk of irreconcilable judgments which might result from separate trials. It is not a requirement that the defendant who is sued where he is domiciled be the principal target of the claim, for if there were a requirement that the local defendant be the main defendant, there would be endless scope for argument. But on occasion a court may suspect that there is no real intention to proceed against the local defendant at all once he has served the claimant's purpose of providing a jurisdictional hook for catching non-local co-defendants. It is regrettable that the Court has wholly failed to decide whether a distinct and additional defence is available by a showing that the proceedings are brought against the local defendant principally to remove the non-local defendant from the court which would otherwise have jurisdiction over him.[222]

As for the degree of connection between the claims, an exercise in judgment is called for. The predominant need to avoid irreconcilable judgments should incline a court to err on the side of joinder, and against taking a restrictive view.[223] There is, however, no analogous right to join co-defendants into proceedings in a court having only special jurisdiction under Article 5, or having jurisdiction by agreement or submission under Articles 23 or 24. It is difficult to see a good reason which excludes these cases from Article 6(1), probably because there is none. It goes

---

[222] Case C-51/97 *Réunion Européenne SA v Spliethoff's Bevrachtingskantoor BV* [1998] ECR I-6511; Case C-103/05 *Reisch Montage AG v Kiesel Baumaschinen Handels GmbH* [2006] ECR I-6827; Case C-98/06 *Freeport plc v Arnoldson* [2007] ECR I-8319; Case C-145/10 *Painer v Standard Verlags GmbH* [2011] ECR I-(Dec 1); Case C-616/10 *Solvay SA v Honeywell Fluorine Products Europe BV* [2012] ECR I-(Jul 12).

[223] Case C-98/06 *Freeport plc v Arnoldsson* [2007] ECR I-839, reinterpreting Case C-51/97 *Réunion Européenne SA v Spliethoff's Bevrachtingskantoor BV* [1998] ECR I-6511.

without saying that there is no joinder by Article 6(1) where jurisdiction is founded on Article 4.[224]

Article 6(2) allows a claim against a *third party* for a warranty, guarantee, contribution, or indemnity, or brought in some other third party proceeding, to be brought in the court hearing the original action unless the original action[225] was instituted with the sole object of allowing the defendant to ensnare the third party with special jurisdiction. It seems probable that the original action must still be live[226] but, by contrast with Article 6(1), the jurisdictional basis of the original action has no bearing on the operation of Article 6(2). The court may refuse joinder of the third party if this is not done for reasons which, in effect, contradict the general scheme of the Regulation.[227] But if there is an Article 23 jurisdiction agreement between defendant and third party, this will preclude reliance on Article 6(2) by the defendant, no matter how inconvenient the overall result may be, for, by contrast with the view taken by the common law, there is no judicial discretion to override Article 23.[228]

Article 6(3) allows a *counterclaim* to be brought in the court in which the original action is pending. The Article is limited to claims which arise out of the same relationship or other essential facts as the original claim, but a pleaded set-off which will not overtop the claim is a defence, not a counterclaim, and need not be justified by reference to this rule.[229] It is not clear whether Article 6(3) extends to a counterclaim against a party other than the original claimant, but in the context of insurance, at least, it has been held that it does not where to allow it would deprive an

---

[224] Case C-51/97 *Réunion Européenne SA v Spliethoff's Bevrachtingskantoor BV* [1998] ECR I-6511.

[225] According to Jenard. But according to Case C-77/04 *GIE Réunion Européenne v Zurich España* [2005] ECR I-4509, the third party claim (instead? as well?) must not have this bad motivation.

[226] *Waterford Wedgwood plc v David Nagli Ltd* [1999] 3 All ER 185; cf *The Ikarian Reefer* [2000] 1 WLR 603 (CA).

[227] Case C-365/88 *Kongress Agentur Hagen GmbH v Zeehaghe BV* [1990] ECR I-1845.

[228] *Hough v P&O Containers Ltd* [1999] QB 834.

[229] Case C-431/93 *Danvaern Productions A/S v Schuhfabriken Otterbeck GmbH & Co* [1995] ECR I-2053.

insured or policyholder of his special jurisdictional privileges.[230]
Article 6(4), which deals with contract actions joined with
actions against the same defendant in *matters relating to rights in rem
in immovable property*, has already been mentioned. It is obviously
sensible that an action against a mortgagor should be able to
enforce the security right as well as the personal covenant to repay
and this is, in effect, what Article 6(4) allows. (Article 7 allows a
court which has jurisdiction 'by virtue of this Regulation'[231] in an
action relating to liability from the use or operation of a ship to
entertain a claim for the limitation of such liability.)

Article 6 still takes too few steps in the direction of the efficient
coordination of claims, and if its provisions are given a restrictive
interpretation, it will be even less successful than it currently is.
Rules which operate in this area have to be accompanied by trust
that the judge will be sensible, a quality which is not ubiquitous
across the continent of Europe. If it is now expected that courts
will trust each other to interpret the Regulation properly, it may
be time to allow judges more general flexibility in this area, and
the provisions for the coordination and consolidation of claims
be made a little more generous.

7. RESIDUAL REGULATION JURISDICTION: ARTICLE 4

If none of the rest of the Regulation has applied, the defendant is someone who has no domicile in a Member State. At this
point, the Regulation gives up the attempt to lay down primary
jurisdictional rules for a claim against a defendant who has no
material connection to a Member State.[232] Article 4 expressly

---

[230] *Jordan Grand Prix Ltd v Baltic Insurance Group* [1999] 2 AC 127.

[231] Which presumably includes a reference to other conventions by way of
Art 66.

[232] Article 4 correlates to Art 6 in Reg 1215/2012, which sets out a fuller list
of provisions which override Art 6 when the proceedings are brought against a
defendant not domiciled in a Member State. A proposal to replace Article 4 with
a rule which would, loosely, have extended something resembling Art 5 to cases
in which the defendant had no domicile in a Member State was not found acceptable. But the organs of the European Union can be expected to reintroduce it at
a future date.

authorizes the claimant to rely on the jurisdictional rules[233] which are native to the court in which he wishes to sue. These rules, which we will encounter in relation to common law jurisdiction, are here incorporated by reference into the Regulation, and may be referred to as rules of 'residual Regulation jurisdiction', that is, the rules which apply to the residue of cases falling within the scope of the Regulation but not dealt with by its primary rules. So Article 4 will allow a claimant to serve process on an Australian defendant present in England, to apply for permission under CPR Part 6 to serve process on an American defendant out of the jurisdiction, and so on. But the Regulation has certainly not washed its hands of the dispute. Article 4 is an integral part of Chapter II, and it is expressly provided that Articles 22[234] and 23[235] prevail over it. Moreover, as Article 4 will result in a judgment enforceable under Chapter III of the Regulation, its operation is also subject to Article 27[236] on *lis alibi pendens*. So a claimant may not rely on Article 4 if proceedings between the same parties and involving the same cause of action were instituted in a court which was seised earlier in time, not even if that court has based its jurisdiction on Article 4 as well.[237] It is therefore wrong to picture Article 4 as opening a door back into the world outside the Regulation. It is better understood as incorporating by reference traditional jurisdictional rules; and the effect of their incorporation into the Regulation means that they have to be tweaked to fit into their new surroundings. Even so, there is room for unease at the combination of residual jurisdictional rules, many of which will appear to defendants as being outrageously wide in their sweep, and the automatic recognition under Chapter III of judgments based on such provisions. The point will be examined when we look at the recognition of foreign judgments.

---

[233] Some of which are set out in Annex I to the Regulation. The list of these rules does not appear in Reg 1215/2012.

[234] Exclusive jurisdiction regardless of domicile.

[235] Jurisdiction agreements for the courts of a Member State.

[236] And presumably Art 28 on related actions.

[237] Case C-351/89 *Overseas Union Insurance Ltd v New Hampshire Insurance Co* [1991] ECR I-3317.

8. LOSS OF JURISDICTION: ARTICLES 27–30

The aim of the Regulation, that judgments should be enforceable in other Member States without impediment, would be jeop-
ardized if there were to be concurrent litigation of identical or
similar disputes in the courts of Member States. Articles 27–30[238]
provide the means of control. Where the *same action, between the
same parties*, is brought before the courts of two Member States,
Article 27 requires the court seised second to dismiss its action;
its only alternative is to stay while any challenge to the jurisdiction of the first court is dealt with (and to dismiss proceedings
once it is confirmed). The rule is simple and clear and is entirely
dependent on which action was first out of the starting blocks.
It takes no account of considerations of comparative appropriateness, for all courts with jurisdiction[239] under the Regulation
are equally appropriate. It takes no account of the particular
rule relied on by each claimant, for despite their hierarchy, all
jurisdictional rules[240] applicable under the Regulation are equally
proper to invoke. Moreover, the court seised second is absolutely
forbidden to investigate whether, still less decide that, the first
erred in concluding that it had jurisdiction: all courts are equally
competent to apply the Regulation, and where the competences
are equal, the first in time prevails.[241] So far as the Regulation is
concerned, one possible exception has been mooted, for the case
where the second court considers that it has exclusive jurisdiction under Article 22,[242] but this has yet to be confirmed. Though
when Regulation 1215/2012 is in force,[243] a true exception will be
made for the case in which the court seised second has exclusive
jurisdiction by agreement: in such a case the court seised first will
be required to give way to the second court, reversing the present

---

[238] Section 9 of Chapter II, correlates to Arts 29–34 of Reg 1215/2012, which
are rather more elaborate, and which make substantial changes which are discussed at p 109 below.

[239] Including Art 4 jurisdiction.

[240] Including Art 4.

[241] Case C-351/89 *Overseas Union Insurance Ltd v New Hampshire Insurance Co*
[1991] ECR I-3317.

[242] ibid.

[243] On 10 January 2015.

position according to which if the first court has been seised in cynical contradiction of a jurisdiction agreement for another Member State, the designated court can do nothing except wait. This wretched tactic or technique saw some 'natural defendants' bringing contrived proceedings in a non-designated court, in which proceedings would move at a glacial pace, in order to 'torpedo' the jurisdiction agreement.[244] Only if the defendant in the first court has contested its jurisdiction is the second court permitted to stay its hand; but once the first court has confirmed its jurisdiction the second court must dismiss the action.

This abrupt solution to the problem of *lis pendens* has always been liable to produce an unseemly rush to commence litigation and seise the court of a party's choice; it may be catastrophic to tell the opposite party that proceedings will be commenced after a period of days.[245] 'Speak softly and hurry a big writ',[246] as Theodore Roosevelt nearly said; *carpe curiam!* as others might prefer.

For its operation, Article 27 requires three identities: of parties (but procedural differences between the formulation of the claimants and defendants are not decisive); of object (the two actions must have the same end in view); and of cause (they must be founded on the same facts and rules of law).[247] So in relation to the identity of parties, an action brought *in rem* against a vessel may still be found to be between the same parties as one *in personam* against those having an interest in the vessel; the critical test is whether the interests of the parties are identical and indissociable.[248] As regards identity of object and cause, an action for damages for breach of contract shares identity with one for a declaration that the contract had been lawfully rescinded,[249] for the one could be raised as a complete defence to the other; an

---

[244] Case C-116/02 *Erich Gasser GmbH v Misat srl* [2003] ECR I-14692 was the classic illustration of the technique. Regulation 1215/2012, taking effect on 10 January 2015, will deal with this, and in effect reverse the effect of *Erich Gasser*: see further, p 109 below.

[245] *Messier Dowty Ltd v Sabena SA* [2000] 1 WLR 2040 (CA).

[246] That is, one drafted with such width and so comprehensively that it is not possible for the opponent to construct a claim or argument which takes advantage of a gap in the claims made.

[247] Case C-406/92 *The Tatry* [1994] ECR I-5439.

[248] Case C-351/96 *Drouot Assurances SA v CMI* [1998] ECR I-3075.

[249] Case 144/86 *Gubisch Maschinenfabrik KG v Palumbo* [1987] ECR 4861.

action by a cargo-owner in respect of damage to cargo shares identity with one against the cargo-owner for a declaration of non-liability.[250] But an action for damages for breach of warranty of quality does not share identity of object and cause with an action for the price of goods delivered, and Article 27 will not apply to it.[251]

Prior to the Regulation, the Brussels Convention made no more than a general attempt to define the point at which a court was seised for the purpose of these Articles. The date on which a court was seised was to be determined by asking when the matter was 'definitively pending' before the particular court, and the question was answered by recourse to the procedural laws of the several courts in which the actions were brought.[252] As a matter of English law, it was held that even though the action had been commenced, a court was not seised until the writ had been served on the particular defendant.[253] Service on a co-defendant would not seise the court of a claim against an unserved co-defendant,[254] nor would the obtaining of interlocutory relief prior to service of process.[255] In other states the rules were different, and in some a court would be seised prior to service of process. The result was unsetting and confusing, not least because it could be difficult for litigants to obtain reliable advice about the seisin of foreign courts for the purpose of this jurisdictional rule, as this is probably not the daily business of the average practitioner. Responding to this concern, Article 30 provides a solution in two parts: (a) in countries where the claimant lodges a document at court before serving it, it is the date of lodging (assuming the claimant has not failed to take the subsequent steps he needs to take for service to be effected); (b) in countries where the document has to be served before being lodged with the court, at the time when it is received by the authority responsible for service (assuming the claimant has

---

[250] *The Tatry.*

[251] Article 28 may apply, though.

[252] Case 129/83 *Zelger v Salinitri (No 2)* [1984] ECR 2397.

[253] *Dresser UK Ltd v Falcongate Freight Management Ltd* [1992] QB 502 (CA).

[254] *Grupo Torras SA v Sheikh Fahad Mohammed al Sabah* [1996] 1 Lloyd's Rep 7 (CA).

[255] *Neste Chemicals SA v DK Line SA (The Sargasso)* [1994] 3 All ER 180 (CA). But see also *Phillips v Symes* [2008] UKHL 1, [2008] 1 WLR 180.

not failed to take the subsequent steps he needs to take for lodging to take place, such as the payment of fees). England is a category (a) country, and the date stamped on the claim form by the court will in principle identify the date of seisin. There may be cases which do not fit easily into this framework at all, such as where proceedings are amended to add a further claim or a new cause of action, or an additional defendant is added into proceedings which are already pending *inter alios*. Difficulty may yet also arise in cases in which a claimant is required to institute a process of mediation before being permitted to commence litigation in the traditional sense. But it would be ungrateful to cavil. The confusion which preceded this reform was ghastly, and if problems emerge with Article 30, they can be tidied up in due course.

If Article 27 is inapplicable, Article 28 may be used if there are *related actions* in the two courts: that is, actions which are so closely connected that it would be expedient to hear them together to avoid the risk of irreconcilable judgments resulting from separate proceedings. If the actions are related, the second court— Article 28 gives power only to the court seised second—may dismiss the action before it if this may be consolidated with the proceedings pending in the first court, or it may stay its proceedings to await the outcome in the first court, or it may do neither and simply proceed to adjudicate. Where Article 28 applies, the English preference is for dismissal for consolidation in the first court.[256] This may well be appropriate if the two actions involve different parties but have essentially the same cause of action: to bind all concerned into the one hearing and one judgment is sensible, and if the cause of action is substantially the same, the joinder of parties may not lengthen the trial in the first court. But if the same parties are litigating different causes of action in the two Member States, it may be more efficient to stay the second action to await the outcome of the first, and apply Chapter III of the Regulation to curtail the second action. By contrast, if the second action is dismissed for consolidation with the first, the effect will be to lengthen the first trial by the length of the second; had there instead been a stay, the second trial may never need to take place.

---

[256] *Sarrio SA v Kuwait Investment Authority* [1999] 1 AC 32.

Where two courts have exclusive jurisdiction regardless of domicile, Article 29 provides that the court seised second must decline jurisdiction in favour of the first court. Although a court with jurisdiction under a jurisdiction agreement is said by Article 23 to have exclusive jurisdiction, it has never been considered that Article 29, as opposed to Article 27, is applicable to such cases.

9. PROCEDURAL POWERS AND REGULATION JURISDICTION

A troublesome set of questions concerns the extent to which an English court may supplement or modify the jurisdictional scheme of the Regulation by recourse to its rules on *forum conveniens*, anti-suit injunctions, and so forth. There may be no clear and easy answer. Certainly confusion has arisen from the search for wide and general solutions, which suggests that the picture must be painted with a fine brush. But it is also important to bear in mind that Regulation jurisdiction and common law jurisdiction are two very different things, and it is dangerous to assume that principles or practices developed at common law can be labelled as procedural and, as a result of this having been done, introduced into a case in which the court is exercising Regulation jurisdiction.

(a) Disputes about jurisdiction

A defendant who disputes jurisdiction *in limine* may deny that the court has the jurisdiction asserted by the claimant. In general, factual doubt on any material point is resolved by asking who has the better of the argument on the jurisdictional question: the court will be well aware that its knowledge of the facts is incomplete, but it is hard to see how one can do better than to ask who made the better showing on the point.[257] Some cases have interpreted this to mean that that the party seeking to disturb the jurisdiction which would otherwise exist must have 'much the better of the argument' on the material before the court:[258] for example, if

---

[257] *Canada Trust Co v Stolzenberg (No 2)* [2002] 1 AC 1.

[258] *Bols Distilleries BV v Superior Yacht Services Ltd* [2006] UKPC 45, [2007] 1 WLR 12; *Konkola Copper Mines plc v Coromin Ltd* [2006] EWCA Civ 5, [2006] 1 Lloyd's Rep 410.

the claimant seises the English court, but the defendant asserts that the case is covered by a jurisdiction agreement for the courts of another Member State, he must have much the better of the argument on the point or points in dispute. But it is hard to see that 'much' adds anything of substance, for when the jurisdictional facts are in dispute and not susceptible to immediate clarification, the less elaborate the test the better.

(b) *Forum non conveniens*

When the claimant invokes a jurisdictional rule other than the residual Regulation jurisdiction provided by Article 4, a court has no discretion to stay its proceedings and encourage the claimant to proceed instead in another Member State on the ground that it is the natural forum.[259] It makes no difference that the claimant is not domiciled in a Member State.[260] But where the natural forum is in a non-Member State, the original instinct[261] of the English courts was that nothing in the Regulation stood in the way of their acceding to a defendant's application for a stay of proceedings on the ground of *forum non conveniens*. This followed from the perception that the Regulation had no application to a question, or a jurisdictional contest, which arose not as between the courts of Member States, but only one as between a Member State and a non-Member State. This view, however, was decisively rejected by the European Court,[262] which probably does not regard jurisdiction as a matter of 'contest'. A claim was brought in England after a grievous personal injury was sustained in Jamaica. Only one of the six defendants was domiciled in England;[263] the natural forum was undoubtedly in Jamaica. The Court ruled that as Article 2 gave the English court jurisdiction, and as the Regulation made no provision for a stay of Article 2 jurisdiction on the ground of *forum non conveniens*, the exercise of such a power was inconsistent with the Regulation. To be sure,

---

[259] Schlosser Report [1979] OJ C59/71 at para 78.

[260] For the Regulation draws no distinction: Case C-412/98 *Universal General Insurance Co v Groupe Josi Reinsurance Co SA* [2000] ECR I-5925.

[261] *Re Harrods (Buenos Aires) Ltd* [1992] Ch 72 (CA).

[262] Case C-281/02 *Owusu v Jackson* [2005] ECR I-1383 (a decision on the Brussels Convention, but directly applicable to the Regulation).

[263] The other five in Jamaica.

the Court laboured under the startling misapprehension that an English court might order a stay even though the defendant had not applied for it, but this schoolboy howler cannot make the rest of the judgment a nullity. And from the perspective of the European Court, it must have seemed incredible that, eight years after he had been rendered quadriplegic by what he claimed was the defendants' fault, a claimant could be ordered by an English court to take his wheelchair and start from scratch in the courts of a third world country, several thousand miles from where he was receiving constant medical care and his defendant lived. For the Court of Appeal to have made the reference to the European Court was ridiculous, but it did so; and if the judgment of the European Court is a wound on the body of English law, it is one which was entirely self-inflicted.

The Court rested its conclusion on the principle of legal certainty, and on the fact that the legislative text made no reference to the doctrine of *forum non conveniens*. But it refused to answer the second question asked, namely whether there was a power to stay in response to a jurisdiction agreement for the courts of a non-Member State, or where there were proceedings already pending before the courts of a non-Member State, or where the claim concerned title to land, the validity of patents, and so forth, in a non-Member State. A superficial reading of the judgment might suggest that such connections to a non-Member State, not being mentioned in the Regulation, are irrelevant and furnish no basis for jurisdictional relief, but this is plainly wrong. The Court had made it clear only a few years earlier that a jurisdiction agreement for a non-Member State took whatever effect it had according to the national law of the court seised.[264] There is little reason to suppose that the Court had changed its mind, and none to suggest that the principle of legal certainty is best served by ignoring agreements on jurisdiction. Nor is legal certainty much advanced by pretending that proceedings pending in the courts of a non-Member State are not happening at all, or by ruling on the validity of a non-Member State patent, or on title to land in a non-Member State. The real surprise is that anyone would

---

[264] Case C-387/98 *Coreck Maritime GmbH v Handelsveem BV* [2000] ECR I-9337.

wish to interpret the Regulation as being liable to produce such ludicrous results. Part of the reason why there is no mention in the Regulation of these particular connections to non-Member States is that the Regulation cannot, any more than the Convention could, direct a non-Member State court to hear or not hear a case: lacking the authority to harmonize the laws of non-Member States, it left these issues unregulated.[265] But there should not be doubt about it: a court seised with jurisdiction under Article 2 is at liberty to apply its own law to give effect to a choice of court for a non-Member State; it may still take the appropriate notice of a *lis pendens* in a non-Member State; and it is not obliged to adjudicate title to land in New York or the validity of patents granted under the law of Japan, just because the defendant to the claim is domiciled in England.

One explanation for this general conclusion, and which finds some support in French doctrinal writing, is that a court seised with Regulation jurisdiction may give 'reflexive effect' to Articles 22, 23, and 27 of the Regulation;[266] a more English idiom would be to apply the Articles by analogy. This, however, is not quite how the Court dealt with jurisdiction agreements for a non-Member State,[267] and it would not be ideal to suggest that the 'reflexive effect' would be as obligatory as the Articles are when they operate within the Regulation. If Regulation jurisdiction is capable of accommodating it, a remission to the more flexible approach of the doctrine of *forum non conveniens* would better reflect the fact that legal systems beyond the borders of the European Union are somewhat variable. But none of this challenges the decision of the Court in *Owusu*.

Unfortunately, Regulation 1215/2012 offers a 'solution' which may be considerably worse than doing nothing at all. A court will be allowed to stay proceedings on the basis of connections to a non-Member State, but only when proceedings before the courts of a non-Member State were pending at the date of institution of proceedings in the Member State. The broad effect is that

[265] Opinion C-1/03 *Lugano* [2006] ECR I-1145.

[266] The argument was first advanced by Mr Droz, which ought to guarantee its credentials. See [1990] Rev Crit 1 at 14.

[267] Case C-387/98 *Coreck Maritime GmbH v Handelsveem BV* [2000] ECR I-9337.

Articles 27 and 28 of the Brussels I Regulation are legislated for application by analogy, but Articles 22 and 23 are not. It remains to be seen whether this new power, set out in Articles 33 and 34 of Regulation 1215/2012, is to be understood as excluding the possibility of granting relief by applying these other provisions by analogy, but the principle of *expressio unius, exclusio alterius* would need to be overcome. If it were to be held that the new Articles 33 and 34 are the limit of what a court can do when there are material connections to a non-Member State, the result will reflect discredit on those who paved the way for it.

Where residual Regulation jurisdiction under Article 4 is concerned, a court must take into account issues of *forum conveniens* in determining whether to grant or to set aside permission to serve out of the jurisdiction, for as a matter of English jurisdictional law service out may only be made, and jurisdiction will only therefore exist, if England is the proper place to bring the proceedings.[268] It has also been held that a stay of proceedings commenced as of right under Article 4 may be granted on the basis of *forum non conveniens*. Where the natural forum is a non-Member State, this makes sense as the doctrine of *forum non conveniens* is an integral part of the jurisdictional rules which Article 4 absorbs into the Regulation. It has also been held to apply where the natural forum is another Member State, which is more controversial,[269] not least because an English court which grants a stay of proceedings remains seised of them,[270] and may at a later stage lift the stay.

(c) Anti-suit injunctions

Given that a court seised second has no right to assess the jurisdiction of a court seised first,[271] it is thought to follow that a court has no right to order a respondent who is claimant in proceedings before another Member State to discontinue his action, for whatever the theory of the matter, the effect would be of

---

[268] CPR r 6.37(3).

[269] *Haji-Ioannou v Frangos* [1999] 2 Lloyd's Rep 337 (CA).

[270] *Rofa Sport Management AG v DHL International (UK) Ltd* [1989] 1 WLR 902 (CA).

[271] Case C-351/89 *Overseas Union Insurance Ltd v New Hampshire Insurance Co* [1991] ECR I-3317.

ruling on the foreign court's jurisdiction and granting relief on the back of a finding that it was lacking. For a while the English courts turned a blind eye to such objections, and ordered injunctions to enforce agreements on jurisdiction without regard to the status of proceedings before the courts of other Member States.[272] Though there was much to be said for summary enforcement of such commercial agreements,[273] reconciling this with the scheme of the Regulation was quite impossible; and as soon as it was given the opportunity to do so, the Court declared that anti-suit injunctions, targeted at proceedings before the courts of another Member State, were inconsistent with the scheme of the Regulation.[274] To the submission that an anti-suit injunction did not depend on a finding that the foreign court lacked jurisdiction, but simply sought to enforce the parties' personal rights and obligations the Court responded, fairly enough, that the effect of the order was to interfere with proceedings before a judge in another Member State, and that the ends thereby condemned the means. In this respect it seems to have departed from an earlier approach to equitable rights and duties, which were understood as operating *in personam* only,[275] but it is undeniable that a judge in a Member State, doing her duty according to her judicial oath, is unlikely to appreciate the subtlety of the distinction between direct and indirect interference with the proceedings before her court, it making little difference whether interfering instructions from a foreign judge are sent directly or via one of the parties at the bar.

The law has been declared by the European Court, and some will say: *Luxembourg locuta, causa finita*, but it is worth reflecting on what caused the misunderstanding in the first place. When an English judge says 'on the application before me I am not asked to decide whether the foreign court has jurisdiction, which I cannot and will not; I am asked to decide whether the parties bound themselves so that the respondent is in beach of his agreement by invoking it, which I can and will' he is performing the 'judge as

---

[272] *Continental Bank NA v Aeakos Compania Naviera SA* [1994] 1 WLR 588 (CA); *The Angelic Grace* [1995] 1 Lloyd's Rep 87 (CA).

[273] *OT Africa Line Ltd v Hijazy* [2001] 1 Lloyd's Rep 76.

[274] Case C-159/02 *Turner v Grovit* [2004] ECR I-3565 (a case on the Brussels Convention).

[275] Case C-294/92 *Webb v Webb* [1994] ECR I-1717.

umpire' role which English procedure, wittingly or unwittingly, ascribes to him. It is misleading to accuse him of doing indirectly that which he may not do directly; he is doing what the parties ask him to do, by acting as umpire in relation to a particular dispute, giving his decision, decreeing the legal consequences of it, and leaving it to the parties to work out what happens next. Any litigator will instantly recognize the way it happens. It is perverse to assert that a judge in such circumstances is deciding whether a foreign court has jurisdiction. He is simply drawing the legal conclusions which flow from his decision as umpire of the matter brought before him for his decision. This may offend the scheme of the Brussels Regulation, but the real basis of the objection, as it is submitted, lies in the failure to appreciate the 'judge as umpire', or limited, nature of judicial adjudication in the common law. It is far from clear that this has ever been explained; it is unclear whether it would have, or should have, led to any different outcome if it had been; and it is now too late to care. Even so, the course of the modern law has been charted in something of a fog for which no-one and everyone is to blame.

The immediate consequence is that an English court may not restrain a wrongdoer, who is subject to its personal jurisdiction, from doing wrong by litigating before a court in another Member State (of course, this limitation on the relief which may be ordered has no relevance to an application to restrain proceedings before the courts of a non-Member State. Such an order may be made just as long as the defendant or respondent is, according to the rules of Regulation jurisdiction, liable to be sued in England). Whatever else justifies this result it certainly weakens the power of an English court to do effective justice according to the law. This is especially noticeable where a party to a binding agreement on jurisdiction brings proceedings in another Member State, which are designed to frustrate reliance on the jurisdiction agreement for so long as the spoiling action may be dragged out in the foreign court. So notorious did this tactic become that it acquired a name of its own: the 'Italian torpedo' is the institution of proceedings in Italy, the courts that time forgot, to forestall the enforcement of a jurisdiction agreement for a court elsewhere.[276] Even so, there appears to be nothing

---

[276] Case C-116/02 *Erich Gasser GmbH v Misat srl* [2003] ECR I-14693. The terminology of torpedo is that of Mr Franzosi: (1997) 7 Eur Int Prop R 382.

clearly standing in the way of an action brought to obtain damages for breach of contract, and while this will not be as effective as the injunction in holding parties to their obligations, it may be better than nothing. Such claims are increasingly seen outside the domain of the Regulation;[277] it remains to be seen whether (and it is far from clear that) they can be accommodated within it. After all, the incentives to forum shop and to prevent forum shopping never die, but simply shift to new ground: *plus ça change, plus c'est la même chose.*

10. PROVISIONAL OR PROTECTIVE MEASURES: ARTICLE 31

Provisional or protective measures obtained before the trial may critically affect the way the dispute is resolved: measures freezing assets and ordering disclosure of their whereabouts, orders for an interim payment, and so on, will affect the balance of power prior to the trial. Yet the jurisdictional control of these measures is touched on only lightly by Article 31[278] of the Regulation, which contents itself with the principle that so long as they are guaranteed to be provisional and reversible, there is no need to impose any jurisdictional restriction on where or when they may be obtained.[279] Where the substantive claim to which they are ancillary falls within the domain and the jurisdiction of the Regulation, that is, within Article 1, it is necessary to distinguish two types of case in which provisional, including protective, measures may be applied for. If the court applied to has jurisdiction over the merits, there is no Regulation limit upon the relief it may order, provisional or otherwise.[280] If it does not, an application may still be made under Article 31 of the Regulation; the only jurisdictional requirements to be satisfied are those which national law places upon the applicant, and there is no objection to the use,

---

[277] *Union Discount Co v Zoller* [2001] EWCA Civ 1755, [2002] 1 WLR 1517.

[278] Section 10 of Chapter II, correlates to Art 35 of Reg 1215/2012, which makes no substantial changes.

[279] Not even where jurisdiction over the substance is governed by Art 22: Case C-616/10 *Solvay SA v Honeywell Fluorine Products Europe BV* [2012] ECR I-(Jul 12).

[280] Case C-391/95 *Van Uden Maritime BV v Deco Line* [1998] ECR I-7091 (where the court did not have merits jurisdiction, an agreement to arbitrate having denied every court merits jurisdiction).

in this context, of traditional or exorbitant grounds of personal jurisdiction. In England, therefore, all that is needed is to serve the respondent with the claim form by which the relief is sought: within the jurisdiction as of right, or out of it with the prior permission of the court (though in deciding whether to grant permission the court may take account of the fact that the trial will not be taking place in England and may ask whether this makes it inexpedient to grant the relief applied for).[281] However, where Article 31 is relied on, it has been held[282] that two further limitations, not strictly jurisdictional in nature, apply. First, the measure must be one which is truly provisional, in that it is guaranteed to be reversible if it turns out not to have been warranted once the merits have been tried. An English freezing order, which will require an undertaking in damages often fortified by a bank guarantee, is a good example of what is meant. Secondly, its scope may not extend to assets within the territorial jurisdiction of another Member State. This is more problematic, for although this limitation makes sense if the order is expressed to take effect directly against assets,[283] an English freezing order does not do so, but merely orders an individual who is or has been made subject to the personal jurisdiction of the court not to dissipate his assets. It remains unclear whether the presence or residence of the respondent within England immunizes such an order from this limitation,[284] or whether the order must instead be taken as one which, in substance and notwithstanding its form,[285] does affect assets in another Member State so that, to that extent, it may not be sought under cover of Article 31.

---

[281] Civil Jurisdiction and Judgments Act 1982, s 25(3): *Credit Suisse Fides Trust SA v Cuoghi* [1998] QB 818. The proposition, advanced in that case and elsewhere, that an English court may properly 'assist' a foreign court in this way is remarkable, and remarkably unconvincing if the foreign court has not requested any assistance. But the objective value of unsolicited English 'assistance' is now a matter of dogma.

[282] Case C-391/95 *Van Uden Maritime BV v Deco Line* [1998] ECR I-7091.

[283] Which is understood to be the way in which a French order of *saisie conservatoire* operates.

[284] This appears to have been the view in *Crédit Suisse Fides Trust SA v Cuoghi*.

[285] For an analogous refusal by the Court to accept that the precise form of an English admiralty action *in rem* renders it different from an action *in personam* in the context of Art 27 see Case C-406/92 *The Tatry* [1994] ECR I-5439.

11. REGULATION 1215/2012

As indicated above, the results of the project to reform the Brussels I Regulation, which began in 2007, were enacted as Regulation (EU) 1215/2012,[286] and take their effect on 10 January 2015. Though a number of the provisions have already been mentioned, it is convenient to summarize the substance of the most important of them here. So far as concerns the law of jurisdiction, the principal lines of reform will be as follows. Article 1 will be elaborated so that arbitration is more completely disentangled and removed from the Regulation. This will mean that arbitrators, and a court dealing with an arbitration matter, will be free to go about their business without regard to the Regulation, even (or so it would be appear to be possible to contend) to the point of being free to order an anti-suit injunction to restrain a party to an agreement to arbitrate from bringing judicial proceedings before a court in another Member State which undermine the agreement. The view which has prevailed was that the legislative exclusion of arbitration from the domain of the Regulation, or the process of getting of the Regulation off the backs of the arbitration industry, had proved to be incomplete, and needed to be reinforced; but as will be seen below,[287] there will still be a duty to recognize a judgment which was given in proceedings brought in breach—as English law would see it—of an agreement to arbitrate, which means that difficulty will still remain to be resolved. In consumer contract and employment cases, jurisdiction over traders and employers not domiciled in a Member State will be directly provided for by Sections 3, 4, and 5 of Chapter II, rather than being left to the residual Regulation jurisdiction of Article 4.

As to jurisdiction agreements, the issue of how to deal with a party who does not take issue with the formal requirements of what is now Article 23, but who contests the validity of the alleged agreement on grounds of substance, will be dealt with in a rather unsatisfactory way. The issue whether the agreement on choice of court is 'null and void' will be referred to the law (including rules of private international law) of the court allegedly

---

[286] [2012] OJ L351/1.
[287] Recital 12 to the Regulation.

chosen. By contrast with the position to which the Regulation has brought the law, which was to ask, in an uncomplicated way, whether the party to be held to it made a formal acceptance, usually in writing, of the jurisdiction of a court, this labyrinthine alternative will contribute nothing to the quick and efficient determination of jurisdictional questions. Of course, it all depends what it comprehended by 'null and void', but whatever it is, the law, and jurisdictional applications, will be more complicated as a result.

In order to deal with the menace of torpedo actions, what are now Articles 23 and 27 will be amended to provide that where there is an exclusive jurisdiction agreement for the courts of a Member State, the designated court will be allowed to go first, and to take and exercise jurisdiction even if proceedings have been commenced before the courts of another Member State once the defendant to the latter proceedings pleads the existence of the jurisdiction agreement. The problem inherent in the idea that there 'is' such a jurisdiction agreement, when its validity and scope may genuinely be a matter for dispute, is evidently regarded as less compelling than the damage which has been done in those outrageous cases in which a jurisdiction clause for a Member State is torpedoed by proceedings brought in another Member State which may take an age to get rid of them again. It remains also to be seen how late in the day this disrupting of the court first sesied will be permitted to be done: will it really be possible that a non-designated court may be required to stay its proceedings even during the course of the substantive trial, if one party, fearing that the case is going badly, then decides to commence proceedings before a court which had been designated by a jurisdiction agreement?

The issue of how to deal with cases in which there are jurisdictional connections to non-Member States will be altered, marginally for the better but also, arguably, for the worse. If on the date proceedings are commenced before the courts of a Member State there are 'identical' proceedings, or 'related' proceedings, pending before the courts of a non-Member State, there will be a power, though no duty, to stay the local proceedings. In this sense, some effect may be given to a jurisdiction agreement for a non-Member State, or some acknowledgment made of the fact that the jurisdictional link to the non-Member State is reminiscent of that in Article 22, *but* this will only be permitted if the proceedings in the non-Member State were started first. If therefore a jurisdiction agreement for a non-Member State is torpedoed by proceedings brought in a Member State before any are started in the agreed forum, there is no evident intention, for there is nothing in the Regulation, to allow anything to be done about it. One assumes that this result proceeds from a rational understanding of what the law should be, but no-one has yet explained what it might be. If the result is that no account may be taken of a jurisdiction agremeent for a non-Member State unless proceedings are already pending before the courts of that non-Member State, there is no defending it.

D. COMMON LAW JURISDICTION

It is now necessary to examine the rules of jurisdiction which apply where the Regulation does not: though they are established by a mixture of statute, judicial decision, and rules of court, it is convenient to refer to them all as 'common law jurisdiction'.

1. DOMAIN OF COMMON LAW JURISDICTION

If the dispute is not a civil or commercial matter, or is otherwise excluded from the scope of the Regulation, the traditional rules of English law, as established by common law and legislation, determine the jurisdiction of the court. *Ex hypothesi*, the Regulation has no bearing on the existence or the exercise of jurisdiction, even in the event of a *lis alibi pendens* before the courts of a Member State; and the judgment will not qualify for recognition in other Member States under Chapter III of the Regulation.

As was said before, if the dispute is in a civil or commercial matter in relation to which Article 4 of the Regulation specifies that the jurisdictional rules of English law are to be applied it is, as was explained above, wrong to suppose that the Regulation is inapplicable. The jurisdiction in such a case is residual Regulation jurisdiction, so the control of *lis alibi pendens* in the courts of Member States, and the recognition of judgments, will still be governed by the Regulation, as will an application for provisional or protective measures. As was also said above, rules which serve as residual Regulation jurisdiction 'receive shape from the subject matter and wording of the Convention itself'.[288] We need say no more about this, but may proceed to examine the traditional approach to the jurisdiction of an English court, that is, the rules of common law jurisdiction. Our focus will be on actions *in personam*.

2. JURISDICTION ESTABLISHED BY SERVICE IN ENGLAND

Common law jurisdiction draws a fundamental distinction between cases where the defendant is and is not within the territorial jurisdiction of the court when the proceedings are commenced. For the jurisdiction of a court is established by the service of process, and the how and when of service of process depends on where the person to be served actually is. A claimant is entitled to serve process on a person who is present in England: jurisdiction may be established as of right. The common law takes the view that any person present in England is liable to be summoned to court by anyone else. The manner of service is prescribed by rules of court, but in principle, service may be made personally, or by post, or by certain electronic means,[289] but the significant consequences of an action having been commenced mean that a degree of formality, and therefore of technicality, is appropriate. Service on a partnership is also regulated by the rules of court. Legislation allows an English company to be served at its registered office[290] (although if in liquidation on its liquidator, and then only with permission of the court[291]). An overseas company may be served by making service on the person authorized to accept service on its behalf, but if this is not possible, process may be

---

[288] Mance LJ in *Raiffeisen Zentralbank Österreich AG v Five Star Trading LLC* [2001] EWCA Civ 68, [2001] QB 825 at [33]. The case concerned the impact of the Rome Convention on common law rules on assignment of intangibles, but the point is important and general.

[289] CPR r 6.3.

[290] Companies Act 2006, s 1139(1).

[291] Insolvency Act 1986, s 130(2).

served leaving it at or posting it to any place of business within the jurisdiction.[292] In this context, a place of business denotes a fixed and definite place from which the business of the company is carried out.[293] If this is a place at which contracts are made which bind the company, the company will probably have a place of business there.[294] But the procedures for service on corporations set out in Part 6 of the Civil Procedural Rules are alternatives to statutory service, and these widen and relax the methods of service on a company.[295]

Jurisdiction for the purpose of an action *in rem*, something which is really confined to admiralty law, is established by effecting service on the vessel while it is within territorial waters.

3. DISPUTING JURISDICTION ESTABLISHED BY SERVICE

A defendant who considers that as a matter of law the court has no jurisdiction over him or over the subject matter of the claim, or who contends that service was irregular, or on some other ground seeks to have service set aside, must first acknowledge the service which was made on him. This is a purely formal step, for he may then make an application within a short fixed period, under CPR Part 11,[296] for a declaration that the court has no jurisdiction, and for relief which follows from that, such as the setting aside of service. Where he has been served within the jurisdiction, the most common ground for objection is that the case is properly one of Regulation jurisdiction and the Brussels I Regulation provides that he is not liable to be sued in the English courts. But he may also plead a personal immunity from the jurisdiction of the

---

[292] Companies Act 2006, s 1139(2).

[293] *South India Shipping Corpn Ltd v Export-Import Bank of Korea* [1985] 1 WLR 585 (CA); *Re Oriel Ltd* [1986] 1 WLR 180 (CA).

[294] cf *Adams v Cape Industries plc* [1990] Ch 433 (CA), a case on the recognition of foreign judgments.

[295] CPR r 6.3(2); *Saab v Saudi American Bank* [1999] 1 WLR 1861 (CA). See further p 373 below

[296] This procedure for contesting the jurisdiction is applicable whether the case is one to which Regulation jurisdiction applies, one based on common law jurisdiction by service within the jurisdiction, or one based on common law jurisdiction established by service out of the jurisdiction.

courts or that the subject matter of the claim is something over which the court has no common law jurisdiction: in any such case service should be set aside. However, if he acknowledges service but makes no application under Part 11, or if he takes a step in the action otherwise than to contest the jurisdiction, he will be taken thereby to have submitted to the jurisdiction, and this submission will itself become the basis for the jurisdiction of the court, no matter that a challenge might have been made successfully.[297] Everything, apart from the question of any provisional or protective measures, is then put on hold, pending the definitive resolution of the challenge to the jurisdiction. Proceedings on the merits only start after that.

4. ADMITTING JURISDICTION BUT SEEKING A STAY

A defendant who cannot argue that the court lacks jurisdiction and that he should not have been served, but who is unwilling to defend in England, may apply to stay the proceedings on the ground that, although the court has jurisdiction over him in relation to the claim, the claimant should nevertheless bring the proceedings before the courts of another country: in other words, England is a *forum non conveniens*. Confusingly to be sure, the application for a stay is generally required to be made within the framework of CPR Part 11, even though the defendant is not contesting the jurisdiction of the court.[298] If his argument succeeds, the English action will not be dismissed[299] but will remain stayed: that is, pending but held in abeyance.[300] Although he cannot be ordered

---

[297] The exception to this proposition is that where there was no subject matter jurisdiction, personal submission cannot remedy the deficiency, and jurisdiction remains non-existent.

[298] However, a later application for a stay may be permitted if, for example, the grounds for it were not apparent at the time of service, but only emerged later: *Texan Management Ltd v Pacific Electric Wire & Cable Co Ltd* [2009] UKPC 46.

[299] Although for the proposition that it may be dismissed if a stay would leave the claimant unable to sue in the foreign court, see *Haji-Ioannou v Frangos* [1999] 2 Lloyd's Rep 337 (CA).

[300] *Rofa Sport Management AG v DHL International (UK) Ltd* [1989] 1 WLR 902 (CA).

to do it, the claimant may have no practical alternative to suing in a foreign court. In principle a stay may be lifted if some problem arises, or if an undertaking given to the court by the defendant is not observed: as the action will have remained pending throughout, there is no problem of limitation. Where service was made within the jurisdiction, two main grounds exist for seeking a stay of proceedings: that the *forum conveniens* is elsewhere, and that bringing the English action is a breach of contract which should be stopped. The relief applied for may be common to both, but the principles which lead to it are sharply distinct.

(a) *Forum (non) conveniens*

If the defendant can show that there is another court which is available to the claimant, and which would be clearly more appropriate than England for the trial of the action, a stay will generally be ordered unless the claimant can show that it would be unjust to require him to sue there. The two limbs of the test are initially distinct, with individual burdens of proof, but in the end, a court will still ask whether the interests of justice require a stay of proceedings.

The English[301] development of this doctrine, principally by the House of Lords, made a distinctive contribution to common law jurisdictional thinking.[302] What underpins it is the proposition of the common law that if the parties are content to have a trial in England, no-one will stand in their way;[303] but if they are not in agreement, there is no compelling reason why the claimant, rather than the defendant, should get his way and have the trial in England. Once that is accepted, all that remains is to elaborate the test which will implement the principle. In England this is done by showing that there is a court, clearly more appropriate than England for the trial of the action, and asking whether

---

[301] It was developed much earlier in Scotland, and embedded in the American constitutional guarantee of due process, long before it was accepted in England.

[302] The leading authorities are *Spiliada Maritime Corpn v Cansulex Ltd* [1987] AC 460, *Connelly v RTZ Corpn plc* [1998] AC 854, and *Lubbe v Cape plc* [2000] 1 WLR 1545 (HL). For the steps which led to *Spiliada*, see *The Atlantic Star* [1974] AC 436, *MacShannon v Rockware Glass Ltd* [1978] AC 705, and *The Abidin Daver* [1984] AC 398.

[303] Unless there is an absence of subject matter jurisdiction.

there would be any injustice in having the trial take place there. In Australia, the same broad principle is accepted but is applied very differently: the immediate focus is not on the comparative appropriateness of the foreign court as against the local one, but on whether the Australian court is clearly inappropriate for the trial:[304] this may be considered a more seemly question for an Australian judge to answer. Even so, it should be observed that the leading Australian cases have tended to be personal injury cases, for which the prospect of making the injured claimant go limping off to a court far away, but preferred by the wrongdoer, is unattractive. The English doctrine, by contrast, was developed in unemotional commercial disputes. But the Australian approach also reflects a view that, if a court is given jurisdiction, it should require clear and convincing grounds before it declines to exercise it; and this is therefore closer to a civilian view that if the legislator has vested the judge with jurisdiction, he has told the judge to adjudicate and the judge should not think he has power to set aside the law, whether on grounds of *forum conveniens* or otherwise. However that may be, the inherent power of an English court to regulate its own procedure is a natural counterpart to the inherent jurisdiction of an English court. It is a necessary counterpart to rules of jurisdiction based on service, which are too broad and insensitive to be acceptable by themselves, but it is a subtle counterpart for it has avoided rigid lines of operation. It is confirmed by statute;[305] has been embraced by the profession; and has been taken up throughout the common law world. Lord Goff of Chieveley, the principal architect of the developed law, described the doctrine as the 'most civilised of legal principles',[306] and he was right: it allows a judge in England to yield to the contention that the courts of another country would be better placed, and are available, to give the parties the adjudication they deserve. It reflects

---

[304] *Oceanic Sun Line Special Shipping Co v Fay* (1988) 165 CLR 197; *Voth v Manildra Flour Mills Pty Ltd* (1990) 171 CLR 538; *Henry v Henry* (1996) 185 CLR 571 (which says that it may well be inappropriate if the foreign action was started first); *Régie Nationale des Usines Renault v Zhang* (2003) 210 CLR 491.

[305] Civil Jurisdiction and Judgments Act 1982, s 49.

[306] *Airbus Industrie GIE v Patel* [1999] 1 AC 119.

judicial comity which acknowledges that where sovereignties collide a sensitive solution is preferable to an abrupt one.

Courts occasionally scold parties for piling resources into a stay application when they would do better, in the opinion of the judge, to be getting on with trying the merits of the claim instead. 'Litigating about where to litigate' is, on this view, a Bad Thing. But this does not convince everybody. A brisk preliminary skirmish on jurisdiction may well allow each side to gauge the strength of the other's case and the stomach each has for the fight. After the issue has been decided, the case may well settle and, if it does, settle on better informed terms than would otherwise have been the case. If this be accepted, the doctrine of *forum conveniens* contributes to efficient dispute resolution, and the odd irritable judge would do well to be grateful for it.

Descending to the detail of the test, the first limb requires that the foreign court be shown to be clearly or distinctly more appropriate than England. Attention will focus on the location of the events and the witnesses to them, the law which will be applied to determine the case, general issues of trial convenience, the relative strength of connection with England and with the alternative forum, and so on. Assessment of these factors is a matter for the trial judge.[307] A foreign court is available if it has, or will have, jurisdiction over the defendant: this may be founded on the defendant's undertaking to submit to it, given as late as the hearing of the application for a stay.[308] The fact that the claimant lacks the resources to sue in the foreign court does not make that court unavailable, although it may well be relevant under the second limb.[309]

Once the defendant has shown the natural forum to be overseas, the claimant may still resist a stay by seeking to show that it is unjust to confine him to his rights and remedies as the foreign court will see them. Arguments that damages will be lower or

---

[307] A point made by Lord Templeman in *Spiliada Maritime Corpn v Cansulex Ltd* [1987] AC 460 (HL), and reiterated periodically since. For a matchless appreciation of the issues as they appear when viewed from the unique vantage point of the courthouse in Galveston, Texas, see *Smith v Colonial Penn Insurance Co* 943 F Supp 782 (1997) (US Dist Ct).

[308] Although this may bear on the issue of costs.

[309] *Lubbe v Cape plc* [2000] 1 WLR 1545 (HL).

civil procedure less favourable to him will not usually be good enough,[310] for as long as the foreign court has a developed system of law, it is inappropriate for the English courts to pass judgment on it, and still less on individual rules self-servingly extracted from it and moaned about. But if funding the action in the foreign court is beyond the means of the claimant, whereas financial support would be available to him in England, it may be unjust to stay, at least in a case which requires substantial labour to prepare the evidence and conduct the trial. Though this may make an inroad on the principle that critical comparison with the foreign court's procedure will not be invited,[311] the interests of justice demand that it be allowed. So also if there is cogent[312] evidence that the claimant will not receive a fair trial, especially on racial or religious grounds: a stay of English proceedings in such a case would be unthinkable. Until very recently, attempts by a claimant to show a court that the foreign court favoured by the defendant was objectively bad were treated by the English courts with icy disdain. But, perhaps under unacknowledged pressure from the European Convention on Human Rights, courts have now accepted that it is permissible and may be proper to point to and find serious fault with the alternative court, and to allow the English proceedings to continue despite the fact that the natural forum lies elsewhere.[313] If that involves passing judgment on the quality of a foreign legal system, that is just the way it is.

The argument that the claimant will lose in the foreign court, because the claim he makes in England will not be available to him in the foreign court or because the defendant will have a good defence to the action, should be an irrelevance: after all, strict

---

[310] *Spiliada* at 482. Although from time to time a court fails to respect this principle, and finds an injustice in, for example, the effect of the costs rules of the foreign court (eg *Roneleigh Ltd v MII Exports Inc* [1989] 1 WLR 619 (CA)), such cases must be wrong in principle. For a ringing statement of rational orthodoxy, see *The Herceg Novi* [1998] 4 All ER 238 (CA).

[311] *Lubbe v Cape plc* [2000] 1 WLR 1545 (HL), explaining *Connelly v RTZ Corpn Ltd* [1998] AC 854. Were the common law otherwise, it probably would have fallen foul of Art 6 of the European Convention on Human Rights.

[312] *The Abidin Daver* [1984] AC 398: attack by innuendo is inadmissible.

[313] *Altimo Holdings & Investment Ltd v Kyrgyz Mobil Tel Ltd* [2011] UKPC 11, [2012] 1 WLR 1804; *Cherney v Deripaska* [2009] EWCA Civ 849, [2010] 2 All ER (Comm) 456.

impartiality should be the watchword, and in every case, in every court, someone has to lose. But there is some support[314] for the view that in this case it would be unjust to order a stay. To favour claimant over defendant in this way is unprincipled and quite wrong: the idea that the rules are different in a case where the claimant has only one court in which he can expect to win is as wrong as it would be if a defendant were to say that the foreign forum is the only court in which his defence can be successfully advanced. No account should be taken of this fact, save perhaps where, in a contract dispute, the foreign court will disregard an express choice of law, so that to try to relocate the case to a foreign court would be for the defendant to engineer a constructive breach of the parties' contract.

If relief is granted, the case is stayed, and remains pending. The stay may well be on terms which reflect undertakings given to the court by the defendant, so that if these turn out to be ineffective the stay can be lifted and the action allowed to proceed. If, by contrast, the action were to be dismissed, it is difficult to see how these undertakings could be enforced, or the action revived, which is why this is not the relief which will be ordered.

(b) Starting proceedings in England in breach of contract

The second ground on which the defendant may seek a stay of proceedings is by pointing to a contract by which the claimant promised to sue in a foreign court and not to sue in England.[315] Now matters stand very differently. Rather than the defendant having to persuade the court to order a stay, a stay will be ordered unless the claimant can establish strong reasons for the court not to.[316] There are two parts to the analysis. First, the agreement must be examined. It will have to be shown that the alleged agreement on choice of court is valid[317] and effective; that on its true construction it applies to the particular action brought by the claimant; and

---

[314] *Banco Atlantico SA v British Bank of the Middle East* [1990] 2 Lloyd's Rep 504 (CA). Moreover, the spurious distinction makes a shadowy appearance in the cases on anti-suit injunctions, such as *Airbus Industrie GIE v Patel* [1999] 1 AC 119.

[315] If the argument is that there is a valid and binding arbitration agreement, the Arbitration Act 1996, s 9 makes a stay mandatory, and no element of discretion arises.

[316] *Donohue v Armco Inc* [2001] UKHL 64, [2002] 1 All ER 749.

[317] Invalidity may be brought about by the Unfair Terms in Consumer Contracts Regulations 1999 (SI 1999/2083).

that on its true construction it means that the bringing of English proceedings is a breach of contract. If so, a stay will usually be the most appropriate remedy. The questions of construction and validity are undertaken by reference to the law which governs the jurisdiction agreement, which will often, though need not, be the law governing the contract of which it forms a part, and any over-riding provision of the *lex fori*.[318] But as a contractual promise, the jurisdiction agreement is construed like any other term of the contract and the law which governs it will determine its effectiveness. So far as concerns its material scope, the defendant will need to show that the words were wide enough to encompass the action brought by the claimant: a term which says it applies to 'all actions under this contract', may, for example, be said not to extend to a claim alleging pre-contractual misrepresentation or claims in respect of equitable obligations. But where the law governing the contract is English, such nit-picking will be very strongly discouraged: there is a very strong judicial instinct to construe the clause and the intentions of the parties widely and inclusively, so that the untidiness, or worse, of two courts having competence over parts of the matter will not arise.[319] So far as concerns the personal scope of the agreement, if on its true construction A had promised B not to bring proceedings against C, C may not be entitled to enforce the contract,[320] but B, as promisee, should be able to. As regards the exclusivity of jurisdiction, there is no breach of contract unless the parties obliged themselves and each other not to sue in the English court.[321] They do not need to have used the

---

[318] *Hoerter v Hanover Telegraph Works* (1893) 10 TLR 103 (CA). Although Art 1(2) (d) of the Rome Convention means that the Convention makes no claim to govern this question, the common law rule is that the agreement is governed by the law of the contract in which it is contained.

[319] *Premium Nafta Products Ltd v Fili Shipping Co Ltd* [2007] UKHL 40, [2007] Bus LR 1719. The authorities are mainly on arbitration agreements, but the principles are common.

[320] Though he may be able to point to the promise of A in aid of an application for a stay on the general ground of *forum non conveniens*: *Global Partners Fund Ltd v Babcock & Brown Ltd* [2010] NSWCA 196, (2010) 79 ACSR 383; cf *VTB Capital plc v Nutritek International Corp* [2013] UKSC 5, [2013] 2 WLR 398.

[321] If they did not, the principles governing a stay will be the ordinary ones examined under *forum non conveniens*, subject to the point that the claimant may not be permitted to point to the court he agreed to nominate with a view to establishing the injustice of a stay.

word 'exclusive', but it certainly helps if they do: inept wording, as where 'the parties submit to the jurisdiction of the courts of X' or 'the courts of Y are to have jurisdiction over all disputes', is harder to construe with any confidence[322] and defeats the whole object of making jurisdiction a matter of certainty rather than lottery.

If the clause is interpreted in such a way as to make it a breach of contract for the English proceedings to have been brought, a stay is probable, although not inevitable.[323] If England is the natural forum, and if there are additional powerful reasons why the claimant should nevertheless be permitted to break his jurisdictional promise, the action will be allowed to continue. A compelling reason for not staying the proceedings will exist if non-parties are also implicated by the facts of the dispute but are not privy to the particular agreement: it may be very inconvenient for the litigation to take place in international fragments.[324] After all, a court has a public duty to secure the proper administration of justice, and this may mean that a private agreement on jurisdiction has to be subordinated to the broader interest. But otherwise, the claimant should not be heard to complain about particular aspects of the legal system which he chose and may have been paid to agree to. If the action is nevertheless allowed to proceed in England despite the agreement on exclusive jurisdiction, it is unclear what, if anything, prevents the defendant counterclaiming for damages for any proven loss flowing from the breach of contract. To permit an action to continue despite a bilaterally-binding choice of court agreement is only to refuse relief by way of specific enforcement; a remedy for damages for breach of contract is a common law right which, in principle, the defendant may assert, and by counterclaim if necessary. It may be difficult to obtain proof of loss, and it is also apparent that it

---

[322] Although it may still be a breach of a non-exclusive agreement on jurisdiction to sue outside the nominated court: *Sabah Shipyard (Pakistan) Ltd v Pakistan* [2002] EWCA Civ 1643, [2003] 2 Lloyd's Rep 571.

[323] *The El Amria* [1981] 2 Lloyd's Rep 119 (CA); *The Pioneer Container* [1994] 2 AC 324 (PC).

[324] *Bouygues Offshore SA v Caspian Shipping Co (Nos 1, 3, 4, 5)* [1998] 2 Lloyd's Rep 461 (CA); *Donohue v Armco Inc* [2001] UKHL 64, [2002] 1 All ER 749.

may be awkward to allow such a claim to proceed. But damages for breach of contract remains a common law right; they have been allowed for breach of jurisdiction agreement by suing overseas;[325] and if the agreement on jurisdiction was bought and paid for, it would denature it to withhold the usual remedy for its breach.

5. JURISDICTION BY PERMITTING SERVICE OUT

If the defendant is not in England he cannot be served with process as of right. Process must therefore be served on him overseas in order to found the jurisdiction of the court; and this requires the permission of the court. The procedure is established by Part 6 of the Civil Procedure Rules, but the authorities on the interpretation of predecessor texts are, inevitably, still pertinent. The claimant will apply for permission, without notice to his opponent, to serve process. The application must state the grounds on which it is made, and must identify the specific grounds relied on.[326] As the application is made in the absence of the defendant, the application must be full and frank in alerting the court to arguments which would be made by the defendant in opposition to the application.[327] Once permission has been granted and service has been made, the defendant is required to acknowledge it, but he may then apply, again under CPR Part 11, for an order declaring that the court has no jurisdiction, and for consequential relief such as setting aside of the permission and the service made pursuant to it. On the hearing of this application, the claimant bears the burden of proof on all those issues which determine whether permission should have been given in the first place: the fact that the application is by the defendant cannot mean that the burden has somehow now shifted to him. Common law jurisdiction

---

[325] *Union Discount Co Ltd v Zoller* [2001] EWCA Civ 1755, [2002] 1 WLR 1517; *National Westminster Bank plc v Rabobank Nederland* [2007] EWHC 1056 (Comm); [2007] EWHC 1742 (Comm), [2008] 1 Lloyd's Rep 16.

[326] CPR r 6.37(1)(a).

[327] Several cases have considered whether breach of this obligation should lead automatically to the setting aside of permission, but the answers are not completely consistent. Evidently it will be a matter of degree.

based on service out is an exorbitant jurisdiction,[328] and the onus of persuasion lies on the party seeking to invoke it.

The claimant must show three things: that each pleaded claim falls within the letter and the spirit of the grounds permitted,[329] lest an exorbitant jurisdiction be widened still further by lax construction of its language; that England is the proper place in which to bring the claim;[330] and that he believes that his claim has a reasonable prospect of success on its merits.[331] These three elements are distinct and must be individually satisfied: a clear success in one cannot condone failure in another.

(a) The grounds for, or gateways to, permission to serve out

The provisions which are now listed in a Practice Direction supplementing Part 6 of the Civil Procedure Rules[332] are variously referred to as 'grounds'[333] for service out, or 'gateways'[334] to jurisdiction. Whatever they are called, they define the claims in respect of which the court is entitled to grant permission to serve out. At first sight it makes sense for the law to have categories of case into which the claims must fit before permission can be given, but at second sight this proves to be an illusion. Permission will not in any event be granted unless England is the proper place to bring, or natural forum for, the claim. If this condition, which emerged as a specific and discrete requirement only relatively recently,[335] is satisfied, it is difficult to see what value is added by these more primitive, pigeonhole, criteria, or why there should not be an

---

[328] So said Lord Diplock in *Amin Rasheed Shipping Corpn v Kuwait Insurance Co* [1984] AC 50, 65. But the High Court of Australia did not agree: *Agar v Hyde* [2000] HCA 41, (2000) 201 CLR 552. It is probably right if service out is subject to *forum conveniens*.

[329] *The Hagen* [1908] P 189 (CA); *Johnson v Taylor Bros* [1920] AC 144, 153; *Mercedes-Benz AG v Leiduck* [1996] 1 AC 284, 289 (PC).

[330] CPR r 6.37(3).

[331] CPR r 6.37(1)(b).

[332] CPR PD 6B, para 3.1.

[333] As the legislation calls them.

[334] As some judges, and presumably counsel, prefer (rather quaintly) to describe them.

[335] In *Spiliada Maritime Corpn v Cansulex Ltd* [1987] AC 460, although there had been occasional trailers for it in earlier cases.

additional, open-ended, provision for any other case in which permission should be given, such as that found in the law of Ontario: 'In any [other case], the court may grant leave to serve an originating process or notice of a reference outside Ontario.'[336] The law still needs to be rethought. The real question is whether, had the central role of *forum conveniens* been appreciated from the outset, the law would have devised these pigeonholes and insisted on compliance with their letter and their spirit before permission to sue in the natural forum was granted. A rational answer would be negative. Nevertheless, the grounds or gateways are the law.

If there is any uncertainty about any fact which is required to bring the claim within the ground relied on, the claimant is required to make out a good arguable case, which is less than satisfying a balance of probability, as to it.[337] So if he applies for permission to serve on the basis that the claim arises from a contract made within the jurisdiction but the defendant, whilst admitting that there is a contract, denies that it was made in England, the claimant must show a good arguable case that England is where it was made. These geographical elements are matters of English domestic law; the broad legal concepts are defined by English law, including its private international law. So in the case just mentioned, if the defendant were to accept that there was a contract as a matter of English domestic law, but deny that it was a valid contract according to the law which actually governs it, the question will be referred to the law which governs the contract. But if he puts in issue the proposition that it was made in England, this will be tested by reference to English domestic law.

Each claim advanced must be distinctly referable to one or more of the grounds listed in the Practice Direction, and any which are not will be deleted.[338] A claimant is not necessarily precluded from adding further claims after service has been made,

---

[336] Rules of Civil Procedure, RRO 1990, r 17.03(1).

[337] *Seaconsar Far East Ltd v Bank Markazi Jomhouri Islami Iran* [1994] 1 AC 438. But *Altimo Holdings & Investment Ltd v Kyrgyz Mobil Tel Ltd* [2011] UKPC 7, [2012] 1 WLR 1804 reinterpreted this as a requirement to have much the better of the argument on the point, which is a retrograde step if England is distinctly shown to be the proper place to sue.

[338] For otherwise the scope of the rule would be extended: *Metall und Rohstoff AG v Donaldson, Lufkin & Jenrette Inc* [1990] 1 QB 391 (CA).

but the court will exercise its discretion to allow or disallow amendment so as to prevent a claimant seeking permission to serve process on a narrow ground, only to seek to amend it once the defendant has accepted jurisdiction, or, as it is more colloquially put, using a sprat to catch a mackerel.

In the account which follows we will deal with only those which are of practical importance. The grounds listed in Paragraph 3.1 of the Practice Direction which are applicable to commercial matters are mentioned first; then those less frequent in commercial litigation; and then the remainder.

So far as concerns claims related to *contracts*, three grounds are available. Under ground (6), service may be permitted where a claim is made in respect of a contract where that contract was made within the jurisdiction, or was made through an agent trading or residing within the jurisdiction, or is governed by English law, or contains a term to the effect that the court shall have jurisdiction to determine any claim in respect of the contract. In principle, the contract must be one by which the parties are bound, but as assignees and third parties may enforce contracts which they did not make, it is not necessary that the claimant and defendant be the original parties. Under ground (7), service may be ordered when a claim is made in respect of a breach of contract committed within the jurisdiction. Ground (8) provides for service where a claim is made for a declaration that no contract exists where, if the contract were found to exist, it would have fallen within ground (6).

As said above, if it is not conceded, there must be a good arguable case that there is a contract, valid according to rules of English law including its rules of private international law;[339] the place of its making is determined by English domestic law.[340] Though the paragraphs are drawn widely, the contract must be one by which the claimant and defendant are said to be bound: it should not suffice that a contract *inter alios* forms the background to the claim.[341] For the purposes of ground (7), breach by a repudiatory act occurs where the act was done; breach by non-performance

---

[339] *Amin Rasheed Shipping Corpn v Kuwait Insurance Co* [1984] AC 50; *Bank of Baroda v Vysya Bank Ltd* [1994] 2 Lloyd's Rep 87.

[340] *Chevron International Oil Co v A/S Sea Team (The TS Havprins)* [1983] 2 Lloyd's Rep 356.

[341] *Global 5000 Ltd v Wadhawan* [2012] EWCA Civ 13, [2012] 1 Lloyd's Rep 239.

where the required act was to have been performed. Ground (8) is a newer addition to the rules, designed to make it straightforward to bring a claim for a declaration of non-liability under an alleged contract. It probably applies generally to claims which deny that a contractual duty is owed to the defendant, but which the defendant alleges is owed, rather than being limited to cases in which it is claimed that no contract ever existed.[342] It is also to be expected that a claim for relief which is consequential upon holding that there is no contract is also covered by this ground: convenience suggests that it should be.

As to *torts*, under ground (9), service out may be permitted where a claim is made in tort where the damage was sustained within the jurisdiction, or where the damage sustained resulted from an act committed within the jurisdiction. A predecessor rule, which required that the claim be 'founded on *a* tort', had been held to require that there be an actual tort, ascertained if it was not conceded, by reference to rules of English law including its private international law.[343] The omission of the indefinite article makes it uncertain whether ground (9) still requires that there must be *a* tort, demonstrable to the standard of a good arguable case. If the paragraph requires only that the pleaded claim be properly formulated in the terminology of tort, or be characterized as tortious, there will be no need to show a good arguable case upon actual liability before service out may be authorized.[344] It is hard to say which view is to be preferred. It is undoubtedly odd that because the term 'contract' does not describe a cause of action, but 'tort' does, a jurisdictional requirement of liability might be imposed by the tort ground which is absent from grounds (6) and (8). No obvious policy requires this and, as a result, it may be preferable to read ground (9) as referring to the characterization of the claim rather than to the existence of liability.

---

[342] A court will not grant leave to serve a claim for a negative declaration unless it is an appropriate case for the seeking of such relief: *Messier Dowty Ltd v Sabena SA* [2000] 1 WLR 2040 (CA).

[343] RSC Ord 11, r 1(1)(f) as interpreted in *Metall und Rohstoff AG v Donaldson, Lufkin & Jenrette Inc* [1990] QB 391 (CA). See Ch 6 below.

[344] Although the requirement of CPR r 6.37(1)(b) will still need to be satisfied, and the claim shown to raise a serious issue on the merits.

Damage is sustained in England if some significant damage is sustained in England: it need not be all, nor even most, of it.[345] There is no particular reason why 'sustained' should reflect or reproduce the interpretation of where damage 'occurred' within Article 5(3) of the Brussels I Regulation, but if it were held to do so, the focus would be on the place of the direct damage done to the immediate victim of it. In the case of purely economic losses or damage to reputation, the location of the damage is to some extent artificial. An act is committed within the jurisdiction if substantial and efficacious acts were committed within the jurisdiction, even if other substantial acts were committed elsewhere.[346] The jurisdictional rule is triggered by the act of the defendant who is to be served, but the act of one joint tortfeasor is the act of all.[347]

So far as concerns *constructive trusteeship* and *restitution*, ground (15) allows service to be authorized where a claim is made against the defendant as constructive trustee and his alleged liability arises out of acts committed within the jurisdiction. The former rule made it explicit that the acts committed within the jurisdiction were not required to be those of the defendant; it is unlikely that their omission from the current version of the rule reflects a desire to narrow the scope of the provision. The acts must still have something to do with the defendant.[348] Only some of the acts, not necessarily the receipt of assets, need take place within the jurisdiction.[349] So as long as a participant in fraud takes part in a scheme where one of the wrongdoers did acts in the jurisdiction, service out may probably be authorized against all of them.[350] Ground (16) allows service where a claim is made for restitution where the defendant's alleged liability arises out of acts committed within the jurisdiction. This provision probably

---

[345] *Metall und Rohstoff AG v Donaldson, Lufkin & Jenrette Inc* [1990] 1 QB 391 (CA).

[346] ibid.

[347] *Unilever plc v Gillette (UK) Ltd* [1989] RPC 583 (CA).

[348] *NABB Bros International Ltd v Lloyds Bank International (Guernsey) Ltd* [2005] EWHC 405 (Ch), [2005] ILPr 506.

[349] *ISC Technologies Ltd v Guerin* [1992] 2 Lloyd's Rep 430; *Polly Peck International plc v Nadir* 17 March 1993 (CA), a case on a predecessor rule.

[350] If one can be served otherwise, it will also be possible to apply for permission under ground (3) to serve a co-defendant as a necessary or proper party to the claim against the defendant served otherwise.

requires that there is a link between the defendant and the acts committed in the jurisdiction, but does not require that the defendant himself do the local acts.[351]

So far as *other types of claim* are concerned, ground (1) is available if the defendant is domiciled within the jurisdiction,[352] though where this is so, the fact will often mean that the jurisdictional rules of the Regulation will apply, and that the case is not one of common law jurisdiction at all. Ground (2) applies if the claim is made for an injunction ordering the defendant to do or to not do an act within the jurisdiction. The injunction must comprise a substantial element of the relief sought,[353] and it must be an injunction in respect of substantive rights: an application for a freezing order, or other relief not predicated on the existence of substantive rights, is not within this provision[354] but is specifically provided for by ground (5) instead. Ground (3) is available if the defendant proposed to be served is a necessary or proper party to a claim against another defendant who has been or will be served;[355] the paragraph is a broad one which serves the coherent adjudication or efficient disposal of claims; the disjunctive wording should not be misinterpreted, for many defendants who are not necessary parties may still be proper parties to the claim.[356] Ground (10) applies if the proceedings seek the enforcement in England of any judgment or arbitral award.[357] Claims relating wholly to property in England fall under ground (11); this provision appears to be of substantial, but largely untapped, width.[358] Claims to execute English trusts come under ground (12); claims in the administration of the estate of an English domiciliary under ground (13); and probate actions under ground (14). Ground (18) applies when

---

[351] *NABB Bros International Ltd v Lloyds Bank International (Guernsey) Ltd* [2005] EWHC 405 (Ch), [2005] ILPr 506.

[352] Within the meaning of the 1982 Act: CPR r 6.31(i).

[353] *Rosler v Hilbery* [1925] 1 Ch 250 (CA).

[354] *Mercedes-Benz AG v Leiduck* [1996] 1 AC 284 (PC).

[355] Ground (4) makes corresponding provision for third parties to be brought in by defendants.

[356] See *Altimo Holdings & Investment Ltd v Kyrgyz Mobil Tel Ltd* [2011] UKPC 7, [2012] 1 WLR 1804.

[357] The judgment or award must have been given by the time permission is sought: *Mercedes-Benz AG v Leiduck* [1996] 1 AC 284 (PC).

[358] *Re Banco Nacional de Cuba* [2001] 1 WLR 2039.

a party seeks an order that costs be awarded to or against someone who was not a party to the proceedings.[359] Grounds (17), (19), and (20) complete a list of other causes of action, almost all statutory and where the statutory duty is reinforced by the right to seek permission to serve out.

(b) England is the proper place to bring the claim

The second requirement cast on the claimant is in rule 6.37(3), that England is the proper place to bring the claim. This echoes, in modified language, an earlier rule[360] that England must be shown, clearly or distinctly, to be the most appropriate forum, or the natural forum. The factors which are relevant when a stay is sought of proceedings commenced by service within the jurisdiction apply, *mutatis mutandis*, here as well. It is unclear why the draftsman elected not to use the 'natural forum' formula which had been hallowed by judicial and professional usage, but little probably turns on it. However, there will be cases in which England may be considered to be the proper place to bring a claim even though England is not the natural forum: if the alternative[361] forum is some war-torn, depraved, or hopeless corner of the globe, a trial in England may be in the proper place.[362] It is less certain whether this condition would be satisfied if financial support for the claim were available only in England and not in the alternative forum. The logic of recent cases on *forum conveniens* would suggest that this is so; and if the defendant is before the court, albeit that he has not yet submitted to the jurisdiction, it would be remarkable, and arguably a breach of the European Convention on Human Rights, for a court to set aside service and leave the claimant without effective remedy.[363] On the other hand, there are manifest points of distinction if the courts do not wish to be pushed this far.

---

[359] Senior Courts Act 1981, s 51.

[360] But which was never so expressed in statutory form. *Spiliada Maritime Corpn v Cansulex Ltd* [1987] AC 460 showed this to be a discrete component of RSC Ord 11, r 4(2), which required that the case be shown to be a proper one for service out. See generally *VTB Capital plc v Nutritek International Corp* [2013] UKSC 5.

[361] In this context this will probably be where the defendant is resident and can, in principle at least, otherwise be sued.

[362] *Cherney v Deripaska* [2009] EWCA Civ 849, [2010] 2 All ER (Comm) 456.

[363] cf *Lubbe v Cape plc* [2000] 1 WLR 1545 (HL).

(c) The claimant has a reasonable prospect of success

Service out will not be authorized unless the claimant states his belief that the claim has a reasonable prospect of success. If the defendant considers that the claim falls below this standard, he should probably challenge the obtaining of permission on the ground that the claimant could not properly have held and stated this belief; and if he succeeds on this point the court will declare that it has no jurisdiction, and set aside the permission and the service of process.[364] It was formerly required of a claimant that he show a good arguable case on the merits of his claim, which, if opaquely, required a higher standard of probability of winning; but this was deliberately relaxed in 1994.[365] It appears to be entirely justified: if England is the proper place to bring the claim, why should a claimant who wishes to serve out be called upon to demonstrate a higher apparent chance of success than the claimant who can effect service within the jurisdiction?

6. PREVENTING LITIGATION OVERSEAS

The rules of common law jurisdiction which we have examined curtail the extent to which a claimant may forum-shop in the English courts, principally by use of the principle of *forum (non) conveniens* to limit inappropriate access to the English courts. But there are two ways in which the common law responds to the practice of forum shopping to a foreign court: by granting injunctions to impede the foreign proceedings, and by allowing actions to be brought for declaratory relief.

(a) Anti-suit injunctions

To start by taking a step back from the common law, one should recall the observation of Lord Goff of Chieveley,[366] to the effect that whereas the jurisdictional scheme put in place by

---

[364] cf *Seaconsar Far East Ltd v Bank Markazi Jomhouri Islami Iran* [1994] 1 AC 438. It may be dangerous to make the argument by means of an application under CPR r 3.4(a) or CPR r 24.2(a)(i), as these are not challenges to the jurisdiction of the court and may therefore be seen as submission.

[365] *Seaconsar Far East Ltd v Bank Markazi Jomhouri Islami Iran* [1994] 1 AC 438.

[366] *Airbus Industrie GIE v Patel* [1999] 1 AC 119.

the Regulation is common to the Member States, and has the European Court sitting above it to ensure the proper interpretation of its rules,[367] the common law world is different. Order and fairness between states is achieved by the doctrine of *forum non conveniens*, by which a court directly limits its own jurisdiction, and by the anti-suit injunction, by which a court indirectly places limits on the jurisdiction of other courts. It is the second of these with which we are now concerned.

A court with personal jurisdiction over a respondent may order him not to bring or to discontinue proceedings in a foreign court, by granting an injunction against suit. The order is not addressed to the foreign judge: after all, he is neither subject to the personal jurisdiction of the English court nor addressed by the order which the court makes, and in any event, the question whether he has been given jurisdiction by his sovereign to adjudicate is probably not even justiciable in an English court. But it is addressed to the respondent, who is ordered to exercise self-restraint or suffer the consequences prescribed by law. Even so, a foreign judge may not appreciate the subtlety of the distinction,[368] and for this reason, a concern for comity controls the court in the exercise of its equitable discretion to restrain wrongdoers.[369] This potent remedy gives the English court an international reach by which to prevent what it finds to be wrongful recourse to a foreign court. Though the remedy is also found in other common law systems, it is largely unknown in civilian systems. It has been held to have no place within the scheme of the Brussels I Regulation,[370] but all this actually means is that it may not be sought or ordered against respondents bringing civil or commercial proceedings in the courts of another Member State. It is necessary to deal separately with two points: personal jurisdiction over the respondent and the exercise of the court's discretion.

---

[367] No irony is intended.

[368] For a telling German refusal to see the point, see *Re the Enforcement of an English Anti-suit Injunction (Case 3 VA 11/95)* [1997] ILPr 320 (Düsseldorf CA). For an even more telling English refusal to see the very same point when the boot is on the other foot, see *Tonicstar Ltd v American Home Insurance Co* [2004] EWHC 1234 (Comm), [2005] Lloyd's Rep IR 32.

[369] *Airbus Industrie GIE v Patel* [1999] 1 AC 119.

[370] Case C-159/02 *Turner v Grovit* [2004] ECR I-3565.

To establish personal jurisdiction over the respondent, he must be served with process in order to be subjected to the personal jurisdiction of the court in respect of the claim for an injunction. An anti-suit injunction is an application for final[371] relief in respect of legal or equitable rights, and process must be lawfully served. Where personal jurisdiction is to be established by reference to common law jurisdictional rules, as just described, it may therefore be necessary to seek permission to serve out of the jurisdiction. None of the grounds set out in the Practice Direction is specifically dedicated to applications for an anti-suit injunction, but there is nothing to prevent the cause of action which founds the claim to relief being brought under any ground which will accommodate it. So if the claim for an injunction is based on the fact that there is a contract falling within ground (6), which gives a legal right not to be sued, this may be relied on in the application for permission. (Of course, where the injunction is sought in relation to a civil or commercial matter within the domain of the Brussels I Regulation, the jurisdiction of the court is determined by the Regulation, and a defendant or respondent may point to the Regulation as a reason why he is not liable to be served with process. In such a case, the court is actually called upon to exercise Regulation jurisdiction, not common law jurisdiction.)

In order to persuade the court to grant the injunction, an applicant may seek to show that he has been wronged by his opponent, on the ground that he has a legal right not to be sued in the foreign court, or an equitable right not to be sued in the foreign court: in short, his complaint is that the respondent is committing a wrong against him, and that this wrongdoing should be restrained. The example of a legal right is easy to comprehend: an exclusive jurisdiction clause will exemplify it, but so also will a settlement agreement, an arbitration agreement,[372] the right to enforce an arbitration award,[373] and even the right to enforce an English judgment.[374] The more challenging development of the

---

[371] Although it is possible to apply for an interim anti-suit injunction to preserve the status quo until the application for a final injunction can be heard.

[372] *C v D* [2007] EWCA Civ 1282, [2008] Bus LR 843.

[373] ibid.

[374] *Masri v Consolidated Contractors International Co SAL (No 3)* [2008] EWCA Civ 625, [2009] QB 503.

law of anti-suit injunctions has been to elucidate what it means to have an equitable right not to be sued overseas. The point of departure is that, in this latter case, a general requirement that England must be shown to be the natural forum for the litigation of the substantive dispute.[375] This is because, if England is where the trial of the dispute should have its natural home, it is not a breach of comity for the English court to make such an order in relation to it. An alternative limitation on the power of the English court might have been developed in the form of a choice of law, by reference to which to ascertain the wrongfulness of behaviour,[376] but it was not. But the means preferred were to utilize a 'natural forum' connection which, when satisfied, makes it singularly appropriate for the English court to exercise its power, and to apply English law and equity in granting relief. Subject to his satisfaction of this condition, the applicant may show that the respondent is vexatious or oppressive in bringing the foreign action.[377] The meaning of these terms retains an element of flexibility, but if the foreign action is brought in bad faith or to harass, or if it is bound to fail if defended but its defence is certain to cause trouble and expense, or if its consequences may be unjustifiably involved or convoluted,[378] the party bringing it may be ordered to restrain himself. The absence of a real link between the acts complained of and the foreign court may help to indicate that there is oppression;[379] if it is otherwise unconscionable to bring the action it may be restrained. Australian equity has held that the foreign action is unobjectionable if it seeks relief which would not be available from a local court,[380] but this seems perverse,[381] for the more foreign the action is, the less it will be possible to order restraint. According to Canadian

---

[375] *Société Nationale Industrielle Aérospatiale v Lee Kui Jak* [1987] AC 871 (PC); *Airbus Industrie GIE v Patel* [1999] 1 AC 119.

[376] cf Briggs [1997] LMCLQ 90.

[377] *Société Nationale Industrielle Aérospatiale v Lee Kui Jak* [1987] AC 871 (PC).

[378] ibid (consequential contribution proceedings would be unacceptably complex).

[379] *Midland Bank plc v Laker Airways Ltd* [1986] QB 689 (CA).

[380] *CSR Ltd v Cigna Insurance Australia Ltd* (1997) 189 CLR 345.

[381] It is also contrary to *Midland Bank plc v Laker Airways Ltd* [1986] QB 689 (CA).

equity,[382] before applying for the injunction, the applicant must make any jurisdictional application to the foreign court: an injunction will not be granted unless the foreign court fails to respect principles of *forum conveniens* but then, having refused to observe comity, it can expect no comity in return.[383] Although this has sometimes been said to be the general rule in England,[384] clarification of the requirement that England be shown to be the natural forum makes it an unnecessary, and possibly undesirable, requirement in England. There is, after all, something rather unattractive in encouraging an English court to sit as if on an appeal from a foreign court;[385] and if the application is delayed until the issue has been fought in the foreign court, it may mean that the time for an injunction has passed.

To revert to the case of a legal right not to be sued in the foreign court, where the claim to an injunction is founded on an allegation of breach of an agreement on jurisdiction, it is debatable whether England must also be the natural forum for the action.[386] If England is the chosen court, there will be no difficulty,[387] but otherwise the answer is less clear. On one view the existence of a legal right not to be sued is enough by itself, but it may also be said that if neither the nominated court nor the action to be restrained is in England, it is none of the English court's business to say where the trial should take place, however much the respondent may appear to be at fault.[388] But where it is appropriate for the court to exercise its discretion, it is unlikely that there is a distinct and further need to demonstrate vexation or oppression: an injunction in support of a legal right not to be sued in the foreign court will be granted unless there is good reason not

---

[382] *Amchem Products Inc v British Columbia (Workers' Compensation Board)* [1993] 1 SCR 897, (1993) 102 DLR (4th) 96.

[383] This may be thought of as the 'Be Done By As You Did' version of comity, in homage to Charles Kingsley, *The Water-Babies*.

[384] *Barclays Bank plc v Homan* [1993] BCLC 680, 686–7 (Hoffmann J) 703 (CA).

[385] cf *The Angelic Grace* [1995] 1 Lloyd's Rep 87, 95 (CA).

[386] The point was left open in *Airbus Industrie GIE v Patel* [1999] 1 AC 119.

[387] *Continental Bank NA v Aeakos Compania Naviera SA* [1994] 1 WLR 588 (CA).

[388] But the Bermuda Court of Appeal displayed no hesitation about it in *IPOC International Growth Fund Ltd v OAO 'CT Mobile'* [2007] Bermuda LR 43.

to do so.[389] To say that there is oppression or vexation whenever there is a legal right not to be sued seems unnecessary and illiterate: an injunction in equity's auxiliary jurisdiction and in support of legal rights does not need to be founded on an equitable right.

By contrast with the cases in which the applicant complains that he is the victim of a wrong, an injunction may also be applied for, and justified and ordered, on the basis that the respondent is bringing proceedings in a foreign court which undermine the established jurisdiction of the English court. In such a case, the basis for the order is not so much the commission of a wrong against the applicant, but that the administration of justice in England is being interfered with. For example, for a creditor to bring proceedings which are designed to secure a benefit which would not be available to him in a pending English insolvency would be for him to interfere with, or undermine, the integrity and effectiveness of the English proceedings. An injunction is plainly appropriate in such a case; the principle that an injunction is necessary to prevent the undermining of the English court's jurisdiction is obviously open to adaptation and to extension and (dare one say) abuse.

A party who is bringing, or who intends to bring, proceedings before a foreign court may have an apprehension that an anti-suit injunction will be sought against him. If the foreign court is one which may grant such relief, he may therefore consider applying to the foreign court for an anti-anti-suit injunction, the point of which speaks for itself. There are even cases in which this apprehension has led to an application for an anti-anti-anti-suit injunction.[390] In cases in which the venue for litigation can be of such surpassing significance, litigation can get very exciting indeed.

(b) Proceedings for (negative) declaratory relief

The development of the doctrine of *forum conveniens* was the first substantial means by which a defendant could challenge the jurisdictional dominance of the claimant; and an anti-suit injunction may be seen as the second: the party sued is not obliged to sit back and wait to be sued, where and when his opponent chooses, but may try to forestall his being sued in a court

---

[389] *Donohue v Armco Inc* [2001] UKHL 64, [2002] 1 All ER 749.
[390] See *Shell (UK) Exploration & Production Ltd v Innes* 1995 SLT 807.

whose jurisdiction he regards as uncongenial. For the sake of completeness, therefore, we should mention the third means which may be resorted to: bringing proceedings on the merits of the claim for a declaration that he, the 'natural defendant', owes no liability to the opponent. This, if successful, will either prevent the opponent bringing proceedings of his own or mean that, if he does, the principles of *res judicata* may forestall the enforcement of a foreign judgment.

The early history of such actions displayed judicial hostility to the very idea.[391] Courts would be slow to exercise jurisdictional discretion in support of them;[392] they ran a serious risk of being struck out as premature or abusive, or otherwise impeded. The suspicion that they were open to abuse by forum shoppers was widely held; and their potential to harass an opponent, who may not have decided whether to sue and who may not yet be ready for the fight, was considerable. But the sea changed, and there is now much less by way of judicial encouragement to disparage such actions. Three principal reasons may be given. First, it became the practice of the Commercial Court to entertain such actions, and to find them justifiable: insurers, suppliers, and others will often need to know whether they have legal obligations to an insured (so they can step in and take over the defence if they do) or a distributor (so they can terminate supplies and retain another if they do not). The practice of the courts simply undermined the contrary view of the law. Second, in the separate context of the Brussels I Regulation, it is well settled that an action for a declaration of non-liability brought in a court which has jurisdiction over the defendant thereto, cannot be objected to on jurisdictional grounds: there is no wrong in suing in a court with jurisdiction under the Regulation.[393] Third, the Court of Appeal has given its seal of approval to this new approach,[394] seeing the merit in such claims, rather than criticizing or obstructing them, as good and useful means of resolving disputes. It is hard to disagree: the legal certainty which can be brought about by a prompt application for a declaration may be far preferable to the limbo of waiting to see

---

[391] *Guaranty Trust Co of New York v Hannay* [1915] 2 KB 536 (CA); *The Volvox Hollandia* [1988] 2 Lloyd's Rep 361 (CA).

[392] By refusing permission to serve out of the jurisdiction.

[393] Case C-406/92 *The Tatry* [1994] ECR I-5439.

[394] *Messier Dowty Ltd v Sabena SA* [2000] 1 WLR 2040 (CA).

whether proceedings are commenced by the other party. Abusive use of the procedure can still be prevented, but there will now be no presumption of abuse; and as this new wisdom beds down in the law, the need for separate mention of proceedings for negative declaratory relief will become a thing of the past.

7. JURISDICTION TO OBTAIN INTERIM RELIEF

For completeness we should revert to the issue of interim relief, which includes provisional and protective measures. This may be ordered in support of actions in the English courts, or of civil or commercial claims in the courts in another Member State (Article 31 cases), or in support of other actions in those courts or elsewhere.[395] If the respondent is present within the jurisdiction of the court he may be served with process as of right: it is irrelevant that he may be domiciled in another Member State and so not be subject to the jurisdiction of the English courts over the merits of the claim. If he is outside the territorial jurisdiction, an application for permission to serve the claim form out of the jurisdiction must be made under ground (5) of the Practice Direction: this is so even in relation to applications falling within Article 31 of the Regulation. But in all cases, the fact that the court may lack jurisdiction to try the case on the merits is a material factor in determining whether it is expedient to grant the relief;[396] and it will also be relevant in deciding whether the court should grant permission to serve out, as rule 6.37(3) also applies to applications under ground (5). As regards whether it may be inexpedient to grant the relief, it has been suggested that where the court seised of the merits could have granted but decided not to grant relief, an English court should be slow to act to contradict it; but where it had no power to grant relief, an English court should be inclined to make an order to assist the foreign court. Not everyone will instantly see that it is right to speak of 'assisting' a court whose legislator has, one supposes deliberately, withheld certain powers from it for a good and proper purpose.[397]

---

[395] Civil Jurisdiction and Judgments Act 1982, s 25.

[396] ibid, s 25(2).

[397] *Crédit Suisse Fides Trust SA v Cuoghi* [1998] QB 818 (CA); *Motorola Credit Corpn v Uzan (No 2)* [2003] EWCA Civ 752, [2004] 1 WLR 113.

3

FOREIGN JUDGMENTS

A. RECOGNITION AND ENFORCEMENT

The most important thing to understand about foreign judgments is that judgments of foreign courts have no direct effect in England, for foreign judges have no authority in England. Unless Parliament has provided otherwise, foreign judgments cannot be enforced by execution, and no person is in contempt of court, or otherwise in dereliction, if he fails to do what he has been ordered to do by a foreign judge. If adjudication is thought of as an exercise of state sovereignty, this will come as no surprise: state sovereignty ends at the border of the state, and while international comity requires respect for the exercises of that power within the sovereign's own territory, it does not acknowledge its direct power to act outside it. But it has long been accepted that there is a general public interest which requires that those who have had a hearing and received judgment should generally abide by its terms, and that the law should discourage or prevent the reopening of disputes which have already had a hearing and adjudication. A related idea would encourage or require litigants to put forward all their issues for adjudication at once, rather than holding some back for a subsequent dispute. This broad principle is not limited to cases where the first judgment was obtained in England but, subject to conditions, applies just as much to foreign judgments.

Accordingly, foreign judgments may be given effect in England according to the rules of the common law as well as the legislative schemes examined in this chapter. But there is more than one way of giving effect to a foreign judgment; and is important to remember the differences. Where statutory registration is provided for, the legislation will normally provide that the foreign judgment itself may be enforced. But where the law relied on is the common law, then although the foreign judgment may be recognized, it cannot be enforced as a judgment. Instead, the judgment creditor needs to use the recognized foreign judgment to obtain an original, if more-or-less derivative, English judgment; and it will be this that may then be enforced and executed upon in England. In these cases, the English court does not rubber stamp or authorize enforcement of the foreign judgment: it does not grant *'exequatur'* to the foreign judgment in the manner in which the civilian tradition has it. It gives a judgment of its own.

So far as statutory registration of foreign judgments is concerned, there are two schemes. The judgments most easily registrable and enforceable are those from other parts of the United Kingdom and from Member States of the European Union in civil and commercial matters.[1] For these, the rules governing registration are easily satisfied and procedures for enforcement, already pretty brisk, are about to become brisker still. The foreign judgment may be enforced by English measures of execution. The second category comprises judgments from a number of states which are party to a bilateral treaty with the United Kingdom or States or territories of the Commonwealth. For these, legislation sets out the conditions for recognition and enforcement; in detail these closely reflect the common law as it was understood at the date of the legislation. However, the process of enforcement is direct; the legislation provides that the foreign judgment may, when registered, be enforced and executed upon in just the same way as may an English judgment.

Where the foreign judgment is not subject to a scheme of statutory registration, the common law alone supplies both the rules for recognition and enforcement and the procedure for enforcement. For these cases, the foreign judgment may be recognized, but if anything is to be enforced, it will be an English judgment derived, by one means or another, from the foreign judgment. It is sometimes said that at common law one enforces a foreign judgment by bringing an action on the judgment. It may be true that this is the effect of the common law, but as it is written the proposition is liable to mislead: one obtains an English judgment, and enforces that.

Another important distinction must be noted at the outset: between the recognition of a judgment and its enforcement;

---

[1] Or states party to the Lugano Convention, for which the rules are substantially the same.

and between these and the other effects which can be derived from a foreign judgment. *Recognition* of a judgment means treating the claim which was adjudicated as having been determined once and for all. It does not matter whether it was determined in favour of the claimant or the defendant, though judgments *in personam* are only ever recognized as effective against particular parties, and the material question will be whether that person is bound to abide by the judgment given. By contrast, judgments *in rem*[2] are recognized generally or universally, and not just against particular parties to the litigation. When the judgment is recognized, the matter is *res judicata*, and the party bound by it will be estopped from contradicting it in subsequent proceedings in an English court.[3] For the foreign judgment to achieve recognition, qualifying conditions have to be met, which specify the connection between the foreign court and the parties, accommodate and limit the scope of objections to the judgment, and define the judgments to which this status of *res judicata* will be accorded. The principles of *res judicata* can operate in relation to entire causes of action ('cause of action estoppel') as well as on discrete issues which arose and were determined in the course of the trial of a cause of action ('issue estoppel').[4] Given a *res judicata*, a party bound by the judgment who brings proceedings in England to try and obtain a ruling which contradicts it may be met with the plea of estoppel by *res judicata*, and stopped in his tracks.

Recognition therefore serves two purposes. A judgment given in favour of the defendant, dismissing the claim, allows the defendant who has won in a foreign court to rely on this to defeat a subsequent action brought by the unsuccessful claimant. A foreign judgment in favour of the claimant is more complex, because the claimant may not have succeeded on every part of his claim. To take the easiest case first, if the claimant[5] obtained judgment in respect of the whole of the claim, he may wish to go

---

[2] For example, on the status of a person, or the ownership of a thing.

[3] See, generally, Spencer Bower and Handley, *Res Judicata* (4th edn, LexisNexis, 2009).

[4] *Carl Zeiss Stiftung v Rayner & Keeler Ltd (No 2)* [1967] 1 AC 853.

[5] Which expression includes counterclaimant or party, not excluding a defendant, in whose favour an order was made.

one step further and bring proceedings for the *enforcement* of the judgment, for example, by collecting money which the foreign court ordered to be paid and which remains unpaid. Not every judgment entitled to recognition may be enforced in England,[6] but to be enforced, a foreign judgment must first be recognized. If it is to be enforced at the behest of the successful claimant, the judgment must meet further conditions; but if the conditions for enforcement are met, a judgment may be executed as if it had been given by an English court if it is ordered that the foreign judgment be registered pursuant to statute which provides for this effect or, if enforcement takes place under the common law, because an English court gives its own judgment which is itself the order which may be enforced.

A third possibility is that the claimant was partially successful. If, for example, he succeeds on his claim but recovers a smaller sum in damages than he had hoped for, he may seek to improve on the first result by suing on the underlying cause of action in the English courts. In this case neither recognition[7] nor enforcement will stand in his way, but the manifest unfairness of his trying to have a second bite at the cherry induced Parliament to legislate to remove the right to sue again.[8]

The tradition of English textbooks is to concentrate on the enforcement of foreign judgments, and to treat recognition as an afterthought of limited practical importance. There is a problem with this, for the logic of the law is that recognition is the necessary primary concern, for without it the judgment can have no effect in the English legal order.[9] In terms of schemes, though, we will first examine statutory registration of foreign judgments: in civil or commercial matters from the courts of Member States

---

[6] If the judgment cannot be enforced, eg because the remedy ordered by the foreign court is not one which can be enforced in an English court, there is nothing to prevent the claimant seeking recognition where enforcement is not available, and using the principles of *res judicata* to short-cut his way to victory in the English action.

[7] For there will be no discrete issue on which the defendant won (but if there is, such as a refusal to award a particular head of damages, issue estoppel in the defendant's favour on this issue will be available).

[8] Civil Jurisdiction and Judgments Act 1982, s 34.

[9] See *Clarke v Fennoscandia Ltd* [2007] UKHL 56, 2008 SLT 33 at [21].

and falling within the Brussels I Regulation,[10] and then under the statutory registration schemes made in 1920 and 1933 to allow registration and enforcement of foreign judgments from certain other countries. Then we examine recognition and enforcement of judgments at common law, where the rules are restricted neither by geography, nor by subject matter, nor by type of court: this will also provide some of the detail which will not be otherwise set out in relation to the 1920 and 1933 registration schemes. In this chapter the main focus of attention will be on judgments *in personam*. However, the recognition of judgments in family law, the administration of estates, and insolvency are dealt with within the chapters which examine this subject matter.

B. REGISTRATION OF FOREIGN JUDGMENTS (1): THE BRUSSELS I REGULATION

Chapter III of the Brussels I Regulation is the mechanism by which judgments in civil and commercial matters from the courts of Member States of the European Union take effect in the English legal order. The Lugano Convention applies to judgments from Iceland, Norway, and Switzerland; its provisions are practically identical to the Brussels I Regulation, which is where attention is primarily to be focused. The Regulation is a legislative instruction to the laws and courts of Member States requiring them, in defined circumstances, to treat judgments from courts of other Member States as legally effective and directly enforceable, almost as though they were not foreign judgments at all. Where the Regulation prescribes the recognition and enforcement of the judgment, what is enforced, and what may be executed upon, is the foreign judgment itself.

The Brussels I Regulation will be superseded by Regulation 1215/2012,[11] which will be in effect from 10 January 2015. The

---

[10] Council Regulation (EC) 44/2001, [2001] OJ L12/1. There will be no systematic examination of the Brussels Convention, which the Regulation has effectively replaced, or of the Lugano Convention, which operates in parallel, but only in relation to Iceland, Norway, and Switzerland.

[11] Regulation (EU) 1215/2012, [2012] OJ L351/1.

changes which are made to the law set out in Chapter III of the Regulation are more organizational than anything else, but their nature makes it problematic to integrate a discussion of it into analysis of the existing Brussels I Regulation. It is therefore dealt with separately, at the end of the examination of the Regulation.

1. RECOGNITION

For a judgment to be recognized under Chapter III of the Regulation, it (i) must be an adjudication from a court in a Member State,[12] (ii) must be given in a civil or commercial matter, (iii) need not be in proceedings which were instituted after the Regulation came into effect, (iv) must not be impeachable for jurisdictional error, (v) must not be impeachable for procedural or substantive reasons, and (vi) must not be excluded from recognition by another treaty. It is often said that if it fails to meet these criteria, there is nothing to prevent an attempt to secure recognition and enforcement of a judgment under the rules of the common law, on the footing that Chapter III of the Regulation is a permissive, not an exclusive, regime. That may be so. But in cases which fall within the domain of the Regulation, whose Article 34 says they 'shall not be recognized', it is just arguable that the Regulation imposes an obligation to withhold recognition which precludes allowing it by other means. Be that as it may, according to Article 33 it is not necessary to bring any form of action or procedure to obtain recognition of a judgment under the Regulation, beyond pleading it, so if a successful defendant wishes to rely on a judgment to which the Regulation applies, all he need do is plead it as satisfying the criteria for recognition. There is no objection to his bringing proceedings for a declaration that the judgment be recognized if this would serve a useful purpose. We will first examine the six points listed above.

2. JUDGMENTS: ARTICLE 32

For the purposes of the Regulation, a judgment is an adjudication by a court of a Member State, including an order as to costs.[13]

---

[12] For the purpose of the Regulation, Gibraltar is treated as part of the United Kingdom.

[13] Article 32.

This excludes judgments from a non-Member State, even after a judge in a Member State has held them to be enforceable:[14] the Regulation applies to original determinations by a judge in a Member State, but not to instances where a judge validates or approves a decision taken by someone who is not. Many Member States have treaties or other provisions dealing with judgments from non-Member States, frequently in relation to former colonial territories; but such bilateral relationships are not enough to admit such a judgment, via the doorway of one Member State's private international law, into the privileged realm of Chapter III of the Regulation. Similar considerations explain why a decision declaring the enforceability of an arbitration award is not a judgment within Chapter III of the Regulation either. Article 32 does include a provisional or interlocutory judgment, and will include the dismissal of a case on jurisdictional grounds, such as by reference to a choice of court agreement for another Member State: there is no requirement that the judgment be *res judicata* in the court which pronounced it. A judgment by consent is included, for it is still an adjudication made on the authority of a judge,[15] as is judgment entered in default of defence when a defendant is debarred for contempt.[16] A judgment which orders a periodical payment imposed as a penalty for disobedience to a court order is included,[17] although it may be enforced only if the sum due has been finally quantified by the court which ordered it.[18] Settlements which have been approved by courts in the course of proceedings[19] and authentic instruments[20] (unknown to English law, they are documents authenticated by a public authority or a notary,

---

[14] Case C-129/92 *Owens Bank Ltd v Bracco* [1994] ECR I-117.

[15] *Landhurst Leasing plc v Marcq* [1998] ILPr 822 (CA). But it does not include a settlement; and if it is desired to make binding the terms on which a claim is compromised, a judgment is much to be preferred to a contractual disposal: Case C-414/92 *Solo Kleinmotoren GmbH v Boch* [1994] ECR I-2237.

[16] Case C-394/07 *Gambazzi v DaimlerChrysler Canada Inc* [2009] ECR I-2563.

[17] Article 49, or other fine imposed to encourage compliance with a court order: Case C-406/09 *Realchemie Nederland BV v Bayer Crop Science AG* [2011] ECR I-(Oct 18), [2012] Bus LR 1825.

[18] Article 49.

[19] Article 58.

[20] Article 57.

and which are enforceable under some laws without the need for legal action) are enforceable under similar, but not identical, conditions.[21]

It is easy to see the final order of a court as a judgment. It is less clear how this applies to a finding made by a court but which is not embodied in its final order: the question is whether 'judgment' includes a decision upon an issue as well as the disposal of a cause of action. In general cases, the answer is unclear, but in principle if a judgment qualifies for recognition under the Regulation, it is then integrated into the English legal order. Once that is done, there is nothing to prevent an English court applying principles of issue estoppel to the judgment and to its parts, although as a matter of English private international law, rather than as a requirement of the Regulation which is *functus officio* once it has brought about the recognition of the judgment. However, in the specific case in which a court rules that it has no jurisdiction because there is a valid and binding jurisdiction agreement for the courts of another Member State, the judgment is *sui generis*, and must be recognized not only as regards its holding that the court seised has no jurisdiction, but also as to its *ratio decidendi* that this result follows from the presence of a valid and binding agreement on jurisdiction for the courts of another Member State.[22] Whether this would extend to a conclusion that a court had no jurisdiction because the defendant had a domicile in another Member State is unclear, but it would be strange if it did not.

3. CIVIL AND COMMERCIAL MATTERS: ARTICLE 1

The judgment must be in a civil or commercial matter, the meaning of which was examined in Chapter 2. Although it has not been stated in clear and explicit terms, it seems certain that the recognizing court must decide for itself whether the judgment

---

[21] For the points of difference, see Case C-414/92 *Solo Kleinmotoren GmbH v Boch* [1994] ECR I-2237.

[22] Case C-456/11 *Gothaer Allgemeine Versicherung AG v Samskip GmbH* [2012] ECR I-(Nov 15): the case concerned the Lugano Convention as the jurisdiction clause was for Iceland, but the principle is general.

was given in a civil or commercial matter, and is not bound at this point simply to accept the view of the adjudicating court. After all, the adjudicating court may not have needed to decide the issue for itself. It may have deduced that if the matter was a civil or commercial one, the Regulation gave it jurisdiction, and if it was not, its own domestic law did instead, and that further decision was unnecessary.[23] Even so, it is to be expected that where the adjudicating court has given such a ruling, its conclusion will at least be persuasive. It follows that a judgment in respect of subject matter excluded by Article 1 from the domain of the Regulation will not be recognized under Chapter III. Where a single judgment deals with included and excluded matter it may be possible to sever it: this may happen when a judgment has provided for maintenance and has determined rights in property which arise out of a matrimonial relationship, or when a criminal court imposes a criminal penalty and orders compensation to a civil party. Where severance is not possible, the substantial presence of excluded matter in an indivisible judgment may wholly preclude recognition under the Regulation.[24] Where the judgment was obtained in breach of an agreement to arbitrate, it is arguable that recognition is not demanded and should be withheld,[25] for else a court would have to contradict its own law on arbitration, which lies outside the domain of the Regulation.[26] On the other hand, if Article 1(2)(d) merely means that no court has adjudicatory jurisdiction over the merits of what is still a civil or commercial claim,[27] and as jurisdictional error is not generally a basis for denying recognition,[28] recognition of the offending judgment may yet be required, though it might in turn be withheld as conflicting with the public policy

---

[23] Case 29/76 *LTU GmbH & Co v Eurocontrol* [1976] ECR 1541; Case 145/86 *Hoffmann v Krieg* [1988] ECR 645.

[24] Case C-220/95 *Van den Boogaard v Laumen* [1997] ECR I-1147; and see Art 48.

[25] Even though the Court of Appeal has clearly and wrongly held the contrary: *National Navigation Co v Endesa Generacion SA (The Wadi Sudr)* [2009] EWCA Civ 1397, [2010] 1 Lloyd's Rep 193.

[26] cf Case 145/86 *Hoffmann v Krieg* [1988] ECR 645.

[27] Case C-391/95 *Van Uden Maritime BV v Deco-Line* [1998] ECR I-7091.

[28] See Art 35.

of enforcing agreements to arbitrate.[29] Further clarification must come from the European Court.[30]

4. DATE OF PROCEEDINGS AND JUDGMENT: ARTICLE 66

The Regulation applies to the recognition of judgments given in proceedings instituted in the then Member States after 1 March 2002. For judgments in proceedings instituted before that date, or before the accession date of a 2004 or 2007 state, but where judgment was given after the accession date, recognition is provided for if the adjudicating court founded itself on rules of jurisdiction which conformed to those of the Regulation.

5. JURISDICTIONAL ERRORS: ARTICLE 35

The adjudicating court may have erred in its application of the Regulation by accepting jurisdiction when it did not properly have it. Save in the exceptional cases mentioned below, this is irrelevant to the recognition of the judgment under Chapter III.[31] At a superficial level the reason is clear: every Member State court is to be trusted to apply the Regulation properly, and it was the responsibility of the defendant to make this very argument to the adjudicating court. That being so, there is no reason to allow a collateral attack on the jurisdiction of the original court at the point of recognition. Indeed, there is every reason not to, for it would impede the free circulation of judgments if it were otherwise.

---

[29] In *National Navigation Co v Endesa Generacion SA (The Wadi Sudr)* [2009] EWCA Civ 1397, [2010] 1 Lloyd's Rep 193 the Court found that recognition was required, and that public policy had no part to play.

[30] It will not be provided by the reform of the Brussels I Regulation (see p 109 above), which will simply say (i) that arbitration is wholly outside the Regulation, and (ii) that a judgment from a court in a Member State which has (contrary to the conclusions of English law) rejected a defence that the parties were bound to arbitrate, will qualify for recognition. The reconciliation of these two points, each individually rational but together contradictory, will have to be left to the European Court. Maybe the legislators provided no answer because, in truth, there is no one answer which is significantly more persuasive than its rivals.

[31] Article 35.

Now while this may be reasonable for defendants domiciled in Member States, whose jurisdictional exposure is defined and limited by Chapter II of the Regulation, it is jaw-droppingly unfair to those not so domiciled, who may be sued on the basis of the residual jurisdiction provided by Article 4. They have no chance to complain about the width of the jurisdictional rules asserted against them: neither at trial, because Article 4(2) makes them expressly subject to the traditional and exorbitant jurisdictional rules set out in Annex I to the Regulation, nor at recognition, because jurisdictional points may not generally be taken at the point of recognition.[32] No European defendant is exposed to this lethal combination of unreconstructed jurisdictional rules, on the one hand, and the absence of right to be heard on the propriety of those rules or their application on the other. This was the calculated act of those who drafted the Convention[33] and the Regulation which adopts it,[34] and it takes the breath away, although to the European bureaucrat or apparatchik, no doubt it makes sense. By humiliating contrast, the Supreme Court of the United States has long held that the constitutional guarantees[35] of due process and equal treatment apply to foreigners as well as to American nationals.[36] But this legislative discrimination is a matter of deliberate policy which shames those who dreamed it up as much as those who maintain it.

Exceptions apply only where the lack of jurisdiction, of which complaint is made, is derived from the provisions on insurance contracts, consumer contracts, and exclusive jurisdiction regardless of domicile:[37] in these cases the original jurisdictional rules enshrine policies of such importance that they call for reinforcement by the recognizing court, though it is striking that this does not extend to the special rules on jurisdiction over employment contracts. Nor does it cover a case in which the adjudicating court

---

[32] Article 35; and it is expressly forbidden to find the jurisdictional rules of the court to be contrary to public policy: Art 35(3).

[33] Jenard was open about it: [1979] OJ C59/20. He should have been ashamed of himself.

[34] Recital 10.

[35] Fifth and Fourteenth Amendments to the American Constitution.

[36] See eg *Asahi Metal Industry Co v Superior Court of California* 480 US 102, 108–9, 113–15 (1987).

[37] Article 35(1). Breach of a jurisdiction agreement is not included.

has failed to give effect to a jurisdiction agreement which should have been regarded as valid by reason of Article 23. This places Article 23 in a relatively low position in the hierarchy of jurisdictional rules;[38] it is not impossible that if the European Union were ever to adopt and bring into effect the Hague Convention on Choice of Court Agreements,[39] this may be reconsidered. In the meantime, breach of an agreement on jurisdiction by one of the parties to it may possibly found a claim for damages.

Those limited cases apart, a plea that the adjudicating court should have realized that it had no jurisdiction is inadmissible. The divergence from the approach of the common law at this point may seem sharp, for where the common law governs recognition, the first line of defence is a plea that the foreign court lacked jurisdiction. But even this is an illusion. Under the Regulation, the defendant may actually make a submission to the adjudicating court that it does not have jurisdiction according to *English* jurisdictional rules: this is because the rules applicable in the foreign court are the same as those of English law.[40] But outside the domain of the Regulation, where it does not apply, such an argument cannot usefully be made to the foreign court, which has no concern with English jurisdictional rules. The first opportunity to air it comes, therefore, at recognition. The schemes therefore converge in agreeing that *this* argument, that the foreign court did not have jurisdiction according to English rules, may be made once, and that it must be made at the earliest sensible point. They diverge only in the identification of this temporal point. The Regulation is in this regard rather less radical than is sometimes supposed.

6. OBJECTIONS TO RECOGNITION: ARTICLE 34

Four procedural or substantive objections to the recognition of a judgment are exhaustively listed in Article 34. Compared with their predecessors in the Brussels Convention, which were

---

[38] Although the protection of the weak may justly be seen as enjoying a higher priority than reinforcing agreements made between equals who ought to be able to look after themselves.

[39] 30 June 2005.

[40] Apart from Art 4 cases, where such concerns of due process are irrelevant.

frequently said to be narrow in scope,[41] those in the Regulation are designed to be narrower still, so as to make the circulation of judgments from and within the Member States even more free. In the Brussels and Lugano Conventions there had been a fifth ground, for the case where the foreign judgment was founded on a conclusion about status which conflicted with the law of the recognizing state. But as questions of marriage and status were excluded from the Convention by Article 1, it was mildly surprising that there was provision for the non-recognition of judgments which had taken a view on an issue which lay outside the domain of the Convention and was unaffected by it. It was best regarded as inept use of belt and braces,[42] and it has not been reproduced in the Regulation. Its omission makes no broader point.

(a) Public policy: Article 34(1)

If recognition of the judgment would be manifestly contrary to public policy, it is precluded by Article 34(1). The content of English public policy is a matter for English law, although the general definition of it is implicit in the Regulation. The European Court has held that where recognition of the judgment would infringe a law which was regarded as fundamental in the recognizing state, such as where the adjudicating court had failed to comply with the standards of the European Convention on Human Rights by refusing one party the right to be heard,[43] recognition could be considered to be contrary to public policy. By contrast, to recognize a judgment which contained a botched application of European competition law could not be considered to be contrary to public policy, especially where the opportunity of bringing an appeal from adjudicating court could perfectly well have put it right.[44] However, in an alarming development, it has been held that a court may refuse to recognize an English default judgment, on grounds of public policy, if the court takes

---

[41] It appears that they are not supposed to overlap, at least where Art 34(1) is concerned: Case C-78/95 *Hendrickman v Magenta Druck & Verlag GmbH* [1996] ECR I-4943.

[42] Article 27(4) BC; Case 145/86 *Hoffmann v Krieg* [1988] ECR 645.

[43] Case C-7/98 *Krombach v Bamberski* [2000] ECR I-1935.

[44] Case C-38/98 *Régie Nationale des Usines Renault SA v Maxicar* [2000] ECR I-2973.

the view that the absence of reasons in the judgment, and the contention that this may make it impossible to bring an appropriate and effective appeal against it, amounts to a manifest and disproportionate breach of the right to a fair trial.[45] The opportunity thereby opened up to an evasive defendant will only be removed if English courts routinely grant summary judgment, which is reasoned, rather than allowing judgment to be entered in default.

The Regulation adds the word 'manifestly' to the corresponding provision of the Convention, which will presumably mean that the scope of Article 34(1) is intended to shrink rather than expand, though proposals to remove it altogether have been resisted by the Member States. Even so, in the related context of the Brussels II*bis* Regulation, it has been reiterated that the public policy bar to recognition has been set particularly high, on the ground that public policy requires the foreign judgment to be recognized save in the most exceptional of circumstances.[46] It must follow that a contention that the judgment was obtained by fraud will fail to trigger Article 34(1) unless—which seems improbable—the foreign state has no provision for allowing such a plea to be raised and investigated. It ought to be possible to argue that if a foreign court has refused to give effect to a commercial arbitration agreement, recognition of the judgment would be considered to be contrary to English public policy as this is set out in the Civil Jurisdiction and Judgments Act 1982, section 32:[47] the wording of the Act mostly supports the argument that respect for arbitration agreements is a matter of fundamental importance in English law.[48] Were a court in a Member State ever to hand one down, recognition of a judgment

---

[45] Case C-619/10 *Trade Agency Ltd v Seramico Investments Ltd* [2012] ECR I-(Sept 6); cf Case C-394/07 *Gambazzi v Daimler Chrysler Canada Inc* [2009] ECR I-2563.

[46] *Re L (A Child)* [2012] EWCA Civ 1157: there is no reason to consider that the approach of the court would have been different in the context of the Brussels I Regulation.

[47] *Phillip Alexander Securities & Futures Ltd v Bamberger* [1997] ILPr 73, 103.

[48] Even though the Court of Appeal has held to the contrary: *National Navigation Co v Endesa Generacion SA (The Wadi Sudr)* [2009] EWCA Civ 1397, [2010] 1 Lloyd's Rep 193. As to 'mostly', the Civil Jurisdiction and Judgments Act 1982, s 32(4) clouds the argument, even though it was intended only to keep the United Kingdom from breaching its obligations in relation to the Convention, now Regulation, rather than anything more assertive.

for multiple damages, to which the Protection of Trading Interests Act 1980 applies, would certainly offend public policy.

(b) Judgments in default of appearance: Article 34(2)

The defence to recognition for certain judgments in default of appearance, as now defined in Article 34(2), has narrowed. If as a matter of fact, and notwithstanding that the adjudicating court did not consider there to be such a default,[49] the judgment was in default of appearance, and the document instituting the proceedings was not served,[50] according to the assessment of the judge in the recognizing state, in sufficient time to allow the defendant to arrange for his defence,[51] recognition will in principle be denied. This provision aims to reinforce[52] the legal protection of the defendant, by giving him the right to be sufficiently and timeously summoned; although if the document was served the requirement is merely that it be in time to allow him to forestall judgment in default of appearance. Whether the time was sufficient may depend on the mode of service: where service has been made on the defendant personally, a relatively short period is probably all one needs to interrupt judgment being given in default. But where 'pretend' service was made on, say, the local consul, or on the *parquet* for onward transmission to the defendant, or by leaving it at a post office or the last known address,

---

[49] This means that there must be an autonomous definition of the term: it essentially covers the case where the defendant was denied a proper right to be heard or represented: Case C-78/95 *Hendrickman v Magenta Druck & Verlag GmbH* [1996] ECR I-4943.

[50] The Brussels Convention had required the service to be 'duly' made, which meant in strict accordance with the law of the original state. But the way this encouraged technical objections was such that the requirement of 'duly' was removed, and this was deliberate: Case C-283/05 *ASML Netherlands BV v SEMIS GmbH* [2006] ECR I-12041; Case C-420/07 *Apostolides v Orams* [2009] ECR I-3571.

[51] Case 228/81 *Pendy Plastic Products v Pluspunkt* [1982] ECR 2723; Case 49/84 *Debaecker and Plouvier v Bouwman* [1985] ECR 1779.

[52] Article 26 obliges the adjudicating court to check, in the case of an absent defendant, that the defendant has been served and has had time to arrange for his defence; the recognizing court must, however, make that assessment for itself, and in doing so it is not bound to accept the certificate of the adjudicating court that service was properly made: Case C-619/10 *Trade Agency Ltd v Seramico Investments Ltd* [2012] ECR I-(Sept 6).

the time period may properly be rather longer. It follows that orders obtained without notice to the respondent will be denied recognition,[53] so a freezing injunction obtained without notice will be denied recognition. The order may lose its original default character if a subsequent application is made to set it aside but this is dismissed:[54] the true answer should depend upon whether the respondent was disadvantaged by the fact that the order had already been made in proceedings in which he could not appear.[55] If he was, with the result that he faced an uphill struggle as a result of the default judgment, an unsuccessful application to set aside should not involve the loss of the shield of Article 34(2); but if the application had the effect of reimposing the original burden of proof on the applicant, any new or confirmed order will not be vitiated by the original taint. Moreover, and in sharp contrast to the predecessor provision of the Brussels Convention,[56] the Regulation provides that the shield of Article 34(2) will be lost if the defendant had the opportunity of bringing proceedings to challenge the judgment but did not do so, though this must be interpreted as meaning that the defendant had a reasonable opportunity to bring proceedings in which he would have been under no appreciable disadvantage when compared with the defendant who did appear.[57]

(c) Irreconcilability with English judgment: Article 34(3)

If recognition of the foreign judgment produces consequences which are incompatible with an English judgment in a dispute between the same parties, whether this was handed down earlier or later than the foreign one, recognition will be refused by Article 34(3).[58] In principle, Article 27 should forestall parallel proceedings at the point when the second action is commenced, or the rules of *res judicata* should apply if the English judgment has not yet been given, so that the English court could therefore recognize the foreign judgment when handed down.

---

[53] Case 125/79 *Denilauler v SNC Couchet Frères* [1980] ECR 1553.

[54] Case C-420/07 *Apostilides v Orams* [2009] ECR I-4207.

[55] cf Case C-474/93 *Hengst Import BV v Campese* [1995] ECR I-2113.

[56] Article 27(2) BC.

[57] Case C-283/05 *ASML Netherlands BV v SEMIS GmbH* [2006] ECR I-12041.

[58] Case 145/86 *Hoffmann v Krieg* [1988] ECR 645.

If all goes according to the plan of the Regulation, there will be little work for Article 34(3) to do. But when this does not quite happen, an English court is entitled to prefer its own judgment. Irreconcilability may involve a measure of evaluation. A judgment that a contract was lawfully rescinded is certainly irreconcilable with an order that damages be paid for its breach,[59] not least because the one might be a simple defence to the other. But a decision that A is liable to B for breach of warranty of quality may not be irreconcilable with a judgment that B was liable to pay the price of goods sold and delivered by A. Again, a decision that A is liable to B for damage to B's cargo is irreconcilable with one that B owes no liability for damage to the cargo, but is not irreconcilable with a claim for damages for short delivery.

(d) Irreconcilability with prior foreign judgment: Article 34(4)

If a judgment from a non-Member State was given in proceedings between the same parties and involving the same cause of action, and satisfies the criteria for its own recognition in England, and was the first to be handed down, and is irreconcilable with a later Member State judgment, Article 34(4) provides that the later, Member State, judgment will not be recognized. The text does not say that proceedings to secure the enforcement of the non-Member State judgment should have been instituted: indeed, as that judgment may well be entitled to recognition without any such proceedings, there would be no reason to infer such a limitation.

Where there is irreconcilability between two different and foreign Member State judgments, the first one is recognized, and the second one, if irreconcilable with it, is not. This is consistent with the view taken in English common law as well.[60]

(e) Australian and Canadian defendants: Article 72

Article 59 of the Brussels and Lugano Conventions permitted states to conclude bilateral treaties with a non-Contracting State to provide for the non-recognition of judgments from other Contracting States, where those judgments were founded

---

[59] Case 144/86 *Gubisch Maschinenfabrik KG v Palumbo* [1987] ECR 4861.
[60] *Showlag v Mansour* [1995] 1 AC 431 (PC).

on the residual jurisdictional rules of Article 4 and which were given against nationals or domiciliaries of the non-Contracting State. The United Kingdom concluded treaties with Australia[61] and Canada,[62] and Article 72 preserves them in force. But there will be no new bilateral treaties, as competence in external relations in the field of the Regulation now reposes in the European Union.[63]

(f) No other grounds for non-recognition

No other ground exists to permit non-recognition of a judgment within the domain of the Regulation. Article 35 precludes any further review of the jurisdiction of the foreign court, and explicitly provides[64] that public policy may not be invoked to launch a collateral attack on the jurisdiction of the adjudicating court. This is obviously aimed at judgments based on Article 4;[65] but it should not prevent the denial of recognition to judgments which disregard a valid and binding arbitration agreement, for in such a case it is not the jurisdiction, but the rejection of the arbitration defence, an excluded matter, which is the basis for objection.

Article 36 absolutely prohibits any review of the merits of the judgment, although this must be allowed to the limited extent required to apply the provisions of Article 34.[66] What may appear to be an exception arises when a court is called upon to recognize a provisional or protective measure which was granted on the basis of Article 31, that is, not by the court with jurisdiction over the merits of the claim. The extent of the permitted review is to ascertain that the order is, as a matter of substance, a provisional or protective one; but if it is not, it will be denied recognition. This limitation appears to be necessary to counter the inherent

---

[61] Reciprocal Enforcement of Foreign Judgments (Australia) Order 1994 (SI 1994/1901), Sch, Art 3.

[62] Reciprocal Enforcement of Foreign Judgments (Canada) Order 1987 (SI 1987/468), Sch, Art IX.

[63] And see Opinion C-1/03 *Lugano Convention* [2006] ECR I-1145.

[64] Article 35(3).

[65] But also Art 5(4): Case C-7/98 *Krombach v Bamberski* [2000] ECR I-1935.

[66] Case C-78/95 *Hendrickman v Magenta Druck & Verlag GmbH* [1996] ECR I-4943.

weakness of Article 31, which simply abnegates any jurisdictional control over such measures. Accordingly, if a foreign court has made an order for an interim payment, but does not have jurisdiction over the merits of the claim (perhaps because the parties have agreed to arbitrate, with the result that no court has merits jurisdiction), an English court, called on to recognize and enforce the order, may and must check that it is provisional or protective: that is to say, limited to assets within the territory of the court which made the order,[67] and guaranteed to be reversible in the event that the applicant does not succeed on the substantive claim.[68]

7. JUDGMENTS UNDER APPEAL: ARTICLE 37

If an 'ordinary appeal' is pending against the judgment in the state of its origin, Article 37 permits, though does not oblige, the recognizing court to stay any proceedings in which the issue of recognition will arise. All English appeals are ordinary appeals.[69] The sense of this is clear: a court must have the power to conclude that it is inappropriate to proceed in a case in which the foreign judgment upon which issues turn may be reversed on appeal. This would appear to require some assessment of how likely it is that the judgment will be reversed, and the degree of prejudice likely to be suffered if the application is or is not stayed; but it may also be that this is impermissible as involving a review of the merits of the judgment.

8. EFFECT OF RECOGNITION

The main consequence of recognition will usually be to pave the way for the enforcement of the judgment, the procedure for which is examined below. But this is not the only effect the recognition of the judgment may bring about. To recognize a judgment means,

---

[67] If that requirement is taken seriously, it may be very rare for such an order ever to be presented for recognition in another country. But in the case of an English freezing order, not made in relation to assets as distinct from being ordered against a defendant personally, this limitation may be an irrelevance, and the order more likely to be presented for recognition in another country.

[68] Case C-99/96 *Mietz v Intership Yachting Sneek BV* [1999] ECR I-2277.

[69] Article 46(2).

in principle at least, to give it the effect it has under the law of the state in which it was given.[70] So if the judgment is in the nature of a provisional order, which would not be taken as binding or conclusive in subsequent proceedings in the adjudicating court, it should be given neither more nor less an effect in England. In certain cases a judgment may be regarded by the adjudicating court as impinging upon non-parties,[71] such as sureties for the defendant, or an insurer; but whether this must be respected and given effect by an English court is unclear. The problems arise at a number of levels. First, it may be argued that, so far as the non-party was concerned, the judgment must have been given in default of his appearance, and so be denied recognition against him by reason of Article 34(2). Secondly, it may be contrary to public policy, as crystallized in the European Convention on Human Rights, for a person to be bound by a judgment in respect of which he had no right to be heard. Thirdly, it may be that once the judgment has been shown to qualify for recognition as between the parties to it, it is thereafter for English private international law, and not for the Regulation, to determine what further effects it may have.

9. ENFORCEMENT

Any judgment which is entitled to recognition and is enforceable in the state in which it was given[72] may be enforced by the procedure set out in detail in Articles 38–52.[73] In England, an application is made to the High Court[74] for an order that the judgment be registered pursuant to the Regulation, by producing an authenticated copy of the judgment[75] and proof in standard form that it is enforceable under the law of the state in which it was

---

[70] Case C-145/86 *Hoffmann v Krieg* [1988] ECR 645. This was not precisely the approach in *Calyon v Michailides* [2009] UKPC 34, where the court asked what would be the effect of a local judgment of the kind which the foreign court had given.

[71] cf Schlosser [1979] OJ C59/71, 127–28.

[72] Article 38.

[73] This part of the Regulation is substantially altered with effect from 10 January 2015 by Reg 1215/2012; see further, p 161 below.

[74] Annex II to the Regulation.

[75] Article 53(1).

given.[76] When registered for enforcement under the Regulation, English law provides that the foreign judgment[77] has the same force and effect for the purposes of enforcement as if it were an English judgment. This is easy to understand when dealing with a money judgment, but enforcement under the Regulation applies also to non-money judgments. In the case of a foreign order of a type close or identical to an English equivalent, there is little difficulty. Where the order is rather different, it is unclear exactly what an English court is to do. The practice of the German courts appears to be to treat the order as though it were its nearest German equivalent, and to use this as the template for enforcement. It is difficult to see that there is a better alternative.

(a) Application without notice

The first stage of enforcement requires the applicant to produce a copy of the judgment and certain other specified documents, and apply, without notice to the respondent, for an order for registration: the respondent has no right to be heard at this stage.[78] The Regulation does not allow the court to refer to Articles 34 and 35 in order to refuse to make the order for registration.[79] This made a departure from the previous law, and was made to counter the prevarication and chauvinism which may be suspected or encountered in some jurisdictions when making an application to enforce a foreign judgment in a local court against local people. Even so, in a truly egregious case there must still be a discretion to refuse to register, a conclusion which is reinforced by the fact that either side may appeal against the decision on the application.[80] But assuming that the court grants the order, it will notify the applicant and serve the order for registration on the respondent, who may learn about it for the first time.[81]

---

[76] In the form in Annex V to the Regulation. But the contents of the certificate may be contested on an appeal against the registration of the judgment: Case C-619/11 *Trade Agency Ltd v Seramico Investments* Ltd [2012] ECR I-(Sept 6).

[77] SI 2001/3929, Sch 1, para 1(3).

[78] Article 41.

[79] ibid.

[80] Article 43(1).

[81] Article 42(2).

(b) First appeal against the decision on the application for registration

If the application for registration was refused, Article 43 allows the applicant to appeal.[82] If the application was granted, Article 43(5) gives the respondent one month if domiciled in the enforcing state, or two months if domiciled in a different Member State,[83] from the date of service, to launch an appeal under Article 43 against the order for registration. This marks the point in the procedure when, in practice, the arguments touching recognition will be raised. According to Article 45(1), the order for enforceability can be refused or revoked only on the grounds specified in Articles 34 and 35, but this cannot be quite right. A court hearing the appeal may conclude that the judgment was not in a civil or commercial matter,[84] or was for a periodic payment which had not been quantified,[85] or was of a measure which should not have been granted under Article 31, or in respect of which there was a bilateral treaty:[86] Article 45 appears to direct the court to ignore all such facts and matters; if it really does, it cannot be taken to mean what it says.

(c) Further appeal on a point of law

The order made on the hearing of the Article 43 appeal may itself be further appealed, but only once, and on a point of law. The grounds on which the court hearing the further appeal may revoke or refuse registration are again defined by Article 45(1).

(d) Other procedural matters

If an appeal has been lodged, or could still be lodged, against the judgment in the court of origin, Article 46 provides that the court hearing the appeal under Article 43 or the further appeal under Article 44 may, on the application of the respondent, stay

---

[82] Annex III to the Regulation. The more usual English usage would be an application to set aside the *ex parte* order for registration, rather than an appeal, but the terminology is established by the Regulation.

[83] It is not said how long is allowed if he is not domiciled in a Member State, but the answer is presumably two months which can be extended.

[84] Article 1.

[85] Article 49.

[86] Article 72.

the appeal proceedings; it is also, presumably as an alternative, empowered to authorize enforcement on the condition of provision of security. After the order for registration has been made, Article 47 permits the court to grant protective measures against the property of the respondent, but pending the final determination of the appeal, only protective measures may be taken. The dominant principle in all these cases will be the need to strike a fair and proportionate balance between the interests of the applicant who, having won, should not be kept out of his money by a prevaricating respondent; and the respondent whose rights to appeal are prescribed by law and should not be undercut by allowing irreversible measures of enforcement to take place in advance of its determination.

10. JUDGMENTS IN UNCONTESTED PROCEEDINGS

For all that enforcement under the Regulation is brisk, it is still possible for a determined judgment debtor to slow down the process of enforcement against him. It is still easier to enforce in London a judgment from Manchester than one from Munich; harder to enforce one from Lisbon than from Liverpool. On the footing that this is not a desirable state of affairs, a Regulation was made to provide for judgments on 'uncontested' claims to be certified by the issuing court with a 'European Enforcement Order'. This allows them to be registered in other Member States, with only minimal rights of opposition before the registering court.[87] So far this is permitted only for judgments in proceedings which the defendant did not contest,[88] but it was only be expected that

---

[87] Regulation (EC) 805/2004, [2004] L143/15. However, for the possible view that the certificate issued by the original court might not be required to be accepted as conclusive, see Case C-619/10 *Trade Agency Ltd v Seramico Investments Ltd* [2012] ECR I-(Sept 6).

[88] However, if the defendant was so elusive that it has not been possible to serve him with process, with the result that the writ was (metaphorically) nailed to the courthouse door, to which he has not appeared, the judgment cannot be certified under this Regulation, even though it was, in a fundamental sense, not contested: Case C-292/10 *G v De Visser* [2012] ECR I-(Mar 15), [2012] 3 WLR 1523.

the scheme would be proclaimed a success and used as the spring-board for a more extensive reform. The eventual aim is not so much that there be free movement of judgments, but that the Member States be understood and organized, for this purpose, as a single law district, in which Birmingham is no more (or less) foreign than Bucharest, with judgments from each being equally reliable.

11. REGULATION 1215/2012

In a further move towards the simpler enforcement of judgments from other Member States given in civil and commercial matters, with effect from 10 January 2015, the Brussels I scheme will be streamlined further. The streamlining of Chapter III may be more procedural than substantive, though it conveys a clear message that Member State judgments should be thought of as being as quick and easy to enforce as truly local ones.

According to Section 1 of Chapter III, recognition of a judgment in a civil or commercial matter from a court in a Member State will be as good as automatic if the court in which judgment was given certifies that the judgment meets the criteria for recognition.[89] As was to be supposed, the EEO procedure of original court certification has been extended.[90]

Where enforcement, rather than simple recognition, of the judgment is required, the mechanism in the original Brussels I Regulation has been inverted. Sections 2 and 3 of Chapter III make it clear that, rather than the judgment creditor being required to apply for a judicial order that a judgment be registered for enforcement, prior to which enforcement is not possible and after and against which the judgment debtor may appeal, the judgment creditor will instead register the judgment by nothing more than a simple administrative act.[91] It will then be for the judgment debtor, who objects to the enforcement to which this will open the door, to make an 'application for refusal of enforcement'.[92] Though the

---

[89] Articles 36–37.
[90] Though cf Case C-619/10 *Trade Agency Ltd v Seramico Investments Ltd* [2012] ECR I-(Sept 6).
[91] Article 39.
[92] Articles 46 *et seq*.

grounds on which this application may be advanced are practically identical to those in the existing Brussels I Regulation,[93] the decision to place the onus of instituting judicial proceedings on the judgment debtor has a symbolic importance. It is justified by the observation, well founded in fact, that the number of cases in which an appeal against a judicial decision to register the judgment for enforcement under the Brussels I Regulation is made and upheld is very small. The conclusion was that such small numbers are an insufficient justification for a general and universal requirement that the judgment creditor must bring judicial proceedings in order to obtain a confirmatory order, or *exequatur*, against the grant of which the judgment debtor may then appeal. The judgment and certificate will instead be served on the judgment debtor; and it will therefore be up to him or her to make an application for an order that the judgment be not enforced.

Two other points merit specific mention. Orders which do not correspond to those found in the law of the recognizing state are to be 'adapted' in the manner sensibly exemplified by the practice of the German courts.[94] Second, the vivid problem which will arise where a court has rejected a contention that the parties were bound to arbitrate and has given judgment, where English law would have disagreed, remains unresolved and, just possibly, insoluble without doing damage to the law of arbitration or to Chapter III of the Regulation.[95] Whatever the answer is, it will have to be provided by the European Court.

Despite the occasional wrinkle, the sum and substance of the law made in Regulation 1215/2012 is that once judgment has been obtained in the courts of a Member State, its non-recognition or non-enforcement will be, and should be, exceptional; and the burden of bringing proceedings to secure such a decision lies on the judgment debtor. Curiously enough, this closely reflects the procedure which applies when a foreign judgment is registered

---

[93] Though including a new defence, that the judgment of the foreign court violated Section 5 of Chapter II, that is to say, the privileged jurisdictional rules for employment contracts.

[94] Referred to at p 158 above; see Art 54 of Reg 1215/2012.

[95] See recital 12 to Reg 1215/2012.

under the 1920 and 1933 Acts, which are considered below,[96] so it can hardly be regarded as a dangerous novelty. Indeed, it may be that the most significant change will be the necessary re-ordering and re-numbering of the provisions of Chapter III of the Regulation, which is recast to reflect the new structure of the law on enforcement. It may all seem rather radical; it is in fact all rather familiar, road-tested, and reassuringly unexciting.

12. LUGANO AND UNITED KINGDOM JUDGMENTS

It is convenient to deal with judgments from the Lugano Convention states (Iceland, Norway, and Switzerland) and from the rest of the United Kingdom, and Gibraltar, as an appendix to the law now set out in the Brussels I Regulation. The provisions of the Lugano Convention are, for all practical purposes, the same as those of the Brussels I Regulation; unless the Lugano Convention is further amended, it will be, at least temporarily, out of line with Regulation 1215/2012.

As well as providing the mechanism for the recognition and enforcement of judgments under the Brussels Convention, which function is now spent, the Civil Jurisdiction and Judgments Act 1982 Act continues to provide for the recognition and enforcement of judgments from Scotland and Northern Ireland, and from Gibraltar. Judgments from other parts of the United Kingdom, whether for money or otherwise, may be registered for enforcement subject to only minor restrictions.[97] For the purpose of the Regulation,[98] Gibraltar is treated as part of the United Kingdom. In England, however, judgments from Gibraltar are recognized and enforced on the basis of provisions derived from and modelled on the rules of the Brussels Convention.[99]

---

[96] Administration of Justice Act 1920; Foreign Judgments (Reciprocal Enforcement) Act 1933; see further, p 164 below.

[97] Civil Jurisdiction and Judgments Act 1982 Act, s 18; Schs 6, 7.

[98] And by contrast with the position under the Brussels Convention.

[99] Civil Jurisdiction and Judgments Act 1982 Act, s 39; Civil Jurisdiction and Judgments Act 1982 (Gibraltar) Order 1997 (SI 1997/2602).

C. REGISTRATION OF FOREIGN
JUDGMENTS (2): THE 1920 AND 1933 ACTS

As explained earlier, there are some countries from which certain kinds of judgment are liable to be registered for enforcement pursuant to two statutory schemes. In some ways it would
have been more convenient to deal with these cases after looking
at the rules of the common law, for the substantive terms of the
statutes which determine the entitlement to register the judgment are very close to the common law as this was understood
at the date of enactment, with the consequencs that in substance,
although not in form, recognition will depend on the rules of
the common law. Indeed, we will postpone the examination of
the precise grounds for registration until we deal with the common law rules, for the geographical reach of the Acts is compara-
tively narrow.

But if registration under the Acts of 1920 and 1933 were to be
quietly subordinated to the rules of the common law, it would
obscure the important fact that under these Acts, it is the foreign
judgment which is registered and which may itself be enforced
and executed upon; and that this makes the scheme very different
indeed from the mechanism, but also from the understanding, of
the common law which does not enforce foreign judgments.

So far as the entitlement to register is concerned, the conditions are close to those of the common law, which are examined
below. But instead of it being necessary to commence original
proceedings by service of a claim form, proceeding from there
to an application for summary judgment, the statutes allow the
judgment creditor to register the judgment for enforcement, it
being thereupon of the same force and effect for the purpose of
enforcement as if it had been an English judgment. The respondent may then, if so advised, make an application to set aside the
registration and the order for registration; and it is on the hearing of this application that the principal issues will emerge: it is
a curious thing that this is the procedural pattern proposed to be
adopted on the amendment of the Brussels I Regulation:[100] *nihil*

---

[100] As to which, see p 161 above.

novi sub sole. But the substantive grounds on which registration may be obtained or set aside closely reflect the common law.

1. ADMINISTRATION OF JUSTICE ACT 1920

Part II of the Administration of Justice Act 1920 applies to many, but mainly smaller, colonial and Commonwealth, territories: of the larger jurisdictions the Act applies to Malaysia, Nigeria, New Zealand, and Singapore.[101] It does not depend on any treaty with the foreign state; it applies to judgments from 'superior courts', which may be registered under the Act within 12 months of their being delivered.[102] Upon an application to set aside the registration, the grounds which satisfy the requirement of international jurisdiction, and the permitted defences to recognition, differ from those of the common law only in minor detail; although if the judgment is still subject to appeal it may not be registered.[103]

2. FOREIGN JUDGMENTS (RECIPROCAL ENFORCEMENT) ACT 1933

The Foreign Judgments (Reciprocal Enforcement) Act 1933 allows for enforcement of judgments in civil and commercial matters from designated courts in countries with which a bilateral treaty has been made. Now that many of the countries to which the Act applied have become Member States of the European Union, or party to the Lugano Convention, which substantially[104] supersede it, the Act now applies to judgments from Australia,[105] Canada,[106]

---

[101] Reciprocal Enforcement of Judgments (Administration of Justice Act 1920, Part II) (Consolidation) Order 1984 (SI 1984/129), as amended by SI 1985/1994, SI 1994/1901, and SI 1997/2601. It no longer applies to Hong Kong. The Act has never applied to South Africa.

[102] Section 9.

[103] Section 9(2)(e).

[104] But not completely: the 1933 Act provides for the registration of judgments giving effect to an arbitral award, whereas the Brussels I Regulation excludes them from its material scope. In this narrow but commercially important area the 1933 Act will still operate in relation to Austria, Belgium, France, Germany, Italy, the Netherlands, and Norway.

[105] SI 1994/1901.

[106] SI 1987/468, 2211; SI 1988/1304, 1853; SI 1989/987; SI 1991/1724; SI 1992/1731; SI 1995/2708. Québec is not included.

India, Israel, and Pakistan, and also to judgments from Guernsey, Jersey, and the Isle of Man. But it applies only to courts identified by name in the order which implements the bilateral treaty: judgments from other courts in these countries may still be enforced by action at common law. The grounds of international jurisdiction and the defences to recognition[107] differ from those of the common law only in minor detail; if the judgment is subject to appeal the application for registration may be stayed.[108]

D. THE INDIRECT EFFECT OF JUDGMENTS FROM THE REST OF THE WORLD: COMMON LAW

By contrast with the closed world of the Member States, whose judgments in civil and commercial matters are recognized under the Regulation, and are declared to be enforceable in other Member States as though they were local judgments, and the schemes for statutory registration made by Parliament in 1920 and 1933, it is left to the common law to determine the effects in England of judgments from the courts of the rest of the world, from Afghanistan to Vietnam; from China to Peru.[109] And although the common law will certainly recognize foreign judgments, the common law does not enforce foreign judgments, even though courts and commentators say that it does: at common law, and by sharp contrast with the Regulation scheme, only English judgments are enforced in England. The fact that the common law does not enforce foreign judgment, the reason why it does not, and a correct understanding of what the common law does do when it comes to enforcement, teaches something important about the common law of private international law.

The basic scheme of common law recognition is that if the foreign court is adjudged to have been competent, as a matter of *English* law, to give a judgment by which the losing party must accept that he is bound, the judgment may, and if there is no other defence to recognition will, be recognized as making the

---

[107] Section 4.

[108] Section 5.

[109] As well as from the Member States if and in so far as the judgment is outside the scope of the Regulation.

cause of action or the issue *res judicata*. If all that a litigant requires is for the foreign judgment to be recognized, it suffices for him to plead it as *res judicata*, but if the judgment creditor wishes to enforce the judgment, as though a sword rather than a shield, he will need to bring an action on it at common law, in the form of original proceedings in the English courts. The action is brought on the basis of the judgment, rather than on the underlying cause of action; but an action is necessary for the common law only enforces English judgments in England, so that the judgment creditor will need to obtain an English judgment.[110]

1. RECOGNITION

A judgment will be recognized at common law if it is the final and conclusive decision of a court which, as a matter of English private international law, had 'international jurisdiction', and as long as there is no sustainable defence to its recognition. There is no requirement that the judgment be that of a superior court: any judicial tribunal will suffice for the common law. But the award of an arbitral tribunal is not sufficient,[111] nor is the decision of an administrative body. The judgment of court, and only a court, will do.[112]

In principle, at least, only orders which are final and conclusive may be recognized. The terminology is more easily used than it

---

[110] *Godard v Gray* (1870–71) LR 6 QB 139.

[111] These do not give rise to issues of recognition in this sense; and their enforcement is regulated by specialist Convention and statute.

[112] For the curious case in which a first instance judgment is annulled by an appellate judgment which is liable to be refused recognition on grounds of fraud or natural justice, and the question whether the obligation created by the original judgment still survives for recognition and enforcement, see *Merchant International Co Ltd v NAK Naftogaz* [2012] EWCA Civ 196, [2012] 1 WLR 3036. If the common law enforces personal bilateral obligations, rather than judgments as such, it should not matter that the original judgment has been adversely affected by a foreign judicial act. The material question is whether this later act affects the obligation resulting from the original agreement; if the later judgment is not recognized, it is certainly arguable that it does not. It might be different if the common law enforced foreign judgments as such, for if there is no judgment there is nothing to enforce. But this is not how the common law works.

is defined, but 'final' means that the decision cannot be reopened in the court which made the ruling, even though it may be subject to appeal to a higher court; and 'conclusive' that it represents the court's settled answer on the substance of the point adjudicated.[113] For this reason, a foreign freezing order will not be recognized, as it is neither predicated upon a final determination of the validity of the claim nor usually incapable of review and revision by the court which ordered it. Likewise, recognition will not be accorded to a decision that there is, for example, a good arguable case on a disputed point, jurisdictional or otherwise: the decision may be final, in that the court will not itself reconsider the question, but is not conclusive if it would not tie the hands of the same court at a later stage when the merits are tried. By contrast, an order made on an interlocutory matter *may* be recognized if it represents the last word of the court on the point in issue. An example may be an order dismissing an action on the ground that it was covered by a jurisdiction agreement for a specific court: if this is the court's final decision on the jurisdictional issue, it is in principle entitled to recognition.[114] A small difficulty arises in relation to default judgments, which will often be liable to reopening in the court in which they were entered, at least on conditions, and not usually only within a fixed time limit. It would appear to follow that these cannot be recognized as final, with the counter-intuitive result that if the defence is so hopeless that the defendant elects to allow judgment to be entered in default of appearance, the claimant may be left with a judgment of reduced effectiveness. The argument may be met by arguing that a default judgment is not, in the material sense, a provisional one which the court expects to reconsider. It represents the court's settled conclusion unless and until something happens which may never happen.[115] On the other hand, the claimant

---

[113] Which may be the whole dispute or a single point: *The Sennar (No 2)* [1985] 1 WLR 490 (HL). There is no reason why it would not extend to a foreign decision that judgment from the courts of a third country was obtained by fraud or by breach of the rules of natural justice, but the Court of Appeal shied away from accepting this conclusion in *Yukos Capital sarl v OJSC Rosneft Oil Co* [2012] EWCA Civ 855, [2012] 2 Lloyd's Rep 208. It was wrong to do so.

[114] ibid; cf *Desert Sun Loan Corpn v Hill* [1996] 2 All ER 847 (CA).

[115] *Ainslie v Ainslie* (1927) 39 CLR 318.

may do better to hurry slowly, and to apply instead for summary judgment on the merits of the claim, even though the defendant is not there to contest them.

2. 'INTERNATIONAL JURISDICTION'

A foreign court has 'international jurisdiction', according to English private international law, if the party against whom the judgment was given submitted to the jurisdiction of the court, or was present—it is not clear that residence is required or would suffice—within the jurisdiction of the court when the proceedings were instituted.[116] The occasional suggestion that the nationality of the defendant is sufficient[117] is not credible today.

(a) Presence

If the defendant was present within the territorial jurisdiction of the foreign court on the date on which the proceedings were commenced he subjects himself to its international jurisdiction, for it is accepted that he is obliged to obey a local judge.[118] The fundamental principles of comity between states require the English court to respect the exercise of sovereign power over a person within the territory of the sovereign. It had sometimes been suggested that the rule should be framed in terms of residence rather than presence, on the supposed basis that it describes a more durable connection with the court, but that would obscure the true relationship between presence and the exercise of sovereign power. It has been suggested that either presence or residence (unaccompanied by presence) on the material date will suffice,[119] but to agree to this would be a very bad idea indeed. An explanation derived from the principles of territoriality and comity recognizes actual physical presence, but if residence means non-presence, these principles do not lead to the recognition of the judgment. Not only that: a defendant served with a foreign

---

[116] Which probably means when process was served: *Adams v Cape Industries plc* [1990] Ch 433, 518 (CA).

[117] *Emanuel v Symon* [1908] 1 KB 302 (CA).

[118] *Adams v Cape Industries plc* [1990] Ch 433 (CA).

[119] *State Bank of India v Murjani Marketing Group Ltd*, 27 March 1991 (CA); *JSC Aeroflot-Russian Airlines v Berezovsky* [2012] EWHC 3017 (Ch).

writ who is told that the judgment will be recognized if he was resident in the country of service may be unsure whether his connection with the state of origin would, or would still, or may later be seen as residence. Residence lacks hard edges; a test of jurisdictional recognition based on residence would not make the common law a better system, but would make it much less certain and predictable.[120] If legislation provides for the registration of judgments from a state in which the judgment debtor was resident, there is nothing to be done but to live with it. But the common law knows, or ought to know, better than to adopt a rule which will simply increase uncertainty.

Of course, if the defendant did not satisfy this condition on the day in question, but did then appear to defend the proceedings, this will be a submission. As to where the presence must be, it has been held that the relevant territorial jurisdiction is defined by reference to the court seised, so that a defendant sued in a state court must be within the territorial jurisdiction of the state, but if sued in a federal court all that is required is that he be within the federation; but insofar as this ascribes an international relevance to rules of local jurisdiction it is debatable whether it is correct.

From one point of view it is odd that this rule acknowledges in a foreign court a jurisdiction effectively wider than English law would assert for itself. For it is irrelevant that the foreign court was a *forum non conveniens* and that, if the roles were reversed, an English court would have stayed its proceedings and declined to adjudicate. But this rather misses the point. The common law admits and avers that a court is entitled to assert jurisdiction over a person present within its territory, whether this means adjudication before the English court or the recognition of the judgment of a foreign court. (And it goes further: it recognizes a judgment *in rem* given by a court at the place where the thing in question was; it regards an acquisition or loss of title to property according to the law of the place where the property was at the time as conclusive.) If an English court may decline to exercise its jurisdiction in a particular case, that is entirely a matter for it; but it is quite wrong to deduce, from that simple and discretionary fact, the conclusion that a foreign court has exceeded what

[120] ibid.

international comity permits and requires if it does not make the same choice: 'we are not so provincial as to say that every solution of a problem is wrong because we deal with it otherwise at home'.[121] If the result is still thought to look odd, the reader should consider getting new glasses. If the defendant was present when proceedings were instituted, comity and respect for sovereignty dictate that he is bound by the judgment.

So to the detail. The presence of a natural person is easy enough to ascertain, but the same rule applies also to corporate defendants. Companies do their business by individuals, and through others: through other companies, which may or may not be in common ownership, representatives, agents, and websites. The presence rule is adapted and applied with as much common sense as possible. The presence of a company entails a reasonably fixed and definite place of business, maintained by the corporation and from which its business is done.[122] So neither the mere presence of the chief executive officer at the golf course, nor that of a peripatetic sales representative, will establish the presence of the company, even if a foreign court may regard it as sufficient for the purpose of its own jurisdictional rules. The same is true of a local representative who merely acts as a conduit for those wishing to transact business with the company which is otherwise out of the jurisdiction.[123] But if the local entity has been given power to make contracts which bind the defendant without further ado, it is probable that the test of corporate presence is satisfied, provided always that the entity does what it does from a fixed place of business.[124] Although a company may therefore be present if another entity is doing its business as well as its own, there is no broader English doctrine which allows all the members of an economic group to be treated on the basis that if one is present all are present,[125] or that one member of the group is the *alter ego* of the others; and English law does not regard a foreign court

---

[121] Cardozo J, *Loucks v Standard Oil Co of New York* 224 NY 99, 120 NE 98 (1918).

[122] *Adams v Cape plc* [1990] Ch 433 (CA).

[123] cf *Littauer Glove Corpn v Millington (FW) (1920) Ltd* (1928) 44 TLR 746.

[124] *Adams v Cape Industries plc* [1990] Ch 433, 531 (CA).

[125] ibid, 532–39.

as having international jurisdiction simply because the company can be said to have transacted, or to be still transacting, business within the territorial jurisdiction of the court. Only if the corporate veil can be lifted can the formal position be departed from, and for English law this is a rather rare event.

The recognition rule therefore reflects the general jurisdictional rule of English law that if a company is present, in the sense of having a place of business, within the jurisdiction it can be sued,[126] and nothing turns on whether the claim arises out of the conduct of the company in the particular place, or arose only after the company started doing business in that place: the company is subject to the unlimited jurisdiction of the court or not at all; there is no middle way. This explains why, given the dramatic consequences of finding of corporate presence, the common law's requirements are purposefully stringent, not satisfied by a casual or delocalized business connection. Were it otherwise, London might become a very risky place for parent companies to incorporate and keep their assets; it is the role of the government, not of the courts, to make damaging changes of that kind.

The larger truth is, however, that where the common law recognizes and enforces the judgment on the jurisdictional basis of presence, what is recognized and enforced is the sovereign act of the sovereign's judge over a person within his territorial jurisdiction.

(b) Submission

On the face of it, no injustice is done to a party who submits to the jurisdiction of a court if its adverse judgment is taken as binding him. So a defendant who voluntarily submits to the jurisdiction of a foreign court is, in principle, subject to its international jurisdiction if the decision goes against him. A claimant, or counterclaiming defendant also clearly submits to the jurisdiction for the purposes of a decision against him; but whether a claimant is taken to submit to any and every counterclaim raised against him will depend on whether the counterclaim arises out of the same facts or transaction as his claim or out of facts which are reasonably connected: a test of broad common sense applies.[127]

---

[126] By being served there: Companies Act 2006, s 1139.
[127] *Murthy v Sivasjothi* [1999] 1 WLR 467 (CA).

A party who agreed by contract to the jurisdiction of a foreign court clearly submits to its jurisdiction.

If a defendant appears in the proceedings for the purpose only of contesting the jurisdiction of the court, or to seek a stay in favour of another court or for arbitration, or to protect property which is threatened with seizure in the proceedings, the Civil Jurisdiction and Judgments Act 1982, section 33(1), provides that the appearance will not on that account be a submission. This departs from the common law which had held[128]—extraordinarily, as it now seems—that to appear before a court simply to apply for jurisdictional relief was voluntarily to submit to its jurisdiction.[129] If the defendant is required, strictly or as a matter of good practice or to make the jurisdictional defence appear genuine, to plead to the merits at the same time as making his jurisdictional challenge, or finds that he is compelled to participate in other interlocutory procedures in order to keep his jurisdictional challenge alive, the statutory protection is not lost.[130] To claim the protection of the statute, it may be that the challenge has to be to the international, rather than to the local or internal, jurisdiction of the court, as the existence or non-existence of local or internal jurisdiction is generally of no relevance to the English law on recognition.[131] So if a defendant argues that she should be tried in another country, this will be protected from being counted as submission, but if she argues that she should be tried

---

[128] *Henry v Geoprosco International* [1976] QB 726 (CA).

[129] The reasoning being that if relief is applied for, the very making of the application involves accepting that the court has jurisdiction to grant it; and there is therefore a submission. A more sophisticated analysis would have been that to submit to the power of a court to rule on its jurisdiction is not the same thing as to submit to its power to rule on the merits: *Williams & Glyn's Bank v Astro Dinamico* [1984] 1 WLR 438 (HL).

[130] *AES Ust-Kemanogorsk Hydropower Plant LLP v AES Ust-Kamenogorsk Hydropower Plant JSC* [2011] EWCA Civ 647, [2012] 1 WLR 920; *Marc Rich & Co AG v Soc Italiana Impianti PA (No 2)* [1992] 1 Lloyd's Rep 624 (CA). If the foreign court does not see the defendant's participation as amounting to submission or appearance, an English court should not do so either: *Adams v Cape Industries plc* [1990] Ch 433, 461 , but cf *Rubin v Eurofinance SA* [2012] UKSC 46, [2012] 3 WLR 1019.

[131] *Pemberton v Hughes* [1899] 1 Ch 781. For a challenge to the existence of a power of attorney to accept service of process and whether this constitutes a challenge to the jurisdiction protected by s 33, see the divergent analyses in *Desert Sun Loan Corpn v Hill* [1996] 2 All ER 847 (CA).

in one city rather than another, or in the High Court rather than a lower court, or in a state court rather than a federal court, these arguments will be less likely to secure the protection of the statute. On the other hand, if the defendant appears under protest, whatever that may mean, to defend the case, her unenthusiastic appearance is nevertheless a voluntary one.

A troublesome argument, which has proved more attractive than it should have, proposes that if a party has made an application to a court for a particular form of relief, issue estoppel may arise out of the decision of the court adverse to the applicant, with such consequences as his opponent may derive from it. It follows, so the argument runs, that if a party applies to a foreign court for a stay or dismissal on the ground that the court has no jurisdiction, the decision of the foreign court that it does, and any finding made in support of this decision, may give rise to an estoppel, and be utilized by the opposite party in an attempt to secure recognition of the consequent judgment. If at first sight this may appear sound—a party who has applied for an order ought to be bound by the court's decision on it—then second thoughts are called for. A party can only be bound to accept a foreign judgment as binding him if he submitted to the jurisdiction of the foreign court in the first place, and if he appeared for the purpose of contesting the jurisdiction, section 33(1) provides him with an answer to the contention that he submitted. It deforms section 33(1) to hold that an adverse decision on the motion to contest the jurisdiction is itself entitled to recognition. The conclusion must be that before any question of recognition as *res judicata* can arise by reason of a party's submission, there must actually be submission; and if section 33(1) provides that there is not, that is the end of the argument.

Submission may also be made by prior contractual agreement. The dispute and the particular court[132] in which the action is brought will need to fall within the ambit of the contractual term. To the extent that this raises a question of contractual

---

[132] There are cases where a court bears the same name as one contractually agreed to at an earlier date, but where revolutionary political change means that it is no longer to be seen as the 'same' court: *Carvalho v Hull Blyth (Angola) Ltd* [1979] 1 WLR 1228 (CA).

construction, the principles will be the same as those examined in relation to jurisdiction. The term itself must have remained valid and contractually enforceable at the date of the action.[133] It has been said that an implied agreement to submit will not suffice.[134] A better view may be that an implied agreement is possible, but will be found to have been made only in the clearest of cases.

The principle which underpins submission as a basis for recognition is that though the defendant was not present within the territorial jurisdiction of the foreign court, with the consequence that the principles of international comity do not require but may actually oppose[135] recognition of the judgment, a court may still find and enforce a personal, bilateral, agreement made between the parties by which they agree to accept the adjudication of the foreign court; and the personal obligations arising from this bilateral agreement form the basis of the law as to recognition *and* enforcement. In this respect, the law reflects the principle first ascertained in *Penn v Baltimore*,[136] namely that a court may enforce a personal agreement made in respect of subject matter the adjudication of which would otherwise lie beyond the competence of the court. This means that where the court recognizes and enforces a judgment on the jurisdictional basis of submission, what is recognized and enforced is not the judgment as such, but the bilateral agreement to accept and abide by the judgment. The notion that foreign judgments are enforced at common law is, on this understanding, a misleading proposition.

(c) Judgments *in rem*

The principles derived from presence and submission as these apply to judgments *in personam* are faithfully reflected in the rules for the recognition of judgments *in rem*. A foreign judgment which purports to decide *in rem* upon, for example, the ownership of property, will be recognized if the property in question

---

[133] *SA Consortium General Textiles v Sun and Sand Agencies Ltd* [1978] QB 279 (CA).

[134] *Vogel v RA Kohnstamm Ltd* [1973] 1 QB 133, not following *Blohn v Desser* [1962] 2 QB 116.

[135] Because the party to be bound will be bound by a judicial act which has effect outside the territory of the sovereign whose judge did it.

[136] See Ch 7 below.

was within the territorial jurisdiction of the court: this closely reflects the principle that title to property is governed by the law of the place where the property was when something happened to it.[137] But if it was not, the judgment may still be given effect between the parties as creating a personal obligation, binding on each by virtue of his agreement to submit to the jurisdiction of the foreign court and enforceable as such.[138]

(d) The difficulty of judicial reform

The grounds stated above are exhaustive; in particular, English law does not recognize a foreign judgment just because the foreign court exercised a jurisdiction which mirrors that which English law would exercise itself,[139] or that the foreign court was the natural forum for the trial of the action: neither comity between states, nor any sense of mutual obligation to accept the judgment, can be found in such facts. Such a step was taken, however, by the Supreme Court of Canada, which has embarked on a sweeping re-examination of the law by which it aims to connect the exercise of jurisdiction, the power to grant anti-suit injunctions, and the recognition of foreign judgments.[140] It saw no reason to narrow the grounds on which a Canadian court will acknowledge the jurisdictional competence of a foreign court, continuing to regard 'tag' jurisdiction as sufficient.[141] Equally, if a defendant submits by voluntary appearance, there will be no question of denying recognition to the judgment. But according to the Supreme Court, recognition should also be extended to judgments from courts having a real and substantial connection

---

[137] See Ch 7 below.

[138] *Pattni v Ali* [2006] UKPC 51, [2007] 2 AC 85.

[139] Traditionally this proposition is supported by *Schibsby v Westenholz* (1870) LR 6 QB 155. The analogy is inexact, for it took no account of the fact that an English court would not have exercised the jurisdiction invoked unless it was also the natural forum for the claim.

[140] See, in particular, *Amchem Products Inc v British Columbia (Workers' Compensation Board)* [1993] 1 SCR 897, (1993) 102 DLR (4th) 96.

[141] That is, jurisdiction established (as people fervently suppose to be the law) by touching the defendant with the writ. It is, however, correct to observe that the decision of the Supreme Court does give effect to its view that the recognition of foreign judgments should be more frequent than it is.

to the dispute.[142] The sentiment is clear enough: if the claimant has sued in the court which is, in Canadian eyes, at least an appropriate place for the claim to have been brought, why should the judgment be denied recognition? To the instinctive, pragmatic, answer, that it makes life awkward for a defendant who may face real difficulty in seeking to predict whether it is safe to allow judgment to be entered in default of appearance, or prudent to appear and defend, it may certainly be said that if this is the right question to be asking, then the interests of the defendant are not necessarily paramount; and if the claimant has played by the rules of *forum conveniens*, it may be that the balance should be held to favour him.

As a matter of English law, such a development would certainly require legislation.[143] And it is important to understand how radical the Canadian departure is. For as has been shown, aside from cases of presence, where international comity requires respect for the adjudication, the English common law asks whether the party to be bound to the judgment has acted in such a way in relation to the other as to have assumed a personal, bilateral, obligation to abide by the judgment, which is then enforced. The Canadian development, however, does not focus on whether the party to be bound has assumed an obligation, but on whether the Canadian court should impose one for reasons of its own. There is nothing inherently wrong with such a law, but far from being a modernization of the details, it represents a fundamental reorientation of the law on foreign judgments. That being so, it is not clear that the Supreme Court fully appreciated what it was doing. Nor is there any reason to think an English court could follow its lead.

3. DEFENCES TO RECOGNITION AT COMMON LAW

A judgment will be denied recognition as *res judicata*, and there can therefore be no question of its enforcement, if any of the defences allowed by English private international law may be

---

[142] *Morguard Investments Ltd v De Savoye* [1990] 3 SCR 1077, (1991) 76 DLR (4th) 256; *Beals v Saldanha* [2003] 3 SCR 416, (2003) 234 DLR (4th) 1.

[143] cf *Owens Bank plc v Bracco* [1992] 2 AC 443; *Rubin v Eurofinance SA* [2012] UKSC 46, [2012] 3 WLR 1019.

made out. It needs to be said at the outset that it is no defence that the foreign court got the law or the facts, or both, wrong or that it tried to apply English law and made a real mess of it,[144] or that it determined the issue by the application of a choice of law rule different from that which the English court would have applied.[145] The merits of the judgment are not reviewable, so the allegation that the foreign court erred in its fact-finding or reasoning is simply inadmissible, no matter how blatant its truth. Were it otherwise, practically every judgment would be re-examinable, and the advantage of the rule would be utterly lost. Common law defences aside, a judgment must be denied recognition at common law if the adjudicating court failed to give effect to a choice of court clause or arbitration agreement.[146] It is unclear whether the common law acknowledged this before the statute was made, but it certainly should have done.

It is arguable that the principal defences—and the contentions which are not accepted as defences—make perfect sense when considered alongside the recognition of judgments on the basis of agreement rather than presence. When parties agree to abide by the jurisdiction of a foreign court, it is most doubtful that their agreement extends to judgments procured by fraud; and it is plausible that they did not agree to abide by judgments obtained by disregard of the rules of natural justice: their agreement is presumably to a judgment arrived at by a reasonably fair procedure, even if it is not the same procedure as one finds in an English court. But they do not agree to abide by the judgment only if it is correct in fact or law, which is why simple error by the foreign court does not carry the judgment outside the terms of their agreement. This approach explains why a judgment obtained in breach of a choice of court or arbitration agreement should not be recognized at common law (though the imposition of a statute has closed down any debate in England), and would also explain why a judgment obtained contrary to an express agreement on choice of law may be seen as one to which the parties'

---

[144] *Godard v Gray* (1870) LR 6 QB 288.

[145] *First Laser Ltd v Fujian Enterprises (Holdings) Co Ltd* [2012] HKCFA 52.

[146] Civil Jurisdiction and Judgments Act 1982, s 32 (unless the other party acquiesced in the breach).

agreement did not extend. As for the defences admissible when recognition is based on presence, the reason why they are no different may simply be the effect of pragmatism. But in principle at least, defences to the obligations which arise by the doctrine of comity need not be identical with those which impeach bilateral agreement.

Whatever theory may suggest, the case law suggests that there are six possible defences to the recognition of a foreign judgment.

(a) Disregard of arbitration or choice of court agreement

If the foreign court was called upon to exercise jurisdiction in breach of a valid choice of court or arbitration agreement, its judgment will not be recognized at common law, even if the foreign court addressed the very issue and concluded, entirely and correctly in accordance with its own law, that there was no breach; it is otherwise if the complaining party acquiesced in and waived the breach.[147] It is obvious that if the court rules against the claimant it is not open to him to complain about the disregard of the agreement, because he brought it about.[148] The justification for this defence is the premium placed on the support of these clauses; but the statutory rule operates only where recognition is governed by the common law. (Where the Regulation provides for recognition, it has no application. Where the judgment comes from a court in a Member State, therefore, it is only the arbitration component of the rule which may be of relevance.)[149]

(b) Lack of local jurisdiction

It is debatable whether the fact that the court did not have jurisdiction under its internal law may furnish a defence, for the authorities are old and inconclusive.[150] But if under the foreign law the judgment is a complete nullity, and not just voidable—presumably

---

[147] ibid, s 32. And see *AES Ust-Kemanogorsk Hydropower Plant LLP v AES Ust-Kamenogorsk Hydropower Plant JSC* [2011] EWCA Civ 647, [2012] 1 WLR 920; *Marc Rich & Co AG v Soc Italiana Impianti PA* [1992] 2 Lloyd's Rep 624 (CA).

[148] *The Sennar (No 2)* [1985] 1 WLR 490 (HL).

[149] As to which, however, see *National Navigation Co v Endesa Generacion SA (The Wadi Sudr)* [2009] EWCA Civ 1397, [2010] 1 Lloyd's Rep 193, which says that it is not.

[150] *Vanquelin v Bouard* (1863) 15 CBNS 341; *Pemberton v Hughes* [1899] 1 Ch 781.

a rare state of affairs, but never mind—it would be odd for it to be recognized in England, particularly if the defendant had been locally well advised to ignore the proceedings. If the judgment is, however, voidable it is, *ex hypothesi*, valid unless and until proceedings are taken to set it aside, which step may never be taken. An English court must therefore recognize the judgment, notwithstanding the fragility of local jurisdiction.

(c) Fraud

For the next two defences, that is, fraud and breach of the rules of natural justice, the dominating question is whether the facts and matters which may be relied on to oppose recognition of the judgment include those things which were put to the foreign court but were rejected by it, and those things which could and perhaps should have been put to the foreign court but which were not. When it is alleged that the judgment was procured by fraud, in particular, the approach taken to defences to recognition becomes more complicated. Although, as said above, the merits of the judgment may not be re-examined by an English court, a different approach prevails if there is a credible allegation that it was procured by fraud.[151] It is an ancient principle of the common law that fraud unravels everything; that fraud is a thing apart;[152] and it is no surprise, therefore, that it can unravel any obligation derived from a foreign judgment. But the definition of fraud and its effect are controversial. It has been held to encompass any misleading or duping of the foreign court. This may include advancing a claim known to be false, fabrication of evidence, intimidation of witnesses, and so on: fraud will generally lie in the use of improper means to defeat, or pervert, the course of justice to prevail over the defendant.[153] Whether this covers the case where a claimant

---

[151] *Abouloff v Oppenheimer* (1882) 10 QBD 295 (CA); *Vadala v Lawes* (1890) 25 QBD 310 (CA); *Syal v Heyward* [1948] 2 KB 443 (CA); *Jet Holdings Inc v Patel* [1990] 1 QB 335 (CA); *Owens Bank Ltd v Bracco* [1992] 2 AC 443.

[152] *HIH Casualty and General Insurance Ltd v Chase Manhattan Bank* [2003] UKHL 6, [2003] 2 Lloyd's Rep 61 at [15].

[153] Although the defendant may also use fraud to support a defence which defeats the claim and, if this happens, the claimant may seek to impeach the judgment which the defendant seeks to have recognized in his favour; cf *Merchant International Co Ltd v NAK Naftogaz* [2012] EWCA Civ 196, [2012] 1 WLR 3036.

pleads a case to which he knows the defendant may have a good answer is unclear, but it cannot realistically be expected that in adversary *inter partes* procedure the claimant has a duty to plead his opponent's case for him. It may, in the end, be a question of degree, with the difficulty that sometimes brings.

The facts and matters which support the allegation of fraud may be put forward to oppose an application for summary judgment in the enforcement proceedings, and if credible will be investigated by trial of an issue,[154] even if they were put before and specifically rejected by the foreign court. In sharp contrast to what is needed to impeach an English judgment for fraud, the defendant need show no new discovery of evidence which could not reasonably have been put forward at trial: he may recycle the very evidence with which he failed to persuade the foreign court. That said, the true position is not quite as stark as this may suggest. In order to have the allegation of fraud investigated, the defendant will have to make a credible case that the foreign court was the victim of, or party to, fraud. The evidence required to reach the threshold of credibility will vary from court to court: it is reasonable to suppose that an English court will take much more persuading that fraud deceived an Australian or American court than where the judgment came from Burma or Guinea-Bissau, or some other place with little international reputation for fearless judicial excellence. The standard which must be met to trigger a review is, on this view of the matter, contextual. Even so, some see in it, and find distasteful, the view that a foreign court was less skilled than the English court at the detection and rejection of fraud; and as a new discovery of evidence is required to impeach an English judgment for fraud,[155] so also should it be, so the argument runs, required for a foreign judgment. Though this criticism has attracted a measure of judicial[156] and other support, the law is sound and the criticism less so. Two reasons may be given. First, it is dangerous for the law, in effect, to require a defendant to make his allegations in a court which may have been selected by the claimant for reasons of his own illicit advantage: the proposition

---

[154] *Jet Holdings Inc v Patel* [1990] 1 QB 335 (CA).

[155] *Hunter v Chief Constable of the West Midlands* [1980] QB 283 (CA).

[156] See, eg, *Owens Bank Ltd v Bracco* [1992] AC 443; *Owens Bank Ltd v Etoile Commerciale SA* [1995] 1 WLR 44 (PC).

that the defendant is entitled to a hearing of a serious allegation in a court over which no suspicion or taint may float is inherently attractive. Second, a finding of fraud in relation to a foreign judgment means only that the judgment may not be recognized in England, just as a finding that an arbitral award was contrary to English public policy means only that the award cannot be enforced in England. The finding of fraud does not impeach the judgment or award *in toto* and *in rem* to prevent its recognition and enforcement outside England. It is less dramatic, and more domestic, a measure than is the setting aside for all international purposes of an English judgment; and the justification for intervention may, for this reason, properly be rather more modest.

But if the allegation of fraud has already had an independent hearing in, and been rejected by, a court of the defendant's own free choosing, this should preclude its being raised *de novo* in England. Either the principles of *res judicata* will mean that the second judgment ties the hands of the party who brought the proceedings in which it was handed down, or it may be an abuse of the process of the English court for it to be advanced (yet) again.[157] Too vigorous a use of the abuse of process doctrine has the potential to overwhelm much of the fraud defence;[158] there is need for caution before the fraud defence is altogether swept away. For even if the defendant has chosen to make the allegation of fraud in fresh proceedings but before the courts of the country of the original judgment, he may only have done so because he faced the prospect of execution against assets which he had in that country. His choice to bring an action to set aside the judgment in the courts of that country will have meant that he faced a far stiffer task[159]—in all probability, needing a fresh discovery of evidence— than he would have done if he had merely defended enforcement elsewhere; and although his choice to bring his action where he did

---

[157] *House of Spring Gardens Ltd v Waite* [1991] 1 QB 241 (CA). There is no reason in principle why the findings against the judgment debtor in the second action should not give rise to an estoppel, but cf the Civil Jurisdiction and Judgments Act 1982, s 33(1)(c).

[158] *Owens Bank Ltd v Etoile Commerciale SA* [1995] 1 WLR 44 (PC); *Desert Sun Loan Corp v Hill* [1996] 2 All ER 847 (CA).

[159] Which may also mean that it was a different cause of action, or issue, from that which arises before the English court in an enforcement context, and that *res judicata* is not applicable.

was technically voluntary,[160] it may have been very much constrained by the fear of execution. Against this background, to find that there is no right to raise the defence anew will require some care.

(d) Breach of standards of procedural fairness

If the proceedings in the foreign court fell short of the standards set by the rules of natural justice such as the right to be sufficiently notified, represented, and heard;[161] or if the procedure violated substantial justice such as by adopting a global and non-judicial assessment of damages for personal injury,[162] or if the foreign court violated the principle of finality by re-opening a final decision for no proper reason,[163] it may be possible to deny recognition to the judgment. The common law provided rather little supporting authority, but it was never doubted that the defence was available.

But the enactment of the Human Rights Act 1998 has raised the profile of this kind of objection, and has given it a new foundation. The Act has been applied in the context of recognition of judgments under the Brussels Regulation, where it has to be regarded as part of the public policy defence.[164] But the Act is a statutory instruction to the judges, and it may well be that it is better understood as separate and distinct from the common law defences whose territory it has taken over. If the English court is called on to ratify or give effect to a foreign judgment which resulted from an unfair judicial procedure, Article 6 of the Convention is directly engaged. This principle has been directly applied to judgments from Contracting States outside the European Union.[165] Very oddly, though, in the context of a judgment from the United States,

---

[160] See p 172 above.

[161] cf, from the context of judgments falling within the Regulation, Case C-7/98 *Krombach v Bamberski* [2000] ECR I-1935.

[162] *Adams v Cape Industries plc* [1990] Ch 433 (CA). No-one ever seems to argue that a non-judicial assessment of damages by a Texas jury makes the judgment unsuitable for recognition. Perhaps they should.

[163] *JSC Aeroflot-Russian Airlines v Berezovsky* [2012] EWHC 3017(Ch); *Pravednaya v Russia* [2004] ECHR 641.

[164] *Maronier v Larmer* [2002] EWCA Civ 774, [2003] QB 620; see p 150 above.

[165] *JSC Aeroflot-Russian Airlines v Berezovsky* [2012] EWHC 3017(Ch). In *Merchant International Co Ltd v NAK Naftogaz* [2012] EWCA Civ 196, [2012] 1 WLR 3036 the Court of Appeal held back from endorsing a similar conclusion in the judgment at first instance.

obtained in proceedings which fell short of what was required by the European Convention on Human Rights, the House of Lords refused to see the 'violation' of Article 6 of the Convention by the American court as reason to refuse recognition of its judgment; it made an order confiscating the defendant's English assets on the back of the objectionable US judgment.[166] This cannot be correct; and the court's view that this provision of the Convention was not engaged unless the violation was 'flagrant' was insupportable.

By contrast with the defence of fraud, where the common law clearly allows the recycling of old material to sustain the defence, it is less certain whether the argument that the foreign judgment involved a breach of the rules of natural or substantial justice may be advanced on the basis of material which was put, or could reasonably have been put, to the foreign court in the original proceedings. It has been judicially suggested that, as with fraud, the view of the foreign court does not preclude the English court from making its own assessment,[167] and that the court may therefore consider or reconsider material rejected by the foreign court; but a more subtle view might be that it depends on the precise nature of the shortcoming complained of:[168] a complaint that the foreign judge should have recused himself on grounds of interest or bias should be something which may be raised again; a complaint that there was no opportunity to cross-examine a witness may not be allowed to be raised again, on the ground that it is just the reflection of a difference in procedural laws. But even if the analogy with fraud is the right one, one supposes that the court will not allow an argument to be advanced past the point where it becomes an abuse of process.

(e) Public policy

If recognition of the judgment would offend English public policy, it is obvious that it will not be recognized. Judgments based on laws repellent to human rights, or producing an outcome which is equally repellent, for example, will be denied recognition,

---

[166] *Barnette v United States* [2004] UKHL 37, [2004] 1 WLR 2241; cf *Pellegrini v Italy* (2002) 35 EHRR 2 (ECtHR).

[167] *Jet Holdings Inc v Patel* [1990] 1 QB 335 (CA).

[168] *Adams v Cape plc* [1990] Ch 433, 564–67.

either on this basis or as a direct result of the statutory instruction implicit in the Human Rights Act 1998.

(f) Prior English judgment

If the judgment is inconsistent with an English judgment, or with a foreign one handed down earlier in time, which is entitled to recognition in England, it cannot be recognized, for there will have remained no issues to adjudicate.[169]

4. THE EFFECT OF RECOGNITION AT COMMON LAW

The most usual reason to seek the recognition of a foreign judgment at common law will be to pave the way for an action by the judgment creditor to bring proceedings against the judgment debtor. If the party in whose favour it was given wishes to collect on it, he may bring an action based on the judgment, subject to the further limitations examined below. However, there are two further consequences of recognition which may be of importance. First, if the party against whom the judgment was given was subject to the international jurisdiction of the foreign court—the claimant will necessarily[170] have been, the defendant may have been—and no relevant defence is applicable, the cause of action or the issue, as the case may be, will be regarded as against him[171] as *res judicata*. This means that he may not contradict it in or by later English proceedings unless some exception to the application of the doctrine of *res judicata* applies.[172] But secondly, if the party in whose favour the judgment was given, and *against whom* there is no *res judicata*, had been hoping for a better outcome, or seeks to rely on a claim which was not put forward the first time around, he may fail: Civil Jurisdiction and Judgments Act 1982, section 34,

---

[169] *Showlag v Mansour* [1995] 1 AC 431 (PC).

[170] Except in his capacity as defendant to a counterclaim which was not sufficiently within the penumbra of the claim he advanced.

[171] And against his privies: those with the same interest or title in the matter, especially if they have stood by, hoping to be regarded as strangers, while one with the same interest as them fights the case: *House of Spring Gardens Ltd v Waite* [1991] 1 QB 241 (CA).

[172] *Carl Zeiss Stiftung v Rayner & Keeler Ltd (No 2)* [1967] 1 AC 853.

now generally prevents a claimant from suing for a second time on the same underlying cause of action in the hope of improving on the result obtained first time around.[173] In the interpretation of the 'same cause of action' it has been held that any claim which arises out of a single contract constitutes the same cause of action as any other, so that a failure to deliver part of a consignment of goods has the same cause of action as the failure to deliver the balance of the cargo. But a claim for damages for one's own injury is not the same cause of action as a claim for damages for a child's loss of dependency;[174] and it is debatable whether a claim for damages for pecuniary loss resulting from personal injury has the same cause of action as a claim in respect of pain and suffering caused by the same injury, for in a tort claim there is no liability without damage, and the two types of damage may indicate two causes of action. Even so, a claimant who manages to steer a careful course around section 34 may still find that his claim or claiming is considered to abuse the process of the court if it raises a matter which could and should have been advanced in the first action.[175]

5. ENFORCEMENT BY ACTION AT COMMON LAW

As a matter of common law theory, a foreign judgment which satisfies the criteria for its recognition against the losing party creates an obligation—it is the obligation, rather than the judgment, which is enforced by action in England—which the judgment creditor may sue to enforce at common law. As the action is brought as one for debt, only final judgments for fixed sums of money can be enforced this way.[176] As for its being final and conclusive, a judgment which may be reviewed or revised by the court which gave it is not final,[177] but its being subject to appeal

---

[173] *Republic of India v India Steamship Co Ltd (The Indian Grace)* [1993] AC 410; *Republic of India v India Steamship Co Ltd (The Indian Grace) (No 2)* [1998] AC 878.

[174] *Black v Yates* [1992] QB 526.

[175] *Henderson v Henderson* (1843) 3 Hare 100.

[176] The Supreme Court of Canada has taken the view that a non-money judgment may in principle be enforced: *Pro-Swing Inc v Elta Inc* [2006] 2 SCR 612, (2006) 273 DLR (4th) 663, although in that case it did not do so. Its decision is sound, its reasoning lacks rigour.

[177] *Nouvion v Freeman* (1889) 15 App Cas 1.

to a higher court is irrelevant. This is for all practical purposes the same requirement as will already have applied to its recognition in the first place, and although it is always stated as an enforcement condition, this reflects only the odd tradition of seeing the law on foreign judgments as concerned with their enforcement rather than with recognition. As a debt claim must be based on a judgment for the payment of a fixed sum in money, if the sum is open to variation by the court which awarded it, it is not final and cannot be enforced.[178] However, if the judgment was final as regards liability but reviewable as regards damages, or if it led to the making of a non-money order, the finding of liability may be recognized as *res judicata* if and when an action is brought on the basis of the underlying cause of action, with the court supplying an original remedy to give effect to the already-established right.

When that is appreciated, it is obvious that the proposition that a foreign non-money judgment cannot be enforced is literally true but a touch misleading. For if a foreign court has given a non-money judgment, such as an injunction, specific performance, or delivery up, the judgment may be recognized as *res judicata* as to the merits of the underlying claim. When the claimant sues on the underlying claim, the merits may be treated as *res judicata*, leaving the court to order the appropriate English remedy; and this order, when made, may be enforced in the usual way. When it is further recalled that a foreign money judgment cannot be enforced as such, but requires an original English judgment on the debt to give the judgment creditor an order on which execution is possible, the line between money and non-money judgments becomes noticeably faint, and the proposition that the former may be, the latter may not be, enforced becomes simply useless.

However, there is no jurisdiction to enforce a foreign penal, revenue, or analogous law; and if the action to enforce the judgment would have this effect it will be dismissed. So if a foreign taxman has obtained a judgment in his favour, enforcement of the judgment by action in England will necessarily fail.[179] Nor, by reason of the Protection of Trading Interests Act 1980, section 5,

---

[178] Although if, for example, instalments already due are now fixed and beyond review, enforcement of these by debt action is possible.

[179] *United States of America v Harden* (1963) 41 DLR (2d) 721 (Can SC).

may an action be brought to recover any part of a foreign judgment for multiple damages, even—perhaps unexpectedly—for the basic, unmultiplied, compensatory element. By curious contrast, it appears that judgments for exemplary damages, unless truly extreme and on that account contrary to public policy, are not covered by the Act and prevented from enforcement by the rule, just so long as the judgment debt has not been calculated by 'doubling, trebling or otherwise multiplying' the sum fixed as compensation.[180] The logic of this is elusive, not only because the difference between multiplication and addition has not been generally thought of as being legally, as opposed to mathematically, significant, but also because the award of such damages is often in partial amelioration of the costly fact that costs are not recoverable.[181]

[180] Protection of Trading Interests Act 1980, s 5.
[181] And see, for the same proposition in the European context, *SA Consortium General Textiles SA v Sun & Sand Agencies Ltd* [1978] QB 279 (CA).

4

CHOICE OF LAW: THE *LEX FORI*

Rules for choice of law, which are considered in the following chapters, will sometimes select the *lex fori* to govern the issue in question. The choice of law for divorce,[1] for the distribution of assets in an insolvency,[2] and until recently (and it has not been completely eliminated, even today) for liability in tort[3] was to apply the *lex fori*: these will be examined in the chapters dealing with these subjects. Aside from these substantive areas of law, issues relating to trial and pre-trial procedure are governed by the *lex fori*, and the scope of this principle is examined immediately below. Moreover, there are instances in which a domestic rule of the *lex fori* may supervene to contradict and negate a choice of law rule pointing to an otherwise-applicable foreign law. It is sometimes said that the application of English domestic law to these significant areas means that English private international law makes less recourse to the doctrine of public policy than it otherwise might. However that may be, it is convenient to undertake a preliminary examination of the role of the *lex fori*.

A. PROCEDURAL ISSUES

The common law took the view that issues which it characterized as procedural were governed by English law, and a rule of the *lex causae* which conflicted with it would not be applied. This is because the *lex causae* governs issues of substance, but not those of procedure. Within the domain of common law private international law, therefore, the first point of characterization in any case may be to ask whether the issue for decision is one of substance or of procedure.[4] But where the substantive choice

---

[1] See Ch 8 below.

[2] See Ch 9 below.

[3] See Ch 6 below.

[4] Dicey, Morris, and Collins, *The Conflict of Laws* (15th edn, Sweet & Maxwell, 2012), Ch 8.

of law rules are provided by European private international law, the technique is, of course, different, for it starts and ends with the interpretation of the legislation. However, most European legislation on choice of law excludes 'evidence and procedure' from the choice of law rules set out in the legislation, leaving a national court free to follow the approach of its own law. One may therefore say that the *lex fori* governs procedural issues, with the only reservation being that the legislative definition of 'procedure' in European Regulations may be rather different, and perhaps rather narrower, than the counterpart definition in the common law of private international law. It is therefore convenient to examine procedural issues as understood by the common law of private international law, and then briefly to note the places in which a European understanding of this expression might be different.

1. PROCEDURAL ISSUES IN THE COMMON LAW SCHEME

(a) Matters regarded as procedural: trials, orders, and remedies

The question whether an intending litigant has such personality and other competence as to allow it to sue or be sued in an English court is a matter of procedure and governed by English law. That said, however, English law will be applied with a measure of flexibility. It does not follow, for example, that juristic persons unfamiliar or unknown to English law may not litigate: although the curator, appointed by a Lebanese court, of a disappeared person was denied *locus standi*,[5] a ruined Hindu temple, which enjoyed legal personality under Indian law, has been recognized as competent to sue;[6] and it may soon follow that entities such as the Whanganui river, which is to be given legal personality under the law of New Zealand,[7] could be a litigant before an English court.

---

[5] *Kamouh v Associated Electrical Industries International Ltd* [1980] QB 199.

[6] *Bumper Development Corpn v Commissioner of Police of the Metropolis* [1991] 1 WLR 1362 (CA).

[7] The New Zealand government undertook to make provision for this in 2012. Two guardians will act for the river.

But the trial process is governed by English law. So its nature and form will be as provided by English law and, in principle at least, the question whether or upon what matters witnesses may or may not be compelled to give evidence is a matter for English law. It has been held that where English law requires evidence to be in writing, this applies equally in cases where the *lex causae* would not have imposed a similar requirement; but this may be due for reconsideration, for if the law which governs the substance sees no need for this, it is not obvious why English law should still insist: after all, the rule of English law will not have been designed with foreign cases in mind.[8] More flexibility may apply to the acquisition of evidence for use at trial. No rule of English law prevents the acquisition of evidence by lawful means not known to English law, or its production and use in England, so the record of depositions taken under US federal pre-trial procedure is admissible at trial in England,[9] as will be documents obtained by disclosure under rules which are more liberal than those of English law. If it is objected that this distorts the balance which each system of civil procedure establishes between the parties to litigation, the answer is that in an extreme case the court may use its inherent power to regulate the trial to prevent it.

An important sub-category of procedure relating to trial is that of interim and interlocutory relief: save where legislation compels a different specific conclusion,[10] orders are made or not according to English law. This represents one of the main prizes at stake when issues of jurisdiction are fought.[11] As a matter of common law, English court has no power to make orders unknown to English civil procedural law; but on the other hand, it will not withhold relief simply because the only connection to England is that the trial is taking place there. Certain limitations

---

[8] *Leroux v Brown* (1852) 12 CB 801.

[9] *South Carolina Insurance Co v Assurantie Maatschappij De Zeven Provincien NV* [1987] 1 AC 24.

[10] *OJSC TNK-BP v Lazurenko* [2012] EWHC 2781 (Ch), which decides that where the substance of the claim falls within the Rome II Regulation, the law which governs the substance of the dispute may limit the availability of relief which would otherwise have been available from the English court: *sed quaere*.

[11] See generally Collins, *Essays in International Litigation and the Conflict of Laws* (Oxford University Press, 1994), Ch 1.

on the power of the court may be imposed by international agreement or assumed in accordance with the principles of comity. For example, an order freezing a defendant's assets worldwide, the making of which is within the procedural power of an English court whenever it has jurisdiction over the defendant, should probably not be made in relation to assets situated within the territorial jurisdiction of another Member State[12] unless the English court is seised of the substantive proceedings,[13] or (perhaps) unless the respondent is resident in England. And an injunction ordering a respondent to discontinue an action in a foreign court, which is no more than another instance of the power of an English court to make procedural orders against someone within its personal jurisdiction, will be made with a measure of restraint which reflects the competing interest of the foreign court in the matter.[14] But in all cases the relief, and the grounds upon which it may be ordered, is entirely a matter for English procedural law.

If the admissibility of evidence is a procedural issue, it may also be argued that the placing of the burden of proof must be treated likewise; and that if this is so, the operation of presumptions must also be included within the category. But the common law was not quite so clear about it. Although the meagre balance of authority held the burden of proof to be a matter for English law as *lex fori*,[15] insisting on this too dogmatically may distort or denature the substantive right to which it relates. If the *lex causae* provides that a particular loss will be held to have been caused by the defendant unless he proves that it was not, it will appreciably alter the rights of the parties if an English court applies its rules on the burden of proof in preference to the foreign presumption. The present state of the common law is uncertain,[16] but its future direction should point to contraction of the category of procedure, at least where this would enhance the effect of the *lex causae* and it can be accomplished without significant adverse effect on the management of

---

[12] Council Regulation (EC) 44/2001 (the Brussels I Regulation), on which see Ch 2 above.

[13] Case C-391/95 *Van Uden Maritime BV v Deco-Line* [1998] ECR I-7091.

[14] *Airbus Industrie GIE v Patel* [1999] 1 AC 119.

[15] *Re Fuld's Estate (No 3)* [1968] P 675.

[16] But for contracts, see now the Rome I Regulation, Art 18; for torts, the Rome II Regulation, Art 22.

the trial process. In this regard, recent decisions of the High Court of Australia are instructive. That court had originally held limitation of actions to be a procedural matter, governed by the *lex fori*, and rules of law which fixed a statutory cap on the amount of recoverable damages to be procedural, both decisions[17] being in line with traditional learning in the common law conflict of laws. It followed that in a tort case, the impact of these two critical factors would be determined by the accident of where the claimant succeeded in bringing the defendant before a court, and not by the location of the accident itself. This was indefensible: there was no reason why the local court should be bound or entitled to apply its rule on these issues in preference to the corresponding rules of the *lex delicti*; and seeing the point, the High Court simply overruled its earlier decisions.[18] Even though there had been a theoretical justification for the earlier decisions, the ends condemned the means, and the High Court put things right at a stroke.

This brings us to the distinction between rights and remedies, and the proposition of the common law that while rights are defined by the *lex causae*, remedies are obtained from the *lex fori*. The High Court of Australia, as we have seen, was not held captive by this historical rule. By contrast, the refusal of the House of Lords[19] to follow that lead, insisting that that the assessment (quantification, calculation) of a head of damages recoverable according to the *lex delicti* was a procedural question, on which provisions of the *lex delicti* limiting damages were irrelevant, was unconvincing. The judgment purported to find this answer in legislation, but it was not there:[20] all the statute provided was that matters which were procedural before the Act was passed were not affected by the enactment, which left a court free to consider whether the procedural characterization was still right as a matter of common law private international law, which the court declined to do. Mercifully, the relocation of choice of law for tort into the domain of European private international law allows us to draw a veil over this calamity.

---

[17] *McKain v RW Miller & Co (SA) Pty Ltd* (1991) 174 CLR 1 (limitation); *Stevens v Head* (1993) 176 CLR 433 (financial cap on damages).

[18] *John Pfeiffer Pty Ltd v Rogerson* [2000] HCA 36, (2000) CLR 203 at [97]–[103].

[19] *Harding v Wealands* [2006] UKHL 32, [2007] 2 AC 1.

[20] Private International Law (Miscellaneous Provisions) Act 1995, s 14(3).

But the common law view that a court may grant only the remedies provided for by its own law is wider than being a rule about the assessment of damages. It was further decided that an English court would award its remedies only where these would dovetail with the rights under the *lex causae* for which they were claimed. Thus at common law an English court would probably not order specific performance of a foreign contract in circumstances where English law would not grant it for an English one, even though no such objection was to be found in the *lex causae*; and it dismissed a claim brought by a Greek daughter seeking an order that her father constitute a dowry, as no English remedy even remotely corresponded to so foreign a right.[21] However, the more constructive approach taken by the Court of Appeal to litigation by entities not known to English law,[22] and the more flexible attitude of the High Court of Australia, suggest that the common law rule that remedies were governed by the *lex fori* even though rights were not, suggests that the common law on this point may not be quite as rigid as authority might have led some to suppose.

(b) Matters no longer procedural: currency of judgment, and limitation of actions

The lesson to be taken from the material just discussed might suggest that the common law rules of private international law were paralysed by authority, and were not likely to be reconsidered by an English court. However, on one notable occasion the House of Lords simply overturned a component of the rule that remedies were governed by the *lex fori*, when it rejected the rule that an English court could only ever give judgment in sterling. Until 1976 an English court awarded damages in it own currency and not in the currency of the *lex causae*: the rule of English procedural law was that the claim was quantified in sterling as at the date of the claim and judgment, years afterwards, would be given for that sterling sum.[23] When sterling went into a period

---

[21] *Phrantzes v Argenti* [1960] 2 QB 19 (CA).

[22] *Bumper Development Corpn v Commissioner of Police of the Metropolis* [1991] 1 WLR 1362 (CA).

[23] Although the judgment would carry interest, and interest rates will bear some relationship to local currency values.

of relentless depreciation it was apparent that this rule would do injustice to claimants, as well as endangering England as a centre for commercial litigation, and all for no obviously good reason. The court therefore held that if, in effect, the loss was sustained in a foreign currency, an English court could give judgment in that foreign currency or in its sterling equivalent as at the date of judgment.[24] Obviously a claimant may not simply ask a court to give judgment in a foreign currency of his fancy, nevertheless, if the recoverable loss is sustained in a foreign currency, a court may give judgment for a sum as if in that currency. This comes as close as makes no real difference to deciding that damages may be awarded in the currency of the law which governs the substance of the claim. If so refreshing an approach could be taken to the currency of judgment rule, nothing stops a court taking a fresh look at other rules currently, but needlessly, treated as procedural.

The procedural rule that English courts gave judgment in sterling was overturned by judicial act. Another ancient procedural rule might have been similarly reformed, but on this occasion Parliament decided not to wait. Prior to the enactment of the Foreign Limitation Periods Act 1984, the approach to time bars and their impact on litigation was complicated. A provision which acted by extinguishing the right or the claim, by prescribing it, was regarded as substantive, with the result that such a provision in the *lex causae* was applicable in an English court. By contrast, a provision which prevented the bringing of proceedings, by limiting the time within which an action might be brought, was regarded as procedural, with the result that such a provision of the *lex fori* was applied by an English court while such a provision of the *lex causae* would not be. English time-bar provisions are enacted in the form of limitation, not prescription; the result was that English limitation periods and foreign rules of prescription applied cumulatively, with the shorter of the two being decisive. Except as the result of logic, the sense of this was impossible to see.

---

[24] *Miliangos v George Frank (Textiles) Ltd* [1976] AC 443; *Services Europe Atlantique Sud (SEAS) v Stockholms Rederaktiebolag Svea of Stockholm (The Despina R)* [1979] AC 685.

The Foreign Limitation Periods Act 1984[25] pre-empted the possibility of reform by the courts, by providing that time-bar provisions are governed by the *lex causae* and not by English law unless it is the *lex causae*. This does not make time-bars substantive; rather, it imposes a statutory rule which overrides the common law doctrine of characterization. English law will still define the point at which proceedings were begun, even where the period is measured by a foreign law;[26] English law will also determine the time period in cases where the application of this rule would yield a result contrary to public policy.[27] Public policy, as defined by the Act, includes cases where the operation of the new rule would do undue hardship to a party, actual or potential. So a period which is too short, and especially one which does not allow for postponement if the claimant is too ill to make the decision to litigate, may offend public policy; conversely, a period which is excessively long, bearing in mind that an English trial relies on oral testimony, may also be inconsistent with public policy; and where this happens, the English time period applies without further ado.[28] The clumsy provision that there is no option to make a *renvoi* on questions of limitation[29] is quite misconceived. One may charitably suppose that its purpose was to ensure that once the rules for choice of law, including any *renvoi* which they may contain and the evidence of foreign law allows, have identified a domestic law for application to the merits, the time-bar provisions of that law will also apply. But if that is what was meant, it is regrettable that the draftsman could not find the words to say so.

2. PROCEDURAL ISSUES IN THE EUROPEAN SCHEME

In assessing the effect of European law on procedure, it is necessary to consider two aspects separately: the manner in which the rule that 'procedure is governed by the *lex fori*' operates when

---

[25] Foreign Limitation Periods Act 1984, s 1.

[26] ibid, s 4.

[27] ibid, s 2.

[28] *Arab Monetary Fund v Hashim* [1996] 1 Lloyd's Rep 589, 599–600 (CA).

[29] Foreign Limitation Periods Act 1984, s 1(5).

the choice of law rules to govern the substance are established by European legislation; and rules of procedural law directly written by the European legislator.

(a) Procedure when the substance is governed by European rules for choice of law

In cases in which the rules for choice of law are provided by the common law rules of private international law, the distinction between substance and procedure is defined by the rules and illustrated by the cases described above. But where the rules for choice of law are provided by European legislation, however, the distinction certainly exists, but it does not work in quite the same way. The Rome I and Rome II Regulations, enacting choice of law rules for the law of obligations in civil and commercial matters provide that they 'shall not apply to evidence and procedure';[30] and in relation to the law on jurisdiction and judgments, the European Court has on several occasions confirmed that the Brussels I Regulation does not affect rules of procedure of national law, save only that these may not be applied to the extent that they would jeopardize the practical effect of the Regulation. On the other hand, certain other Regulations, enacted in greater detail, are more prescriptive in relation to matters which might be seen as procedural, and tend not to use the language which makes the matter clear in the context of the Rome I and Rome II Regulations. Nevertheless, it seems reasonable to suppose that where a matter is to be regarded as procedural, all these Regulations, whether by words or the absence of words, allow a national court to apply its procedural law.

But what qualifies as a procedural matter is, *ex hypothesi*, a matter of legislative definition. The Rome I and II Regulations do not define their scope so as to exclude themselves from issues which *national* law would regard as procedural, but from those matters which the *Regulation* treats, or leaves to be treated, as procedural, which is a rather different thing.[31] For example, the burden of proof and the impact of presumptions is, in a matter within the scope of the Rome Regulations, governed by the *lex causae* and not

---

[30] Rome I Regulation, Art 1(3); Rome II Regulation, Art 1(3).
[31] The expression 'same same but different', otherwise heard in the markets of the East, makes the point surprisingly effectively.

by the *lex fori*, no matter what the common law might otherwise have said, for where the Regulation has spoken the common law has no voice.[32] For another example, the assessment of damages is governed by the *lex causae*, so excluding the contrary rule of the common law from application.[33] The question whether it would be open to an English court to order specific performance where the *lex contractus* would not provide for such an order to be made, or withhold it on grounds which are sufficient in English law but which would be disregarded by the *lex contractus*, is unclear for, as we shall see, the wording of the material rule in the Rome I Regulation[34] is in need of clarification, but whatever the answer proves to be, it will be defined by elaboration of the Regulation, and not by the common law. In the context of the Brussels I Regulation, the proposition that it had no application to procedure was stated by the European Court rather than the legislature. It was held that national rules on admissibility of proceedings—in that case, whether a proposed joinder of a third party could be refused on the ground that it was sought to be made too close to the trial—were liable to be applied, as the issue was procedural, not jurisdictional, and the only restriction was that its application might not jeopardize the practical effect of the Regulation.[35] This qualification means, for example, that an English court may not grant an anti-suit injunction, even on an interlocutory basis and even though it might be thought of as a procedural order, where this would have the effect of interfering with the right and duty of a judge in another Member State to apply the Regulation to the proceedings in his court;[36] an English court may not grant a procedural stay of proceedings in favour of a court in a non-Member State where the order means that it will, in effect, not exercise the jurisdiction which the Regulation confers upon it.[37] But it is almost certainly the case that a national court is at liberty to make or to not make orders for interim or protective relief according

---

[32] Rome I Regulation, Art 18; Rome II Regulation, Art 22.

[33] Rome I Regulation, Art 12(1)(c); Rome II Regulation, Art 15(c).

[34] Rome I Regulation, Art 12(1)(c).

[35] Case C-365/88 *Kongress Agentur Hagen GmbH v Zeehaghe BV* [1990] ECR I-1845.

[36] Case C-185/07 *Allianz SpA v West Tankers Inc* [2009] ECR I-663.

[37] Case C-281/02 *Owusu v Jackson* [2005] ECR I-1383.

to its procedural law: though the Regulation might authorize a claimant to apply for such relief, it does not require the court to grant it.[38] These instances go to make the general point, which is that within the domain of European private international law, certain issues which may arise are liable to be seen as procedural and as governed by national law, but that this happens because and to the extent, and only because and to the extent, that this is provided for by the Regulation itself.

(b) Procedural law directly made by Regulation

Even if procedure is governed by the *lex fori*, the *lex fori* may contain rules of European law which alter the overall shape of a Member State's procedural law. There is no doubt that this is now happening; it is unclear how far this process may yet go. Two examples may be chosen to make a broader point.

First, a Regulation[39] has been made to provide a mechanism for the service of process in other Member States. The 'Service Regulation' supplements national law otherwise to be found in the Civil Procedure Rules but also in international Conventions[40] to which the United Kingdom is party, providing for service to be requested and made by transmitting agencies in the Member States. Second, a procedure for obtaining from overseas evidence for use in local proceedings is provided by Regulation. The 'Taking of Evidence Regulation'[41] also supplements law otherwise principally to be found in international Convention[42] and provides a mechanism for obtaining evidence in other Member States for use in national proceedings. There will be others, but these two examples make the point that the European Union is legislating to bring closer into parallel the procedural laws of Member States, at least in civil and commercial

---

[38] This follows from Case C-391/95 *Van Uden BV v Deco-Line* [1998] ECR I-6511, though cf Case 119/84 *Capelloni v Pelkmans* [1985] ECR 3147.

[39] Regulation (EC) 1393/2007, [2007] OJ L324/79, replacing Regulation (EC) 1348/2000, [2000] OJ L160/37.

[40] Particularly the Hague Convention on the service abroad of judicial and extra-judicial documents in civil and commercial matters (1965).

[41] Regulation (EC) 1206/2001, [2001] OJ L174/1.

[42] The Hague Convention on the Taking of Evidence Abroad in Civil and Commercial Matters (1970).

matters. A pervasive question is whether the mechanisms put in place by the Regulations are exclusive, or exist to add to, but not to derogate from, other procedural laws existing in the Member States which regulate these matters. It is probably fair to say that in some circumstances[43] compliance with the provisions of the Service Regulation is taken to be mandatory (though as it itself allows for other means of service to be made, mandatory may be a misleading term), but the European Court has clearly ruled that the Taking of Evidence Regulation was not designed to, and did not prevent a court in a Member State using other means existing in its procedural law to obtain evidence located in another Member State which might have been sought by means of the Regulation.[44] This seems right, and it is certainly welcome.

B. PENAL, REVENUE, AND PUBLIC LAWS

The second broad area in which the common law of private international law applies the *lex fori* or (if this is different) ignores any provision of what might otherwise have been the *lex causae*, is in the area of penal, revenue, and other public laws: the usual formulation of the rule is that an English court has no jurisdiction to enforce a foreign penal law or a foreign revenue law, or an 'other public law', though it is widely understood that the matter is not one of jurisdiction in the strict sense.[45] The identification of a penal or revenue law is in principle straightforward; the meaning of 'other public law' is less so. The greatest difficulty is separating enforcement, which is prohibited, from recognition, which is not. We will look separately at the effect of penal laws and revenue claims within the domain of European private international law at the end of this section.

A penal law is one which imposes a fine or forfeit or other obligation upon a lawbreaker and is ordered to be made to the state. Its identification as penal is a matter for English law as *lex*

---

[43] cf Brussels I Regulation, Art 26.

[44] Case C-170/11 *Lippens v Kortekaas* [2012] ECR I-(Sept 6), [2012] ILPr 808 somewhat departing from its earlier decision in Case C-104/03 *St Paul Dairy Industries BV v Unibel Exser BVBA* [2005] ECR I-3481.

[45] Dicey, Rule 3.

fori.[46] It is unlikely that a law which requires a payment to be made to a private individual is in this sense a penal law, even if one of the avowed purposes of the law is to deter wrongdoing by ordering a payment to be made which is a multiple of any loss suffered. On this basis, the Roman law action which the owner had against a thief for twice or fourfold the value of the thing stolen, or the award of damages trebling the loss inflicted on the victim by violation of US anti-trust laws, would not be considered as penal laws whose enforcement is prohibited by the common law. This conclusion might be debatable, but if one state legislates to enforce standards of behaviour by imposing civil liabilities at a deterrent level, the money being payable to a victim,[47] while another imposes fines, payable to the state, the penal nature of the latter need not cast doubt on the non-penal nature of the former.[48] It is tolerably clear that where a regulatory body brings a civil action on behalf of a class of persons who have sustained losses at the hands of a criminal wrongdoer, this will not involve the enforcement of a penal law.[49] But it is irrelevant that the defendant has agreed to make the payment liable to be imposed in respect of a crime, so the forfeit of a voluntary bail bond involves enforcement of a penal law;[50] and the payment of an agreed sum to prevent criminal prosecution will be treated likewise.

It is not very illuminating to define a revenue law as a tax law, but it is hard to improve on it; and in this context the rule is sometimes described as the 'revenue rule'. Income and capital taxes, sales and service taxes will be revenue laws, and their enforcement cannot be by action in the English courts. More marginal cases may arise from the collection of state medical insurance payments from employees, for it may be thought that if the state

---

[46] *Huntington v Attrill* [1893] AC 150.

[47] In states in which the court has no power to order the winning party to recover his costs, an enhanced level of compensation may, in its own way, serve as compensation for the financial loss of litigating. From this point of view, one can see the danger of leaping from 'penal' to 'incapable of enforcement in England'.

[48] But in the case of multiple damages, statute precludes enforcement: Protection of Trading Interests Act 1980, s 5; *Lewis v Eliades* [2003] EWCA Civ 1758, [2004] 1 WLR 692.

[49] *Robb Evans v European Bank Ltd* (2004) 61 NSWLR 75.

[50] *United States of America v Inkley* [1989] QB 255 (CA).

provides a benefit in return for the payment, the demand is not so much a tax as a charge for services; the same analysis may be applied to payments made to a state monopoly utility. But such an argument would be unhelpful, not least because it is capable of being applied to practically all income taxes: every taxpayer is said to get something—national defence, social security, the incalculable benefit of the Olympic Games, that sort of thing—in return for his payment. The more incisive question is whether the payment is voluntary in the sense that the law, which creates and imposes the charge on a person who meets the criterion for payment, nevertheless permits her to avoid liability to pay by disclaiming the benefit. Whatever the practicalities may otherwise be, if a person has no power in law to disclaim the right to take advantage of the hospitals, national defence, etc, which are paid for and provided to her from her income taxes and national health insurance, and thereby be released from liability to pay for them, the laws in question will be revenue laws. Likewise, if she is not entitled to disclaim or hand back whatever it is[51] which is said to be provided to the public in return for value added tax and thereby be released from liability to pay VAT, this identifies the liability as imposed by means of a revenue law. So also with a state provider of utility services: if a homeowner is legally entitled to tell the water utility that he does not want its services, and as a result to avoid the liability to pay a charge, the payment is not made under a revenue law, no matter how unlikely it is that the person could take advantage of his technical freedom of contracting and non-contracting. But if the owner of a television remains liable in law to pay the licence fee even though he forswears any reception of the state broadcasting service, the payment is demanded and made under a revenue law. It is nothing to the point that a householder can avoid liability for payment by having no television, or that an employee can avoid income tax by giving up his job, or that a customer can avoid VAT by not buying shoes, for on that basis the only true revenue laws would be death duties. The real question is whether the person may satisfy the condition which renders him liable to tax but renounce the benefit which is offered in return for the payment, and by

---

[51] Does anybody actually know?

so doing avoid the liability to pay. If he cannot, the law is a tax law and is not a contractual liability. Or if there is a better test, no-one has yet identified it.

English private international law prevents only the enforcement[52] of such laws; it does not deny them recognition[53] unless they are so offensive that even to notice that they have been enacted would shock the conscience of the court.[54] It is easy to see the action as an enforcement one when a foreign attorney general seeks to enforce a dishonoured bail bond, or when a foreign collector sues for unpaid taxes.[55] But while the exclusionary rule also applies to indirect enforcement, the recognition of a penal or revenue law is not prohibited. For example, if performance of a contract is illegal under the criminal law of the place where performance is due, that should render the contract unenforceable in the English courts: a result which would be impossible if the penal law were to be denied even recognition.[56] The separation of recognition from indirect enforcement is, however, not always easy to explain, and the case law is not as helpful as it should be. Take an easy case first: the exclusionary rule applies if the state first obtains a judgment against a defaulting taxpayer in regular civil form from its courts, and then seeks its enforcement in England,[57] for the court will not be blinded by a coat of whitewash. What, then, of a claim by a foreign state[58] which sues for a civil wrong such as conspiracy, where the loss complained of is the non-payment of taxes? For though the question is one

---

[52] Save where legislation (which can make country-by-country provision) gives an answer which the common law could not give. In fact, much of the law on the effect in the United Kingdom of foreign tax laws will be legislated as the consequence of bilateral and multilateral treaties.

[53] *Re Emery's Investment Trusts* [1959] Ch 410.

[54] cf *Kuwait Airways Corpn v Iraqi Airways Co (Nos 4 and 5)* [2002] UKHL 19, [2002] 2 AC 883, where the court refused to recognize Iraqi legislation purporting to dissolve Kuwait and to seize the assets of the Kuwaiti state airline, in flagrant breach of international law.

[55] *Government of India v Taylor* [1955] AC 491.

[56] *Ralli Bros v Compania Naviera Sota y Aznar* [1920] 2 KB 287; *Regazzoni v KC Sethia (1944) Ltd* [1958] AC 301.

[57] *United States of America v Harden* (1963) 41 DLR (2d) 721 (Can SC).

[58] Whether suing to establish liability, or bringing proceedings to enforce an original judgment from its courts.

of substance rather than form, civil wrongs are civil wrongs. The difficulty is that some rather loosely-reasoned authorities have stated that if judgment in the action 'would increase the likelihood' that a tax would be paid, the action is prohibited by this rule.[59] If this view is motivated by anything other than distaste for taxes, it is hard to see what it is. But it has been used to justify the dismissal of a claim brought by a company against a director who stripped its assets, on the spurious ground that sums recovered would be used to discharge a corporation tax liability.[60] For a supposed rule of the common law to license theft from a company is anarchic, the very antithesis of law.[61] A more sensible approach has allowed a foreign tax authority to obtain an order for the taking of evidence in England, even though the entire purpose of the application was to assist the foreign state in collecting taxes, on the presumed basis that a right to obtain evidence was legally and conceptually distinct from any purpose to which that evidence might be put, but also because the House of Lords was not horrified by the idea that a foreign state might raise revenue by taxing gains.[62] Next, consider a claim brought by a seller or provider of services, upon an unpaid invoice, which contained an element of value added or service tax. It would be unhelpful to see in this the indirect (because brought at the instance of a person obliged by law to levy the charge and collect the dues on behalf of the state, to which an account must be made) enforcement (because it seeks an order to pay money which belongs to the defendant) of a revenue law. Were it otherwise, and were the court to deduct the tax element from the sums claimed, the claimant would presumably still have to account to the state for the proper fraction of this reduced sum, which would then have to be further reduced, and so on, *ad absurdam*; a similar analysis would make impossible an action brought by an employee for unpaid but taxable wages: *res tota ridicula est*. The better test would simply be to ask whether the right upon which the

---

[59] *Rossano v Manufacturers' Life Insurance Co Ltd* [1963] 2 QB 352; *QRS 1 ApS v Fransden* [1999] 1 WLR 2169 (CA).

[60] ibid.

[61] *Williams & Humbert Ltd v W & H Trade Marks (Jersey) Ltd* [1986] AC 368.

[62] *Re Norway's Application (Nos 1 and 2)* [1990] 1 AC 723.

claim is founded, the *jus actionis*, was a revenue law, or something else, such as a contractual promise to pay money, or the liability of a thief or other wrongdoer that he account for his wrong, or a right to the return of property. If the claim may be pleaded and sustained without mention of any tax law, it cannot involve the enforcement of a revenue law; if a foreign revenue law is pleaded as mere datum, the answer should probably be the same. Similar care, and a similar approach, will be required in relation to governmental seizure of property, where close attention needs to be paid to whether law which provided for the seizure is being pleaded as due for enforcement[63] or is merely part of the history of an accomplished fact, with the claim being based on a property right.[64]

To picture this as the *lex fori* supervening to defeat a claim which was otherwise well founded under a foreign *lex causae* may not, however, be the best way of looking at it, not least because the common law never derived a choice of law rule for penal and revenue issues in the first place. It may be better to say that penal and revenue claims are governed by the *lex fori*: if the claim is of that nature, it must be founded on the domestic law of the court in which it is brought. Liability for a crime may be enforceable under the English law of extradition, or under those rare English laws which criminalize conduct taking place overseas or which allow effect to be given in England to a specific criminal law of another state. A revenue claim may be enforceable in accordance with a treaty with the foreign state implemented in England by domestic legislation. Seen in these terms the application of the *lex fori* in this context is part of, and does not contradict, the common law rules for choice of law. These cases would be integrated into the mainstream of the common law conflict of laws, and would no longer need to be explained as some sort of overriding exception to the general scheme for choice of law.

As indicated above, there is a third category, of 'other public laws'.[65] It makes sense for claims based on and calling for the

---

[63] *Banco de Vizcaya v Don Alfonso de Borbon y Austria* [1935] 1 KB 140.

[64] *Williams & Humbert Ltd v W & H Trade Marks (Jersey) Ltd* [1986] AC 368; *Islamic Republic of Iran v Barakat Galleries Ltd* [2007] EWCA Civ 1374, [2009] QB 22.

[65] *AG (UK) v Heinemann Publishers Australia Pty Ltd* (1988) 165 CLR 30; *AG of New Zealand v Ortiz* [1984] AC 1 (CA).

enforcement of foreign laws which are analogous to penal and revenue laws, such as confiscation and nationalization, exchange control, laws regulating the duties of those employed in the security services, and so forth, to be dealt with similarly. For example, if a householder is obliged by law to pay utility charges, whether he wishes to take the service or not, to a private or privatized company, it would be odd if the private character of the payee meant that as the payment was not under a revenue law, it could be enforced. If it is treated as quasi-revenue, as an 'other public law', the difficulty goes away.

Whether it is beneficial to call these 'other public laws' is debatable: indeed, whether they have any conceptual unity is unclear. In some cases, a useful test may be to ask whether the relationship relied on, or the interest to be vindicated, is governmental in nature. It is hard to see how else one may explain why a foreign state may not sue one of its former spies who has spilled the beans and made a profit, pretending to rely on the service agreement to do so, or why a repressive government may not sue the liberation movement which has damaged the infrastructure of the state, pretending to rely on the ordinary law of tort to do so. There is an understandable reluctance to allow courts to be used by a foreign secret service,[66] or to allow a state to sue those who seek to overthrow it or eject it from occupied territory.[67] The fact that the claim may be got up as a private law action of the kind any master could bring against a disloyal servant, or any property owner against a trespasser who did damage, or any victim of a conspiracy to injure its economic interests by unlawful means, gives rise to a problem for which the answer must be found elsewhere. The High Court of Australia[68] saw this first, declining to adjudicate on claims brought to vindicate a friendly foreign 'governmental interest' for fear of the more dubious state which might try to rely on the precedent. The English courts have, in substance if not quite in form, adopted it, holding that a claim founded on a right which is uniquely governmental will not be adjudicated. So a state may bring proceedings to recover

---

[66] *AG (UK) v Heinemann Publishers Australia Pty Ltd* (1988) 165 CLR 30.
[67] *Mbasogo v Logo Ltd* [2006] EWCA Civ 1370, [2007] QB 846.
[68] *AG (UK) v Heinemann Publishers Australia Pty Ltd* (1988) 165 CLR 30.

its property by relying on the kind of title—possessory, derivative, finder's—that any other owner may. But where its right to recovery or delivery up is based on its right to divest a prior owner who still has possession, its claim will be uniquely governmental, and there will be no jurisdiction at common law to give effect to it.[69]

Where jurisdiction or choice of law may be governed by European legislation, the applicability of the common law rules just described depends on the legislation authorizing or permitting that to be done. In practice there will rarely be difficulty, for Regulations which are defined so as to apply only to civil and commercial matters will not apply where the claim is a penal or a revenue one, or one of public law, or one which arises *jure imperii*. A claim to recover taxes would fall outside the jurisdictional provisions of the Brussels I Regulation, as would an attempt to enforce a Member State judgment ordering the payment of a tax liability; a claim for compensation for property damage arising from enemy action in time of war will be outside the domain of the Regulation, for the right to wage war, and the duty to reparate, is all a matter of public law, unique to governments and states.[70] But a claim for payment of sums to reimburse for the discharge of another's customs liability, which the defendant had contracted to make, is within the domain of the Regulation, for the claim is founded on an ordinary contractual promise to pay for services rendered;[71] and it is impossible to believe that a claim against a thieving former director, brought by a company acting by a liquidator appointed at the behest of a taxing authority, would be considered to fall outside the domain of the Brussels I Regulation.[72] If the court is given[73] jurisdiction to adjudicate according to provisions of the Brussels I Regulation, it would be most surprising if the court were nevertheless free to

---

[69] *Equatorial Guinea v Bank of Scotland International Ltd* [2006] UKPC 7; *Iran v Barakat Galleries Ltd* [2007] EWCA Civ 1374, [2009] QB 22.

[70] Case C-292/05 *Lechouritou v Germany* [2007] ECR I-1519.

[71] Case C-266/01 *Préservatrice foncière TIARD SA v Netherlands* [2003] ECR I-4867.

[72] cf *QRS 1 ApS v Fransden* [1999] 1 WLR 2169.

[73] This may be important: the jurisdiction is given by the European legislator, as distinct from being inherent in the authority of the High Court according to the common law. The point was developed at p 53 above.

decline to adjudicate the claim on the basis that the court lacked jurisdiction to enforce a foreign revenue law. Likewise, if a claim is, according to the Rome I Regulation, considered to be a civil or commercial matter and governed by a particular foreign law, it would be surprising if the court could nevertheless decline to apply that law on the ground that it was, as it saw it, a foreign penal or revenue law. However, the right of a court under the Regulation to not apply foreign laws where the application would contradict public policy might be pressed into service if any such case—which could only be rare—were to arise.

C. PUBLIC POLICY

At various points in our examination of private international law we will encounter the proposition that a particular result otherwise provided by choice of law may be departed from by reason of public policy. It is helpful to set out some lines of demarcation. The public policy engaged is only ever that of English law, but where it is engaged it overrides or displaces the application of a foreign *lex causae*. As an illustration which relates to the previous material, if an English court is called upon to recognize a foreign law which is so repellent to English standards that even to know that it was made is unbearable, it will be completely ignored. So if a defendant resists a claim for the return of property, otherwise good, by relying on a law which divested the claimant on grounds of race, the defence will be struck out on the ground that, as a matter of English public policy, the law is too corrupt even to be recognized as datum.[74] If a defendant denies liability for personal injury on the basis that a torturer owed no duty of care under the foreign law, the foreign law should be wholly ignored. With that introduction, we may examine how and when English public policy overrides an otherwise-applicable foreign rule. We will look separately at public policy within the domain of European private international law at the end of this section.

As indicated above, where foreign rules are picked out for application by choice of law rules, a rule of the *lex causae* will not

---

[74] *Oppenheimer v Cattermole* [1976] AC 249; *Kuwait Airways Corpn v Iraq Airways Co (Nos 4 and 5)* [2002] UKHL 19, [2002] 2 AC 883.

be applied if its content is repugnant to English public policy, or if the result of its application in the given context would be contrary to English public policy. 'Public policy' in this sense refers to the fundamental values of English law; and it is clear that these may change with time. It was not so long ago that English law took little or no notice of discrimination on grounds of sex or sexual orientation, but today foreign laws which appear to be stuck in that version of the past will be liable to offend the public policy of English law, which has (with the occasional Jurassic survivor, now bound for extinction) adopted the values of the new enlightenment with the zeal of the convert. Though it is often said that public policy should be given a restrictive meaning, the Human Rights Act 1998 is bound to broaden and better define certain aspects of English public policy.[75]

The history of prejudice has given a few ghastly illustrations. A law depriving a racial group of its property,[76] or one invalidating marriage across racial or religious lines will, or should, be regarded as so offensive to English public policy that it will be treated as if it had never been enacted, no matter the context in which it arises; alternatively, a court will refuse to receive evidence of such foreign law and will therefore not be placed in a position to apply it. Iraqi laws purporting to seize Kuwaiti assets in time of war and in defiance of United Nations sanctions which demanded to have mandatory effect have also been denied recognition.[77] There are less obvious examples, which are less persuasive. It has been held that although a contract containing a covenant restricting the freedom of a party to take employment elsewhere may be valid and enforceable according to the *lex causae*, it may still conflict with the English doctrine that such agreements are illegal restraints on trade;[78] and the English rule of freedom may prevail.[79] We are still

---

[75] Although it may be more correct to understand the Human Rights Act 1998 as applying part of the *lex fori*, by virtue of a direct instruction from legislature to judge, rather than as something which relies on the common law doctrine of public policy.

[76] *Oppenheimer v Cattermole* [1976] AC 249.

[77] *Kuwait Airways Corpn v Iraq Airways Co (Nos 4 and 5)* [2002] UKHL 19, [2002] 2 AC 883.

[78] *Rousillon v Rousillon* (1880) 14 Ch D 351.

[79] The issue will be reconsidered in the context of the Rome I Regulation, in Ch 5 below.

waiting for a judge to hold that a foreign 'religious' law, by which a husband may repudiate his marriage and divorce his wife without allowing her a right to be heard, or by which he invokes religious grounds to refuse his wife the freedom of a divorce, should not be recognized. Discrimination on grounds of sex is peculiarly rank when 'justified' by the obscurantist nonsense of religion; clarification is long overdue.

By contrast with indisputably wicked or evil laws, other laws may need to be evaluated in their context and the facts shown to have a sufficient connection to England before any similar conclusion can be drawn about them. For instance, though a law giving a husband, but not a wife, a unilateral right to divorce should certainly be considered to be contrary to public policy when applied to a wife who is resident in England[80] it may, just possibly, be regarded differently, and not immediately disqualified from application, when applied to parties who have no material connection with England. Likewise, a law which allows marriage of uncle and niece will not be regarded as so objectionable that it will be overridden by English public policy when the marriage has nothing to do with England.[81] Clarity may result from separating the two ways—the first absolute, the second contextual—in which public policy may work; and it may be that the restraint of trade example considered above would be better seen as falling into the contextual category.

Another way to express this idea might be that the first category of public policy applies whatever the *lex causae* or connection to England, whereas the second applies only if the issue has a real and substantial connection with England. This could be seen either as a disguised choice of law rule, or as analogous to the 'sufficient connection' principle which must be satisfied before an English court will grant certain forms of equitable relief, such as an anti-suit injunction.[82] And if this were to be accepted, attention could be focused on the question which ought to lie at the heart of the analysis, namely what degree of connection with England ought to be required before this context-dependent form of public policy might be invoked.

---

[80] cf *Chaudhary v Chaudhary* [1985] Fam 19 (CA).

[81] *Cheni v Cheni* [1965] P 85.

[82] See p 133 above.

The common law has no mechanism for applying the rules of public policy of a country whose law is not the *lex causae*, or one of the *leges causae*, for the very rule is expressed as one which exists to prevent the application of a rule of foreign law which the common law rules of private international law would otherwise have picked up. Of course, where a provision of the *lex causae* is described under that law as, or as enshrining, a rule of public policy, there is no reason whatever for an English court to decline to give it effect, for it is still part of the *lex causae*, whatever else it may be said to be. And as a matter of common law, there is no such thing as 'European public policy'.

Where the issue in question falls within the domain of European private international law, the initial question may be formulated a little differently, but the substance is almost exactly the same: one may go in through a different door, but they open into the same room. Recourse to English public policy—again, the Regulations do not make any provision for a European public policy as such—will be dependent upon the legislation first authorizing it: in a civil or commercial matter, there is no possibility of departing from the answer given by the Regulation unless the Regulation says so itself. But for practical purposes, the legislation with which we will be concerned does permit a court to veer away from the answer to which the Regulation is otherwise steering it by reference to its own public policy. For example, a judgment may be denied recognition where recognition would be manifestly contrary to public policy;[83] the application of a law otherwise required by the Rome I and Rome II Regulations may be refused if the application would be manifestly contrary to public policy;[84] a divorce or annulment may be refused recognition if recognition would be manifestly contrary to public policy;[85] and even insolvency proceedings in another Member State may be refused recognition on this ground.[86] Given the restrictiveness of the doctrine of public policy in any event, it is unlikely that 'manifestly' adds much to the operation of the law. However, as the Brussels I

---

[83] Brussels I Regulation, Art 34(1).
[84] Rome I Regulation, Art 21; Rome II Regulation, Art 26.
[85] Regulation 2201/2003, Art 22(a).
[86] Regulation 1346/2000, Art 26.

Regulation does not make specific provision for the application of the European Convention on Human Rights, those cases in which a court considers that it is required to implement a provision of that Convention will need to be identified as those where recognition of the judgment would manifestly conflict with its public policy. The same may be true in the context of the Rome I and Rome II Regulations, for example, though in the case of these instruments, provision is also made for the application of a law of the forum as one which is of mandatory application, and the Human Rights Act may be accessed by this means instead. When looking at the various substantive issues which form the remaining chapters of this book, it will be necessary to look at the individual ways in which each piece of European legislation authorizes the application of laws of the forum as mandatory laws. But it does not call for any more by way of introductory treatment.

5

OBLIGATIONS: CONTRACTUAL

A. INTRODUCTION

From the beginning of time until 1991, the rules of private international law in respect of contractual obligations were established by the common law: the common law doctrine of characterization decided what fell within the choice of law rule or rules for contracts, and the common law rules for choice of law determined the law which applied to them: most issues were referred to the 'proper law of the contract', with marginal roles for the law of the place of performance, the personal law of the contracting party, and the law of the place where the contract was made.

All that came to an end when European legislation displaced the common law and provided uniform European rules for choice of law in relation to contractual obligations arising in civil and commercial matters. The legislation defined the area within which it was to be applied as well as providing the rules for choice of law when a question of choice of law arose within it. For contractual obligations in civil and commercial matters arising from contracts made after 1 April 1991,[1] the choice of law rules are found in the Rome Convention on the law applicable to contractual obligations 1980, which was enacted into law by the Contracts (Applicable Law) Act 1990.[2] The Rome Convention harmonized the choice of law rules for contractual obligations in civil and commercial matters for the then Member States of the European Union. The justification for legislation was that if choice of law rules were made predictable and uniform this would encourage the free movement of persons, goods, and services throughout the Member States. There was, however, no prior empirical research to vouch for this assertion, nor much sign afterwards that European shoppers were now flocking to Tottenham Court Road to buy their televisions because of it. But there it is.

[1] SI 1991/707, Art 17.
[2] A consolidated version of the text of the Convention was printed at [1998] OJ C27/34.

The Rome Convention was only ever intended to be an interim stage in the larger project of harmonization of choice of law rules across the Member States. In 2007 a Regulation for choice of law for non-contractual obligations was adopted and is known as 'Rome II':[3] it is examined in the following chapter. Parallel negotiations to convert the Rome Convention into a 'Rome I' Regulation made rather slower progress. Perhaps this was attributable, at least in part, to an ambition to expand the existing Convention to include some issues of considerable complexity which had hitherto been left outside it. But in 2008 the Rome I Regulation was adopted, and came into force in such a way that it applies to contracts made after 17 December 2009.[4] The immediate result is that, subject to the date in relation to which the question has to be addressed, choice of law for obligations in civil and commercial matters is governed by the Rome I and Rome II Regulations.

It was sometimes said that the Rome Convention had been influenced by the common law's choice of law rules for contracts. But even if this dubious claim were true,[5] it would have been wrong to interpret the Convention by the fading light of authorities on the common law, not least because the status of the Convention as an international text meant that the need for it to have as uniform an interpretation as possible[6] would draw it away from any common law ancestry which some say it had. So far as its detailed interpretation was concerned, the report of Professors Giuliano and Lagarde[7] served as the authorized[8] aid to its interpretation. So far as the operation of the Convention was concerned, it was irrelevant that none of the parties had any connection with England or even with the European Union, or that the law which the Convention made applicable was that of a country not party to the Convention.[9]

---

[3] Regulation (EC) 864/2007, [2007] OJ L199/40.

[4] Regulation (EC) 593/2008, [2008] OJ L177/6.

[5] It was almost certainly said by the promoters of the Convention in order that it not scare the horses.

[6] Article 18.

[7] [1980] OJ C282/1.

[8] Contracts (Applicable Law) Act 1990, s 3(3).

[9] Article 2.

The Rome I Regulation applies to contracts concluded after 17 December 2009:[10] in the very rare case in which the date of concluding is in dispute, it may be pragmatic just to apply English law on when contracts are made, and never mind the more complicated answers which could also be recited. The content of the Regulation is not greatly different from the Convention which preceded it, though this makes for more difficulty than might be supposed, for where a provision of the Convention appears to have been replicated in the Regulation, it should not be too quickly assumed that it will invariably have precisely the same meaning and effect as it had in the earlier instrument. The principle of legal certainty will favour stability in interpretation, but as only one among a number of other principles of interpretation or canons of construction. Likewise, legal certainty of a different kind may favour consistency of interpretation as between the Rome I Regulation and the Brussels I Regulation.[11] But consistency does not necessarily mean identity. To take one example: the privileged jurisdictional rules which allow a consumer to sue in his or her home courts have been held by the European Court to require a restrictive interpretation, as they derogate from the important principle that the defendant should be sued where he is domiciled. But the rules which determine choice of law for certain contracts made by a consumer are more complex and fragmented, and even if they were not, it is not clear that the purpose which they are intended to serve is met by giving them a strict or restrictive construction. If a contract is made by an individual for mixed purposes—for the re-roofing of the house and buildings used for work purposes, as an entire contract, for example[12]—a claim against the roofing contractor will fall outside the privileged jurisdictional rules in Section 4 of Chapter II of the Brussels I Regulation. It is not immediately clear that it would, or would have to be held, to fall outside the provisions for choice of law in Article 6 of the Rome I Regulation: it may do, but the issue needs to be analysed in terms of the policy of the Rome I Regulation, which may be autonomous in its own way.

---

[10] Article 28.
[11] Recital 7 to the Regulation.
[12] Case C-464/01 *Gruber v BayWa AG* [2005] ECR I-439.

For convenience of explanation, rather than for any other reason, this chapter is organized on the footing that the primary legislative text is the Rome I Regulation, that is to say, it concerns itself with choice of law for contracts made after 17 December 2009. But the litigation of such contracts is not yet as common as disputes arising out of those made on or before that date, and it will therefore be necessary to continue to make some reference to the Rome Convention.

1. JURISDICTION OVER CONTRACT MATTERS

The majority of contractual claims will arise as civil or commercial matters, and jurisdiction over defendants in respect of them will fall within the domain of the Brussels I Regulation.[13] It is reasonable to suppose that the definition of 'contract' in the Brussels I Regulation and Rome I Regulation will be very similar, maybe completely congruent, and it is probable that these two European instruments, together with the Rome II Regulation,[14] may be considered side-by-side in determining whether a particular cause of action (say for a payment of a sum of money on the unilateral termination of a distribution agency,[15] or a claim for damages for fraudulently inducing the claimant into a contract which he is not now able to rescind) is contractual for the purposes of these Regulations. But it is arguable that the interpretation of the term 'contract' in CPR Part 6, Practice Direction 6B will be different, and will continue to be defined by the common law rules of the conflict of laws.[16] Accordingly, a claim founded on the principle that a person who gives negligent professional advice to another who relies on it may incur liability[17] may yet[18] be held to be contractual if the question arises in the jurisdictional context of the

---

[13] Regulation (EC) 44/2001, [2001] OJ L12/1; see Ch 2 above.

[14] Regulation (EC) 864/2007, [2007] OJ L199/40; see Ch 6 below.

[15] Case 9/87 *Arcado v Haviland SA* [1988] ECR 1539.

[16] For the view that statutory reform of choice of law does not affect issues which are procedural (which service out must surely be) see *Harding v Wealands* [2006] UKHL 32, [2007] 2 AC 1.

[17] *Hedley Byrne & Co Ltd v Heller & Partners Ltd* [1964] AC 465.

[18] No case has yet held this to be so.

Brussels I Regulation, and may also be governed by the choice of law rules of the Rome I Regulation when it comes to determine which law governs the substance of the claim made, but will be seen as a claim in tort if it arises in the context of an application for permission to serve the claim form out under CPR Part 6: this makes for a rather untidy law, but it appears to be correct.

2. AUTONOMY AND CHOICE OF LAW

As will be seen, the general principle which underpins the choice of law for contracts at common law, and choice of law for contractual obligations under the Rome I Regulation, is that so long as the parties have contractual capacity, they have very substantial contractual autonomy,[19] and that if they can choose to make any contract they wish, it follows that they can choose any law they wish to govern it. But this seductive proposition almost immediately leads into a logical thicket. For whether they made an effective choice must be, if it is disputed, determined by reference to a law: but which one? Will that law which makes that assessment do so finally or only provisionally? Can the law whose status or significance derives from the proposition that it was chosen also be the law which determines whether a permissible choice was made? If the parties purport to alter the law they have chosen, which of the various available laws determines whether they have executed that change lawfully and effectively? If the parties dispute whether a contract has been made, can the law which would govern it if it were found or assumed to be valid properly answer the anterior question whether it *is* valid, or whether an alleged choice of law is effective? If the identification of a governing law does not depend on express choice but on the terms of the contract, but the terms of the contract depend on the governing law, where does the analysis begin? The principle of party autonomy cannot be self-justifying: some external point of reference is required to explain why and when recourse or reference to party autonomy is justified. The theoretical difficulties which can be spun out of such self-absorbed navel-gazing can obscure the fact that the rules work satisfactorily, certainly where it is common ground that the parties are

---

[19] Nygh, *Autonomy in International Contracts* (Oxford University Press, 1999).

contractually bound, and the only issue concerns the interpretation and performance of their agreement. But, as will be seen, there are other places, especially where the very existence of the contract is a matter of dispute, in which the theoretical underpinnings of the law are not as firm as they might be.

B. THE ROME I REGULATION

The Rome I Regulation applies to contractual obligations in civil and commercial matters where the contract was concluded after 17 December 2009, except for the matters specifically excluded from its material scope by Article 1. The Regulation is an instrument which defines its own domain or sphere of operation *as well as* providing rules for choice of law for issues falling within that domain; and Article 1 defines that domain. But even in the areas which are outside the material scope of the Regulation (or, for contracts made before 18 December 2009, outside the material scope of the Rome Convention), there is no reason why the common law rules for choice of law operating in this unclaimed territory may not, on their own authority, refer some or all of the excluded issues to the governing law as identified by the Regulation for issues which do fall within its scope. For example, arbitration agreements are excluded from the Rome I Regulation by Article 1(2)(e). The Regulation therefore makes no claim to impose its rules for choice of law upon a court which has to determine the validity of such an agreement. Nevertheless, an English court, applying principles of common law private international law where the Regulation does not intrude, is at liberty to decide on its own authority that the law which governs an arbitration agreement will often be the law which governs the contract of which it is a term, and this law may be identified by the Regulation. The process is the inverse of what is done by Article 4 of the Brussels I Regulation on jurisdiction.[20] That provision co-opts the jurisdictional rules of the common law to form a component part of the Regulation's rules on jurisdiction. In the context of the Rome I Regulation, the common law may

---

[20] Regulation (EC) 44/2001.

be seen to incorporate the Regulation for purposes which are, and remain, its own. A dynamic equilibrium is at work.

The Rome I Regulation applies to cases involving a contractual obligation in civil and commercial matters litigated before an English court and involving a choice between the laws of different countries.[21] It applies in all the Member States and in order to secure uniformity of interpretation and application its scope and terms of art will be interpreted independently of national laws.[22]

The material scope of the Regulation is defined inclusively and exclusively: to determine whether an issue is regulated by the choice of law rules of the Regulation it must be within the general scope of the Regulation and not specifically excluded from it. It is to this that we first turn.

1. DOMAIN OF THE REGULATION

The Regulation applies to identify the law applicable to 'contractual obligations' in contracts concluded after 17 December 2009. It will be apparent, even obvious, that the meaning of this expression is not taken from national law, and that the definition of contractual obligation has no need to be, and is not, precisely the same as its meaning in the common law of private international law. It is necessary to define 'contractual obligations' for the purpose of the Rome I Regulation without looking backward to the common law, whose detail but also whose definitions it has supplanted. For those inclined to more graphic imagery, the definition is an autonomous one, drawn out on squared, not foolscap, paper.

(a) 'Contractual'

The definition of 'contractual obligations' will encompass most obligations regarded as contractual in English law, and will exclude most which are not. If, as in principle will be the case, the definition of contractual obligations follows that used for special jurisdiction under the Brussels I Regulation, the defining

---

[21] Article 1(1). For this purpose the separate parts of the United Kingdom are treated as separate countries: Art 22 provides that a Member State may do this if it wishes to, and SI 2009/3064, reg 5, does it.

[22] Article 18.

characteristic of a contractual obligation will be one that was freely entered into with regard to another, identified, person.[23] On the basis of the jurisprudence of the European Court in relation to the Brussels I Regulation, the obligations of a member to his trade association or of a shareholder to his company will be contractual even if national law might categorize them differently, because the relationship between the parties is one in which the obligations were freely undertaken in relation to identified others.[24] Conversely, the claim of a sub-buyer to enforce the manufacturer's warranties of quality will not be based on a contractual obligation, even where so understood in national law, and even though the manufacturer's obligations were undertaken by him freely and voluntarily, because the sub-buyer seeking to enforce them was not identifiable by the manufacturer.[25] It seems probable that any obligation said to be contractual must be tested by reference to both components of this definition— the voluntariness of the assumption of obligation, the ability to have foreseen or identify the counterparty—though the extent to which it must always satisfy them is less easy to say.

The proposition that the obligation be one which was freely and voluntarily assumed cannot mean that it must be one which was expressly agreed to, or one which could have been excluded by the choice of the parties. Were it otherwise, the obligations of a supplier in a consumer contract, which are often incapable of exclusion by contractual term, would not be contractual, nor would some of the terms and conditions implied by law into a contract for the sale of goods. Instead, it appears that the relationship created, as distinct from the individual terms found within it, is probed to see whether it was voluntarily assumed. Indeed, it has even been held that a claim for damages for breach of warranty of authority is within the scope of a contractual obligation, even though English law appears simply to impose it on an agent

[23] Case C-26/91 Soc Jakob Handte & Co GmbH v Soc Traitements Mécano-Chimiques des Surfaces [1992] ECR I-3967.

[24] Case 34/82 Martin Peters Bauunternehmung GmbH v Zuid Nederlandse AV [1983] ECR 987.

[25] Case C-26/91 Soc Jakob Handte & Co GmbH v Soc Traitements Mécano-Chimiques des Surfaces [1992] ECR I-3967.

who has acted as though he had his principal's authority.[26] It is probable that the relationship or obligation is still contractual, with its choice of law determined by the Rome I Regulation, even if it is argued by way of defence that the agreement was vitiated from the outset,[27] or even that it was void *ab initio*.[28] It is a common usage in domestic law to talk of a void contract, even if it is, from one point of view, something of a nonsense to do so. And the Rome I Regulation, as we shall see, indicates the choice of law rule for application when it is alleged that a party did not consent,[29] and when dealing with the consequences of nullity.[30] On this view, if a claim is raised on the basis that the claimant was entitled to rescind a contract for misrepresentation, or avoid it for duress or undue influence, the matter should be seen as one of contractual obligation, for the whole point of the litigation is to establish the validity or otherwise of a contractual obligation. But where the claim is for monetary compensation for loss caused by being tricked into contract or for the failure of the counterparty to negotiate the conclusion of a contract in good faith,[31] the obligation which forms the matter in dispute is non-contractual, a matter of pre-contractual fault. For these, the Rome II Regulation will provide the applicable rule for choice of law. However, as will be seen in the following chapter, the solution arrived at by the application of the Rome II Regulation will almost invariably be the same as that which the Rome I Regulation would have yielded, so even if there is any doubt about the line of demarcation just drawn, it will not much matter.

Even so, the following seven propositions appear to be justified. (1) If it is common ground that there was a contract between the parties, the Rome I Regulation will in principle apply to determine issues of choice of law. (2) If the claimant seeks to enforce

---

[26] *Golden Ocean Group Ltd v Salgaocar Mining Industries Pvt Ltd* [2012] EWCA Civ 265, [2012] 1 WLR 3674. But should it not be seen as a case of pre-contractual fault by the agent, who misrepresented his authority to the third party?

[27] cf *Agnew v Länsförsäkringsbolagens AB* [2001] 1 AC 223.

[28] But cf *Kleinwort Benson Ltd v Glasgow City Council* [1999] 1 AC 153.

[29] Article 10.

[30] Article 12(1)(e).

[31] cf *Fonderie Officine Mecchaniche Tacconi SpA v Heinrich Wagner Sinto Maschinenfabrik GmbH* [2002] ECR I-7357.

a contract, but the defendant counters with an assertion that the alleged contract was not valid or made, the obligation relied on and sought to be enforced is contractual, and the Rome I Regulation will again in principle apply. (3) If the roles are reversed, and the claimant seeks to rescind a contract for pre-contractual fault, or applies for relief predicated on the basis that he has rescinded the contract, the defendant contending by way of answer that the contract is valid, the obligation in dispute between the parties is contractual, and the Rome I Regulation will in principle apply. (4) If the claimant seeks to enforce a contract but the defendant denies that he is party to it, the obligation in question is still a contractual one, and the Rome I Regulation will in principle apply. (5) If it is common ground that a supposed contract was a nullity, the dispute concerns the consequences of nullity of a contractual obligation, and the Rome I Regulation will in principle apply.[32] (6) If claimant seeks monetary compensation for being tricked or pressured into a contract which he cannot now escape from, the claim is founded on an allegation of pre-contractual fault and does not require the court to enforce or assess the validity of the contract, with the consequence that the obligation in question is non-contractual and the Rome II Regulation will in principle apply to identify the law which governs it. (7) If the claimant seeks monetary compensation for the counter-party's wrongful failure to negotiate in good faith towards the conclusion of a contract, the obligation in question is non-contractual and the Rome II Regulation will deal with the question of choice of law.

Civil or commercial obligations can be freely assumed outside the domestic law of contract, and dealing with these is, for an English lawyer, slightly more problematic. Liability for statements negligently made to someone who was expected to rely on them can be explained, as a matter of domestic law, as resting on a voluntary assumption of responsibility,[33] which idea comes very close to replicating the autonomous definition of contracts. Moreover, if liability under this principle of domestic law is said to arise from a relationship 'equivalent to contract', which is not contractual only because of the absence of consideration,[34] it is plausible

---

[32] Article 12(e).
[33] *Henderson v Merrett Syndicates Ltd* [1995] 2 AC 145.
[34] *Hedley Byrne & Co Ltd v Heller & Partners Ltd* [1964] AC 465.

that these may be contractual obligations for the purpose of the Rome I Regulation. After all, English private international law long acknowledged that a promise unsupported by consideration counted as a contract.[35] It might even be argued, for example, that the question whether A, who has agreed to provide a confidential reference on behalf of B to C owes liability to B[36] or to C,[37] if he is said to have been careless in what he writes, would be a matter for the Rome I Regulation. Similarly, the liability of someone who volunteers to assume fiduciary duties, in relation to another may be seen as resting on obligations freely entered into, and the existence of these duties, their extent, and their consequences will be subject to the choice of law rules of the Rome I Regulation; likewise a former employee said to owe obligations of confidentiality to his former employer.[38] After all, the fact that such obligations are treated as equitable obligations in domestic law is an historical and doctrinal accident which cannot be reflected in the Rome I Regulation. The eventual answer in relation to the 'contractual' part of the autonomous definition will be to ask whether the relationship out of which the liability is said to arise can be described as one in which the defendant freely assumed obligations in relation to another and, if he did, the law which governs the relationship will be likely to be that specified by the Rome I Regulation. If in the end this all seems rather more difficult than it needs to be, there are two things to remember which palliate the headache. First, even when the law was far simpler than it is today, the division of the law of obligations between contract and delict was difficult for Gauis and Justinian,[39] so it is not just common lawyers who toil all day and still feel uneasy about the result of their labours. Second, in many of the cases which one may feel

---

[35] *Re Bonacina* [1912] 2 Ch 394.

[36] *Spring v Guardian Assurance plc* [1995] 2 AC 296.

[37] *Hedley Byrne & Co Ltd v Heller & Partners Ltd* [1964] AC 465.

[38] *OJSC TNK-BP Holding v Lazurenko* [2012] EWHC 2781 (Ch) (alleged equitable obligation of confidentiality arising from contract of employment governed by *lex contractus*, a case on the Rome Convention, but the principle will be the same).

[39] All the more so as the Rome Regulations do not have, as Justinian did have, the benefit of quasi-contract and quasi-delict to accommodate some forms of liability.

inclined to locate within the Rome II Regulation but where the Rome I Regulation remains within easy reach, the choice of law generated by the Rome II Regulation is the same as it would have been if the issue had been accepted as contractual and governed by the Rome I Regulation.

The second aspect of the definition of 'contractual' appears to require that the obligation be assumed in relation to another who can be identified, so that if the defendant has no idea who the other party is, the relationship is not contractual.[40] But this really cannot be correct, and cannot comprise part of a workable definition. Were it to be taken at face value, Mrs Carlill, through whose legendary purchase and use of the carbolic smoke ball, and influenza, every first year law student discovers the law of contract,[41] would not be party to a contractual obligation. The Carbolic Smoke Ball Company neither knew nor cared who its customers were any more than does anyone else who advertises a reward,[42] or the fire brigade which responds to a call for help,[43] or the transport company which sells more than one ticket at once. Nor would an assignee or other successor in title ever have a contractual claim to enforce against the original obliged party, for in none of these cases is the identity of the other party known to, or probably even discoverable by, the supplier or advertiser or debtor; and that would appear to carry the obligations of the relationship outside the Rome I Regulation. The trouble is that these cases must be contractual, for private international law has no other category into which it would be even remotely realistic to accommodate them. The supposed requirement that there be an identified or identifiable 'other' is therefore unstable. An obligation is contractual if the defendant freely assumes a promissory obligation to another or to others, but that if the promisor does not know or wish to know[44] the identity of the other this is

[40] Case C-26/91 *Soc Jakob Handte v Soc Traîtements Mécano-chimiques des Surfaces* [1992] ECR I-3967 ; Case C-543/10 *Refcomp SpA v Axa Corporate Solutions Assurance SA* [2013] ECR I-(Feb 7).

[41] *Carlill v Carbolic Smoke Ball Co* [1893] 1 QB 256 (CA).

[42] *Gibbons v Proctor* (1891) 64 LT 594.

[43] *Upton-on-Severn RDC v Powell* [1942] 1 All ER 220.

[44] Such as where an offer is made to the world for acceptance without the need for communication, or where the offer is made to a single promisee, but without restraint on assignment.

immaterial to its characterization. But it does entail the conclusion that the claim of the sub-buyer to enforce the original seller's obligations against him might yet be contractual for choice of law purposes.[45] So also will be an obligation undertaken with the deliberate intention that it be enforceable by a non-party: there is no reason to suppose that after the partial abolition of the English doctrine of privity of contract,[46] consensual obligations enforceable by non-parties will be excluded.

(b) 'Obligations'

The Giuliano–Lagarde report stated that gifts were included within its scope of the Rome Convention where they are seen as contractual: this will also be true for the Rome I Regulation. This may be, if only at first sight, a curious proposition for an English lawyer.[47] It does, however, underline the rather different contours of the autonomous conception of contract. The sense in which gifts give rise to promissory obligations is obscure, especially as the Regulation does not apply to the constitution of trusts,[48] but a challenge to the validity of an assignment of an intangible done by way of gift will be within the choice of law regime of the Regulation, at which point the inclusion of gifts begins to make rather more sense.[49] There may be requirements of formal validity; if there is a right to revoke a gift on account of ingratitude,[50] perhaps this right (or the obligation to be grateful to a donor) is contractual.

Property rights, not being part of the law of obligations, are excluded from the scope of the Regulation. So the regulation of intellectual property lies outside the scope of the Regulation, although contracts to create or transfer such property will be within it, in just the same way as are contracts to transfer land and cars. A more troublesome question arises in connection with the assignment of intangible movable property in general, such as shares,

---

[45] Not least in the case where the rights of the buyer are voluntarily assigned to the sub-buyer; cf Art 14.

[46] Contracts (Rights of Third Parties) Act 1999.

[47] [1980] OJ C282/1, 10.

[48] Article 1(2)(h).

[49] *Gorjat v Gorjat* [2010] EWHC 1537 (Ch).

[50] A rule which would greatly contribute to the civilization of teenagers.

policies of insurance, contractual debts, and so forth. There is a respectable view that all these are property, albeit that they were created by a contract, and that their status as property is separate and distinct from the contract which created them: a contract may well be needed to give birth to the right, but once this act of creation has taken place what results is a right of property which can be bought, sold, mis-sold, mortgaged, pledged, assigned, alienated, bequeathed, confiscated, discharged, interfered with, and obtained by deception. From this it follows, so the argument runs, that the legal relationships thus created, at least between donor and donee, or assignor and assignee, are proprietary and are not contractual, and that the issue of what law governs dealings with these rights is therefore not governed by the Rome I Regulation.

The difficulties presented by this argument arise on two levels. True, the process conveniently[51] regarded as transfer or assignment of some forms of intangibles, such as shares and intellectual property rights, is undeniably proprietary and is distinct from any contract which created them. And in English law, and perhaps in others, there are many contexts, of which insolvency is certainly one, where it is convenient for contractual debts to be regarded as property rights. But the view that there is a difference between owning a debt (which is a statement made in proprietary language) and being owed a debt (which is expressed in contractual language) requires the fiery certainty of faith, for it looks awfully like an illusion: the question of who owns a debt is the same as the question to whom the debt is now owed, and there is no easy way in which the two can be separated so as to make a distinction between them. At a more general level, it is easy to see the distinction between contract and property where, in the real world, the conclusion of a contract will be followed by delivery or conveyance; but when dealing with simple contractual obligations there is no clearly separate item to regard as 'intangible property'. The whole of the question may be contractual, there being neither need nor room for a separate property; after the

---

[51] But not always accurately: in the case of some, such as registered shares, there is no transfer or assignment of the shares. As far as the technicalities go, there is a surrender to and re-grant by the company, but no actual assignment of shares from the former to the new shareholder.

contract has been executed, nothing remains to be done;[52] it is difficult to accept that we are dealing with things rather than obligations when the 'property' is a simple contractual debt. But even if that were not so, Article 14 of the Rome I Regulation contains a rule to deal with choice of law for the voluntary assignment of contractual obligations. Although it extends only to the single question of which law governs the assignment of such rights, it overrides any objection that a contractual choice of law rule is inapplicable to an issue which the Rome I Regulation considers, as did the Convention before it, as contractual. There is therefore no basis for excluding the assignment of contractual rights from the scope of the Rome I Regulation; the law which governs their assignment is that specified by Article 14 of the Regulation.[53]

(c) Concurrent obligations

In some contexts—in the field of employment law[54] and in the provision of professional services,[55] for example—English domestic law permits a claimant to frame his claim concurrently in contract and in tort, or to elect between them; and the common law approach to private international law was understood to allow this as well. Despite the view of the Court of Appeal that this approach was consistent with the Rome Convention,[56] it was not clear that it really was. For if the claimant formulates in tort a claim which would otherwise have fallen within the four corners of what is now the Rome I Regulation—he alleges that his employer breached the common duty of care, rather than pleading a broken contractual promise to take care; he alleges carelessness on the part of the company from which he bought his holiday,

---

[52] Except, perhaps, notification to the debtor. See *Raiffeisen Zentralbank Österreich AG v Five Star Trading LLC* [2001] EWCA Civ 68, [2001] QB 825. See also p 308 below.

[53] The content of the rule is examined in Ch 7 below. An intense debate, which began in 2005 and which is continuing, took place within the negotiations to settle the terms of the Rome I Regulation. In the event, no change could be agreed to, and it was decided to return to the question after everything else in the Rome I Regulation had been agreed to.

[54] cf *Coupland v Arabian Gulf Oil Co* [1983] 1 WLR 1151 (CA).

[55] *Henderson v Merrett Syndicates Ltd* [1995] 2 AC 145.

[56] *Base Metal Trading Ltd v Shamurin* [2004] EWCA Civ 1316, [2005] 1 WLR 1157.

rather than pleading a broken contract to exercise skill and care; he alleges negligent misstatement on the part of his investment adviser, rather than a breach of a contractual promise to use reasonable care and skill—it means that a claim between two contracting parties, capable of falling within the material scope of the Regulation, may be subjected to a law other than that specified by the Regulation, with the result that the seemingly mandatory words of Article 1 will have been by-passed. A similar argument could be advanced if a claimant were to elect to enforce fiduciary duties owed by his counter-party, rather than the contract between them.[57] The traditional[58] common law approach that a claimant is free to elect how to formulate his claim, and that this freedom continues in full force and effect, with the Rome I and Rome II Regulations applying only after this freedom has been exercised, cannot be considered as sound.[59] It reflects a view which is not common across all the Member States and it will therefore perturb the uniform application of the Rome I Regulation. It would certainly be ameliorated if any claim formulated as based on a non-contractual obligation were, by the Rome II Regulation, governed by the law which applied to the contract with which it was closely associated, but the proposition that a claimant may choose his choice of law may not be how the Regulations work. After all, the special jurisdictional rules of the Brussels I Regulation provide in effect that if the claim is one which does relate to a contract, it may not be repackaged so as to be brought under or take advantage of the special jurisdictional rule for torts.[60] It would be surprising if this approach was not reflected in the relationship between the choice of law rules of the Rome I and Rome II Regulations.[61]

---

[57] Assuming for present purposes (but see Ch 6 below) that there is a different choice of law rule for claims based on fiduciary duties. For the conclusion that there is not, reference should be made to the actual result, as distinct from the reasoning, in *Base Metal Trading Ltd v Shamurin*.

[58] Although this is not exactly what it seems, for there is also a general view that concurrency as between the principles of common law and equity is not conducive to the rational development of the law: see Burrows (2002) 22 OxJLS 1.

[59] If it were a procedural matter, but which it surely cannot be, it would be unaffected by the Regulation: Art 1(3).

[60] See p 86 above.

[61] cf recital 7.

(d) Excluded issues

The Regulation does not apply to revenue, customs, or administrative matters. It will, however, apply to a contract by which A agrees to reimburse B for discharging customs duties for which A was liable, as the obligation relied on as the foundation of the claim is an ordinary contractual one, and relies on no principle of customs law to support it.[62]

The Regulation eschews any authority over choice of law for the matters set out in Article 1(2), and to these the appropriate choice of law rule must be found elsewhere: in other European legislation, or in default of that, in the common law rules of conflict of laws. Many of these matters would not be seen as contractual in any event, so Article 1(2) largely confirms what would already have been known without it. They are: status and the capacity of natural persons;[63] obligations arising out of family and analogous relationships, including maintenance;[64] obligations arising out of matrimonial property regimes, also wills and succession;[65] obligations arising from bills of exchange and promissory notes and other negotiable instruments where the obligations arise from their negotiable character;[66] questions governed by the law of companies, such as creation, capacity, and winding-up;[67] the question whether

---

[62] Case C-266/01 *Préservatrice Foncière TIARD SA v Netherlands* [2003] ECR I-4867.

[63] Article 1(2)(a); though this is subject to Art 13; see below.

[64] Article 1(2)(b). Maintenance will generally be covered by the Maintenance Regulation, Regulation 4/2009, [2009] OJ L7/1.

[65] Article 1(2)(c). Succession to the estates of those who die after 17 August 2015 will fall, for most Member States, within Regulation (EU) 650/2012, [2012] OJ L201/107. But this day is some way off, and in any event the United Kingdom has expressed its decision not to be bound by it. Common law choice of law rules will therefore apply. Negotiations toward the adoption of a matrimonial property Regulation led to a proposal from the Commission (COM(2011) 126, 16 March 2011), but no further. In default of legislation, common law choice of law rules will therefore apply.

[66] Article 1(2)(d). But contracts pursuant to which these instruments are issued are not excluded: [1980] OJ C282/1, 10.

[67] Article 1(2)(f). In many cases these issues will be referred to the *lex incorporationis*. It is possible that the liability of a director to the company for wrongful acts or breaches of his duties to the company, whether fiduciary or otherwise, will therefore be excluded from Rome I (and therefore also from Rome II) by this rule; cf *Base Metal Trading Ltd v Shamurin* [2004] EWCA Civ 1316, [2005] 1 WLR 1157.

an agent can bind a principal, or an organ bind the company, in relation to a third party;[68] the constitution and internal relationships of trusts;[69] obligations arising out of dealings prior to the conclusion of the contract;[70] a very specific category of insurance contracts;[71] and evidence and procedure.[72] Although the Rome Convention excluded insurance where the risk was situated in the territory of the European Union, this exclusion is not carried forward into the Rome I Regulation.

Where choice of law in relation to any of these issues arises for decision in an English court, choice of law rules specified by other European Regulations will apply if there are any; in default of such legislation, common law conflict of law rules will continue to apply. As explained in the chapters where they arise for examination: as a matter of common law, the *lex domicilii* has a dominant role in relation to wills, succession, and family matters; the *lex situs* in relation to negotiable instruments; the *lex incorporationis* in relation to companies; the proper law of the trust in relation to trusts; and the *lex fori* over issues of evidence and procedure: none of these was traditionally seen as a contractual issue, and their exclusion from the Rome I Regulation is not surprising. In relation to the power of an agent to bind a principal to a third party, the exclusion was probably brought about by the complexity of the issue and the irreconcilable differences between the common law and civilian analyses of agency; but it will remain open to the common law conflict of law rules to decide that this issue is governed by the law which governs the contract of agency, which may in turn be identified by the Rome I Regulation. For though the Regulation makes no claim to govern this issue it does not

---

[68] Article 1(2)(g). But in so far as they are contractual, relations between principal and agent and agent and third party are not excluded as such: [1980] OJ C282/1, 13. Though see fn 70 below.

[69] Article 1(2)(h).

[70] Article 1(2)(i): the Rome II Regulation will apply. This may now be a better place for claims of breach of warranty of authority: cf *Golden Ocean Group Ltd v Salgaocar Mining Industries Pvt Ltd* [2012] EWCA Civ 265, [2012] 3 All ER 842, decided under the Rome Convention which did not contain a specific exclusion in these terms.

[71] Article 1(2)(j).

[72] Article 1(3).

prevent a national law taking that step in the exercise of its own legal authority.

In the same way, although Article 1(2)(e) excludes agreements on arbitration and choice of court from the domain of the Regulation,[73] the common law takes the view that these are usually terms of a larger contract, usually assessed for their validity by the law which governs the larger contract of which they are a part, that law usually (though not always) serving as the 'proper law' of the arbitration or jurisdiction agreement.[74] An agreement on jurisdiction or arbitration will generally be valid if effective under its proper law, and not if not. The *lex fori* can in certain cases override this answer: by denying effect to an agreement valid under its proper law[75] or by regarding as valid an agreement invalid and ineffective under its proper law.[76] Indeed, the reason for this exclusion from the material scope of the Regulation is that under the laws of many countries, the validity of such agreements is seen as a procedural matter, concerned with allocation of jurisdiction as a matter of public law, and not a private contractual one (and in the case of arbitration, principally regulated by specialist international convention). But again, the Regulation presents no obstacle to common law private international law deciding on its own authority to treat jurisdiction and arbitration agreements as being governed by the law which applies to the contract in which they are found, and this therefore remains the position in England.

---

[73] Although they may be taken into account in the determination of the governing law.

[74] See *Sulamerica Compania Nacional de Seguros SA v Enesa Engenharia SA* [2012] EWCA Civ 638, [2012] 2 All ER (Comm) 795. The 'proper law' is the term which was used at common law to signify the law by which the validity of the contract was tested, and is used in this context to acknowledge that the identification of the law which governs a jurisdiction or arbitration agreement is a matter for the common law rules of the conflict of laws.

[75] See *The Hollandia* [1983] 1 AC 565 (which would be decided differently today) on the Carriage of Goods by Sea Act 1971; and the provisions of the Brussels I Regulation controlling jurisdiction agreements in insurance, consumer, and employment contracts.

[76] cf Case 25/79 *Sanicentral GmbH v Collin* [1979] ECR 3423, where what is now Art 23 of the Brussels I Regulation overrode a rule of the proper law which denied that a jurisdiction agreement could oust the jurisdiction of the employment tribunals.

Because the status of a person is predominantly the concern of the law of the domicile, so generally is her capacity. Contractual capacity, as a distinct part of the broader question is, according to the common law conflict of laws, satisfied if the person had capacity either by the law of the country with which the contract was most closely connected or by the law of her domicile.[77] But the Regulation intrudes on this in one respect. Article 13 provides that where two individuals make a contract in the same country, and one later relies on a personal incapacity according to some other law to plead the invalidity of that contract, she may do so only if the other party was, or should have been, aware of it. For corporations, the existence and extent of contractual capacity is a matter for the *lex incorporationis*. But the legal effect, if any, of a contract made by a corporation without capacity to do so is a matter for the *lex contractus*.

2. *LEX CONTRACTUS* (1) CHOICE MADE BY THE PARTIES

Article 3 of the Regulation provides that a contract is governed by the law chosen by the parties, provided that this choice is express or may be clearly demonstrated[78] by the terms of the contract or the circumstances of the case. In every contract falling within the domain of the Regulation the parties are at liberty to choose the governing law, and in every case except for contracts for the carriage of passengers[79] and certain kinds of contract of insurance,[80] for which cases the menu of laws which may be chosen is restricted, they may choose a law which has no other connection to the facts of the contract. The only qualification stated in Article 3, that where all other elements relevant to the situation at the time of choice are located in a country other than that which has been chosen,

---

[77] *Charron v Montreal Trust Co* (1958) 15 DLR (2d) 240 (Ont CA).

[78] The Rome Convention had referred instead to this version of choice being 'demonstrated with reasonable certainty', which may mean that the test has become slightly more stringent.

[79] Article 5(2).

[80] Article 7(3). In the negotiations leading to the conclusion of the Regulation, it had also been proposed that a free choice of law should not be possible for consumer contracts, but this was not agreed to.

the choice of the parties shall not prejudice the application of provisions of the law of that country which cannot be derogated from by agreement, is so unlikely to be satisfied in real life that it is more apparent than real. But if two English residents purport to make a contract to gift a bicycle, and purport to choose the law of Scotland to circumvent the English doctrine of consideration, theirs would be the first reported awakening of this provision, which may therefore be put to one side and left undisturbed.

The parties may choose different laws for separate parts of the contract and, so far as the Regulation is concerned, may alter the governing law at any time. The Regulation adopts the principle of party autonomy: indeed, in the recitals it refers to the parties' freedom to choose the law as 'one of the cornerstones' of the rules for choice of law in matters of contractual obligation.[81] The Regulation draws certain conclusions from it, allowing a choice to be decisive except only in relation to limited and clearly specified matters;[82] but it makes two requirements: the choice must actually be made, and that choice must be expressed or be so clearly demonstrable from the contract or the circumstances of the case that it did not require further expression. This will preclude the argument that the parties, as reasonable people, 'must have' made a choice but which they did not trouble to express, or 'would have been bound to agree' on the governing law. The freedom to choose is a freedom which must be affirmatively exercised; like all freedoms, if it is not exercised it will be lost.

A choice expressed in the form 'this contract shall be governed by the law of France' will be effective to make French law the governing law; and a less artful choice, such as 'this contract shall be construed in accordance with French law', will probably be taken the same way. Life is easier when parties take advantage of the freedom to choose and express that choice clearly: Article 3 helps those who help themselves. But one could be forgiven for thinking that some draftsmen regard a clear expression of choice as being just too easy, rejecting it for something more likely to generate work for the litigation department. A choice of the law of the United Kingdom, or of British law, for example, cannot

---

[81] Recital 11.
[82] Examined below.

be given effect according to its terms, because there is no such law to be chosen; and to interpret this as an express choice of English law is to make an assumption which is almost always factually correct[83] if politically incorrect.

Article 3 is capable of validating a purported choice which is expressed formulaically, such as where the contract is expressed to be governed 'by the law of the place where the carrier has its principal place of business'. If there is no dispute about these identifiers, the expression of choice will be effective. But there may be genuine disagreement about who (shipowner, charterer) is the carrier, or which is the principal place (of day-to-day decision-taking, of supervision and overall direction) of business.[84] If ever it were to matter, the governing law will be charged with answering these questions, for they go to the interpretation[85] of a term of the contract. The trouble arises where answers to these questions are required in order to identify the governing law in the first place. Although the European Court has held, in the context of the Brussels I Regulation, that a provision in such terms may be effective as an agreement on jurisdiction,[86] this presupposes that the court seised has been able to identify the geographical place which is referred to. But if one asks the simple question whether these words choose a law, either expressly or in a way which can be said to be clearly demonstrated from the terms of the contract or the circumstances of the case, the answer may be that they do not. It is no help to say that, as a matter of English law, the carrier will be regarded as the charterer, or the principal place of business that from which day-to-day control is exercised: the Rome I Regulation is meant to operate independently of national law, and to be a full, complete, and sufficient code for the identification of the governing law. From that point of view, some forms of words, although superficially intelligible, do not achieve it.

When the choice of law was being determined by the application of common law principles, in cases in which the parties had not mentioned a choice of law but selected English

---

[83] cf *The Komninos S* [1991] 1 Lloyd's Rep 370 (CA).

[84] *The Rewia* [1991] 2 Lloyd's Rep 325 (CA).

[85] Article 12(1)(a).

[86] Case C-387/98 *Coreck Maritime GmbH v Handelsveem BV* [2000] ECR I-9337.

jurisdiction, this was not understood as an unequivocal and express choice of English law but would be taken to be of equivalent effect unless substantially all the other factors in the case came together in pointing to another law.[87] But where the question is whether parties who make such a choice have brought themselves within Article 3, the Regulation offers surprisingly poor guidance. It is said[88] that a contractual choice for the courts of a Member State, giving them exclusive jurisdiction, 'should be one of the factors taken into account in determining whether a choice of law has been clearly demonstrated'. This is surprisingly unhelpful: words like 'should be', 'one of', and 'whether' are bound to leave the national court guessing as to the real intention of the European legislator, and only the clarification of the European Court can rescue the situation. In the meantime, it is probably a safe prediction that an English court, needing to arrive at a decision of some sort, will fall back on the common law to reach it; and whatever else may be right, this cannot be considered as best practice. The better course, but which involves paying little attention to recital 12, is to regard the choice of court as playing a part within the framework of Article 4, the case not being one falling within Article 3 at all. That said, if the parties contract on the basis of a standard form, which is known in the trade as being founded on English law, this may be a case in which the parties' actual choice may be deduced from the terms of the contract or the circumstances of the case.[89]

(a) Split, deferred, and altered choices

Although it allowed for freedom to choose the proper law of a contract, the common law was reluctant to permit two laws to govern different parts of the contract, no doubt to avoid the risk of contradiction which might arise from allowing it. And it denied the validity of an agreement to defer until later the making of an actual choice of law: it was not open to the parties to specify that no choice of law was to be made until, at some point

---

[87] *Compagnie Tunisienne de Navigation SA v Compagnie d'Armement Maritime SA* [1971] AC 572.

[88] Recital 12.

[89] Giuliano-Lagarde Report [1980] OJ C282/1, 17.

after the formation of the contract, one party nominated it.[90] Such a 'floating' choice of law was axiomatically precluded, on the footing that if a contract must be a source of obligation from its inception, the absence of a governing law would mean that it contained no mechanism to impose any obligations. But there appeared to be no obstacle to prevent the parties changing the proper law: if it was open to them to vary the contract, it must surely have been open to amend their choice of law as well.[91]

The position under the Regulation is simpler and more complex. Proceeding from the view that the parties are permitted to exercise freedom of choice, it is provided that they may agree to have separate parts of the contract governed by different laws.[92] They may agree to alter the governing law at any time.[93] It is implicit, perhaps even explicit, that a purported variation is validated by the text of the Regulation itself, and that this must override any contrary indication from the law originally chosen to govern which, therefore, cannot be 'locked in'. It is less clear whether the parties may assume restrictions or conditions on the choice of a replacement law to govern their contract, whether in terms of time or country. A pragmatic answer would be that if the parties agree today to alter the governing law for a contract made some time ago, there is no reason to impugn their exercise of choice. Where by contrast they do not act together in this way, and one of them acts pursuant to a power conferred by the contract to nominate a replacement law to govern the contract, the nomination must comply with the conditions laid down in the contract itself.

It is not clear from the Regulation whether the parties may choose not to have a law at the outset. Logic suggests a negative answer, for a contract without a law makes no more sense under the Regulation than it did under the common law;[94] but if in default of choice the governing law is initially supplied by Article 4, there will be no problem: if they agree to change it

---

[90] *Armar Shipping Co Ltd v Caisse Algérienne d'Assurance* [1981] 1 WLR 207 (CA).

[91] *Whitworth Street Estates (Manchester) Ltd v James Miller & Partners Ltd* [1970] AC 583.

[92] Article 3(1).

[93] Article 3(2).

[94] *Amin Rasheed Shipping Corpn v Kuwait Insurance Co* [1984] AC 50.

later, they may; and if they cannot agree, then it will remain governed by whatever Article 4 provided as governing law.

(b) The meaning of 'law'

According to the Regulation, 'law' means the domestic law of the country chosen by the rules of the Regulation.[95] This has a number of consequences. First, certain items which the parties may have wished to choose and express are not on the menu. The Regulation limits the choice which may be made to the law of a country, or to state law.[96] This in turn excludes the possibility of choosing the *lex mercatoria*, as well as the principles, whether or not regarded by adherents as law, of a religion or other cult. The parties may have what they conceive to be sound personal or business reasons for wishing their contractual relationship to be governed by Jewish law,[97] or sharia law,[98] or the *lex mercatoria*, or whatever else, but if they say so they still cannot expect to have this choice given effect by a court: if they want adjudication in accordance with this material, they are free,[99] but also need, to provide for arbitration before a tribunal of their designation. Quite apart from the fact that the courts are not likely to be equipped to deal with the proof and reliable application of this kind of stuff, allowing any role for non-state law would be incoherent in cases falling within Article 4, considered below. Take for example a contract made between two members of the Muslim community in England, in circumstances in which both were keen to comply with the principles of Islamic finance. That contract may be closely connected to England, as the country in which they reside, and with the sharia as the social value system to which they adhere. Given that the contract could not be governed by both 'laws', which would govern it? Could the contract be said to

---

[95] Provision has been made, in Art 23 and recital 14, to allow the parties to choose a set of rules which may be made by the Community as an 'optional instrument'. This is liable to cause trouble unless the instrument is as comprehensive in its coverage as is the law of a Member State.

[96] Article 2 and recital 13.

[97] *Halpern v Halpern* [2007] EWCA Civ 291, [2007] 2 Lloyd's Rep 56.

[98] *Beximco Pharmaceuticals Ltd v Shamil Bank of Bahrain EC* [2004] EWCA Civ 19, [2004] 1 WLR 1784.

[99] *Jivraj v Hashwani* [2011] UKSC 40, [2011] 1 WLR 1872.

have a closer connection to the one than to the other? The impossibility of answering the question means that the Regulation has to exclude the possibility of a non-state law governing at all, while allowing parties who wish to do so to incorporate as terms the principles (assuming them to be sufficiently clear to serve as terms) of a non-state body of rules as terms of the contract.[100] It is not a bad solution; all others would be far worse.

The restriction to a choice of domestic law is deduced from the fact that the possibility of *renvoi* to the law of another country is precluded by Article 20: of course, if the law of the country which they have chosen would apply, as part of itself, the rules of a text such as the Vienna Convention on Contracts for the International Sale of Goods, this does not involve a *renvoi* to the law of another country, rather the application of the appropriate chapter of the law of the country chosen.[101] The general justification for this rejection lies in the pragmatic argument that if the parties went to the trouble of choosing a law it would be unlikely to the point of perversity for them to have chosen anything other than the domestic law of the nominated country, and if they were so perverse as to choose anything else, there is no good reason to indulge them. Where they have not chosen and expressed their choice, they may have been perfectly content to accept a default option; but for this version of the governing law to mean something different would be unacceptable. One might question the wisdom of excluding *renvoi* in the case where the parties have not chosen a law but have chosen a forum for adjudication. Common law orthodoxy, which some may consider to have influenced the Regulation,[102] is that this is a pretty powerful indicator of choice for the domestic law of the court chosen. This looks odd, for what it clearly is is a clear and unambiguous choice for whatever law the court at the place

---

[100] *Halpern v Halpern* [2007] EWCA Civ 291, [2007] 2 Lloyd's Rep 56. But there is nothing to prevent a choice of the law of a country which has chosen to incorporate into it the principles of a non-state system, whether secular, conventional, or superstitious.

[101] To put it another way, Vienna is not a country, and the Convention is not the law of Vienna. See also *Dallah Real Estate & Tourism Holding Co v Pakistan* [2010] UKSC 46, [2011] AC 763.

[102] Giuliano-Lagarde Report [1980] OJ C282/1, 17.

of trial would itself have applied. But this pattern of reasoning is apparently precluded by Article 20.

3. *LEX CONTRACTUS* (2) ABSENCE OF EXPRESS CHOICE

Leaving aside for the moment the four categories of contract for which particular provision is made, and which are considered below, Article 4 provides the governing law in cases in which that law has not been chosen and expressed in accordance with Article 3. By contrast with its predecessor in the Rome Convention, which had opened with the statement that the governing law was the law of the country with which the contract is most closely connected, Article 4 of the Regulation provides, first, a more detailed and specific identification of governing law by reference to categories of contract, and then, second, an escape clause. It is designed to make the identification of the governing law in cases in which the parties have not made and expressed a choice more predictable than it will have been under the Rome Convention, and though the solution is not perfect, it is really rather sensible. A 'basic rule with escape clause' scheme may well be easier and more manageable than a single rule which is, at first sight, more elegant, but which risks asking a question to which no really clear answer, or for the solution of which no clear and learnable technique, can be given.

The default rules are set out in Article 4(1). For contracts which may be identified by a particular kind of performance it makes specific provision for the governing law. In general terms, it appears that the person whose performance under the contract will 'identify' the contract is the person whose place of habitual residence identifies the governing law.[103] As to the meaning of habitual residence, a partial definition is provided by Article 19, which assists with the identification of a person's habitual residence, but also attempts to iron out divergences in interpretation between Member State courts. The starting point is that habitual residence is assessed as at the date on which the contract was concluded. For a natural person not acting in the course of business, no further definition

---

[103] It may be argued that the contract is (in English at least) named after, or designated by, the party whose performance is stated in Art 4(1).

is given. For a natural person acting in the course of his business activity, it will be his principal place of business; for a company or other body, it is the place of central administration; and where the contract is concluded in the course of operation of a branch or agency (or if under the contract, performance is the responsibility of a branch or agency), the place where the branch or agency is located will be the place of habitual residence.

The drafting makes for a somewhat cumbersome set of individual rules, but as a point of departure it is perfectly sensible. To descend to the particulars, contracts for the sale of goods,[104] contracts for the provision of services, franchise contracts, and distribution contracts will be governed by the law of the country in which the seller, supplier, franchisee, and distributor has his habitual residence. For contracts concerning land, the *lex situs* is predictably dominant. So a contract relating to a right *in rem* in land, or a tenancy of land, is governed by the law of the country in which the land is situated; by way of exception, a short private letting taken by a tenant who is a natural person is governed by the law of the country in which landlord and tenant have their habitual residence, but if this condition is not met, the earlier rule applies.

Where the contract is more complex, in the sense that it would fall within two of these special rules, such as a contract for the supply and installation of goods, or where it falls within none of these rules, such as with a contract of barter, Article 4(2) provides that it will be governed by law of the country in which the person whose performance is characteristic of the contract is habitually resident:[105] it is only at this point that the Regulation adopts what was the general rule in the predecessor Convention. The identification of a performance as characteristic will, in these cases, be relatively difficult, and this rule may have little real scope: under a contract of barter, the obligations of each party mirror each other. The reason is that the usual examples which exemplify the idea of characteristic performance are those of sale (it is the seller, not the buyer) and supply (it is the supply, not the

---

[104] But where the sale is by auction, the governing law will be the law of the place of the auction if this is capable of being determined.

[105] If the contract falls within two categories, but each would have pointed to the same law, the answer will be easy to arrive at.

receipt). These cases being covered by the more specific rules in Article 4(1), there may not be much for this rule to cover.

So much for the first or general part of Article 4. Article 4 then provides escape clauses for two cases: where these rules yield the 'wrong' answer, and where they yield no answer at all. If the contract is manifestly more closely connected to a country other than that identified by the rules just described, Article 4(3) provides that the law of that other country shall apply as the governing law; and where the law which governs the contract cannot be ascertained from the rules just described, Article 4(4) provides that the contract shall be governed by the law of the country with which it is most closely connected.[106] The framework within which the governing law is identified in the absence of an express choice is firmly based on the identification of connections and points of contact to *countries*, rather than on connections to *laws*: once the connection to a country has been ascertained, the law of that country applies to govern the contract.[107] This may mean that although a contract would be seen to be most closely connected to English *law*, it may still be more closely connected to another *country*, and it will be the latter which identifies the governing law. However, in considering these escape clauses, and by textual contrast with the predecessor Convention, recital 21 to the Regulation tells the court that it may properly examine whether the contract in question has a close relationship with another contract, the law of which other contract may exercise a gravitational pull over the question of governing law.[108] So where the case is one involving connected contracts, such as a bill of lading and contracts made in accordance with it,[109] or letters of credit

---

[106] Case C-133/08 *Intercontainer Interfrigo SC v Balkenende Oosthuizen BV* [2009] ECR I-9687.

[107] *Crédit Lyonnais v New Hampshire Insurance Co* [1997] 2 Lloyd's Rep 1 (CA). The fact that the parties 'would have chosen' a different law if they had made a choice, which they did not, should not trigger the application of Art 4(3): *Lawlor v Sandvik Mining & Construction Mobile Crushers & Screens Ltd* [2012] EWHC 1188 (QB), [2012] 2 Lloyd's Rep 25 (a case on the Rome Convention).

[108] Recital 20 to the Regulation; *British Arab Commercial Bank plc v Bank of Communications* [2011] EWHC 281 (Comm), [2011] 1 Lloyd's Rep 664.

[109] *The Mahkutai* [1996] AC 650 (PC).

or of comfort, issued as part of a larger financial transaction,[110] or contracts of reinsurance made back-to-back with contracts of insurance,[111] in which an express choice of law is made in some but not all contracts, common sense would say that all were probably intended to be governed by the same law, to prevent the dislocation which would otherwise be risked. The statement in the recitals now provides cover and justification for a court which wishes to follow that line of reasoning.

Where a court is called upon to evaluate degrees of connection to a particular country, it is debatable how precisely these are to be assessed. The common law developed an informal hierarchy of connection, so that the place of arbitration was seen as a strong connection, the places of domicile of the parties as weakish ones, and the others arranged along the spectrum between the two. This was probably based on an unarticulated reflection of how far, if at all, each allowed the court to read something of the parties' minds as regards intended proper law. If this is correct, it will be inapplicable in the context of Article 4, where the search is not for clues to intention as to law, but for connections to a country, where intention is not relevant.

Article 4(3) is seen by some as having the potential to undermine the system intended to be made predictable by Article 4(1). The general question is what is meant by the contract being, from all the circumstances of the case, 'manifestly more closely connected' to another country. In a case dealing with the predecessor rule in Article 4(5) of the Rome Convention the European Court,[112] in apparent rejection of a stringent view found in Dutch[113] and Scottish[114] case law, but aligning itself more obviously with an English approach to the effect that the escape clause would apply when and whenever there was good reason for it to do so,[115] said

---

[110] *Bank of Baroda v Vysya Bank Ltd* [1994] 2 Lloyd's Rep 87.

[111] cf *Forsikringsaktieselskapet Vesta v Butcher* [1989] AC 852, where the contracts were governed by different laws.

[112] Case C-133/08 *Intercontainer Interfrigo SC v Balkenende Oosthuizen BV* [2009] ECR I-9687.

[113] *Soc Nouvelle des Papéteries de l'Aa v BV Machinefabriek BOA* (25 September 1992).

[114] *Caledonia Subsea Ltd v Microperi Srl* 2003 SC 70.

[115] Which actually came close to saying nothing at all: see *Samcrete Egypt Engineers and Contractors SAE v Land Rover Exports Ltd* [2001] EWCA Civ 2019, [2002] CLC 533; *Ennstone Building Products Ltd v Stanger Ltd* [2002] EWCA Civ

that a finding that another country was more closely connected was all that was required to permit a court to use the escape clause of the Convention. No doubt this decision will, in the interests of legal certainty, continue to be taken seriously, though as the current version of the escape cause includes the word 'manifestly', and as the rules in Article 4(1) and 4(2) of the Regulation which are to be escaped from are formulated in rather more careful detail than was the case before, it is natural to suppose that there will be rather less escaping from the governing law identified by Article 4(1) in particular.

At common law it was occasionally said that a presumption of validity meant that where the issues were finely balanced, a contract should be governed by a law under which it would be valid.[116] The legitimacy of such a presumption was debatable, but could be defended as reflecting the presumed intention of the parties. There is therefore no obvious basis for including such a presumption where Article 4 of the Regulation identifies the governing law, and party intention has no formal role.

4. *LEX CONTRACTUS* (3): SPECIFIC CONTRACTS

Although a choice of law made by the parties which satisfies Article 3 cannot[117] be denied effect there are certain contracts, and other issues, for which the rules of another system of domestic law may be superimposed so as to limit the hegemony of the *lex contractus*. It is also worth making it plain at this point that there are certain contracts where, if the parties do not make an express choice of law, Article 4 does not supply the governing law. There are four kinds of contract for which special legislative provision is made.

916, [2002] 1 WLR 3059; *Ophthalmic Innovations International Ltd v Ophthalmic Innovations International Inc* [2004] EWHC 2948 (Ch), [2005] ILPr 109.

[116] For example, *Coast Lines Ltd v Hudig and Veder Chartering NV* [1972] 2 QB 34, 44, 48 (CA).

[117] Save for certain prohibited choices in the context of contracts for the case of carriage of passengers and certain contracts of insurance, considered below.

(a) Contracts for carriage

Article 5 makes modifications to the general rules for the identification of the governing law in a contract of carriage. If the contract is one for the carriage of goods, the parties are free to choose any law to govern their contract, but if they do not exercise that freedom, a somewhat convoluted, but mainly carrier-focused rule, applies.[118] If the contract is one for the carriage of passengers, the range of laws which may be chosen is limited to five: the country of the habitual residence of passenger or of carrier, the country in which the carrier has his or its central administration, or the countries of the place of departure and of destination.[119] This is, no doubt, to prevent the selection of the law of a country which allows carriers to evade their proper responsibilities. If no such choice is made, the law of the country of the passenger's habitual residence will apply if either the place of departure or of destination was in that country; if not, the country where the carrier has habitual residence will apply. If the contract is manifestly more closely connected to another country, the law of that other country shall apply.

It is obvious that there may be contracts which do not fall neatly into this framework, such as contracts which contain multiple obligations, such as a cruise-and-hotel package,[120] or a contract for carriage by sea and rail. It seems that such cases will be approached as though each element in the contractual package is discrete for the purposes of choice of law, at least if they can be regarded as independent obligations;[121] if they are not independent, then in principle the law which governs the contract of carriage will govern the whole of the contract. But it would be wrong to be too clear or confident as to how this will actually work in practice.

(b) Certain consumer contracts

Article 6 makes modifications to the general rules for the identification of the governing law in certain consumer contracts. It

---

[118] Article 5(1).
[119] Article 5(2).
[120] cf Article 6(4)(b).
[121] cf Case C-133/08 *Intercontainer Interfrigo SC v Balkenende Oosthuizen BV* [2009] ECR I-9687.

is probably fair to say that the current wording of Article 6 is as untidy and problematic as it is because it was a compromise between views and interest groups which were polarized; the same could be said of its rather different predecessor in the Rome Convention. It is well to be aware, especially as the provision is expressed in oddly grudging language, that the parties may choose any law to govern their contract even though it is a consumer contract.

A consumer contract for the purpose of Article 6 is defined negatively and positively. Negatively,[122] it excludes a contract of carriage[123] and contracts of insurance, for which special rules are provided elsewhere.[124] It also excludes a contract for sale or rent of land other than timeshare-use contract, as well as a contract for the supply of services to a consumer exclusively in a country other than that in which he has his habitual residence. Positively, it includes a contract concluded between a natural person for a purpose outside his trade or profession with another person who is acting within his or its trade or profession; and the parties to such a contract are designated as consumer and professional respectively.

If that threshold condition is met, the identification of governing law then depends on whether the professional pursues his commercial or professional activities in the country of the consumer's habitual residence, or if he by any means—which certainly includes electronic means—directs his activities to that country or to several countries including that country. If the professional does do so, and if the contract falls within the scope of such activities, then unless a law has been chosen to govern it, the contract will be governed by the law of the country in which the consumer has his habitual residence. Indeed, if a law has been chosen to govern such a contract, the choice may not deprive the consumer of legal protection which would have been afforded to him by the law which would have applied if there had been no such choice, though for this to be so, the protective rule in question must be one which may not be derogated from

---

[122] Article 6(4).

[123] Other than a package holiday: Art 6(4)(b). Certain financial contracts are also excluded: Art 6(4)(d), (e).

[124] This exclusion is explained in recital 32.

by agreement, or contracted out of, as one might say in English. But if by contrast these 'directing' conditions are not satisfied, choice of law is determined in accordance with Articles 3 and 4.

It is necessary to say a little more about this plausible but troublesome notion of 'targeting' or 'directing' professional activities into the country of the consumer's habitual residence as this is elaborated in the recitals 24 and 25 to the Regulation.[125] First, the contract must be concluded within the framework of this targeting, which seems to mean that there must be a connection rather than a bare coincidence of targeting and contracting, though it is not necessary that the consumer respond specifically to an individual targeting. Second, the accessibility of an internet site will not by itself establish targeting, but if the internet site solicits the conclusion of distance contracts, that will be different. It has also been said that the language of the website or currency referred to does not constitute a relevant factor. No doubt this reflects pressure by internet sellers, ever anxious to avoid laws they dislike. But really, it is very hard to see how an internet site legible in Hungarian is not targeted at Hungarian consumers: the diaspora population is, one imagines, numerically insignificant, and no-one else can even hazard a guess at what the words actually mean. If a website has a page in Portuguese, who apart from Portuguese residents can it credibly be said to be directed at? Is it really aimed generally at the world at large, just in case any of them has Portuguese as a first language? One may understand that a website in French or German might be seen to aim at consumers in several countries, or if in English, at practically the whole world, but to exclude language and currency from the list of factors which are material is, one would think, wrong. One does not need to be much of a sleuth to suspect that special interest groups ganged up and got their way by predicting the death of the internet if they did not get what they wanted.

(c) Insurance contracts

Article 7 makes modifications to the general rules for the identification of the governing law for certain insurance contracts.

---

[125] See also Joined Cases C-585/08 *Pammer v Reederei Karl Schluter GmbH & Co KG* and C-144/09 *Hotel Alpenhof GmbH v Heller* [2010] ECR I-12527 on the Brussels I Regulation.

But the particular rules for insurance contracts in Article 7 are, it is submitted, too complicated for a book whose purpose is to outline the principles of the subject. However that may be, they do not apply to reinsurance, to which the ordinary rules of the Regulation apply.[126] For insurance, a primary distinction is drawn between insurance of large risks other than life insurance, and the rest. In the case of such large risks, no matter where the risk is situated,[127] the law governing such insurance may be chosen according to Article 3, or in default of such choice, it will be governed by the law of the insurer's habitual residence.[128] In the case of insurance of non-large risks, if the risk is not situated in a Member State, the rules for choice of law are those of Articles 3 and 4; but if the risk is situated in a Member State, an express choice of law may be made from a restricted list, the broad justification for which is to protect the policy-holder from outlandish choices of law, and in default of such choice, the governing law shall be the law of the Member State in which the risk is situated at the time of the conclusion of the contract.

(d) Individual employment contracts

Article 8 makes modifications to the general rules for the identification of the governing law for individual contracts of employment. An express choice of law is effective, but the choice may not deprive the employee of legal protection which would have been afforded to him by the law which would have applied if there had been no such choice, though again, for this to be so, the protective rule in question must be one which may not be contracted out of.[129] If the law is not chosen, the contract will be governed by the law of the country in which (or failing that, from which) the employee habitually carries out his work in performance of the contract,[130] or, if no such single country can be determined, by the law of the country where is situated the place

---

[126] Article 7(1).

[127] The location of the risk is dealt with in Art 7(6).

[128] Article 7(2).

[129] Article 8(1).

[130] Article 8(2) For cross-border cases, and the recourse to a centre-of-gravity approach, see Case C-29/10 *Koelzsch v Luxembourg* [2011] ECR I-1595.

of business which engaged him,[131] unless (in any case) the contract appears to be more closely connected to another country, in which case the law of that country shall apply.[132]

5. *LEX CONTRACTUS* (4): GENERAL DISPLACEMENT

(a) *Lex contractus* overridden by laws of other countries

Apart from the cases just mentioned, there are two general instances in which the hegemony of the governing law is encroached upon by the substantive laws of another country. The Regulation identifies these laws as 'overriding mandatory provisions': that is to say, laws the respect for which is regarded by a country as so crucial for safeguarding its public interests (political, social, or economic organization) that they are applicable to any contract falling within their scope, regardless of the law which might otherwise be applied.[133] Where such a law has been identified, choice of the governing law is certainly not annulled, but its operation is to this extent overridden by and subordinated to the rules of another system of law; the same applies to a governing law identified otherwise than by express choice. It may be appropriate to picture 'mandatory laws' as directions given by the legislator directly to the judge, as distinct from laws which are made relevant because of the way a party puts its case. Their definition is deliberately restrictive;[134] it is intended to define a category of laws narrower than those which cannot be contracted out of by agreement.

Article 9(1) provides that any such law of the forum will be applicable notwithstanding any other provision of the Regulation. The operation of this provision is therefore entirely determined by the court in which the trial takes place, and provides, notwithstanding the uniformity in choice of law created by the Regulation, a limited incentive to forum-shop. In the context of a trial in England, examples *may* include legislation controlling contract terms

---

[131] Article 8(3).
[132] For cases in which the duties are carried on outside the territorial jurisdiction of any state (such as on an oil rig) see [1980] OJ C282/1, 26.
[133] Article 9(1).
[134] Recital 37.

which purport to limit or exclude liability.[135] An example would be the Carriage of Goods by Sea Act 1971, which gives the force of law to the Hague-Visby Rules,[136] though it is not completely easy to see these as satisfying the restrictive definition in Article 9(1). A better example might be those provisions of the Financial Services and Markets Act 2000 or similar and successor legislation, which make unenforceable an investment agreement made through an unauthorized person.[137] These are not to be sidelined by the simple expedient of choosing a law other than English to govern the contract, but may be necessary to stop unauthorized salesmen of snake oil and Ponzi schemes from running amok and wrecking the economy, a task reserved to Her Majesty's government. Even so, if a judge concludes that Parliament has made a law and directed the judge to stop any attempt to contract out of it, even if the wording of Article 9(1) is still out of reach, it is really rather hard to see that an English judge could consider himself at liberty to not apply them. It may be, therefore, that Article 9(1) should probably be seen as an exhortation towards restrictiveness, not more.

Obviously a court cannot be expected to apply the laws of a foreign country simply because the legislature of that foreign country regards them as of overriding importance to the organization of itself as a state: in principle, a legislator speaks directly to his own judges but not to anyone else. Article 9(3) of the Regulation, therefore, cannot and does not impose a similar obligation upon a judge to apply the overriding mandatory laws of a foreign country. But insofar as a contract requires[138] performance in a foreign country, and the overriding laws of that country would make performance unlawful, a court may give effect to those laws.[139] In this respect, the Regulation recalls, perhaps surprisingly and perhaps

---

[135] Unfair Contract Terms Act 1977, s 27(2); Unfair Terms in Consumer Contract Regulations 1999 (SI 1999/2083) (although Art 23 expressly provides for the application of such rules as those which derive from Directive 93/13/EC, [1993] OJ L95/29).

[136] cf *The Hollandia* [1983] 1 AC 565.

[137] Financial Services and Markets Act 2000, ss 26, 27.

[138] If the common law is to be taken as any guide, it must be *required* rather than intended or expected: *Libyan Arab Foreign Bank v Bankers Trust Co* [1989] QB 728.

[139] Article 9(3).

not so surprisingly,[140] a rule of common law private international law to the effect that an English court would enforce or order performance of a contract where that performance would be illegal—in a more than technical sense[141]—under the law of the country of performance.[142] The common law could never have countenanced enforcing a contract to smuggle alcohol into the United States during prohibition[143] (or, for that matter into a Muslim country which has the same outlook), or to export goods from India destined for a South Africa legislating itself into a state of utter depravity,[144] for example. It is inconceivable that the Regulation would have taken a different view, and it does not.

(b) Non-application of *lex contractus* by reason of public policy

A provision of the governing law will not apply where its application would be manifestly contrary to public policy of the adjudicating court.[145] The relationship between this rule, stated in Article 21, and Article 9, may not be immediately clear, but whereas Article 9 provides for the governing law to be overlaid by a rule found in the domestic law of the forum, Article 21 proceeds by the blanking out of a provision of the governing law, with the result that the governing law applies as if that provision were not part of it. So if the governing law allows damages to be claimed for breach of a contract to sell slaves or narcotics, Article 21 will prevent its being applied by a court in English

---

[140] Rumour has it, and reason would corroborate it, that Art 9(3) was adopted in order to encourage the United Kingdom to exercise its discretion to opt into, rather than remain outside, the Rome I Regulation.

[141] It will depend on the nature and degree of the illegality, and probably on the awareness of the party prepared to make a contract to perpetrate it; see also *Royal Boskalis Westminster NV v Mountain* [1999] QB 674.

[142] A different view, that the non-enforcement rule was confined to contracts whose proper (governing) law was English law, is plainly ridiculous. It is no part of the function of Her Majesty's judges to make orders which require the commission of crimes on the territory of foreign friendly states.

[143] *Foster v Driscoll* [1929] 1 KB 470.

[144] *Regazzoni v KC Sethia (1944) Ltd* [1958] AC 301. See also *Lemenda Trading Co Ltd v African Middle East Petroleum Co Ltd* [1989] QB 728; *Euro-Diam Ltd v Bathurst* [1990] 1 QB 30.

[145] Article 16.

proceedings. Such a case would fit less easily into Article 9(2), for no easily stated substantive rule of English law—as opposed to the principles of English public policy—demands application in such a case. A foreign contractual law which upheld as valid a covenant in restraint of a person's freedom to take employment with a rival, which would be found to be illegal as in restraint of trade as a matter of English domestic law, might conceivably be refused application—with the consequences that there was no binding restraint—on this ground;[146] the same might conceivably be said of a rule of the *lex contractus* which provided for the payment of a sum which would in English law be seen as a penalty and therefore as unconscionable.

6. DOMAIN OF THE *LEX CONTRACTUS*

Subject to those reservations, the Regulation provides, in various places, that the governing law, ascertained as above, applies in particular to the interpretation and performance of the contract; to the consequences of a partial or total breach of obligations, including the assessment of damages so far as this is governed by rules of law; to the various ways of extinguishing obligations, including limitation and prescription; and to the consequences of nullity of the contract. The fact that the list in Article 12 is introduced by the expression 'in particular' means that this is not to be understood as an exhaustive list. Where the law of remedies is concerned, the intention is that all questions of the law of compensation should be obtained from the *lex contractus*, and that the contribution of the *lex fori* be as modest as possible: nothing else is consistent with the imperative of ensuring that the Regulation applies equally, and equally predictably, in all Member States. There is no earthly reason why the determination of the heads of damages, or their quantification, should not be attempted and done in accordance with the *lex contractus*, at least where the content of this law is proved to the satisfaction of the court. Of course, if the *lex contractus* provides, in effect, that damages are to be assessed by a civil jury, as one finds in Texas and probably elsewhere in the United States, there *is* no rule of the *lex contractus* which could be

---

[146] The common law certainly said so: *Rousillon v Rousillon* (1880) 14 ChD 351.

applied by an English court: when assessment takes the form of an unelaborated figure given without reasons, the assessment is not governed by a rule of law in the sense of Article 12(1)(c), but by a purely procedural mechanism which the Regulation does not direct the court to pick up and apply.[147] Likewise, if the *lex contractus* would not provide for or permit an injunction to restrain conduct said to amount to a breach, an English court should probably refrain from ordering the injunction which English procedural law would otherwise have permitted.[148]

The Rome Convention had provided that the *lex contractus* applied to the consequences of nullity of the contract, but it also provided that this rule might be excluded from the Convention as adopted by Contracting States.[149] The United Kingdom duly opted not to enact it, but it was not clear what resulted from this; and in any event, this legislative freedom has now disappeared from the Regulation.

In addition to the matters listed in Article 12, the governing law will also settle the burden of proof and the operation of any presumptions.[150] In relation to formal validity, compliance with the governing law is sufficient; otherwise compliance with the law or laws of the place where the parties were when they made the contract will also suffice.[151] The effect is that, subject to the specific points made below, practically all points of construction, interpretation, and discharge (by performance, agreement, frustration, and breach) are within the domain of the governing law as, in principle, is the availability of remedies for breach. It seems probable, as was said at the beginning of this chapter, that the question whether a contract is valid in the light of complaints of pre-contractual wrongdoing is governed by the *lex contractus*, though the existing of any obligations arising from this wrongdoing will be governed by the Rome II Regulation.

Subject to the fact that the formal validity of a contract is, by Article 11, assessed by a rule of alternative validating reference, the

---

[147] Article 1(3).
[148] *OJSC TNK-BP Holding v Lazurenko* [2012] EWHC 2781 (Ch).
[149] Contracts (Applicable Law) Act 1990, s 2(2).
[150] Article 18.
[151] Article 11.

governing law as the Rome I Regulation identifies it will, in general, determine whether the contract is valid. But the concept of 'validity' covers a range of possible objections, ranging from breakdowns in formation to the effect of a change in the law making performance illegal; and disputes about contractual validity are invariably difficult to deal with. Nevertheless, the point of departure is that the contention that there was, or is now, no binding contract is one which will be resolved by the law which would govern the contract if it were taken or found to be valid. So if X enters into negotiations with Y, and at the point where these terminate, X's law would say that no contract had been concluded, while Y's law would take the opposite point of view, the dominant approach would be to ask what law would govern the supposed contract if there really were one, and to use this law to determine whether the parties had reached contractual agreement. This, at any rate, is the effect of Articles 3(5) and 10(1) of the Regulation,[152] and it is broadly in line with what some took to be the solution given by the common law. When references are encountered to the 'putative' governing law, or the governing law of the putative contract, they are references to this 'law'.

It does not take much to see that the methodology involved in this approach is open to objection. If we suppose that Y will be contending that there was a valid and binding contract, while X says that there never was any such thing, it is not immediately easy to see why one would proceed by assuming, conditionally but still significantly, that Y's submission is correct and that the appropriate rule or tool of decision is the law which would have governed the contract if it were, as Y says it is, valid; the idea that a judge should begin the adjudication by taking sides is not one which will leap to every mind. The reverse proposition, which respects another aspect of the parties' autonomy (namely the right to walk away from negotiations which have not reached agreement), appears equally convincing: X will presumably say that the remedies lie in the law of restitution or not at all, so one

---

[152] Which also provides that whether a particular term is valid is determined by the law which would govern it on the footing that it was valid: a proposition which is particularly challenging where each party has proposed a contract term, including a choice of law, which contradicts that of the opposite party.

should assume the contract to be invalid, and look to the law which would govern the restitutionary claim. If that law considers that there was indeed no valid contract, and that the claim is for restitution, the choice of law will be the restitutionary one. If instead it considers that there was a contract, and no cause for restitution, the *lex causae* will be the contractual one. So why should one side's vantage point be preferred to that of the other? If this is an intelligible question, the answer will be that there is no reason, and the solution must lie elsewhere.

But alternative solutions are not attractive, either. One possibility might be to characterize the facts to see whether they disclose, or feel like, an issue falling within a broad understanding of contract; but this is liable to degenerate into little more than a judicial sniff test; and on these facts, never mind any more commercially complex ones, it is quite unpredictable how it would work. Another might have been to apply the *lex fori* to decide whether there is a contract and, if there is, to use the proper law which it must necessarily[153] have to decide whether there was a valid contract. That would mean that if according to the *lex fori* there is no contract, that would be an end of it: but why should the *lex fori*, which might be the law of neither party, have even that much of a role?

Yet another might be to apply the putative governing law, but with a saving provision made for people whose own laws would have reassured them that there was no contract and that they were not bound.[154] In effect, this is the solution adopted by the Regulation. Article 10(2) qualifies the approach in Article 10(1) by allowing the party who contends that he should not be bound to rely on the law of his habitual residence 'to establish that he did not consent' if it would be unreasonable to apply the governing law to the question.[155] But if he has dealt by reference to the foreign law before, or maybe simply because he was prepared to make an international contract, he may be found to have forfeited a protection designed

---

[153] *Amin Rasheed Shipping Corpn v Kuwait Insurance Co* [1984] AC 50.

[154] Foreshadowed by Jaffey (1975) 24 ICLQ 603.

[155] It is unclear whether this reference to habitual residence excludes parties who are not natural persons, for whom the corresponding point of reference is the place of business.

for the innocent abroad.[156] It is only fair to concede that, by contrast with all the possible rules of single reference, this rule of double reference has a lot to be said for it. It is, after all, quite hard to come up with a set of facts for which it will produce a result which is plainly wrong. And in the context, that is saying something. And leaving the novice aside, for whom Article 10(2) is good enough, perhaps it is true that if the parties have allowed themselves to get so close to the point where one possibly-closely-connected law would say they had made a contract, they have only themselves to blame if it is held that they did so.

The precise scope of what is encompassed by the argument, licensed by Article 10(2), that 'he did not consent' is, however, not altogether certain. As a matter of first impression, any argument which has at its root the proposition that X did not in law consent to bind himself to Y seems to be covered, and therefore any assault on the legal effectiveness of the alleged consent might be brought within the material scope of Article 10(2). Giuliano-Lagarde expressed a narrower view in relation to the corresponding rule of the Rome Convention,[157] claiming that the scope of what is now Article 10(2) was confined to the existence, as distinct from the validity, of consent: that is, to offer and acceptance and mistake, but not to factors which render the contract voidable and the consent vitiated. It is unclear whether this is tenable; it remains to be seen whether Article 10(2) will be confined to the limited role proposed by Giuliano-Lagarde. But exceptions are construed narrowly.

7. THE ROME I REGULATION IN CONTRACT LITIGATION

One of the curious things about the private international law of contract is that whilst the domestic law of contract divides its subject up into familiar and everyday pieces—offer and acceptance, consideration, mistake, misrepresentation, and so on—the rules of private international law use categories and address concerns which cut across these more practical issues, or make disproportionate provision for issues (such as formal validity and capacity)

---

[156] cf *Egon Oldendorff v Libera Corpn* [1995] 2 Lloyd's Rep 64.
[157] [1980] OJ C282/1, 28.

which are only rarely of practical importance. As a result, it is instructive to take a quick look at the issues which might be raised in an ordinary contract action in an English court, and to examine how and where these points fit within the Regulation. We will proceed on the assumption that C is suing D, a defendant habitually resident in England, for breach of contract, and examine the elements of the law of contract as if raised by D as a defence to the claim. We will also assume that by the governing law, which will be ascertained on the basis that the contract is, for this purpose at least, assumed to be valid, the contract would be valid and enforceable, and all the defences raised by D would fail; but that as a matter of English domestic law, the several defences raised by D would be well founded and that, also on the facts, D would satisfy the requirement of its being reasonable for him to rely on his own law.

If D argues that he is not bound and cannot be liable because there was no binding *offer and acceptance*, this plea is a matter for the governing law, for it goes to the validity of the contract; but D may in a proper case rely on his own, English, law to demonstrate that he did not consent, by reason of Article 10(2). If D argues that there was no *intention to create legal relations*, the effect of this plea will primarily be a matter for the governing law. But if D formulates the argument to say he did not consent to, nor had any reason to suppose that he was, entering into legal relations at all, because under English law such an agreement would not be legally enforceable, Article 10(2) may avail him. If D argues that the alleged contract cannot be enforced because the price was never agreed, and there was therefore no *certainty of contractual terms*, the governing law may possibly be displaced by the argument that D cannot be held to have consented to something which, as a matter of his own law, he could never have been bound by; and if this is so, Article 10(2) is in principle available to him. All these issues go to the existence of consent to bind oneself to enforceable obligations; but if the conditions of Article 10(2) are not met by D, he has no answer to whatever the *lex contractus* would provide.

If D argues that he is not bound because there was no *consideration* for the promise, and that he knew that if he asked for nothing of value in return for C's promise, then he could not be said to have given his consent to be legally bound to C, it is arguable that Article 10(2) will apply here also, even though the governing law would not regard this as a necessity for the formation of a contract. Even so, is a statement that 'I asked for nothing in return, by which I ensured that I could not have become bound' really a means of establishing that D did not consent? If C argues that he contracted in order to benefit C2, who was not a party to the contract, nor mentioned in it, nor known about by D, and that under the governing law C2 may sue in his own name, D may say that under the English doctrine of *privity*[158] he would not be bound to, and did not consent to be bound, to C2. After all, one cannot just be contractually bound: one must be contractually bound to another. Likewise, if C argues that he contracted with D2 and the effect of their contract under its governing law was that D was bound by an obligation in it, D may argue that under the English doctrine of privity he is not taken to consent to be bound to an obligation in a contract to which he was a stranger. Article 10(2) may preserve his right to argue that he did not consent to be bound by the obligation created by the contract. These issues may not go to the question whether D agreed something with somebody, but if D submits that he did not consent to an agreement which would have legal effect or that he never consented to be bound to C2 or by D2, it is arguable, despite the clear and contradictory view of Giuliano-Lagarde, that these arguments go to the very existence of the consent which C asserts and D denies.

If C argues that D is bound despite the fact that there was a *limitation or exclusion clause* in the contract, the validity of this defence will be a matter for the governing law to assess. But in the reverse case, if the governing law would regard the limitation clause as valid, it may yet be struck down as a matter of English law by reference to Article 9(2), assuming that the provision of English law relied on is one which must be applied by a judge whatever the governing law, and that the legislative purpose is taken to be sufficiently important to override the *lex contractus* in this way.

If D argues that his agreement was procured by *fraud*, or *negligent or innocent misstatement*, or by *material non-disclosure*, or by *duress*, or by the exercise of *undue influence*, the legal effect of his plea is that his consent was vitiated and, subject to conditions,

---

[158] But cf the Contracts (Rights of Third Parties) Act 1999 for modification of English common law.

is capable of being wiped away. If the governing law would nevertheless regard these pleas as insufficient to ground relief, may D rely on Article 10(2) to establish that he did not consent and that as a result he is not contractually bound? Perhaps not: unlike issues relating to offer and acceptance, these are not factors where D will have known or believed at the time, or if asked at the time would have said that his own law provided that he was not bound to the other; to put it another way, he cannot deny that he did, albeit as a result of fraud, originally consent. Yet D may know that he has been the victim of what may be duress or undue influence; he may know that as a matter of English law he has no need to check the accuracy of representations made by another, or that he was entitled to rely on C to make disclosure in a contract made in the utmost good faith, so that he will not have to be bound if he relies on misrepresentations; and he may rely on the security of his own law accordingly, just as he does when he throws away an offer letter, knowing that he cannot be bound by it. Seen in those terms it is arguable that Article 10(2) should be relevant here too, for an alleged consent which does not bind D, and which D is right to assume does not bind D, is no consent at all. If D argues that the alleged contract was void on the basis of a mutual *mistake*, or his own unilateral mistake, this is, in effect, a confusion which prevents the parties coming to an agreement, and Article 10(2) is applicable in principle. If he argues that the alleged contract was void on the basis of fundamental common mistake or should be set aside on the basis of less fundamental common mistake, D is arguing that he did not consent to the terms of the contract alleged by C, because there was nothing to consent about.

If D argues that he cannot be made to perform because the contract was one which required him to perform an act which would be *illegal* under the law of the place where performance was called for, the validity of the contract is in principle a matter for the governing law, and if under that law the illegality renders the contract unenforceable there is no more to be said.[159] Though the governing law may not accept this as an excuse for non-performance, Article 9(3) allows a court to find that if performance would involve a sufficient degree of illegality under the law of the place

---

[159] Article 12.

where the contract was to be performed, this renders the contract unenforceable, whatever its proper law: an English court could hardly make an order on the basis that D was required to commit a crime in the place of performance. Alternatively, to apply the provision of the governing law which required performance of a criminal act, or an act tainted with illegality, may well be manifestly contrary to English public policy, and therefore precluded by Article 21.

If D argues that he cannot be sued because C's action is barred by *limitation* or prescription, this plea will be determined by the governing law. Article 12(1)(d) so provides, but the Foreign Limitation Periods Act 1984 had already brought English private international law into line with this answer.

If D argues that the contract was *discharged by performance* or by C's *breach*, or by *frustration*, the plea will be dealt with by the governing law, according to Article 12. If D denies that C is entitled to the particular *remedy* claimed, the answer will come, and in principle come only, from the governing law: it would be wrong in principle for an English court to grant a remedy in circumstances in which the *lex contractus* would refuse it. The extent to which an English court is required to grant remedies available under the governing law but which an English court would not grant is uncertain, but an English court will probably be expected to follow and apply the remedial provisions of the governing law unless this is simply too inconvenient to be practicable, or would contravene some fundamental policy of English law.

C. CONTRACTS CONCLUDED BEFORE 18 DECEMBER 2009

Though it will eventually fade from the law reports, litigation concerning contracts made prior to the material date of the Rome I Regulation but after 1 April 1991, which were within the temporal scope of the Rome Convention, will continue for some time to come.[160] It is therefore necessary to say something

---

[160] By contrast, it does not seem appropriate to discuss the common law rules of private international law, as in the field of contracts in civil and commercial matters, these can only apply to contracts made over 20 years ago.

brief about the principal[161] respects in which the provisions of the Convention differed or differ from the corresponding provisions of the Rome I Regulation.

The power of the parties to choose and express a law to govern their contract set out in Article 3 of the Convention was for all practical purposes the same as in the Regulation, but the provisions of Article 4, which identified the governing law in the absence of such choice, were significantly different. The point of departure was that the contract would be governed by the law of the country with which it was most closely connected; but it was presumed that this would be the country of habitual residence of the party whose performance was characteristic of the contract.[162] The difficulty generated by this rule was not insubstantial, for it required one side of the agreement to be identified as the 'characteristic' one, while the other side was not. The paradigm was, no doubt, the contract of sale, for which sale was characteristic, on the footing that all that the buyer was obliged to do was to pay the price. Even if this was a fair representation of most contracts of sale, it will not have been true for all; and for contracts which were more complex than the sale of sweets in a corner-shop, a template of performance against the payment of money would not necessarily fit: distributorship,[163] barter, and reinsurance, for three, suggested that the notion of a characteristic and an 'non-characteristic' performance was not as helpful as it may have seemed when it was first invented. Not only that: for contracts made in the course of a trade or profession the governing law was presumed to be the country

---

[161] It should also be noted that the provisions for consumer, employment, and carriage contracts were slightly different, and that the Rome Convention did not apply to insurance or risks situated in the Member States of what was then the EEC. These points are not dealt with here. Nor is the requirement in Art 18, that the Convention be given a uniform interpretation, for the replacement of the Convention by a Regulation has ensured that this does not need to be separately and specifically enacted.

[162] Article 4(1).

[163] For which the supplier, rather than the distributor, was the party whose performance was held, by courts in England (*Print Concept GmbH v GEW (EC) Ltd* [2002] CLC 382) and France (*Optelec SA v Soc Midtronics BV* [2002] Rev Crit 86) to be characteristic. This was an odd way of looking at a contract generally called 'distribution', rather than 'supply for the purpose of distribution by another'.

of the principal place of business, except where under the terms of the contract, performance was to be effected through a place of business other than the principal place of business, which led to a complication in cases in which it was implicit, but was not contractually obligatory, that performance be through a secondary place of business.[164] The escape clause in Article 4(5) applied if the characteristic performance could not be determined, or if the contract as a whole was more closely connected to another country than that indicated by the rules on characteristic performance; it was held in England,[165] and in Luxembourg,[166] that this escape clause was not intended to be restrictive or particularly narrow, for if the contract really was more closely connected to another country, it would be surprising for the law of that country not to govern it: but Article 4(5) could not be satisfied by showing that the parties 'would have chosen' a different law if they had made a choice.[167] It was said above,[168] but it bears repetition, that the less satisfactory the default rule, the more work the escape clause would have to do. If one takes the view, as one should, that Articles 4(1) and 4(2) of the Rome I Regulation are more likely to produce a sensible choice of law to begin with, it would be justifiable for Article 4(3) of the Regulation to have a narrower sphere of operation than Article 4(5) of the Convention.

The Rome Convention provided for the permissive application of the mandatory[169] laws of a country other than that of the forum or of the applicable law. The power to apply such laws, picked up from the law of a country 'with which the situation has a close connection', was provided for by Article 7(1), but the contracting states were permitted to enact the Convention without this provision, which was how it was done in the United

---

[164] *Iran Continental Shelf Oil Co v IRI International Corpn* [2002] EWCA Civ 1024, [2004] 2 CLC 696; *Ennstone Building Products Ltd v Stanger Ltd* [2002] EWCA Civ 916, [2002] 1 WLR 3059.

[165] *Samcrete Egypt Engineers & Contractors SAE v Land Rover Exports Ltd* [2001] EWCA Civ 2019, [2002] CLC 533.

[166] Case C-133/08 *Intercontainer Interfrigo SC v Balkenende Oosthuizen BV* [2009] ECR I-9687.

[167] *Lawlor v Sandvik Mining & Construction Mobile Crushers & Screens Ltd* [2012] EWHC 1188 (QB), [2012] 2 Lloyd's Rep 25.

[168] See pp 242–43 above.

[169] The definition of 'mandatory' which is now in Art 9(1) of the Regulation had not appeared, in terms at least, in the Convention.

Kingdom.[170] It was thought, and probably rightly, that the principle was as unsound as the drafting of Article 7(1) was woolly. The odd result was that the question whether an English court might apply the provisions of a law other than the applicable law was left to be determined by the common law, on the footing that where a hole had been cut in the fabric of the Convention as enacted in English law the common law remained, uncovered and intact. Accordingly, provisions of the law of the place of performance could be given effect to the extent that they rendered performance of the contract unlawful;[171] it is gently ironic that such a provision was, in substance, made and incorporated as part of the Rome I Regulation.[172]

The Rome Convention also extended to Contracting States the power to not enact the provision which stated, as the Rome I Regulation also provides, that the governing law was to be applied to the consequences of nullity of the contract. Why the United Kingdom took advantage of this was and remains a mystery, for it was pretty plain[173] that if the governing law was used to derive the conclusion that a supposed contract was void, the same law would—however one understood the theoretical[174] basis for the conclusion—determine the restitutionary or other consequences. But the point is now just a wrinkle in the blanket of legal history, which description may, in time, be extended to the Convention itself.

---

[170] Article 23 of the Convention; Contracts (Applicable Law) Act 1990, s 2(2).

[171] *Ralli Bros v Compania Naviera Sota y Aznar* [1920] 2 KB 287.

[172] Article 9(3) of the Regulation.

[173] To the English, at least; for a rather odder and decidedly arid-looking view from the romanist perspective of Scots law, see *Baring Bros & Co Ltd v Cunninghame DC* [1997] CLC 108.

[174] That is, that the issue of recovery is contractual, or that the issue of recovery is not contractual but still governed by the law which governed or would have governed the contract.

6

OBLIGATIONS: NON-CONTRACTUAL

A. INTRODUCTION

Where a court is called upon to deal with a question of choice of law which is concerned with obligations in civil and commercial matters, which are not contractual in the sense of the Rome I Regulation examined in the previous chapter, and which arise out of events which occur after 11 January 2009, the choice of law rule applicable to them will be, subject to limited exceptions, provided by the Rome II Regulation rather than by the common law rules of private international law. It is for this reason that this chapter is entitled 'non-contractual obligations' as distinct from 'tort' and as further distinct from 'unjust enrichment': the days when these familiar terms would have been helpful have been and gone and their obituary written. As was explained in the previous chapter, the two Rome Regulations aim to divide up choice of law for the whole of the field of obligations arising in civil and commercial matters into contractual and non-contractual obligations. It is for this reason—because litigation of claims which the common law would consider to lie in tort or in unjust enrichment, or even as certain varieties of equitable[1] obligation, is now governed by the Rome Regulations—that it is appropriate to state the law by taking the Rome II Regulation as the point of departure.

It is not necessary to repeat the points which explain the technique of interpretation and application of the Rome II Regulation, as these follow directly from what was said about the

---

[1] This can be very difficult. A claim based on knowing receipt, for example, will certainly fall within Rome II, but does it do so as a tort or delict (that is to say, as a claim based on wrongdoing), or as a species of unjust enrichment ? In other words, does it fall within Chapter II or Chapter III of the Regulation? English domestic law is notoriously unclear on the question, and choice of law has to live with the consequence. Dishonest assistance, by contrast, will count as a tort, within Chapter II of the Regulation; cf *OJSC Yugraneft v Abramovich* [2008] EWHC 2613 (Comm).

Rome I Regulation which must be read so as to be consistent with it.[2] However, the exclusions of material from the scope of the Rome II Regulation are in some respects wider and more significant than the exclusions from Rome I. In particular, the Regulation does not apply to non-contractual obligations arising out of violations of privacy and rights relating to personality, including defamation. There is therefore a substantial body of material left outside the Regulation and to which the common law[3] principles of choice of law still apply. As privacy and defamation cannot be regarded as peripheral to the law of non-contractual obligations, it is necessary to say something about the choice of law rules preserved and reserved for such cases. It is, however, a singular misfortune that the law which the Regulation left untouched is pretty unsatisfactory. This will mean that the account of common law choice of law, which will appear after an examination of the Rome II Regulation will appear to be distinctly unimpressive by comparison.

The Rome II Regulation applies to non-contractual obligations in civil and commercial matters which fall within its scope in terms of subject matter and time; but its choice of law rules draw an internal distinction between non-contractual obligations in torts and delicts, and what one might call 'other', *sui generis*, non-contractual obligations. For the purposes of this chapter, it is convenient to start with those aspects of the rules for choice of law which are common to these two categories, and then to deal with the tort/delict and 'other' cases of non-contractual obligation. At the end of the chapter there will be a need for an explanation of the common law rules in sufficient detail to show how they apply, as they still apply, to matters falling outside the scope of the Regulation.

The Rome I and Rome II Regulations are designed to make a smooth and seamless whole, to make a complete statement of the choice of law rules for obligations arising in civil and commercial matters. Seamlessness is achieved, in part at least, by channelling the choice of law for those issues which lie in the area of overlap between the Regulations into the *lex contractus* as this is identified

---

[2] Recital 7 to the Rome II Regulation. And, no doubt, vice versa.
[3] In this context, 'common law' means 'common law as amended by statute'.

by the Rome I Regulation. This does not mean that in every case in which the litigants in a tort matter are parties to a contract the law governing the tort claim will be the law which governs the contract—for example, where the claimant is an employee run down by his employer while crossing the road outside the factory gate it is unlikely that the tort will be governed by the law which governed the employment contract, for the tort has nothing to do with the employment contract[4]—but in those cases in which the tort is in some sense associated with the contract, there will be little incentive to seek to formulate the claim by reference to the one Regulation or the other, for they are designed to be complementary and coherent. But compared with the common law, the methodology is refreshingly clear. One asks whether the matter raised before the court is civil or commercial. If it is, one asks whether it is based on the law of obligations. If it is,[5] one asks whether the obligation in question is contractual or non-contractual, there being no *tertium quid*. These questions are asked, and answered, without regard to national law, but by reference to the autonomous definition of terms used in the Regulation.

As the definition of 'contractual' was considered in Chapter 5, there is no need to repeat it here. But some issues are so instructive that they are worth addressing twice. Although French domestic law has disallowed the cumulation of remedies in contract and delict—that if the claim may be founded on the contract there is no parallel or concurrent claim in tort—it has also persuaded itself that if A's failure to perform his contractual duty to B causes loss to C, C may be able to rely on this 'fault' to establish a delict claim against A.[6] Indeed, English law has toyed with this idea, and has very occasionally upheld a claim alleging the commission of a tort.[7] If such a set of facts does arise,

---

[4] A proposition which is more intuitive than it is easy to define.

[5] And assuming that is it not an obligation specifically excluded from the material scope of the Regulation under which it would otherwise have fallen.

[6] Based on Art 1382 of the Civil Code: *Loubeyre v SARL Myr'Ho* Cass ass plén, 6.12.2006; JCP 2006.II.10181. But there were earlier decisions of chambers, and there have been subsequent decisions, to the same effect as this decision of the Full Court. It is understood that French commentators are pretty unimpressed, and that this seems to have no effect upon the court.

[7] *White v Jones* [1995] 2 AC 207.

and the question has to be addressed whether a claim raised by C against A is, for the purposes of choice of law, a matter of contractual or non-contractual obligation, there are two plausible answers. Seen from the perspective of C, the answer ought to be that his claim is non-contractual and presumptively governed by the place where his damage occurs, for it would be wrong in principle for a choice of law made between A and B to prejudice his rights and interests. Seen from the perspective of A, it makes sense for it to be contractual: he should realize that if he makes a contract governed by French law, he exposes himself to being blamed for non-performance by more people than just his contractual counter-party. Each view seems clear and rational; they cannot both be admitted as right. No doubt the domestic laws of the other Member States wrestle with similar issues in similar ways; and the idea that an answer could be derived from national law is fanciful. There are bound to be cases in which the European Court just has to settle the answer, with the rest of us being grateful for the clarity. This is likely to be one of them.

B. THE ROME II REGULATION

The Rome II Regulation[8] was adopted in July 2007, as part of the larger project to establish uniform choice of law rules for obligations in civil and commercial matters. Though the negotiations started from scratch, in the sense that there was no precursor analogous to the Rome Convention which paved the way to the Rome I Regulation, which was made a year later, the strange truth about choice of law for tort is that almost all possible solutions are open to serious objection. An understanding of the law put in place by the Regulation must acknowledge that basic truth, for it shows that the Regulation may succeed in achieving something which no other national system ever managed to pull off: putting in place a choice of law rule which works sufficiently well that courts and commentators just leave it alone. For this reason, though, a digression into the history of choice of law in tort is called for.

1. BACKGROUND

Despite the fact that it appeared to generate little judicial interest in England until the end of the 20th century, choice of law in tort claims produced an enormous amount of academic examination and, particularly in the lush litigation grasslands of the United States, some highly creative thinking. A contract is an agreement, and if the law to be applied is not one which the parties had chosen, it will still be deduced from points of connection which the parties knew or should have known about from the start: choice of law for contract is easy and uncontroversial, with only the detail needing debate. Torts, by contrast, are the law's accidents, messy and unplanned, and covering a far more diverse set of interests and duties. A single or uniform choice of law rule may struggle to encompass and deal convincingly with personal injury, negligence, economic torts and conspiracies, unfair competition, liability for fires and animals, defamation, nuisance, and conversion; but when causes of action arising under foreign laws of tort and delict are added in, a single and reliable choice of law rule, whether very flexible or very inflexible, will be difficult to devise. Whereas the parties to a contract know of each other, and the range of persons with a potential claim will be limited and predictable; the parties to a tort claim, often flung together or strewn about by the tort, will not always be known to each other in advance. In devising choice of law rules this has to be borne in mind.

As a matter of history, choice of law rules in tort tended to centre on the *lex fori* or the *lex loci delicti commissi*. The justification for the *lex fori* was sometimes said to lie in the similarity between torts and crimes, but this was rarely convincing, and a better view was that the imposition of legal duties and civil obligations without regard to the will of the parties was a matter on which each court was entitled to prefer the standards of its own law. Justification for the *lex loci delicti commissi* was the homely advice that when in Rome one should do as Romans do. At this level of generality each has an attraction, which may even be the reason English law wove them into a rule of double actionability.[9] But the objection that either rule could result in the application of a law which had

---

[9] *Boys v Chaplin* [1971] AC 356.

little genuine or durable connection with the parties or the facts of the claim does not need illustration. This led some to suggest that, just as a contract was governed by a proper law, so also should a tort be.[10] The immediate objection was that while it was one thing to subject a consensual, pre-litigation, relationship to a proper law, it was quite another to subject an unplanned or non-relationship to the same process. But the sense that only a 'proper law' could guarantee that the law eventually applied was the 'right' law was palpable, and manifested itself in different ways. In England, it prompted the development of a flexible exception to the rigid rule of double actionability, thus resulting in a rule with a high degree of predictability which could nevertheless yield in the face of unusual facts.[11] The United States brought about a more fundamental re-casting of the choice of law rule, where the uniform application of the *lex loci delicti commissi* was largely given up for a variety of alternative techniques. These alternatives took took root there, mainly because the application of the law of the place of the tort is less attractive within a federation in which each of the states is legally foreign but not noticeably geographically so: whereas it may be obvious that one is in Rome, it may not be so obvious in the United States that one is not in Kansas any more. Borderless inter-state trade and traffic are such that a rigid preference for the law of the place where the tort occurred has an appreciable chance of pointing to a law which was in every sense accidental. Various alternatives were developed to deliver the elusive goal of an intuitively right answer derived nevertheless from scientific theory. In the first case of significance[12] the New York Court of Appeals toyed with a test of closest connection, and with a more complex approach which asked (and sought to answer) which state or states had laws which were intended, or 'interested', to apply to the particular issue before the court for decision: a method generally labelled, if rather surprisingly, as 'governmental interest analysis'. The debate later extended to inquire which state's law might be the most impaired if not applied;[13] to the use of a

---

    [10] Originating in Morris, 'The Proper Law of a Tort' (1951) 64 Harv LR 881.
    [11] *Boys v Chaplin* [1971] AC 356; *Red Sea Insurance Co Ltd v Bouygues SA* [1995] 1 AC 190.
    [12] *Babcock v Jackson* 191 NE 2d 279 (1963), [1963] 2 Lloyd's Rep 286 (NY CA).
    [13] *Bernard v Harrah's Club* 546 P 2d 719 (1976).

'better law' approach,[14] a technique tending to make it difficult for a court not to apply its own domestic law; and whatever else all this experimentation may have achieved, it was hard to claim that the result promoted the goal of legal certainty.[15] A European lawyer may recoil from the thought that a clear rule, with provision for an exception to serve as a pressure valve, should be abandoned in favour of a more individual approach. After all, although torts may be accidental and unplanned, the taking of insurance against liability for torts is a public good; and an approach which makes it uncertain which law will govern a claim makes the risk more difficult to insure against. But the American jurisprudence demonstrated that one size of choice of law rule did not fit all torts equally well, and it did a useful job.

In Canada and Australia, by contrast, the fact that many torts take place elsewhere within the federation moved the courts in precisely the opposite direction from that which drew support in the United States. Faced with the need to fashion a choice of law rule for torts committed elsewhere in Canada, the Supreme Court of Canada opted for a rigid and unbending *lex loci delicti* rule,[16] on the footing that this was both correct in principle and in line with Canada's sense and understanding of its own sovereignty. Faced with similar questions in relation to intra-Australian torts, the High Court of Australia also opted for a rigid and inflexible *lex loci delicti* rule,[17] spurning the path taken in the United States and expressing specific disapproval of the pragmatic English common law amalgam of rule and exception. Even so, experience shows that the need to make an exception in the interests of flexibility becomes irresistible when the facts are sufficiently unusual; and the courts in Canada and Australia may yet have to eat some of their words.[18]

---

[14] *Cipolla v Shaposka* 262 A 2d 854 (1970); *Clark v Clark* 222 A 2d 205 (1966).

[15] For an annual survey of choice of law in the American courts, see Symeonides in the *American Journal of Comparative Law* from Vol 36 (1988) to the present.

[16] *Tolofson v Jensen* [1994] 3 SCR 1022.

[17] *John Pfeiffer Pty Ltd v Rogerson* (2000) 203 CLR 503; *Régie Nationale des Usines Renault v Zhang* (2003) 210 CLR 491.

[18] It can be argued, although it is not convincing to do so, that the adoption of the principle of *renvoi* into the Australian *lex loci* rule, in *Neilson v Overseas Projects Corpn of Victoria* (2005) 233 CLR 331, was a surrogate for the flexibility which the court was at pains to reject. This does not appear to be based on a fair or accurate reading of the analysis contained in the judgments.

England was not immune. Prompted by the Law Commission,[19] Parliament decided to abandon the rule of double actionability and the excessive burden it was seen to place on the claimant. But it opted neither for a *lex loci delicti* rule, nor for a proper law approach. It took its cue from the acute observation of the Law Commission that the search for the place of the tort may be to look for something that is not there:[20] after all, not all torts are of the 'mind that car' 'what car?' 'splat' variety: in commercial litigation in particular the elements making up the cause of action may be widely dispersed, and the notion that the tort has a location is, perhaps in the cases most likely to result in litigation, something of a fiction: it may be a useful fiction, but it should be possible to do better than that. The legislation[21] therefore adopted a rule which applied the law of the place of the damage, supplementing this with a rule of exception where this somewhat crude initial rule did not yield the right solution.

The sum and substance was that, by contrast with the Rome I Regulation, the Rome II Regulation was not able to draw on an existing consensus, and still less on one in which a single choice of law rule could be devised and applied across the board. It was inviting to conclude that the best solution would be a general choice of law rule with as much certainty as possible, but allowing for clear and measured exceptions where the facts called for it, together with particular choice of law rules for torts or relationships which are so driven by their own particular concerns that a general rule will not work well for them. By and large that is exactly what the Rome II Regulation delivers.

2. ROME II REGULATION: APPLICATION IN TIME

The Rome II Regulation was adopted in July 2007. There was some initial confusion as to its temporal scope: by contrast with the law of contract, for which the date on which the contract is concluded serves as a neat and comprehensible starting date, cases involving torts and other non-contractual obligations do

---

[19] Law Commission Report 193 (1990).

[20] The point is made in more prosaic form in recital 12 to the Regulation.

[21] Private International Law (Miscellaneous Provisions) Act 1995.

not start so cleanly; and anyone reading Articles 31 and 32 would be entitled to be puzzled as to what they were supposed to mean. The European Court ruled that the Regulation does not apply to events (which give rise to damage) occurring before 12 January 2009,[22] which is fine as far as it goes, though it is not hard to imagine cases in which the events which give rise to damage occur both before and after 11 January 2009, as to which the ruling is unhelpful. It may be open to a claimant to select and selectively plead the facts and matters on which he proposes to rely to establish his claim, confining himself to pleading only those which occur before (or after, as serves his purpose) the material date; but even if he does not do so in so self-serving a way, there will be cases which are just problematic to deal with. Take a case of product liability, for example. If a pharmaceutical drug is manufactured before 12 January 2009, but sold and used on or after that date, would the Regulation apply? Though the common law conflict of laws cannot be a proper guide to the Regulation, it took the view that the gist of the tort was sale to a purchaser without a proper warning, as distinct from the faulty scientific research and development of the drug. It is, however, not hard to imagine that another law might take the view that the event which gives rise to the damage is the manufacture of a thing with the potential to cause harm to anyone who ingests it; and if one therefore asks whether a case like this, where the actions or omissions of the defendant, and the pre-damage acts of the claimant which form an essential part of the story, fall on each side of the dateline, the answer is not yet there to be seen. It may be harder still: take the cases of liability for injury in which death from mesothelioma has resulted from exposure to asbestos fibres over a period of years, or (if domestic law ever draws the necessary conclusions) from gradual self-destruction courtesy of the tobacco industry. If the acts attributed to or alleged against the defendant fall on both sides of the dateline, the plain and simple ruling that the Regulation does not apply if (all the) events which give rise to damage take place before 12 January 2009 will not answer all the questions which need to be answered.

---

[22] Case C-412/10 *Homawoo v GMF Assurances SA* [2011] ECR I-(Nov 17), [2012] ILPr 49.

Perhaps one should simply reflect that torts are like that. It is reasonable to suppose that the answer must be uniform, and will not reflect national laws and their understanding of what constitutes the tort, and in some respects the problem will cure itself as the commencement date recedes into history. As matters currently stand, if a centre of gravity approach, or balance of the events approach, can be made to work, it will be attractive. In relation to non-contractual obligations other than torts, the same commencement date rule applies, but it is less likely to cause problems.

3. ROME II REGULATION: MATERIAL SCOPE

The Regulation applies to non-contractual obligations in civil and commercial matters; it applies whenever there is a choice of law to be made between the laws of states, including in the case of the United Kingdom, choice of law as between the parts of the United Kingdom.[23] It applies to torts and delicts, and to non-contractual obligations which are not torts, which is to say, to obligations arising from unjust enrichment, from *negotiorum gestio*, and from pre-contractual fault. Assuming that the events complained of took place after the start date of the Regulation, choice of law for any non-contractual obligation will, unless excluded by the Regulation from its material scope, be determined by the Regulation.

Some of the exceptions from the material scope of the Regulation are similar to those of the Rome I Regulation. Accordingly, it excludes non-contractual obligations arising: out of family relationships, including maintenance;[24] out of matrimonial property regimes, also wills and succession;[25] under bills of exchange, cheques and promissory notes, and other negotiable instruments to the extent that the obligations to the extent that the obligations arise out of their negotiable character;[26] out of the law of companies such as creation, capacity, and winding up;[27] and out of the relations between settlors, trustees, and beneficiaries.[28] It does not

---

[23] Which in this context includes Gibraltar: Art 25; SI 2008/2986, Art 6.
[24] Article 1(2)(a).
[25] Article 1(2)(b).
[26] Article 1(2)(c).
[27] Article 1(2)(d).
[28] Article 1(2)(e).

apply to evidence and procedure,[29] and for all of these, what needs to be said was said in the previous chapter.

Other exclusions from its material scope are more obviously peculiar to the Rome II Regulation, and in several cases, respond to particular interests and issues recently exposed. First, the Regulation does not apply to the liability of the state for acts and omissions in the exercise of state authority (*acta jura imperii*).[30] This may have been prompted by a case under the Brussels I Regulation in which a Greek claimant sought to bring tort proceedings against Germany for loss and damage caused by the armed forces of the German state. Though the European Court ruled that the matter did not arise in a civil or commercial matter,[31] it was presumably thought by Member States that they had better do something. The Rome II Regulation will not apply to any non-contractual obligations arising from such acts; the exclusion extends to those who act on behalf of states, including office-holders. So choice of law in a tort claim against a state torturer will be governed by the common law rules of private international law: the rule is clear enough, though it is harder to understand why it made sense to leave choice of law in such cases to the unpredictable variety of national rules. Second, the Regulation does not apply to non-contractual obligations which assert the personal liability of auditors to a company or to its members in the statutory audit of accounts.[32] No explanation is given as to why this should be, but again, the common law rules for choice of law will apply in such cases. Third, it does not apply to non-contractual obligations arising out of nuclear damage.[33] No doubt the choice of law rule for non-contractual obligations in respect of environmental damage was considered to pose too much of a threat to those states whose nuclear activities are liable to cause catastrophic damage in other countries. Fourth, it does not apply to non-contractual obligations arising out of violations of privacy and rights relating to personality, including defamation.[34] The explanation for this exclusion of

---

[29] Article 1(3).
[30] Article 1(1).
[31] Case C-292/05 *Lechouritou v Germany* [2007] ECR I-1519.
[32] Article 1(2)(d).
[33] Article 1(2)(f).
[34] Article 1(2)(g).

this lively and topical area of non-contractual liability[35] appears to lie in the particular sensitivities raised by privacy and self-esteem, on the one hand, and the freedoms of speech and of the press, on the other. For there are some Member States in which the dignity and self-esteem of persons in public life appears to outweigh the so-called right of the press to publish and of the prurient to poke their noses in; in other states the freedom of the press is considered to be a vital part of the struggle against corruption in high places. It was little surprise that agreement on choice of law was not reached at the first attempt; the effort to find a basis on which the European Union might harmonize choice of law in these areas continues; in the meantime, non-contractual obligations arising out of these matters are governed by the common law rules for choice of law.

4. ROME II REGULATION: GENERAL AND COMMON PROVISIONS

(a) Habitual residence

As is the case with the Rome I Regulation, the principal point of reference between a person and a law is defined in terms of habitual residence. Article 23 defines this in terms which are functionally identical to those in Article 19 of the Rome I Regulation. The only differences are that the Rome II Regulation does not specify the date for the assessment of habitual residence, but it seems reasonable to suppose that it will be the date of the accrual of the cause of action rather (if it be different) the date on which legal proceedings are begun; and that the language in which Article 23 is drafted is more conspicuously gender-neutral than that used in Rome I. The true significance of this conspicuous difference in drafting remains elusive.

(b) Agreements on choice of law

Whether the non-contractual obligation in question is a tort or not, Article 14 of the Regulation sets out the circumstances in

---

[35] It is also observed that the jurisdiction rules applicable in such cases, which will frequently take place in mass media with global reach, have been very awkward to manage: see eg Joined Cases C-509/09 *eDate Advertising GmbH v X* and C-161/10 *Martinez v MGN Ltd* [2011] ECR I-(Oct 25), [2012] QB 654.

which the parties may submit it to the law of their choice. This means that they may[36] make an agreement as to the governing law. In confirming or conferring the autonomy of the parties in this way the Regulation makes a mighty improvement on the choice of law rules which previously held sway in England, where the notion that parties could choose the law to resolve their dispute insofar as it involved litigation of a tort was never seriously developed. The freedom conferred on the parties by Article 14 is not, however, unfettered. The choice of law may be made by an agreement entered into after the event giving rise to the damage, but if the agreement is made before the occurrence of the event giving rise to the damage, it will be binding only if all parties are pursuing commercial activity and the agreement was freely negotiated. In any event, it must be expressed, or demonstrated with reasonable certainty by the facts of the case. Where the agreement is contained in a contractual term, any question of construction of the scope of that agreement will, no doubt, be answered by giving the choice of law as broad a construction as reasonably possible, the better to achieve uniformity of governing law.

A limitation of this freedom to those engaged in commercial activities makes sense if the aim is to prevent choice of law 'agreements' being imposed on parties whose non-contractual obligations are the equivalent of contracts made by consumers: there being no such thing as 'consumer torts', this was probably the best way to produce an analogous rule. Where all the elements relevant to the situation at the time of the event giving rise to the damage are in a country other than that whose law has been chosen, the choice cannot prevent the application of rules of law of that country which cannot be derogated from by agreement.[37] As far as English law is concerned, this provision is long overdue.

So much may have been expected. But because the Regulation also applies to non-contractual obligations which are not torts, it opens the door to the possibility, in principle at least, that parties negotiating towards a possible contract may agree upon the law which will apply to any non-contractual obligations arising from their pre-contractual dealings. This freedom is likely to be

---

[36] Subject to specific exceptions: Art 6(4), Art 8(3) (and by implication, Art 13).
[37] Article 14(3).

most useful in commercial relationships, for the idea of agreeing after the breakdown of relations upon a specific law to govern pre-contractual obligations seems improbable, but it opens the door to the selection of a law which limits, or perhaps extends, the duties which each negotiating party owes to the other: duties of disclosure, care, truthfulness, good faith, and so on. While this law will not of itself govern the validity of the contract,[38] it offers an opportunity to parties to manage the risks to which each is exposed in the negotiation phase of their relationship.

(c) Scope of applicable law

According to Article 22, the applicable law applies to determine who bears the burden of proof; it also determines the application of any presumption, such as may relate to causation or fault. Article 20 provides that the *lex causae* will govern the extent to which a debtor, who has himself satisfied a claim which existed against several debtors, may recover compensation or contribution from the other debtors.

In addition, Article 15 states a long list of issues which will be governed by the *lex causae*; this long list is not exhaustive. The *lex causae* will govern the basis and extent of liability, including the determination of who may be held liable for acts done, including the imposition of vicarious liability for the acts of a servant; also, the grounds for exemption from liability, including any limitation of liability and division of liability, such as the effect of contributory negligence and the apportionment of liability as between multiple tortfeasors. Also, the existence, nature, and assessment of damage or the remedy claimed: in other words, it will govern all the component parts of the remedies.[39] There is therefore no reflection of the awkward division drawn by the corresponding provision of the Rome I Regulation;[40] the assessment and calculation of damages is simply a function of the applicable law. It will govern the measures which a court may

---

[38] Because the Rome II Regulation applies only to *non*-contractual obligations.

[39] It has been held that this means that if the *lex causae* does not allow for a particular interim remedy, which would be otherwise available under English law, it may not be awarded: *OJSC TNK-BP Holding v Lazurenko* [2012] EWHC 2781 (Ch), which has the attraction of logic and the appearance of a bad decision.

[40] Article 12(1)(c) of the Rome I Regulation.

take to prevent or terminate injury or damage or to ensure the provision of compensation, though in this case, there is a necessary limitation in that the court is not required to go beyond an exercise of the powers which it has under its own procedural law. It will also answer the question whether a right to damages or a remedy may be passed on or inherited, which appears to include the assignment of rights even where this would be considered champertous; and it will determine the persons entitled to compensation for damage sustained personally and liability for the acts of another person: a point which seems to have been provided for previously, but this makes the point with double force. And it will determine the manner in which an obligation may be extinguished, as well as prescription and limitation, which includes the rules relating to the commencement, interruption, and suspension of time.

There will be some cases in which the application of a provision of the applicable law, say the *lex delicti*, is impossible. If that happens, the court will simply have to apply its own law in default. This may be significant in a case in which a claim in tort is found to be governed by American law according to which the assessment of damages would simply involve leaving the issue to a civil jury. In such a case an English court cannot apply the *lex delicti*, for it is either a rule that the measure of damages is whatever the trier of fact feels and finds to be the right figure, or it takes the form of a procedural mechanism rather than a rule of substantive law capable of being proved and applied as such. Though it would not be wholly unthinkable, it does not seem plausible to try to show the court that a 'typical' jury award would fall within a particular range, for this would not be the application of a rule of law so much as a prediction as to the bare result of applying it, which is not the same thing at all.

Nevertheless, the basic scheme of the Regulation is clear enough to see: it is to refer practically all issues to the law identified by the Regulation as applicable, and to leave it to the public policy or mandatory laws of the forum, considered below, to make the exceptions necessary. In other words, the technique is to establish a broad general rule controlled by an exception formulated by reference to the particular needs of the individual case.

(d) Overriding the applicable law

Just as is the case with the Rome I Regulation, the law identified as applicable by the Rome II Regulation may be displaced. Article 16 provides for the application of overriding mandatory provisions of the *lex fori* where that law requires their application irrespective of the law otherwise applicable. The definition of 'overriding mandatory provisions' which is given by Article 9(1) of the Rome I Regulation is not reproduced in Rome II. The argument for consistency of interpretation would suggest that the two expressions should have the same scope, but this may not be right. The reasons to allow a law to override the *lex contractus* may not be identical with those which are persuasive in the law of tort, for the degrees of hold and legitimacy which each has may not be precisely the same; and Article 16 may therefore operate less restrictively than Article 9(1) of the Rome I Regulation.

A rule of the *lex causae* may be refused application where this would be manifestly incompatible with the public policy of the *lex fori*;[41] it is obviously no objection that a rule of the *lex causae*, proposed to be applied, articulates the public policy of that foreign country. Recital 32 indicates that a rule of the *lex causae* which would lead to the recovery of 'non-compensatory exemplary or punitive damages of an excessive nature' may be found to be objectionable in this way. The primary aim of this provision is awards of damages which are excessively large, though if the approach of the Canadian courts were to be at all instructive, damages would need to be truly astronomic[42] before some judges would be shocked into reaching for their own sense of public policy. There is no reason, however, to confine the operation of this provision to cases in which the *lex causae* would lead to very high damages. It must be open to a court to find that a rule of the *lex delicti* capping damages at a level regarded as unfeasibly low to be contrary to public policy. For this reason, provisions of Australian law which cap damages for personal injury resulting from motor accidents should not be applied by English courts, at least in circumstances in which the

---

[41] Article 26.

[42] cf *Beals v Saldanha* [2003] 3 SCR 416, where the damages ordered by the US court were not contrary to Canadian public policy despite their extraordinary size in relationship to the original loss.

claimant had only a transient connection with the state in which the accident took place.[43]

(e) The meaning of law

Law, in the context of the Rome II Regulation, means the domestic law of the country whose law is identified as applicable. Article 24 means that there is no room for *renvoi* in the law of non-contractual obligations.

Only in one sense is this a pity. The High Court of Australia, in a thoughtful judgment on choice of law for torts committed overseas, had taken the view, on grounds which seemed unassailable, that the law of the place of the tort should mean the law, including foreign law, where it was sufficiently proved that the foreign judge would apply it, which would be applied by the judge at the place of the tort.[44] It saw that this was a sensible way to prevent forum-shopping as well as being an intelligent understanding of what 'the law of the place of the tort' actually meant: it is perfectly rational to consider that 'law' actually is what a judge would apply to resolve the matter before him. This thinking, however, is not relevant to a scheme of the kind proposed by the Regulation. For the Regulation does not look to the place of the tort in order to apply its law as a rule of single reference. Instead, it selects a law by pinpointing the law of the location of a specific element within the cause of action as a rule of first reference, and offering a series of measured exceptions to meet the needs of cases in which this rule of first reference does not or would not yield a satisfactory answer. It is so different a technique for choice of law that the more intellectual reflections of the High Court of Australia upon common law technique can have no part to play in it.

(f) Insurance and other third party issues

The question whether the victim of damage may bring his or her claim directly against the insurer of the wrongdoer is answered

---

[43] *Harding v Wealands* [2006] UKHL 32, [2007] 2 AC 1 (where the cap was inapplicable according to the common law as it was regarded as a procedural rule going to quantification).

[44] *Neilson v Overseas Projects Corpn of Victoria* (2005) 223 CLR 331.

benevolently: Article 18 provides that a direct claim may be brought if this is permitted by the law which governs the non-contractual obligation or by the law which governs the insurance contract. It therefore follows that a direct claim may be brought even though the law of the insurance would preclude it.

A rather cumbersome provision in Article 19 deals with subrogation. In effect, if an insurer has discharged a liability of its insured, the law which governs the insurer's duty to satisfy the claim also determines whether it may exercise against the debtor (wrongdoer) the rights which the insured party had against the wrongdoer.

5. ROME II REGULATION: CHOICE OF LAW FOR TORTS

The general approach taken to choice of law in Chapter II of the Regulation, which applies to torts and delicts, is to establish a rule for general cases, and to provide special rules for particular kinds of tort for which the general rule is either not appropriate or not sufficient. Sensibly enough, the choice of law rules in Chapter II of the Regulation apply to torts which have occurred as well as to those which are likely to occur.[45] Given the wide variety of torts, and the correspondingly wide variety of geographical connections displayed by some tort cases, it is unsurprising that the choice of law regime is sometimes complex; but it is undoubtedly wise that there be a general rule as well as specific ones.

There is a need to distinguish between torts, to which Chapter II applies, and other non-contractual obligations which fall under Chapter III; and this may[46] be problematic in cases which English domestic law might simply see as tortious while other national laws do not. The cases which call most obviously for the application of this line of distinction are causes of action for damages which arise from being wrongfully induced to enter into a contract, such as (in terms of English law, for the purposes of

---

[45] Article 2.2.

[46] However, according to Art 13, where the non-contractual obligation results from the infringement of an intellectual property right, it falls under Art 8, and not within Chapter III.

illustration) fraud, negligent misrepresentation, and the strict-ish liability imposed by the Misrepresentation Act 1967; and causes of action in which the claimant decides to treat the wrongdoer as unjustly enriched without legal cause by the profit which he has gained, so waiving the tort which has been committed. As to the first, it seems pretty clear that the Regulation intends these cases to fall within Article 12, and therefore to be regarded as falling outside Chapter II. As to the second, it may be better not to worry, for if the claim alleging unjust enrichment arises as the consequence of a tort, Article 10(1) will be likely to mean that it will be governed by the *lex delicti* in any event; and if that is so, further analysis is without practical utility.[47]

(a) General rule

Article 4 establishes a choice of law rule for general cases in slightly complicated form. The point of entry depends on whether the defendant and victim are habitually resident in the same country when the damage occurs. If they are, the law of that country will be the applicable law for the non-contractual obligations arising out of the tort;[48] but if they are not so resident, the applicable law will be that of the country in which the damage occurs, irrespective of the country in which the event giving rise to it occurred, and further irrespective of country in which the indirect consequences of the event giving rise to the damage occur.[49] In this latter respect the rule will almost certainly reflect the distinction drawn, and now well established, in the context of the Brussels I Regulation between the place where damage occurs, which is significant, and the place where it is (afterwards) suffered, felt, written up, recorded, or resented.[50] Even so, it is not hard to pose challenging questions which probe the difficulty of ascribing a location to the occurrence of damage. In personal injury, is the place where the damage occurs (for example) where the malign substance is ingested, or the place where the victim is when the symptoms first manifest themselves? Where does the damage occur when a claimant receives advice in

---

[47] And for the problems with knowing receipt, see fn 1, p 263 above.

[48] Article 4(2).

[49] Article 4(1).

[50] See p 88–89.

country A, sends a message to his broker in country B directing him to make an investment in property in country C which will be paid for by transferring funds from the claimant's bank account in country D? If the property acquired by way of investment is worthless, did the damage occur in A, where the fatal decision was taken, or in B, where the consequences of that decision were transmitted, or C, where the worthless asset was acquired, or D from which the funds to pay from it were sent and lost for good? So far as authority is any weak guide, where the loss is purely financial in the sense of a parting with money, in consequence of which the unwanted property is acquired, it may be seen as the place where the money passed out of the control of the claimant, everything else being a consequence of that irreversible loss of finance, or financial loss.[51] To take another example, how does one locate the place where damage occurs if that damage is moral, emotional, or reputational? For that matter, how does Article 4(1) work where the damage to the claimant is nervous shock, or psychological damage sustained as the arguably-indirect consequence of injury to another? Or to cases of bereavement? For all that one may ask these questions, the truth really is that, in most cases, a place of the damage rule works as well as any other, and probably better than most: the Law Commission[52] came to a similar conclusion in 1990, so there appears to be something in it. It is possible to construct difficult cases, and a good deal easier in tort than elsewhere, but this does not call into question the sense of the general rule devised to try to make sense of them. It is still a pity, though, that the Regulation does not define 'damage' if this is to be the fact or factor on which the application of the general rule will turn.

But whichever initial version of the general rule applies, Article 4(3) provides that if from all the circumstances of the case it is clear that the tort is manifestly more closely connected with another country, the law of that other country shall apply instead. This rule, which it may not be helpful to regard as an exception,[53] applies only if the tort as a whole is manifestly more

---

[51] See p 270 below.

[52] Law Commission Report 193 (1990).

[53] For 'exceptions' are given a restrictive interpretation, so as not to derogate from the general rule, and it has yet to be held that Art 4(3) should be so treated.

closely connected to another country; by contrast with what the common law appeared to countenance,[54] it does not permit one specific issue within the broad framework of the claim to be hived off from the corpus of the claim and made subject to a different law. It is also provided that the requisite degree of closer connection may be seen in the existence of a pre-existing relationship between the parties, such as a contract. Where, therefore, the contract is governed by a law which the parties have chosen and expressed, it would be rational for a tort associated with the contractual relationship to be governed by the same law, though whether this can be explained as there being a connection linking the tort to a country, as distinct from a system of law, is unclear.[55] It is submitted that this would not contradict Article 14, which lays down fairly strict conditions for the validation of a choice of law made to govern a tort. That is a separate and distinct process from what is involved when Article 4(3) enquires into whether there is a pre-existing relationship between the parties, governed by a law which they may have chosen, which has a manifestly close relationship with the tort.

Apart from cases in which Article 4(3) is triggered by a pre-existing relationship between the parties, recourse to the exception will be rare, but it will be more likely to serve as an exception to Article 4(1) than to Article 4(2). In relation to Article 4(2), the cases in which a tort will be manifestly more closely connected to a country other than that of the parties' shared habitual residence will presumably be where the fact that the parties have the same habitual residence is unplanned and coincidental, as distinct from the case being one in which friends or partners habitually resident in one country go on holiday together to another. But in relation to Article 4(1), the country of the occurrence of the damage may not be the country which lies at the heart of the tort. In cases in which this is so, the reference to Article 4(3) will allow a more suitable law to be chosen. Though

---

[54] Perhaps under the influence of American thinking: *Boys v Chaplin* [1971] AC 356.

[55] For a common law view that this distinction may be more apparent than real, see *Morin v Bonhams & Brooks Ltd* [2003] EWCA Civ 1802, [2004] 1 Lloyd's Rep 702; for a common lawyer's view that it is not, see *Credit Lyonnais v New Hampshire Insurance Co Ltd* [1997] 2 Lloyd's Rep 1.

it is doubtless an unintended coincidence, this is pretty much the pattern established in England by the Private International Law (Miscellaneous Provisions) Act 1995, sections 11 and 12.

(b) Product liability

Try as one might, it is not easy to find sympathetic things to say about the *lex specialis* provided by the Regulation for non-contractual obligations arising out of damage caused by a product which is set out in Article 5. It may appear at first reading that the Article is intended to mean that all cases of damage caused by a product are dealt with within Article 5; but the trouble is that the provisions in Article 5 do not cover the whole of ground.

The starting point is that if the defendant and victim are habitually resident in the same country when the damage occurs, the law of that country will apply. If they are not, then Article 5(1) offers four sub-rules by which to identify the applicable law for the non-contractual obligation. The law will be that of the country in which the victim was habitually resident when the damage occurred, provided that the product was marketed there. Failing that, it will be the law of the country in which the product was acquired if the product was marketed there. Failing that, it will be the law of the country in which the damage occurred if the product was marketed there. But an answer derived from any of these possibilities may be displaced in favour of the law of the country in which the tortfeasor is habitually resident if he could not reasonably foresee the marketing of the product, or a product of the same type, in the law of the country otherwise applicable by reason of the provisions described. And finally, where Article 5(1) has given its answer, if the tort is manifestly more closely connected with a country other than that derived from Article 5(1), Article 5(2) allows that law to apply instead. The opening words of Article 5 suggest that these provisions cover the whole of the ground, leaving no room for any other law to deal with non-contractual obligations arising out of product liability.

This is rather awkward. Some of the problems can be illustrated if we take the example of a person injured by a mobile telephone which has an electrical fault, and which causes physical injury to a person who uses it. The point of departure must be to understand what it is meant by 'marketed', for though the meaning of this term shapes the heart of the rule, 'marketed' is not defined. If the actual handset was sold, at least commercially, it was presumably marketed. But is it sufficient if the product line is advertised and put on sale, while the individual handset was acquired somewhere else? If it is advertised that the new generation yPhone mobile device will be in English shops a month before Christmas, would this allow it to be said that where the damage is caused by one such handset, acquired outside the United Kingdom, it had still been marketed in England? Second, even if we understand what 'marketed' means, it is not clear whether it matters who needs to have done the jurisdictionally-significant marketing: manufacturer, main dealer, re-seller, or individual private entrepreneur. Third, even if the individual handset was marketed in a country, does the user have to have acquired it as a result of this marketing? Suppose she received it as a gift, rather than obtaining it in any form of market? Fourth, is it necessary that the specific model which did the damage was marketed, or is it sufficient that a similar model was? And in light of the emphasis on marketing, there will be some cases which fall within none of the hypotheses in Article 5(1). One might then suppose that the *lex specialis* had no further interest in providing a rule for choice of law, and in default of such provision, one would presumably wish to fall back on Article 4(1). But the wording of Article 5(1) appears to exclude this possibility.

There is, of course, sense in Article 5(1). If a manufacturer[56] releases his product into the stream of commerce it should not be held to complain when a law other than that of the place of the occurrence of damage applies, if the degree of foreseeability which is inherent in the notion of 'marketing' the product meant that it could have foreseen it. But where these special conditions are not met, the general answer which would otherwise have been provided by Article 4(1) should apply. This may be how Article 5(1) has, in the end, to be understood, though it will require some muscular manipulation of its language to get us there.

(c) Unfair competition; acts restricting free competition

Article 6 deals with non-contractual obligations arising out of unfair competition and acts which restrict free competition. For

---

[56] Though Art 5(1) is not necessarily confined to claims against a manufacturer.

these torts, the general solution provided by Article 4 is excluded altogether, except for the single case in which unfair competition affects the interests of a specific competitor. Otherwise, for unfair competition, the basic choice of law is to apply the law of the country in which competitive relations or the collective interests of consumers are likely to be affected; it is not said how this rule is to work where the tort has this effect in more countries than one.

For cases of restriction of competition, the basic orientation of the rule is to apply the law of the country where the market is, or is likely to be, affected: this reflects the broader general rule in Article 4(1) in favour of the place where the damage occurs. However, if the restriction affected more than one market, the victim may choose to base his claim instead on the law of the court seised, just so long as the market in that state is one of those substantially affected by the restriction in competition. The result will be that where, for example, a cartel has engaged in a price-fixing conspiracy, and has put this into practice across several national or regional markets, the claimant may choose to base his claim on the law of the country in which proceedings are brought. It is a pragmatic solution for cases which are almost inevitably complex.

No choice of law is permitted for torts falling within Article 6.[57]

(d) Environmental damage

For non-contractual obligations arising out of environmental damage,[58] including damage sustained by persons or property as a result of such damage, Article 7 specifies as applicable the law of the country in which the damage occurs unless the victim opts to found his claim on the law of the country in which the event giving rise to the damage occurred. In other words, the only two possible laws to be applied are that of the damage and that of the event giving rise to it: there may be a closer connection with a third country, but that country's law is shut out from potential operation.

Once again, at first sight, the choice of law rule, and in particular the option which it gives to the claimant, who may be but

---

[57] Article 6.3.

[58] See also recital 24 for the alarmingly amorphous definition of 'environmental damage'.

need not be a personal victim, reflects the special jurisdictional rule given by the Brussels I Regulation for cases of tort. But this rule opens up the possibility that when toxic effluent escapes from an industrial plant just across the border, a claimant may ask the courts for the place of the defendant's domicile to apply the law of the place where the fish or birds were killed. No doubt the possibility that something similar might be done accounts for the exclusion of non-contractual obligations arising out of nuclear damage, for Member States which have these terrifying machines for generation of electric power tend to site them on the remotest edges of their territory, whence it is hoped that wind and tide will carry the consequences away. The idea that residents from Ireland might come and bring proceedings against the company running a nuclear plant on the coast of Cumbria, complaining of radiation escaping into the Irish Sea and be entitled to have the English court apply Irish law, will not have been an attractive one.

(e) Infringement of intellectual property rights

For non-contractual obligations arising from the infringement of intellectual property rights, Article 8 provides that the applicable law is the law of the country for which the protection is claimed; it is not open to the parties to purport to depart from this rule by agreement pursuant to Article 14.

(f) Industrial action

Non-contractual obligations arising from industrial action are governed by the general rule in Article 4, but with one modification: in place of Article 4(1), with its reference to the law of the place where the damage occurs, Article 9 makes its reference to the law of the country where the action is to be or has been taken. The rule applies whether the claim lies against a worker or a workers' organization, and whether the action is past, or pending. It is a sensible rule, for two among many reasons. First, there is a closer association between criminal law and civil law in the area of industrial relations than in most other areas: the idea that the law of the place determines the presence or absence of criminal liability for organizing strikes and other campaigns of industrial warfare is so well entrenched that it is natural to allow the law of the place where the action is taken to determine the civil law consequences as well. Second, there will be cases in which the place of the damage would in any event be hard to discern. If one surveys the campaign of industrial action organized by or on behalf of the maritime trade unions against shipowners and ship operators who flag or re-flag their vessels in convenient places, the industrial action has its employer-damaging effects in several countries at the same time: indeed, it would be liable to fail if it did not. This is more than enough to justify the terms of Article 9.

6. ROME II REGULATION: CHOICE OF LAW FOR OTHER OBLIGATIONS

Chapter III of the Rome II Regulation provides a choice of law rule to deal with non-contractual obligations arising in three cases which evidently are not at home within a chapter dealing with torts.[59] It seems probable that their appearance in Chapter III is a matter of organizational convenience, and that Chapter III should simply be regarded as *sui generis*. It would be particularly problematic if their treatment for purposes of choice of law were to be taken to say anything about their relationship to the special jurisdictional rules in Article 5 of the Brussels I Regulation. For example (and it is only one example), it has generally been assumed that when a claim is made for the recovery of sums paid under a failed contract, the claim falls within the special jurisdictional rule for matters relating to a contract in Article 5(1) of the Brussels I Regulation, but if the location of unjust enrichment in Chapter III of the Rome II Regulation were to suggest that this kind of claim was neither based on a contractual obligation nor on a non-contractual obligation in the nature of a tort, it is more difficult to see how it could fall within Article 5 of the Brussels I Regulation at all. For this among other reasons, it is suggested that recital 7 to the Rome II Regulation, which calls for consistency in interpretation, should not be pressed beyond the limit of what is sensible. Consistency across the provisions of the Regulations does not necessarily mean that technical terms must bear identical meanings.

---

[59] For the problems of locating knowing receipt within Chapter III or Chapter II, see fn 1, p 263 above.

The three cases placed within Chapter III share two characteristics. First, they arise, or are liable to arise, in territory adjacent to or overlapping with other categories of case for which a choice of law rule is separately prescribed. Unjust enrichment claims may arise in connection with a contract which has been rescinded, or with a contract which was supposed, but mistakenly, to have been made, or with a payment made on the misunderstanding that the person paid was the counterparty when he was not, or when it was not realized that the contract had been discharged. They may arise in connection with a tort, such as the conversion or misuse of another's property to make a gain; and they may arise without any such connection. Uninvited intervention in another's affairs may take place between contracting parties, or in the circumstances in which a tort is committed, such as where the claimant intervenes to prevent a fire carelessly started from doing damage to another's property, or in response to a danger for which no-one is to blame. And pre-contractual fault almost always arises in connection with a contract, even though in some cases the fault prevents the conclusion of the valid and binding contract which was foreseen.

In other words, these three causes of action are not as free-standing and insulated from the rest of the world as some others may be. This has the potential to be problematic, but the practical sense of the Regulation is to construct choice of law rules for these cases which mean that in these adjacent cases, the choice of law rule takes its colour from the relationship which stands in close proximity to it.

Second, the three cases are dealt with by a series of sub-rules, addressed in sequence, and finishing up with a default sub-rule. It is not exactly elegant, but it seems to offer the best opportunity for connecting the issue to a law which might rationally have been expected to govern it, which is a virtue in its own right.

And lest it should have been forgotten or overlooked, it should not be forgotten that the freedom of the parties to choose the law to govern their non-contractual obligation, which is conferred by Article 14, applies to Chapter III as it applies to Chapter II of the Regulation.

(a) Unjust enrichment

Choice of law for non-contractual obligations arising out of unjust enrichment, which expression includes obligations arising from the payment of amounts wrongly received (or, perhaps more correctly, anyhow received but wrongfully retained), is covered by a four-part rule set out as Article 10. If the obligation concerns a relationship between the parties, such as a contract or a tort, it will be governed by the law which governs that prior relationship. Otherwise, if the parties had their habitual residence in the same country when the event giving rise to the unjust enrichment occurred, the law of that country will apply, failing which the applicable law will be that of the country in which the unjust enrichment took place. And whichever of those rules provided the answer, if the non-contractual obligation is manifestly more closely connected to another country, the law of that country shall apply instead.

If one accepts that unjust enrichment is little more than a debatable label applied to a diverse collection of individual cases in which a law might properly require payment or repayment, but which fit neither individually into another legal category nor together as a unified class, a choice of law regime of alternate reference seems most rational. The effect of the scheme in Article 10 is that those obligations closely connected to contracts or torts will be governed by the *lex contractus* or the *lex delicti*, with the result that there is no need to worry whether they should be regarded 'as' contractual or tort claims: that may be, as said above, still a controversial issue in the interpretation of the Brussels I Regulation, but it has been taken care of and put to bed for the purpose of choice of law. As to the escape clause which allows reference to the law of another country, this will be the most likely to happen in the case for which the applicable law would otherwise be selected as the place of the enrichment. For the place of enrichment may be difficult to locate or artificial where the 'enrichment' takes the form of electronic crediting of bank or other accounts: particularly in the case in which funds are instantaneously transferred—except that nothing except data, whatever that is, is actually transferred—from one account to another (and all the more so if the real beneficiary of the bank account is cloaked in mystery), it may hard to say where 'the' unjust enrichment took place, and impossible to believe that it actually matters.[60] Even so, the fact that this default rule is pretty

---

[60] cf *Fiona Trust & Holding Corpn v Privalov* [2010] EWHC 3199 at [179].

close to what the common law or private international law would have said on the same question simply goes to show that this rather uncomfortable rule of last resort may be the least bad option for the solution of the choice of law problem.

(b) *Negotiorum gestio*

The choice of law rule for non-contractual obligations arising from acts performed without due authority in connection with the affairs of another (*negotiorum gestio*, benevolent interference, or uninvited intervention) is, according to Article 11, framed in the same general way. The first rule is to apply the law which governs the relationship existing between the parties if there is one; if not, the law of the shared habitual residence when the event giving rise to the damage occurred, if there is one; if not, the law of the country in which the intervener's act was performed; and in any event, an escape clause allows the application of the law of the country which with the obligation is manifestly more closely connected.

(c) *Culpa in contrahendo*

Article 12 of the Rome II Regulation deals with non-contractual obligations arising from dealings prior to the conclusion of a contract, regardless of whether the contract was concluded. The Regulation labels this *culpa in contrahendo*, though pre-contractual fault, which will include misrepresentation and non-disclosure, would be more familiar to English eyes. As was said above, this rule deals with the non-contractual obligations which arise from such dealings. It will not apply to the question whether the contract is valid, voidable, or non-existent, for those are issues of contractual obligation (or not) to which the *lex contractus* as identified by the Rome I Regulation will usually apply.[61] This rule is left to deal with choice of law for claims for compensation for fraud, misrepresentation, non-disclosure, failure to negotiate or to contract in good faith, and so forth, where these arise from dealings prior to the making or possible making of a contract. Insofar as there was an obligation to do or to refrain from

---

[61] If the contract was concluded after 17 December 2009.

doing any of these things, the obligation is a non-contractual one: adjacent to contractual, perhaps, but non-contractual.

The principal rule enacted by Article 12 is that the non-contractual obligation in such cases is governed by the law which applies to the contract or would have applied to it had it been entered into. Where the applicable law cannot be determined on that basis—presumably in circumstances in which it is just not possible to say or predict with sufficient certainty which law would have governed a contract which never came into being—the applicable law is determined on the basis of a three-part rule which is, for practical purposes, a copy of the three-part rule in Article 4. Presumably, if this process results in a choice of law which seems completely unfair to the court, public policy will serve as the rule of last resort.

C. NON-CONTRACTUAL OBLIGATIONS OUTSIDE THE ROME II REGULATION

Left outside the scope of the Rome II Regulation, and governed by the rules of the common law and English statute, which the Regulation otherwise displaces for non-contractual obligations falling within its scope, are obligations arising from events occurring before 12 January 2009; obligations arising otherwise than in civil and commercial matters; and all non-contractual obligations arising out of violations of privacy, and rights relating to personality, including defamation.[62] Although it is hoped or anticipated that the last of these may yet be brought within the scope of the Rome II Regulation, it is necessary to say something about the non-Regulation rules for choice of law which apply to them. When the Rome II Regulation is expanded to cover such cases, as it is assumed that it soon will, the saving provision for local mandatory laws and national public policy should be sufficient to safeguard important national interests in freedom of speech and rights to privacy and personality. There seems to be no real reason why these torts should not be accommodated within the

---

[62] It is not certain, but claims which allege economic loss resulting from negligence, for example, by carelessly writing a 'kiss of death' job reference (cf *Spring v Guardian Assurance plc* [1995] 2 AC 296), will not be excluded from the Rome II Regulation, as the basis of liability is not defamation, and the damage is economic rather than moral, reputational, or personal.

domain of the Rome II Regulation; and the summary of the common law below simply adds to the reasons why they should be, and quickly, too.

1. DEFAMATION

Choice of law for defamation is governed by the rules of the common law, unamended by statute: defamation was also excluded from the Private International Law (Miscellaneous Provisions) Act 1995.[63] In principle, at least, the common law regarded every communication of defamatory material to another as an individual tort, separate and distinct from every other communication of the same information. The logic of this is impeccable; the bad outcomes to which it gave rise are legendary. It meant, among other things, that an individual who fancied himself to have been defamed in a newspaper or other journal might pick and choose which 'publications' he wished to complain of. If, for example, the principal place of publication is in the United States, under the laws of which there would generally be very limited civil liability for publishing material about a person in the public eye, the claimant may decide to complain only of the sales or circulation of the newspaper in England. True, this may limit the size of the damages he hopes to recover, for if there is only a small readership, the measure of damages might be expected to be rather small. But the science by which damages for defamation are assessed is obscure,[64] and it is far from clear that the practice reflects the theory of the arithmetic. In one ridiculous case a deranged German princeling, in exile in Paris, sent his manservant to London to purchase a seventeen-year-old copy of a magazine, in the pages of which he claimed to have

---

[63] Section 13 of the 1995 Act. The Defamation Bill 2012–13, which is expected to pass into law in 2013, will place limitations on the jurisdiction of the court, but does not appear to affect the approach to choice of law for those cases which the court does have jurisdiction to hear.

[64] In one famous case, a judge warned a jury against awarding 'Mickey-Mouse damages'; the jury duly awarded £1 million. It always seemed probable that the judge thought he was issuing a warning against excessive or fantastic damages; it is plausible that the jury took it to be a warning against awarding only tiny damages; and none of it reflected any credit on lawyers or the law.

been defamed. The servant having discharged his duty, it could be held, and was held, that the sale amounted to a fresh publication by the magazine, for which a fresh claim could be brought.[65] The whole thing is ridiculous, but claimants in modern times have evidently felt it no shame to tread in the footeteps of the mad duke.[66] It is notorious that defamation claims having no rational connection to England routinely turn up in the Strand, it being alleged in all seriousness that there were readers or listeners in England, who heard the terrible things which the one foreigner said about the other and who now hold the latter in ridicule and contempt, and that on account of this publication or reading in England, the case is to be dealt with for choice of law purposes as though it lay between two members of the Tunbridge Wells Lawn Tennis Club. If the claim survives any jurisdictional challenges, or contentions that the proceedings are an abuse of process,[67] defamatory publication in England is governed by English law.

For a tort committed in England is governed by English law. The question where it is committed was, for the purpose of the common law rules of private international law, answered by enquiring where the cause of action 'in substance' arose;[68] but in the context of defamation, that place will be where the individual transfer or delivery of information took place.[69] And if that was in England, English domestic law applies, no matter how otherwise foreign the facts may be. Not only does this selective pleading skew the question of choice of law, it also means that an

---

[65] *Duke of Brunswick v Harmer* (1849) 14 QB 185. He was awarded £500, on any view of the matter a ludicrous sum for a single sale to the claimant's own servant sent to make the purchase.

[66] *Schapira v Ahronson* [1998] ILPr 587 (CA); *Berezovsky v Michaels* [2000] 1 WLR 1004 (HL). The same principle has been applied to defamation by internet publication: *Dow Jones Inc v Gutnick* (2003) 210 CLR 575. It was pretty shameless, though the antics of those involved certainly added to the gaiety of life: *King v Lewis* [2004] EWCA Civ 1329, [2005] ILPr 185; *Richardson v Schwarzenegger* [2004] EWHC 2422 (QB), on which see (2004) 75 BYIL 565.

[67] *Dow Jones & Co Inc v Jameel* [2005] EWCA Civ 75, [2005] QB 946.

[68] *Metall und Rohstoff AG v Donaldson Lufkin & Jenrette Inc* [1990] QB 391 (CA).

[69] *Bata v Bata* [1948] WN 366 (CA); cf *Shevill v Presse Alliance SA* [1992] 2 WLR 1 (CA), and as Case C-68/93 *Shevill v Presse Alliance SA* [1995] ECR I-415.

argument that the natural forum for the claim is outside England can be completely derailed.[70]

For torts committed outside England, the claimant faces the obligation of meeting the requirements of the rule of double actionability: he must show that the facts and matters relied on would give rise to tortious liability under the domestic law of England, and would be sufficient to establish civil liability for the same head or heads of damage according to the law of the place where the cause of action arose. In an extreme case, in which the factual connection with one or the other of these laws is remote, the claimant may be dispensed from the requirement of satisfying it,[71] but in principle the requirement of double actionability means that the claimant must in principle win twice over in order to win once.

2. PRIVACY, AND EVENTS PRIOR TO 11 JANUARY 2009

The common law rule which applied a rule of double actionability for claims characterized as torts was abolished for torts other than defamation, malicious falsehood, and similar causes of action arising under foreign laws, and was replaced by a statutory choice of law rule laid down by the Private International Law (Miscellaneous Provisions) Act 1995. Though there are flaws in its conception and its drafting, its role is a fast-vanishing one, and it needs only summary treatment for the two main issues to which it applies: causes of action based on a violation of privacy and other rights relating to personality, excluding defamation; and to causes of action where the events giving rise to liability occurred before 11 January 2009.[71a]

The general choice of law rule applied by section 11 of the Act is to apply the law of the place where the events constituting the tort in question occurred. Where these events are not all located in a single country, the applicable law will be the law of the place

---

[70] This proposition may be amended by legislation in the form of the Defamation Bill 2012–13, but the proposal there is to deal with the question by removing jurisdiction rather than by adapting the rules for choice of law.

[71] *Red Sea Insurance Co Ltd v Bouygues SA* [1995] 1 AC 190.

[71a] For a detailed analysis, see *VTB Capital plc v Nutritek International Corp* [2013] UKSC 5, [2013] 2 WLR 298

where the person was when he or she sustained the injury or was killed; the law of the place where the property was when it was damaged; and in cases not falling within either of these, the law of the country in which occurred the most significant element or elements of the events comprising the tort: in this last case, and for want of any better solution, the identification of the events comprising the tort will be done by reference to the claimant's pleaded claim. Where the answer given by section 11 is not persuasive, because the tort, or the issue, in question is so much more closely connected to another country that it is substantially more appropriate for the law of that other country to be applied to determine the issue or question, section 12 allows that law to be applied instead. The applicable law will determine most aspects of liability, but it will not be applied to the quantification of damages, which is a procedural matter on which an English court applied English domestic law.

For torts which complain about the violation of privacy, the applicable law will be either that of the place where the events constituting the tort occurred, or if they are not all in the same place, the law of the country in which occurred the most significant element or elements of the events comprising the tort. It seems inevitable that this choice of law rule lends itself to manipulation by a claimant, who may identify the invasion of his personal space, or the broadcasting of material acquired, as the element of the events which has the greatest significance, framing the claim so as to take advantage of the choice of law rule in general and the way it will operate in particular.

For torts which arise from events which took place prior to 11 January 2009, the choice of law rules outlined above will apply. The problem of the difficult case, in which the events which gave rise to the damage lay on both sides of the dateline, has no obvious solution.

3. UNJUST ENRICHMENT PRIOR TO 11 JANUARY 2009

The common law never developed a robust choice of law rule for claims based in essence on the notion of unjust enrichment. Perhaps it never needed to; but aside from cases where the enrichment was closely connected to a contract (real, terminated, rescinded, frustrated, supposed, intended, void), for which cases the *lex contractus* would be pressed into service,[72] and cases concerned with land, for which the *lex situs* was practically bound to be applied, it asserted that that the proper law of the obligation would govern, and in default of any better idea, this might be the place of the enrichment. But the case law did little to suggest judicial satisfaction with this rule, or set of rules;[73] and its passing into history is no loss. It is striking, however, how close to the provisions adopted in the Rome II Regulation this actually is, which may suggest that those who laboured to discern the common law, and who came to this conclusion, deserve more credit than was given to them.

---

[72] cf *Baring Bros & Co v Cunninghame DC* [1997] CLC 108 (Outer House), where the judge made extremely heavy weather of the point, but got there in the end.

[73] *Barros Mattos Jr v Macdaniels* [2005] EWHC 1323 (Ch), [2005] ILPr 630.

7

PROPERTY

The private international law of property is a large topic, or several topics. It has to cover a diverse range of property: immovable and movable, tangible and intangible, as well as intellectual and matrimonial. It has to deal with a variety of transactions: voluntary and involuntary, *inter vivos* and on death, marriage and divorce. It can raise difficult questions about the relationship between jurisdiction and choice of law, and between property and the law of obligations. In most cases in which a court is called upon to adjudicate it is asked to settle a dispute about title, and to make an order which is good and reliable against the world, not just as between the parties to the action. Most of the rules are established by the common law: although it has sought to intervene to harmonize choice of law in the fields of succession to property and may to do likewise with matrimonial property, the European Union has not yet proposed the general reform of choice of law in relation to *inter vivos* dispositions of property, which is perhaps slightly surprising. Where choice of law is a matter for the common law rules of private international law, a court may be entitled[1] to apply any foreign law which its rules tell it to in its *renvoi* sense, that is, as the law would be applied by a judge sitting in the foreign country and hearing the case himself. Even though parties will frequently place no reliance on the principle of *renvoi*, this cannot be taken as a decision that the doctrine is inadmissible in the context of property law.

The private international law of property traditionally divides into immovable and movable property, and movables sub-divide into tangible things and intangible property. Whether property is an immovable is determined by the law of the place where it is, the *lex situs*.[2] It may be thought that this offends against the

---

[1] If the rules of foreign law are pleaded and proved to the satisfaction of the court.

[2] Dicey, Morris, and Collins, *The Conflict of Laws* (15th edn, Sweet & Maxwell, 2012), Ch 22; *Re Hoyles* [1911] 1 Ch 179, 185.

principle that characterization is a matter for the *lex fori*, and that in cases of potential disagreement, such as where the property is an oil rig, the interest of a mortgagee in the property mortgaged, the interest of a beneficiary under a trust of land, and so on, this question should be answered by the law of the forum. But in a context in which, as will be seen, the *lex situs* is broadly applicable, and *renvoi* applies also, it would be somewhat self-defeating to distort the very law which a court is seeking to apply with particular faithfulness. The result is that the question whether property is movable or immovable is determined by the *lex situs*.

A. IMMOVABLE PROPERTY

Although claims involving immovable property are mostly liable to be civil or commercial, with jurisdiction simply following the rules of the Brussels I Regulation, it is justifiable to look separately at jurisdiction at this point. Where the land in question is in another Member State, Article 22(1) means that an English court will lack jurisdiction which it might otherwise have had if the proceedings have as their object a right *in rem* in, or a tenancy of, that land.[3] A second issue arises where the land is in a non-Member State but the court has personal jurisdiction over the defendant under, say, Article 2, of the Regulation. It can be argued that it is bound to adjudicate, and that it may not look back to its common law rules of jurisdiction, which are considered below, for a justification for not adjudicating; the application of Article 22(1) by analogy or reflexive effect is yet to be confirmed.

A third issue arises when the court is exercising residual jurisdiction in accordance with Article 4 of the Brussels I Regulation. At this point the common law rules of jurisdiction will be used; and it is instructive for various reasons to consider them in a little detail. The common law held that an English court has no jurisdiction to determine questions of title to immovable property situated outside England, and had no jurisdiction to entertain tort claims in which such an issue would arise for decision.[4]

---

[3] See above; and Chapter III of the Regulation requires the non-recognition of judgments which conflict with this rule.

[4] *British South Africa Co v Companhia de Moçambique* [1893] AC 602; *Hesperides Hotels Ltd v Aegean Turkish Holidays Ltd* [1979] AC 508.

So where a claim was brought which alleged trespass to a hotel and its furniture, in the northern part of the island of Cyprus by defendants claiming authorization by the authorities of the *soi-disant* and illegal 'Turkish Republic of Northern Cyprus', the court could not entertain the action concerning trespass to the land, but could hear the claim alleging conversion of the chattels. The decision shows the width of the rule, for under the *lex situs*, a connecting factor defined by English law and which acknowledged only the laws of the Republic of Cyprus, there could be no dispute about title, as the illegal ordinances of the non-state were not law. But the exclusionary rule still operated.

The common law jurisdictional rule was amended by statute to remove the bar to jurisdiction in relation to tort claims where the issue of title was not the principal issue;[5] but otherwise the preclusion prevails.[6] So a claim alleging trespass may be defeated on jurisdictional grounds if the defendant pleads that the land was his and this question needs to be adjudicated. The historical basis of the rule lay in a common law rule that such actions were 'local', and had to be tried in the place where the land was situated, but a more pragmatic, private international legal, reason is that most laws impose similar limitations for reasons of public policy. And as titles to land are increasingly recorded on a register, only the court with personal jurisdiction over the registrar has any sensible basis for accepting or exercising jurisdiction over an action which may result in the registrar being told to amend the register of title. It follows that, so far as the common law is concerned, disputes about title to foreign land must be tried in the courts of the *situs*, no matter how inconvenient this is, and notwithstanding that the parties would be willing to submit to the personal jurisdiction of an English court. It probably follows that foreign judgments which purport to rule on title to English land will not be recognized in England.[7]

   [5] *Re Polly Peck International plc (in administration)(No 2)* [1998] 3 All ER 812, 828 (CA).

   [6] Civil Jurisdiction and Judgments Act 1982, s 30.

   [7] Although for the possibility that they may be recognized between the parties as judgments binding them *in personam*, see *Pattni v Ali* [2006] UKPC 51, [2007] 2 AC 85.

A very important common law exception to the exclusionary rule exists. If a claim may be framed as one to enforce a personal obligation, albeit one relating to a foreign immovable, there is no jurisdictional impediment to it, even though it may appear that the court is doing indirectly what it cannot do directly. It derives from the ancient case of *Penn v Baltimore*.[8] The parties had made a contract to go to arbitration to settle the boundary between two American proto-states of which they were proprietor. Though the court had no legal power to draw colonial boundaries, it had jurisdiction to order parties to perform their contractual agreements, and it did just that. Despite these unlikely origins, the principle is plain enough: if the claim is brought to enforce a contract, or in respect of a pre-existing equitable obligation, such as a trust, between the parties, the court does not lack jurisdiction to enforce it even if the obligation derives from, or is created by, a transaction relating to land;[9] a similar principle applies if a court is administering an estate which includes foreign land. Indeed, it is only because there is no contract or equity between trespasser and proprietor that statute was required to bring the law of tort into line with this general principle. So if it is claimed that the vendor has failed to perform his contract for sale of land, or that a bare trustee should convey legal title to the claimant beneficiary, the court has jurisdiction to make an order against the defendant in person, which it may back up with its considerable coercive powers, requiring the conveyance of the land; or awarding damages for the breach. Likewise, a court should have jurisdiction to assess shares in the equitable ownership of foreign land to the purchase of which the parties have contributed, and to decree the performance of the duties of any trust. The court is not doing indirectly what it cannot do directly; it is doing, directly, exactly what it is asked to do.

So much for jurisdiction in common law terms and in its residual role. If one asks whether this common law exclusionary rule still operates in cases in which jurisdiction is based on the Brussels I Regulation otherwise than under Article 4, the

---

[8] (1750) 1 Ves Sen 444.
[9] cf Case C-294/92 *Webb v Webb* [1994] ECR I-1717 (a case on what is now Art 22(1) of the Regulation).

only safe answer is that the question has yet to be authoritatively decided. However, if Article 22(1) of the Regulation were to be applicable by analogy, the question would be practically redundant.

So far as regards choice of law in those cases in which the court does have jurisdiction, the inevitable choice of law is for the *lex situs* as this would be applied in a court at the *situs* to any question concerning immovable property: this may, of course, result in the application of the domestic law of country other than that of the *situs*. The usual justification for this is the futility of doing otherwise than what a local judge would do, for she alone has control of the immovable, and her view on the correct answer is inevitably destined to prevail: even those whose distaste for *renvoi* sends the needle off the scale will accept that it has a proper role in questions of immovable property. In fact, and rather ironically, as a justification this one is not as convincing as it may seem. The real question for the foreign judge (as, were the roles reversed, it would be for an English judge) is whether to accept that a judge in another country had the right to make an order concerning local land at all, rather than asking whether that judge arrived at the right substantive answer: she may still refuse to recognize a foreign judgment, even though its reasoning and the result appear to be unimpeachable; and the recognition of a judgment does not usually depend on the conclusion that the adjudicating judge decided correctly. But, that said, it is impossible to maintain a serious argument for the application of anything other than the *lex situs*, and in its *renvoi* sense, where the question is properly one concerning title to the land.[10] Where the court has jurisdiction under the *Penn v Baltimore* exception, the law governing the contractual issue may not be the *lex situs* of the land.[11] But this will be the presumed governing law for contracts concerning land; and only on issues of formality or personal capacity, for example, is there any real prospect of applying a law other than the *lex situs*.

---

[10] *Bank of Africa v Cohen* [1909] 2 Ch 129 (CA).
[11] Though it usually will be: Rome I Regulation, Art 4(1)(c).

B. MOVABLE PROPERTY

The reason for the application of the *lex situs* in the case of immovables is that, because the land cannot be moved, the *lex situs* combines expectation with reality. By contrast, movables move: the clue is in the name. True as this is, it does not affect the choice of law, only the justification for it. Private international law treats tangible and intangible movable property separately.

1. TANGIBLE THINGS

Questions of title to, or the right to possession of, tangible movable property are governed by the *lex situs* of the thing at the date of the event which is alleged to have affected title to it.[12] In the leading classic case, when goods rescued from a shipwreck on the coast of Norway were auctioned and sold by the local magistrate, the buyer acquiring a good title under Norwegian law, English private international law concluded that the title of the former owner was displaced. Certainty and security of title are paramount and are best achieved by the general application of the *lex situs*: if you take a good title according to the law of the place where the thing is, that really should be decisive against the world of claimants. Recognizing this, and understanding that hard cases will inevitably make bad law, the courts have been resolute in refusing to develop exceptions to add to the one established by authority. So if the parties are together in one place but the thing is elsewhere, the law of the place of the transaction, the *lex loci actus*, will not be applied but the *lex situs* will.[13] Of course, if the parties have made a contract which specifies when property will pass, this may be effective, but only if its validity and effect are acknowledged by the *lex situs* applying (one presumes[14])

---

[12] *Cammell v Sewell* (1860) 5 H & N 728; *Winkworth v Christie, Manson & Woods* [1980] Ch 496.

[13] *Glencore International AG v Metro Trading Inc* [2001] 1 Lloyd's Rep 283.

[14] The argument to the contrary is that the Rome I Regulation, Art 20, does not allow for this. One response might be that as the Regulation does not apply to proprietary issues, it does not affect the operation of the *lex situs* in its full, *renvoi*, sense.

its own choice of law rules to assess the effect of the contract. The *lex situs* prevails.

As to whether *renvoi* does so as well, one understanding of the principle of security of title would suggest that our concern is with law as a local judge would apply it to the matter at hand; and if it is pleaded, *renvoi* should be apply in order more perfectly to support the policy underpinning the choice of law rule itself.[15] However, a couple of first instance decisions have cast first-instance doubt upon this proposition.[16] According to this view, recourse to the principle of *renvoi* may actually weaken the reliability of local advice and the expectation that local law will be applied, and will damage the expectation that titles obtained in accordance with local domestic law will be indefeasible. That is undeniably a point of view.

By way of difference from dealings with land, there are many cases in which a succession of transfers of, or other dealings with, a movable takes place, and in a series of countries with conflicting laws. There are two basic possibilities which may have been used to underpin the law. Suppose that X delivers a car to Y on terms of hire purchase, according to which X remains owner during the period of hire, but that Y drives the car to a second country where he sells the car to Z. Suppose also that under the law of the second country, a person in possession of a chattel with apparent ownership of it can sell and confer a good title on a buyer in good faith, but that under the law of the first country, the governing principle of *nemo dat quod non habet* would mean that Y had no title to give, nor capacity to confer the title of another. Under the law of the first country X had an indefeasible title, which could not be affected by a purported sale by a

---

[15] In this respect the methodology is that of *Neilson v Overseas Projects Corpn of Victoria* (2005) 223 CLR 331.

[16] *Iran v Berend* [2007] EWHC 132 (QB), [2007] 2 All ER (Comm) 132; *Blue Sky One Ltd v Mahan Air* [2010] EWHC 631 (Comm). *Dornoch Ltd v Westminster International BV* [2009] EWHC 889 (Admlty), [2009] 2 Lloyd's Rep 191, is open-minded on the issue. Despite what has been said, this conclusion derives no serious support from the first instance decision in *Macmillan Inc v Bishopsgate Investment Trust plc (No 3)* [1995] 1 WLR 978, which was reversed on appeal ([1996] 1 WLR 387) on the issue of choice of law and in which the point concerning *renvoi* was not raised for decision.

non-owner. Under the law of the second country, the principle of indefeasible titles does not prevail, and a buyer in good faith, Z, may acquire a title which was not the seller's to give. If one were to adopt a strictly chronological view, and regard each *lex situs* as having sole control over the issues as arose within its territory, one might say that the transaction in the first country reserved to X an indefeasible title to the car; and that when it was taken to the second country, that second law must have taken the indefeasibility of X's title as given, with the result that Y will have been unable to defeat the indefeasible title by conferring title on Z: anything else allows the law of the second country to trespass on the role of the first country's law.

It is evident that the analysis can be stood on its head, by pointing out that the law of the first country is purporting to dictate to the law of the second country in relation to a transaction taking place in the second. An alternative analysis would therefore be that the eventual question, who owns the car, is as to the legal effect of the second transaction; that this is exclusively governed by the law of the second country, and any anterior questions are answered by looking through the eyes of this eventual *lex situs*, leaving it to the law of obligations to remedy, as best it may, any losses sustained from wrongdoings along the way. This is the solution adopted by the English conflict of laws. It therefore follows that the main question will be answered by the *lex situs* at the time of the final transaction, and any earlier issues will be regarded as incidental, and resolved by looking at them through the lens of the law governing the main, ultimate, question.

As a result, the question whether A obtained good title to a camera which he bought in Ruritania is governed by Ruritanian law, even if the camera had been delivered on hire purchase terms or under a conditional sale to A's seller in England; whether B lost his title to a painting stolen from him in England and sold by auction in Italy to another is governed by Italian law, even though the theft took place in England;[17] whether C succeeded in reserving and retaining title to steel after its use or on-sale by D is answered by the *lex situs* at the time of D's use of or dealing

---

[17] *Winkworth v Christie, Manson & Woods Ltd* [1980] Ch 496.

with it, which law will also decide whether it is still steel or is a completely different thing.[18]

The rule as it applies to transfers allows for one exception. If the goods are in transit and[19] their *situs* unknown there is a case for saying that the case for applying the *lex situs* has gone, and that it makes better sense to apply instead the law which governs the transaction which is alleged to have affected title.[20] By contrast, where a disposition of goods is effected by document, it is not yet, and may never be, accepted that the *lex situs* of the goods can be overlooked in favour of (say) the law of the place of the documents, or the law of the place of the handing over or endorsing of the documents. In principle, the answer should be that if the *lex situs* of the goods considers the purported disposition by dealing with the documents as effective, that will be conclusive; but that if it does not, that is conclusive also.[21] Any uncertainty in the minds of those involved in the trade or transaction will presumably be reflected in the price or in the taking of insurance.

Although the choice of law rule was originally established in the context of derivative titles, that is, transfers, in principle it will also apply to original modes of acquisition, to establish the claim of title to things found (*occupatio*), new things made (*specificatio*), things incorporated into something else (*accessio*), and to things mixed and blended (*commixtio* and *confusio*).[22] But the simple moving of a chattel from one country to another will not have any effect upon its title; to hold otherwise would be most inconvenient. If goods are transported across several countries, and under the law of one of them an existing title is not recognized, it would be unhelpful for the thing thereafter to be regarded as

[18] *Re Interview Ltd* [1975] IR 382; *Armour v Thyssen Edelstahlwerke AG* [1991] 2 AC 339; but both cases are weak authority for the proposition advanced in the text.

[19] In its established form, this is conjunctive, not disjunctive. Although there is a case for restating the exception in disjunctive form, the increased scope for uncertainty which this would create will make it unlikely to be adopted.

[20] Dicey, Rule 133, exception.

[21] There will naturally be consequential contractual claims.

[22] *Glencore International AG v Metro Trading Inc* [2001] 1 Lloyd's Rep 283. The *situs* rule also applies to seizure by way of nationalization or confiscation of property by governments; see below.

ownerless and as available for *occupatio*. It may be necessary to adapt the exception, described in the last paragraph, to produce this result.

Actions to recover movable property, or to obtain damages for its wrongful loss, are brought in the form of tort actions: in the domestic common law, as claims alleging the tort of conversion; in terms of private international law, one supposes, as claims based on the non-contractual obligation of the defendant to the claimant, and therefore as claims which fall within the material scope of the Rome II Regulation. Of course, this does not mean that the law which governs the obligation asserted by the claimant also determines the question of title. Title still has to be determined—where it is material to the obligation relied on—by the common law rules of private international law, for the Rome II Regulation applies only to the obligation, not to answer the questions of property law upon which that obligation may depend.

The choice of law rule for tangible movables also applies to negotiable instruments.[23] As the instrument, being negotiable, is as good as the right to which it is the key, transfers of the document are, in effect, transfers of the thing. The same principle applies to bearer shares, which are treated as tangible things, and where transfer of the instrument is effective to transfer all rights or property inherent in it.

2. INTANGIBLE PROPERTY

(a) General

Choice of law in relation to intangible property—the rights arising from a debt owed by a bank to an account-holder, the rights under a policy of insurance, the rights of an investor in a unit trust, and so forth—have traditionally raised issues of abstract complexity, for three among many reasons. First, it was sometimes difficult to see why or on what basis intangibles were characterized under the common law as property at all, as distinct from their being the simple contractual or analogous right which

---

[23] Whether the document is negotiable is determined by its *situs* at the time of its purported negotiation.

they almost always are. If the question is who is now entitled to a debt or other contractual obligation, which means asking who may therefore insist on performance of the obligation owed by the debtor or obliged party, this is really to ask little more than who stands in a relationship equivalent to privity with the debtor or obliged party. From this perspective there will be no substantial distinction between owning a debt and being owed a debt. This analysis would suggest that the issues which arise are really only facets of the law of contract, albeit with a particular gloss supplied by laws regulating security and insolvency, but which may allow them to be got up to look like something else; and today, whatever the common law might have thought, one would expect to find the answer legislated in the Rome I Regulation. Second, the universe of intangible things is almost certainly too wide for a uniform choice of law rule to be applied to everything in it. A choice of law rule developed in the 19th century for the assignment of spousal insurance policies, and interests under family trusts and dynastic settlements, was not designed for, and may not adapt to, dealings with interests in financial instruments held in indirect holding systems; and it may really, really struggle with delocalized or dematerialized 'securities' of the sort which now serve to underpin or undermine the global financial system. Either a choice of law rule has to allow for pragmatic exceptions, so that doctrinal dogmatism does not defeat the expectations of commerce, or the law must develop new (sub-)rules for choice of law.

Third, when dealing with choice of law for the assignment of intangibles, the common law authorities were remarkably opaque. As editor of Dicey, Dr Morris asserted, in the face of some really useless case law, that the law governing the underlying obligation would determine its assignability; the law governing the actual assignment would govern the effect of the relationship between assignor and assignee; and when the two answers were combined, the answer would emerge.

Article 14 of the Rome I Regulation now provides a statutory rule for choice of law in voluntary assignments which is similar in effect to the common law as ascertained by Dr Morris. Article 14(2) states that the law governing the right or claim assigned, which really means the law under which the obligation was created, determines its assignability, the relationship between assignee and debtor, the conditions for invoking the assignment against the debtor, and the discharge of the debtor. Article 14(1) states that the mutual obligations of assignor and assignee are governed by the law applicable to the contract between them. In other words, issues involving the debtor and enforcement against him are governed by the law which governs the debt; any residual or consequential issues between the creditors, or between those trading in the debt owed by the debtor, are for the law governing their bilateral relationship. This has the basic elements of good sense about it, for it accords due weight to the law which created the thing being dealt with. It defends the expectation of the parties who created the obligation that it has all, but has only, the characteristics with which they endowed it, thereby reflecting the essentially contractual nature of the thing assigned; and it invites the conclusion that, as Article 14 embraces these matters within the Rome I Regulation as matters relating to contractual obligations in the autonomous sense, it precludes any argument that they are, in any exclusionary sense, proprietary.

It might once have been possible to read down Article 14, by contending that while it regulates contractual issues properly so called, it had no relevance to the proprietary aspects of intangibles. The difficulties with this argument were many, but for reasons set out in the discussion of the meaning of contractual obligations, it is untenable today.[24] On the other hand, this analysis causes problems for those who trade in bundles of debts (receivables), and for whom the task of ascertaining the law under which each separate debt was created is discouraging. From this perspective it may be argued that the property which is passed from one to another may be seen not as the debt, as such, but as the right to have the debtor directed to discharge the debt by paying to A or to B or to C as the case may be. If an 'assignment of the debt' is understood as a passing of the right to give instructions to the debtor, giving the assignee the right to tell the assignor to direct the debtor to pay the assignee, it is then less obvious that this 'property' is the same 'property' as the debt

[24] *Raiffeisen Zentralbank Österreich AG v Five Star Trading LLC* [2001] EWCA Civ 68, [2001] QB 825, see p 225 above.

itself. The differences in approach are fundamental, and it is hard to see how they may be reconciled. For practical purposes, however, the 'contractual' approach seems to be more easily reconciled with the Rome I Regulation; and if it has to be concluded, as it does have to be, that the particular issue now has, like it or not, a legislative solution, there is little more to be usefully said about it.

Article 14 will be applicable where a contract is made to assign a contractual right or claim. Where the assignment is not by way of contract, the rule still applies, for Article 14(3) extends the meaning to outright transfers (which must include gifts), and transfers by way of security. It is less clear that Article 14 can apply where the right assigned is not a contractual one, for it will appear that in such a case, the Rome I Regulation is simply not engaged. Certainly, where the right assigned is a right to sue another in respect of a non-contractual obligation, its transferability will be determined by the law governing that non-contractual obligation;[25] but in principle, in any case in which the Regulation does not apply, there is no objection to the common law using it to help bring order to the common law. In any case, as Article 14 is probably a reflection of the state of the common law as it was best understood, in the cases in which the common law rules on assignment of intangible property continue to apply, they may well be indistinguishable from those set out in Article 14.

(b) Special cases

Transfers or assignments of registered shares are governed by the *lex incorporationis* for the pragmatic reason that any solution which departs from the law of the place of the share register is futile. In such cases, the general rule in Article 14 of the Rome I Regulation is inapplicable.[26] This may be deduced from the exclusion in Article 1(2)(f) or, perhaps more persuasively, from the argument that it is inaccurate to say that shares are ever assigned: as they comprise a bundle of duties and obligations as well as rights, simple assignment of them is impossible, and the

---

[25] Rome II Regulation, Art 15(1)(e).
[26] *Macmillan Inc v Bishopsgate Investment Trust plc (No 3)* [1996] 1 WLR 387 (CA).

process mis-described as 'share transfer' is in fact the surrender and new-grant of rights in the company. If this be accepted, then the nomenclature of 'share transfer' might be better not used. For shares and other instruments held in holding systems, according to the terms of which a 'shareholder' has only an interest as co-claimant with others in relation to a pool of similar assets registered in the name of someone else (a process which may be replicated upwards through several levels of holding), it seems inevitable that a mechanical solution, derived from a rule made for cases of much less complexity, is inappropriate, especially where this would, for no compelling reason, defeat the expectations of all those who participate in the system. Because private international legal science appeared unlikely to produce a universal solution suitable to those whose business is founded on such speculations, a Convention was concluded at The Hague in 2003 which would, if ever adopted, apply a dedicated, if rather complicated, rule for choice of law. The proposed rule would not 'look through' to find and apply the law under which the ultimate or original intangible was issued, but would treat the rights of an investor against the entity with which he holds a securities account as being the property or thing with which dealing is done, which seems fair enough. But the Convention has not yet been adopted or brought into force and its future does not look bright.

(c) Intellectual property

In relation to intellectual property rights, to the extent that a question is not governed by convention or statute, and is not outside the jurisdiction of an English court, issues of choice of law concerning patents, copyright, and trade mark rights are governed by the law of the place of the right of protection, or the law of the place for which protection is claimed (*lex protectionis*); and that law will determine whether and on what terms they are assignable. This seems inevitable. Contracts which deal with intellectual property are, of course, just contracts, and they fall within the domain of the Rome I Regulation.

In the small number of cases in which jurisdiction is governed by the residual rules of common law, there was thought to be a complication resulting from the view that an English court had no jurisdiction to adjudicate the validity of a foreign intellectual property right. But though said over and again, it was not supported by significant English[27] authority; and at least in relation to copyright, the Supreme Court concluded that there never had been any such exclusionary common law rule.[28] As the issue of validity would frequently be raised by a defendant sued in proceedings alleging infringement, it was inconvenient that a court could be deprived of jurisdiction over a tort claim, especially in relation to a defendant over whom it had personal jurisdiction under the Brussels I Regulation. Certainly, where the right in question is granted by the law of a Member State, and the question of validity has to be determined, Article 22(4) of the Brussels I Regulation gives exclusive jurisdiction, even where the issue simply arises as a defence to a claim alleging infringement, to the Member State of deposit or registration.[29] But where the right arises under the law of a non-Member State, the question whether a court may apply Article 22(4) by analogy, or may look over its shoulder and apply what remains of the common law exclusionary rule, or do neither, remains obscure. The jurisdictional rule is therefore, at present, in a bit of a mess.

As to choice of law for infringement and other non-contractual claims, the Rome II Regulation applies the *lex protectionis* to non-contractual obligations arising from the infringement of intellectual property rights, and excludes the right of the parties to choose another law to govern them.[30]

C. TITLE BY SEIZURE AND CONFISCATION

The treatment of nationalization or other expropriation or seizure of property by governments starts with the application of the general *lex situs* rule set out above. If the property is within

---

[27] *Potter v Broken Hill Pty Co* (1906) 3 CLR 479. But this was reinterpreted, and doubt cast on the width of the proposition as a matter of Australian law, in *Habib v Commonwealth of Australia* (2010) 183 FCR 62.

[28] *Lucasfilm Ltd v Ainsworth* [2011] UKSC 39, [2012] 1 AC 208. The rule may therefore survive for patents; though if it does, the exception in *Penn v Baltimore* will apply to it as well.

[29] Case C-4/03 *GAT v LüK* [2006] ECR I-6509.

[30] Article 8.

the territorial jurisdiction of the state, the *lex situs* rule, to say nothing of the respect which international comity requires to be given to the acts of sovereigns executed within their territory, will lead to the recognition of the title acquired by this legislative or executive act according to local law.[31] There is no question of an English court being called upon to 'enforce' the foreign law: once that law, the *lex causae* according to the rules of the English conflict of laws, has done what it set out to do and has vested title to the property in the state, there is nothing else left in it to need enforcing.[32] So if property is seized by a state pursuant to a confiscatory decree, and is then sold by state authority to a buyer who takes good title under that law and who then brings the property to England, the former and dispossessed owner has no maintainable claim for its delivery up from the person who, as a matter of the English conflict of laws, has a complete title; he has no maintainable claim for damages for conversion as his dispossession was lawful because in accordance with the law of the place where it was done. The transfer of ownership and loss of possession and of any right to possession were all completed under the *lex situs* of the property at the time of the act, and any claim which asserts a right which follows from the claimant's lost ownership will be defeated by the good new title and the lawful taking of possession. Likewise, if a government passes a decree to take to itself ownership of shares in a company incorporated and registered under its law, it may, as new controlling shareholder, direct the management of the company to recover debts and property abroad.[33]

But, by contrast, had the decree provided that overseas property vested in the state, the ordinary application of the *lex situs* rule would mean that title to the property in England, at least, would be unaffected or changed by this legislative act, and that any action in the English courts would be founded on an irrelevant law, not part of the *lex situs* at the time of the relevant act. Likewise, if a foreign state purports to confiscate English

---

[31] *Luther Co v James Sagor & Co* [1921] 3 KB 532 (CA); *Princess Paley Olga v Weisz* [1929] 1 KB 718 (CA).

[32] *Williams & Humbert Ltd v W & H Trade Marks (Jersey) Ltd* [1986] AC 368.

[33] ibid.

copyright, its law will have had no effect on title to it.[34] It follows that any action brought to complete what the foreign law had sought to accomplish would have to be seen as seeking the enforcement of that law; and if that is so, the rule against the enforcement of a foreign penal, revenue, or other public law will, as was shown above,[35] be precluded on that ground too.

The result is less clear where the property lies outside the territory of the legislating state but the law of the *situs* would regard the (to it) foreign legislation as effective in the particular case.[36] Where the *lex situs* rule collides with the rule against the extra-territorial enforcement of penal laws, one or the other has to give way; it seems, in principle at least, that if the *lex situs* confirms that the legislative decree was sufficient to alter the ownership of property within the territory of the *situs*, there is again nothing left to enforce, and nothing to which enforcement can be denied. In such a case, it would be only if the confiscating law were so abhorrent that it should be refused even recognition as law,[37] and title acquired by reference to it and the *lex situs* rule treated to a complete ignoral, that the result will be different.

Something similar may be true where the Human Rights Act 1998 directs an English court not to apply its law, which expression certainly includes its rules for choice of law, to give effect to its usual choice of law rule in a way which would place the English court in breach of its obligations under the European Convention on Human Rights. Whether the Convention actually has this effect is hard to tell. One might have supposed that an English court was precluded from giving a judgment which would have the effect of condoning behaviour (and giving it effect in the English legal order), wherever committed, which violated the standards of the European Convention. But when faced with a submission substantially in those terms, the House of Lords

[34] *Peer International Corpn v Termidor Music Publishers Ltd* [2003] EWCA Civ 1156, [2004] Ch 212.

[35] See Chapter 4.

[36] Such as where the law is regarded as being effective in relation to nationals of the expropriating state.

[37] *Kuwait Airways Corpn v Iraqi Airways Co (Nos 4 and 5)* [2002] UKHL 19, [2002] 2 AC 883, refusing to recognize an Iraqi law dissolving Kuwait and assuming ownership of Kuwaiti-owned property.

demurred, requiring instead that the offending conduct amount to a 'flagrant' breach of the standards of the Convention.[38] It seems probable that this question will need to be revisited. In the meantime, unless the Convention is found to be the source for one, there is no rule of English private international law which withholds recognition from a foreign expropriatory law unless compensation is paid for the acquisition;[39] the fact that there may be such an obligation in public international law is of no general relevance in private law.

It is sometimes suggested that the answer to the question of title is more complicated if the property is spirited away from the territory of the seizing state before it has been taken into the possession of the authorities. In cases where the *lex situs* requires possession to be taken as a precondition to the acquisition of title under it, it is uncontroversial that title will not have been acquired while the property was within the territory of the state, and will not be acquired by legislative decree once it is outside it.[40] There is, however, no wider justification for imposing such a requirement that possession have been taken as a condition which limits the ability of the state to enforce its title when title has been vested under its own law. At the very least, there is no such limitation where the property in question was ownerless when the state legislated to vest title in itself. Where the state legislates to acquire title to ownerless property within its territory, the vesting of title to local and ownerless property will be regarded as good, perfect, and reliable for the purpose of English private international law.[41] By contrast, where the state has demanded and acquired its title by expropriating a person who was, until then, the owner, or has nationalized the property of an individual—vesting by divesting, so to speak—the approach will be different. The rule which prevents an English court enforcing foreign public laws will mean that unless the state has already taken possession of the property (in which case it can simply rely upon its prior lawful possession), an application for delivery up

---

[38] *Barnette v United States of America* [2004] UKHL 37, [2004] 1 WLR 2241.

[39] *Williams & Humbert Ltd v W & H Trade Marks (Jersey) Ltd* [1986] AC 368.

[40] *AG for New Zealand v Ortiz* [1984] AC 1.

[41] *Islamic Republic of Iran v Barakat Galleries Ltd* [2007] EWCA Civ 1374, [2009] QB 22.

will be understood as the state calling on the English court to order that it be given the possession which it had not hitherto taken. It will be seen as asking the English court to enforce a right which is peculiar to a state, a foreign public law; and the court will not oblige it.[42]

The rules about seizure apply easily to immovable property, and to tangible property. In relation to intangible property it certainly applies to shares situated where the company is incorporated in, seized in, and acquired in, in accordance with the law of that country.[43] It is less obvious how it will apply to simple contractual intangibles, but the *situs* of a debt is in general the place of residence of the debtor, for it is there that he may generally be sued, and the *situs* rule will probably apply to it in this sense. Article 14 of the Rome I Regulation, dealing as it does only with voluntary assignments, is irrelevant to the issue.

D. TRUSTS

The private international law of trusts is substantially contained in the Hague Convention on the Recognition of Trusts, given force in England by the Recognition of Trusts Act 1987.[44] From the perspective of English law, however, the Convention has much more to do with the identification of the governing law than with the recognition of foreign trusts. The Convention defines a trust as the legal relationship, created, *inter vivos* or on death, voluntarily, and evidenced in writing, when the settlor places assets under the control of a trustee for the benefit of a beneficiary or for a specified purpose.[45] However, the Act extends this Convention definition to encompass trusts of property arising under the law of any part of the United Kingdom, and to trusts created by judicial decision;[46] and applies it to trusts falling within its definition whatever the date of their creation.[47]

---

[42] ibid explaining *Brokaw v Seatrain UK Ltd* [1971] 2 QB 476 (CA); *AG for New Zealand v Oritz* [1984] AC 1, 20 (CA); aff'd on different grounds, 41.

[43] *Williams & Humbert Ltd v W & H Trade Marks (Jersey) Ltd* [1986] AC 368.

[44] Dicey, Ch 29.

[45] Article 2.

[46] Recognition of Trusts Act 1987, s 1(2).

[47] Article 22.

Its application to implied, resulting, and constructive trusts is therefore clear. Accordingly, the implied or constructive trust arising from the joint purchase of property will fall squarely within the scope of the Act; but where a constructive trust is sought against or imposed upon a defendant found answerable to what the common law would regard as an equitable claim, the relevant choice of law rules are probably those examined under the law of obligations in the previous two chapters.

A trust is, for practical purposes, governed by the law chosen by the settlor; in default of such a demonstrable choice it is governed by the law with which it is most closely connected.[48] In identifying the latter, regard is to be had to the place of administration of the trust, the *situs* of the assets of the trust, the place of residence of the trustee, and the objects of the trust and the places where they are to be fulfilled. The governing law regulates the trust, its construction, effect, and administration,[49] but gives way to mandatory and conflicts rules of the *lex fori*, and to public policy.[50] It is not clear that these are sufficient to deal with cases in which the law of trusts, and the freedoms which it extends to the settlor, are used to magnify greed at the expense of the public good.

E. PERSONAL STATUS AND PROPERTY RIGHTS

1. MARRIAGE AND PROPERTY RIGHTS

The impact of marriage on property rights is only a fragment of a larger picture.[51] When a marriage is annulled or dissolved, most systems of law allow the court to make orders in relation to the property of the spouses which may override property rights created or existing prior to or independently of the marriage, or which would arise if there had been no marital regime to

---

[48] Articles 6, 7. Note that it is the connection to a law, and not to a country, which is the determining factor. See also *Gómez v Gómez-Monche Vives* [2008] EWCA Civ 1065, [2009] Ch 245.

[49] Article 8.

[50] Article 18.

[51] Dicey, Ch 28.

supervene;[52] and where a marriage is terminated by death, many systems employ rules of succession, perhaps modified by restricting the testamentary freedom of a deceased, to provide for those left behind. Others, more commonly civilian systems, employ the institution of a matrimonial property regime, often but not always community of property, to regulate the property rights of the quick and the dead. Our concern at this point is simply with the effect which marriage has on the property rights of spouses up to the point when an event such as divorce or death may displace or even override the matrimonial regime; the property rights of civil partners whose relationship falls within the scope of the 2004 Act will be treated in the same way.[53]

Where the parties to a marriage make a matrimonial contract to govern their property rights *inter se*, the proper law of that contract obviously governs its creation, validity, interpretation, and effect, including the identification of the property which does[54] and does not[55] fall within it,[56] and including whether foreign land falls within it.[57] Such contracts were excluded from the material scope of the Rome I Regulation: partly because they are intimately connected with status, which is also excluded, but also because it was intended that they would be dealt with in a dedicated Regulation. This projected Regulation, proposed originally to be designated as Brussels III, latterly as Rome IV, has made halting progress. In any event, the United Kingdom is unlikely to opt into any Regulation which may eventually be adopted. It follows that the private international law of matrimonial property rights is a matter of common law, the principal

---

[52] For example, Matrimonial Causes Act 1973, s 24(1)(c); cf *Radmacher v Granatino* [2010] UKSC 42, [2011] 1 AC 534.

[53] Civil Partnership Act 2004. The regimes of foreign law which the Act regards as civil partnership are listed in Sch 20.

[54] *Re De Nicols (No2)* [1900] 2 Ch 410; *Murakami v Wiryadi* (2010) 268 ALR 377.

[55] *Slutsker v Haron Investments Ltd* [2012] EWHC 2539 (Ch). If the property in question does not fall within it, any question concerning rights to and in it will be determined by the default rule for choice of law which, in the case of land, will be the *lex situs*.

[56] *Re Fitzgerald* [1904] 1 Ch 573 (CA).

[57] *Murakami v Wiryadi* (2010) 268 ALR 377, following *Re De Nicols (No2)* [1900] 2 Ch 410 and followed by *Slutsker v Haron Investments Ltd* [2012] EWHC 2539 (Ch).

characteristic of which is that the proper law may be chosen. In the absence of such choice, the proper law will be that with which the marriage contract has its closest and most real connection, the law of the matrimonial domicile.[58] As to this, there was an historical preference for this law being that of the husband's domicile, but this has been indefensible at least since the abolition of the wife's dependent domicile at the end of 1973. The capacity of a person to make a marriage contract is governed by the law of his or her domicile at the date of marriage.[59] It is consistent with principle that once a matrimonial contract has been made, a change in matrimonial domicile cannot alter its content and the rights created under it;[60] but there is nothing in principle, or probably in law, to prevent the spouses exercising their joint autonomy to vary their contract by agreement.

Where the parties do not make a matrimonial contract it was once thought that the factual and legal basis for analysing the proprietary aspect of their relationship was different, and that a distinct set of answers was applicable. It was once proposed that the law by reference to which they married (the law with which the marriage had its closest connection; the matrimonial domicile) applied to determine the proprietary consequences of marriage,[61] but that this original property regime did not necessarily survive a change of spousal domicile. By far the better view always was,[62] however, that on marriage the spouses simply expect, receive, and adopt the scheme which is imposed or implied by the law of the original matrimonial domicile.[63] This may be a system of community of property, or separation of property, or some other variant. Whether this is conceptualized by the law of the matrimonial domicile as a tacit contract or default provision is immaterial, though as the regime will be held to continue to apply after a change in personal domicile, and for the same reasons, as where

---

[58] *Duke of Marlborough v AG* [1945] Ch 78 (CA). The connection is to a law, not to a country.

[59] *Re Cooke's Trusts* (1887) 56 LT 737; *Cooper v Cooper* (1888) 13 App Cas 88.

[60] *De Nicols v Curlier* [1900] AC 21.

[61] *Re Egerton's Will Trusts* [1956] Ch 593.

[62] Goldberg (1970) 19 ICLQ 557.

[63] It might be better to refer to this as the proper law of the marriage, but little turns on that.

there is an express contract, it may be understood as a tacit contract. So when two Indonesian parties married in Indonesia, they expected without fuss or bother that the joint property regime of Indonesian law would apply to any acquisition of real property outside Indonesia. It followed that land acquired by them in New South Wales was subjected to a regime which, as a matter of the private international law of that state, should be regarded as assumed by means of a tacit contract.[64]

A seeming problem may arise when two systems of proprietary provision come into contact and become entangled. If spouses marry into a system of community, when one dies the community rules will determine what portion of the marital property accrues to the survivor, and what falls into the estate of the deceased. But if the deceased dies domiciled in a country where separation of property, and particular provision for inheritance, is the basis of the law, that law may give the survivor a claim to a portion of the estate of the deceased, with the result that, in principle at least, the survivor can claim more than either system would have provided. A practical solution would be for characterization of the issue or issues to lead to the result that only one of these schemes applies, but if the court is unable to see past the analysis that tells it, correctly enough, that there are two, sequential, issues—what did the deceased own when he died? who succeeds to the estate of the deceased?—each having its own choice of law rule, this will be hard to achieve. And in any case, can one really be certain that this generosity to the survivor was not what the parties sought to bring about?

2. DIVORCE AND PROPERTY RIGHTS

The private international law rules for (post-)matrimonial property orders, which, as a matter of domestic law, give a court very wide powers to adjust and override property rights, and which, for the purposes of private international law, are closely related to the dissolution of marriage, are best examined as part

---

[64] *Murakami v Wiryadi* (2010) 268 ALR 377, following *Re De Nicols (No2)* [1900] 2 Ch 410 and followed by *Slutsker v Haron Investments Ltd* [2012] EWHC 2539 (Ch).

of family law. It is nevertheless telling that when the Supreme Court had to consider the validity and effect of an express matrimonial contract upon the parties at the date of their divorce, it simply subsumed the contract, the intrinsic validity of which it did not question, within the set of data to be taken into account within the statutory regime for dealing with financial relief on divorce.[65]

3. BANKRUPTCY AND PROPERTY RIGHTS

The private international law rules for personal bankruptcy form an important part of the law on change of status and property rights. However, because of the tendency of states to legislate for bankruptcy and corporate insolvency together, is best examined as part of the law of corporations. It is not logical, but for convenience of exposition, it will appear in the final chapter of this book.

4. DEATH AND PROPERTY RIGHTS

When someone dies and the question arises of the ownership and devolution of his or her property, it is necessary, at least for the purposes of English private law, to deal separately with two issues, each having its own rules for choice of law,[66] as well as jurisdiction and the recognition of foreign orders and judgments.

The first stage is the administration of the estate of the deceased: the interim process during which the assets are identified and collected, the proven debts paid in the order of their priority, and the balance of the estate calculated. If the deceased was subject to a regime of community of property, the effect of this on his estate will be calculated at this stage of administration. During this period, legal systems differ on the question of who owns the property: in some, the property vests immediately in those who will ultimately take it, but in England it vests in those charged with the administration of the estate.

---

[65] *Radmacher v Granatino* [2010] UKSC 42, [2011] 1 AC 534.
[66] Dicey, Ch 26.

The second stage is the substantive devolution of the estate: once the administration is complete, a further set of rules determines who actually takes which property. Substantive devolution sub-divides into three kinds: testate succession, where devolution is governed by a will left by the deceased and proved in the administration; intestate succession, where the deceased left no valid will or a will which left some of his estate ungifted, where the law steps in to allocate the property according to a formula which usually incorporates a descending scale of relationship; and *bona vacantia* where, because there is no succession (because there is no will and according to the rules on intestacy there is no relative to whom the property will pass by operation of law), the property is regarded as truly ownerless and will be taken by the state as a matter of last resort.

The European Union has now adopted a Regulation for Succession,[67] which will cover both the administration of estates and rights of succession of those who die after 17 August 2015. However, the United Kingdom elected not to be bound by it, with the result that the private international law of administration and succession remains that of the common law. The objection of the United Kingdom was not that the completion of the internal market required no legislation to secure the free movement of the dead. Instead, it found fault with specific parts of the Regulation. These points of objection included the preference for habitual residence over domicile as the main connecting factor for succession to the estate of the deceased; the perception that the proposed rules for choice of law would permit a foreign law to intrude on English domestic law as to testamentary freedom (and in particular, that freedom from the provisions of a foreign law which would allow the clawing back of gifts and transfers made prior to death); the threat which claw-back rules would

---

[67] Regulation (EU) 650/2012, [2012] OJ L201/107. It was originally understood that this would be known as Brussels IV, but as there will not be a Brussels III Regulation, this designation having been discarded for the Regulation still intended to be made for matrimonial property but which will be known as Rome IV, the system of nomenclature which used a capital city as short title appears to have been quietly abandoned.

pose to the integrity of trusts,[68] and to the court-based system of probate. It was therefore decided to leave this particular measure of harmonization of private international law to those who were content to live and die with it.

(a) Administration of deceased estates

The administration of estates is the process by which the estate of a deceased person is organized and settled prior to its distribution to those to whom the assets will pass by way of succession. As a matter of English law, administration requires an order of the court to empower a person to deal with the assets of a deceased, whether this is done by proving a will in order to appoint a named and willing executor or by obtaining a grant of letters of administration.[69] Although the court may make a grant of representation of any deceased, only rarely will it do so if there is no property of the deceased in England. The making of a grant confirms or vests the property of the deceased in the grantee. Where the deceased died domiciled in a foreign country, the court will usually make a grant to the person who, under the law of the domicile, has been or is entitled to be appointed to administer the estate.[70] Once appointed, the representative may take all steps to get in all property, wherever situated, of the deceased. The substance of the administration is governed by the law of the country under which the grant of representation was made.[71] As a matter of English law, in the paying of the deceased's debts foreign creditors and English creditors are treated alike; the admissibility of and priority between claims is governed by English law as *lex fori*.

A foreign grant of representation has no direct effect in England: the person appointed overseas must also obtain an English grant.[72] This stands in curious contrast to the fact that the

---

[68] It seems that this means trusts established to avoid the lawful claims of the Revenue or of deserted and former wives. It is not clear that the opting out of the United Kingdom was done with a view to protecting the interests of those who give off the odour of sanctity.

[69] *New York Breweries Co v AG* [1899] AC 62.

[70] Supreme Court Act 1981, s 25(1).

[71] *Re Kloebe* (1884) 28 Ch D 175; *Re Lorillard* [1922] 2 Ch 638 (CA).

[72] *New York Breweries Co v AG* [1899] AC 62.

status of a foreign-appointed trustee in bankruptcy is recognized without the need for further order; and it would have been removed as a requirement by the Succession Regulation in respect of the cases to which it applied. Although it has been said that the current English system is the best way to secure the interests of English creditors, it is hard to see how this can explain the difference in treatment between different types of representation.

(b) Succession to property

Except where its rules lead to the conclusion that there was no valid will and no relative of the deceased to take on the intestacy, it is the law of succession which determines who takes the property of a deceased who may have died with or without leaving a will.[73] When disputes about succession arise, if a duly appointed representative is before the court, an English court has jurisdiction to determine a question of succession.[74] A foreign court is regarded as having jurisdiction to determine succession to the property, wherever situated, of a deceased dying domiciled in that country, and its decision will in principle be recognized in England;[75] it will also be recognized as having jurisdiction to determine the right of succession to all property within its territorial jurisdiction, regardless of the domicile of the deceased. The potential overlapping of decisions will require the principles of estoppel by *res judicata* to regulate it.

Where the deceased died having left a will, any question of her testamentary capacity is governed by her domicile at the date of making the will,[76] and the capacity of a legatee to take is conferred by the law of either his own or the testator's domicile.[77] The formal validity of the will is satisfied if it is formally valid according to the law of the place when and where it was executed, or by the law of the place (at the time of either execution or death) where the deceased died domiciled or habitually

---

[73] Dicey, Ch 27.

[74] *Re Lorillard* [1922] 2 Ch 638 (CA).

[75] *Re Trufort* (1887) 36 Ch D 600; *Ewing v Orr-Ewing* (1883) 9 App Cas 34; *Ewing v Orr-Ewing* (1885) 10 App Cas 5.

[76] *Re Fuld's Estate (No 3)* [1968] P 675.

[77] *Re Hellmann's Will* (1866) LR 2 Eq 363.

resident or of which she was a national.[78] The same laws govern
the formal validity of a will revoking an earlier will.[79] Wills of
immovables are formally valid if they conform to the *lex situs*.[80]
The material validity of a will is governed by the law of the testator's domicile at death,[81] except for immovables, where this
is governed by the *lex situs*.[82] It follows that if it is argued that
the testator was limited as regards the fraction of her estate over
which she had testamentary freedom, as is the case in systems
which provide a statutory portion for spouses and children, this
question will be treated as one going to the material validity of
the will. But the interpretation of the will is governed by the law
of the domicile at the date of making the will.[83] The validity of
an act of revocation is governed by the domicile of the testator
at the date of revocation.[84] So the question whether subsequent
marriage, or the tearing up or burning of a will, serves to revoke
an earlier will is determined by the *lex domicilii* of the testator at
the date of the marriage or other revoking event.

Where the deceased dies without leaving a valid will or fails to
will a part of her estate, the intestate succession is governed by
the domiciliary law of the deceased at the date her death, except
that succession to immovables is governed by the *lex situs*.[85] It is
inherent in the nature of intestate succession that it means the
taking of property, by operation of law, but by a relative of the
deceased who did not make a will.

Where there is no will and no person to take by way of intestate succession, the property still has to pass. In this case the principles can no longer be those of succession, for there is no-one
to succeed to it. Instead, a state will assume title to local ownerless property as *bona vacantia*, and the question of which state is
governed in all cases by the *lex situs* of the property. An illusory

---

[78] Wills Act 1963, s 1.

[79] ibid, s 2(1)(c).

[80] ibid, s 2(1)(c).

[81] *Whicker v Hume* (1858) 7 HLC 124; *Re Groos* [1915] Ch 572; *Re Ross* [1930] 1
Ch 377.

[82] *Nelson v Bridport* (1846) 8 Beav 547; *Freke v Carbery* (1873) LR 16 Eq 461.

[83] *Ewing v Orr-Ewing* (1883) 9 App Cas 34.

[84] *In bonis Reid* (1866) LR 1 P & D 74.

[85] *Balfour v Scott* (1793) 6 Bro PC 550.

problem arises when the application of the law of the domicile would vest the property of an intestate deceased in the state of his domicile, it being provided that the state is the 'final heir' of a deceased. It has been said that in this context it is necessary to characterize the rule of law relied on by the claiming state to determine whether it is a succession rule or a rule about *bona vacantia*, and that this is a matter of ascertaining the substance of the foreign rule rather than being persuaded by its form.[86] This is the product of muddled thinking. Quite apart from the fact that the process of characterization is directed at issues as distinct from rules of law, the law requires a characterization line to be drawn to separate intestate succession from the devolution of *bona vacantia*, to which a different choice of law rule, the *lex situs*, applies. The court must first decide whether the issue concerns property which is owned by way of succession, or is ownerless for failure of succession: only in the latter case does an issue arise of its devolution as *bona vacantia*. Thus understood, there is no need to characterize rules rather than issues. The misunderstanding arises where the process of taking property upon death is seen in every case as succession. Once it is accepted that the true characterization category is the devolution of property on death, which in turn sub-divides into three possibilities, each with its own choice of law rule, there is no real difficulty.

---

[86] *Re Maldonado's Estate* [1954] P 233 (CA).

8

PERSONS

A. ADULTS

Family law, and the private international law of marriage in particular, is the one area in which the *lex domicilii*, the law of the domicile, still has a significant role to play. Not every issue is answered by recourse to it, and statutory reform has made inroads into its territory. But family law is substantially about status; status is traditionally determined by the personal law; and as far as the common law conflict of laws is concerned, the personal law is the *lex domicilii*, the law of the domicile.

It should not be supposed, however, that this means that there will be international agreement on the status of an individual. For although most systems agree in a general sense that status is a matter for the personal law, there is no agreement about which law—domicile, habitual residence, nationality, law of a religious group, and so on—actually is the personal law; and even as between countries which use the *lex domicilii* as the personal law, there are differences in the way it is defined. In the context of family law, the reference to *law* is liable to indicate the whole law, including the rules of the conflict of laws, which would be applied by a judge hearing the case in his own court: the principle of *renvoi* is generally taken to be relevant to those family law cases in which it is pleaded and proved.

It is sensible to confront at the outset an issue which follows from this, but which also lurks deeply[1] in the private international law of persons, for if it is unaddressed the law risks being found to lack the coherence for which it claims to strive. The issue is whether 'personal status' still is a concept of any use in helping to formulate the rules of private international law. One

---

[1] Though as will be shown, coming much closer to the surface than it has previously done.

approach would have been to refer all or most of the issues to be discussed in the first half of this chapter to the personal law, that is, to the law of the domicile. If that law were to determine the validity of marriage, the effect of a divorce or nullity decree, and so on, it would be easy enough to defend the view that status was an issue in its own right, having its own legal value, and was a matter determined by the law of the domicile: in other words, one broad issue would be dealt with by one generally applicable law.

But if one regards the milestones of personal life as, well, just a succession of individual events, the picture of uniformity is changed. The first crack came when it was accepted, first by the common law and then by legislation, that the validity of a divorce (and later, also the validity of an annulment of marriage) could be referred to a number of possible laws in addition to the law of the domicile, and that as long as it could be validated by reference to one of them it was sufficient for the purpose of English private international law. But such changes to the law of divorce instantly mean that the view of status which might be taken by the personal law is not reliable: if the divorce is recognized as effective by reference to one of the laws available for its validation, but the *lex domicilii* would not share that view, the idea of having a single law to determine status is to travel down the path to illusion. Indeed, if life is a length of time during the course of which marriage, divorce, annulment, and so on, are regarded as transactions, each tested according to the law or laws to which it seems sensible to refer them, personal status is simply what results from these events from time to time. And if that is so, the idea that adults may choose the law by which these separate transactions are to be governed, or to which these transactions are to be referred, becomes much more plausible. The common law of private international law never countenanced such a thing (save in the underappreciated sense that parties with the means may choose where to go to marry or to petition for divorce); but if these processes really are the contracts and engagements one makes to get through life, why should the right to choose the law associated with them be available only to those with the means to travel? To be sure, the legislation and proposals for legislation coming from the institutions of the European

Union[2] would open the door to substantially greater choice of law to govern the effect of life-changing events. But if these are just events, mostly entered into by choice, whether happily or unhappily, why on earth should adults of sound mind and the age of discretion not be allowed choose the law to determine the effects of what they are doing? Does personal autonomy and respect for private life not entail the right to choose the law to govern these events? Is it not enough to use public policy as the means to override the unpalatable consequences of a choice of law which has been made, but to intervene no further than that? Perhaps the idea of a progression of law from status to contract has a part to play here too; perhaps the suggestion from Europe that one should be able to choose how to make one's private life is one to be looked at with increased respect.

But one must take the law as it is. The plan of this chapter is therefore to examine adult relations: marriage, matrimonial causes, and financial provision, and to examine the most important parts of the highly complex law relating to children.

1. MARRIAGE

Assessment of the validity or invalidity of marriage requires a preliminary distinction to be drawn between formal validity, capacity to marry, and other impediments to marriage.[3] The first is concerned with the ceremony and its components, the second with whether the person is in law free to marry, or free to marry the other, and the third with a miscellany of unhappy factors not falling within the scope of the other two. An advantage of this division is that it reflects the plausible and legitimate interest of a number of countries in the validity of marriage, but seeks to limit that interest to those particular matters with which they are most closely concerned. On the other hand, the disadvantage of making reference to a number of laws may lead to complexity; and if more laws are given the opportunity to make an objection, this may increase the likelihood of the marriage being invalidated. If this were fair criticism, it might be preferable to have

---

[2] See further, p 344 below.
[3] Dicey, Morris, and Collins, *The Conflict of Laws* (15th edn Sweet & Maxwell, 2012), Ch 17.

marriage governed by a single law, maybe that with which the marriage is most closely connected. It is generally assumed that this should not be the law of the place of celebration, although this potential rule is not without significant support in the laws of the United States and elsewhere. But a rule which focused on the marriage as if it were a self-contained contract, as opposed to a step in a chain of status-determining events, would help to weaken of the idea of status as an enduring, organic concept.

From time to time it is said that English law makes a presumption of the validity of marriage.[4] All this appears to mean is that where there is room for any flexibility in the rules for choice of law, and the parties believe that they have gone through a valid ceremony of marriage, any doubt should probably be resolved in favour of validity. This is not because marriage is a higher and more developed state of human existence, but because it reflects the pragmatic view that where there has been a wedding ceremony, and reliance has been placed on its validity, there needs to be good reason to surprise the parties and any interested third parties by finding it to have been invalid all along.

Once an issue has been characterized, and the relevant choice of law rule invoked, it is necessary to decide what precise question is to be formulated for answer by reference to the chosen law. Suppose facts are characterized as raising an issue of formal validity, and that this requires reference to a foreign law which, in the particular case, governs formal validity. The question to be referred to the foreign law for answer will be either 'is this marriage formally valid despite …?' or 'is this marriage valid despite …?', the difference being whether the characterization which led to the choice of law remains in place as a constraint on the formulation of the question. It was proposed above[5] that it does not: that where the English court may be trying to decide the case as the foreign judge would, there is no sense in pre-empting the foreign law on the first stage of the analysis which it would have to undertake. The question is therefore whether the alleged defect makes the marriage invalid.

---

[4] For example, *Radwan v Radwan (No 2)* [1973] Fam 35.
[5] At pp 19 and 24 above.

(a) Formal validity of marriage

The formal requirements of a marriage ceremony and the effects of non-compliance are governed by the law of the place of celebration of the marriage, the *lex loci celebrationis*.[6] The question whether there is need for a public, civil, or religious ceremony,[7] whether particular words need to be read or spoken in the course of the ceremony, whether the ceremony must be held in temple, registry, or out in the fresh air, whether a religious practitioner need be in attendance, whether it is necessary for either spouse to be present in person or by proxy,[8] or whether it is necessary for the parents or other third parties to give their consent,[9] are all characterized as issues of formal validity. They are all answered by recourse to the *lex loci celebrationis*, and the consequences in terms of nullity or otherwise are determined by it as well. If the marriage would be invalid by the domestic law of the place of celebration, but would be valid by reference to the law to which a judge at the *locus celebrationis* would look if he were trying the issue, the marriage will be formally validated via the principle of *renvoi*.[10] Although theoretically possible, it is improbable that the reverse proposition would invalidate a marriage, for it is hard to believe that there is a system of family law anywhere which would not regard compliance with its own forms as sufficient.

There is an exception to the proposition that a marriage is formally valid only if it complied with the *lex loci celebrationis*. In two cases a marriage will be formally valid by virtue of having complied with the rudimentary formal requirements of the English common law as this stood prior to 1753. This extraordinary proposition—that a marriage is formally valid if it complied with the forgotten requirements of a (to them, foreign) law prior to its first alteration by statute over 250 years ago—is only a little less startling if it is remembered that this is in substance

---

[6] *Simonin v Mallac* (1860) 2 Sw & Tr 67; *Berthiaume v Dastous* [1930] AC 79 (PC).

[7] *Taczanowska v Taczanowski* [1957] P 301 (CA).

[8] *Apt v Apt* [1948] P 83 (CA); *McCabe v McCabe* [1994] 1 FLR 257 (CA).

[9] *Simonin v Mallac* (1860) 2 Sw & Tr 67; *Ogden v Ogden* [1908] P 46 (CA) (both parental consent); cf *Sottomayor v De Barros (No 1)* (1877) 2 PD 81 (CA) (papal consent, although this may instead be a question of personal capacity).

[10] *Taczanowska v Taczanowski* [1957] P 301 (CA).

a reference to the canon law which prevailed across much of Europe, and in England until 1753. The requirements of the pre-1753 common law appear to involve no more than the public declaration of intention to marry in the presence of witnesses with no need for a priest,[11] which comes close to saying that there are no formal requirements at all. This suffices to establish formal validity where it was impossible for the parties to comply with local forms, or where the place of celebration was under belligerent occupation and the parties belonged to or were associated with those occupying forces.[12] Impossibility may be invoked where two persons wish to marry in a place where civil order has wholly broken down or where there is no human population; but it is much less clear that it applies if the parties have rational objections to the form—say, that only religious or superstitious marriage is permitted—of local marriage ceremony. Not everyone will accept that parties should be able to opt out of the local law; but if the parties do not come within the local formality criteria for marriage, it is hard to deny that marriage is impossible for them there. As regards belligerent occupation, it would have been revolting to common sense to require Poles or other victims of barbarism, who wished to marry while serving in forces in belligerent occupation of enemy territory in 1945, or in groups associated with them, to comply with the formal requirements of German or other axis laws, even if the marriage would not have been technically impossible: the exception allows decency to prevail over dogmatism. Statutory provision is made for members of HM forces to marry while serving abroad, and for consular marriages.[13]

(b) Capacity of persons to marry

Each party is required to have capacity to marry the other according to the law of his or her ante-nuptial domicile, the *lex domicilii*.[14] The reason is said to be that whether and when someone is

---

[11] *Wolfenden v Wolfenden* [1946] P 61; *Penhas v Tan Soo Eng* [1953] AC 304 (PC).

[12] *Taczanowska v Taczanowski* [1957] P 301 (CA); *Preston v Preston* [1963] P 411 (CA).

[13] Foreign Marriage Act 1892, s 22 (as amended) and s 1, respectively.

[14] *Brook v Brook* (1861) 9 HLC 193; *Sottomayor v De Barros (No 2)* (1879) 5 PD 94.

ready for marriage is determined by the society in which he or
she has the longest roots. Some authorities suggest that the law
of the intended matrimonial home might be a more appropriate
test, but none has so decided, and the inherent uncertainty of
such a test makes it difficult to support, at least when the question
arises prospectively.[15] But it must be admitted that there is much
to be said for the view that the law of the society in which the
would-be spouses are going to live has the most obvious interest
in saying whether they have capacity to live there as husband and
wife. The category of capacity includes the age of marital capacity[16] and the prohibited degrees of relationship.[17] But the distinct
issue of the effect of a previous marriage arguably dissolved or
annulled by decree is examined below, as it deals with a more
complex conflict of laws and of judgments.

The concurrent role of the *lex loci celebrationis* in the regulation of capacity is also a bit of a puzzle. The first question is
whether it is necessary to comply with the capacity rules of the
lex loci as well as with those of the personal law or laws. If the
marriage takes place in England it is natural that the parties must
also satisfy the capacity requirements of English law,[18] at least if
the issue arises prior to the celebration of the marriage, in the
form of judicial review of a registrar's refusal to license the marriage. So if the registrar refuses to permit the marriage of two
foreign-domiciled persons, one of whom is under 16, he will not
be ordered to marry them even if each has domiciliary capacity.
But if the marriage has taken place in England, the parties having
had capacity by the relevant personal law, and subject to what is
said below about marriages celebrated overseas, it is hard to see
the proper interest of English law in then regarding it as invalid.
If the marriage takes place overseas, the dominant,[19] although
questionable, view is that the parties do not need capacity under
the *lex loci* in addition to satisfying their personal laws.

---

[15] For its use retrospectively, see *Radwan v Radwan* [1973] Fam 35.
[16] The Marriage Act 1949, s 2 applies to any marriage in England and requires
that neither party be under 16.
[17] *Brook v Brook* (1861) 9 HLC 193.
[18] There is no judicial authority to this effect, however.
[19] *Breen v Breen* [1964] P 144.

Even so, there is a respectable argument that capacity by the *lex loci*, whether English or foreign, ought generally to be required for a marriage to be valid. It feels strange to say that the law of the place is uniquely concerned with formal validity, and that it is completely unconcerned with personal capacity. Moreover, if the law under which the celebrant is vested with authority considers that, on account of the parties' lack of capacity to marry, his purported act of marriage was a nullity, it is hard to see how English law could disagree. If it is correct to understand marriage as something which is brought into legal being by a marriage officer, rather than something done by the parties themselves, the law which defines the officer's powers appears to be uniquely interested in the question whether he has altered the status of the parties, even though reference to an additional law will tend to increase the invalidity of marriages.

By contrast with the possibility that the *lex loci* may invalidate a marriage, otherwise valid, for lack of capacity, it may also validate a marriage even though one of the parties lacks domiciliary capacity. If the marriage takes place in England and one party is domiciled in England, it suffices for the other to have capacity according to English domestic law, even though he or she lacks capacity under the foreign domiciliary law.[20] This controversial principle is justified on the shaky footing that injustice would otherwise be done to an English domiciliary. Its weakness is all the more obvious when it is noted that the foreign incapacities which the court indicated it was prepared to override were of a kind which were offensive to English freedoms and public policy—prohibitions on inter-racial marriage, and the need for the pope of the Roman Catholic Church to consent—and which could have been better accommodated under that exceptional rule. Tellingly, the rule has no counterpart for a marriage taking place overseas in the domicile of one of the parties.

(c) Other impediments to marriage

There remain a number of other factors which may lead to the invalidity of marriage, but which it is not helpful to see as raising

---

[20] *Sottomayor v De Barros (No 2)* (1879) 5 PD 94; *Ogden v Ogden* [1908] P 46 (CA) (alternative ratio).

issues of personal capacity, and which are not the subject of a uniform choice of law rule. They are grouped together for convenience rather than coherence. First, each party must consent to marry, or become married to, the other. Any argument that there was no consent, whether this is said to follow from mistake, fraud, concealment, or duress, will in principle be governed by the *lex domicilii* of the party said not to have consented, as though this were a question of personal capacity.[21] Second, it is rational, though not clearly established by law, that physical impediments such as inability or refusal to consummate the marriage by sexual intercourse are referable to the law of the allegedly incapable party,[22] although contrary views are not untenable: it may be argued that if the willing-and-able party has no capacity to marry a person who will refuse to consummate, that party's law should apply instead. However that may be, as absence of consent and refusal both render a marriage voidable rather than void, and as the evidence is likely to be problematic, there is certainly room for the further alternative view that the case should be treated as though it were one of divorce, for which the appropriate choice of law would currently be the *lex fori*.

Third, there are special rules which apply to the validity of polygamous marriages in so far as the polygamy is alleged to be an impediment. For the purpose of the rule, it is first necessary to identify a marriage as polygamous. This will be the case[23] if two conditions are met: it must be celebrated in polygamous form[24] and the husband's *lex domicilii* must give him personal capacity for polygamy.[25] The first condition means that a marriage celebrated in England is inevitably monogamous, but if celebrated overseas the nature of the marriage will depend on the nature of the ceremony. The second condition needs no further explanation, save that if the husband loses his personal capacity for polygamy, for example by changing his domicile, the nature of the marriage

---

[21] *Szechter v Szechter* [1971] P 286, but cf *Vervaeke v Smith* [1983] 1 AC 145.

[22] *Ponticelli v Ponticelli* [1958] P 204.

[23] Subject to the Private International Law (Miscellaneous Provisions) Act 1995, s 5, a marriage is polygamous if actually or potentially so.

[24] *Lee v Lau* [1967] P 14.

[25] *Hussain v Hussain* [1983] Fam 26 (CA).

will be changed to monogamy.[26] When the matter was regulated
by the common law, the second condition meant that a marriage
celebrated overseas by an English domiciled man was not polygamous, for he had no personal capacity for polygamy, but if celebrated by an English-domiciled woman it could be polygamous,
as the husband may have personal capacity for polygamy and it
would on that account be invalid if her capacity to enter it was
governed by English law as her *lex domicilii*. It is now provided
that if a potentially polygamous marriage is actually (in the sense
of arithmetically) monogamous, an English woman does not lack
capacity to enter it, and the domiciliary incapacity is restricted
to actually polygamous marriages. Moreover, while a woman
domiciled in a country which permits polygamy may contract
a polygamous marriage, and an Englishwoman has no personal
capacity for actual polygamy,[27] it has been held, in a decision
ostensibly designed to uphold the validity of a marriage which
had endured for 20 years, that her personal capacity to have contracted a polygamous marriage should be governed by the law of
what was the intended matrimonial home.[28]

Fourth, if a previous marriage has been dissolved or annulled
by a decree recognized by English law otherwise than under the
Brussels II Regulation,[29] the subsequent remarriage of either
party is not invalidated by the refusal of some other system of law
to recognize the decree.[30] So if an Irish domiciliary is divorced
by a decree recognized by the Family Law Act 1986 but denied
recognition under Irish law, the remarriage will be valid even
though Irish law, as the law of the domicile, would regard the

---

[26] *Ali v Ali* [1968] P 564; *Parkasho v Singh* [1968] P 223. This still seems rather
odd, especially if polygamy is seen as an institution which is quite different and
distinct from monogamous marriage. After all, if the husband to a monogamous
marriage changes domicile and acquires personal capacity for polygamy, it is improbable that the marriage changes its nature and risks becoming invalid; and if
a married man undergoes a change of sex, it is equally improbable that the marriage is turned into a civil partnership.

[27] Private International Law (Miscellaneous Provisions) Act 1995, s 5.

[28] *Radwan v Radwan (No 2)* [1973] Fam 35.

[29] Regulation (EC) 2201/2003, [2003] OJ L338/1. It replaces the original
Brussels II Regulation, Regulation (EC) 1347/2000, and is on that account sometimes known as Brussels II*bis*. It is discussed at p 346 below.

[30] Family Law Act 1986, s 50.

first marriage as subsisting and the second marriage as bigamous and void: this result is brought about by the Family Law Act and the deduction that a divorce is hardly being recognized in accordance with Parliament's instruction if it leaves a spouse incapable of remarriage. In this it reverses the understanding of the common law which, although allowing the recognition of a divorce to break the bonds of matrimony, accepted that capacity to remarry was a distinct issue having a different, and domiciliary, choice of law. The inverse position, where the *lex domicilii* recognizes the validity of a decree which English legislation does not, is not legislated for. But if the *lex domicilii* regards an individual as capable of remarriage it is hard to see the rational interest of English law in contradicting it just because English private international law would not recognize the decree.[31] On the other hand, the wording of the Family Law Act 1986, section 45, may stand in the way of this result, on the ground that to accept the remarriage as valid is to grant constructive recognition to the divorce; and section 45 states that a divorce may not be recognized except in accordance with the Act. It is all a bit of a muddle.

But where recognition of the decree of a court in a Member State is mandated by the Brussels II Regulation,[32] the provisions of the Family Law Act 1986 do not apply,[33] and the impact of the decree on the parties' capacity to remarry is even more uncertain. As the Regulation governs the dissolution of matrimonial ties, and disclaims any effect on related issues,[34] the conclusion that the right to remarry is an incident or consequence of recognition may not follow if the personal law of the (former) spouse refuses to recognize the decree. The issue is whether to regard the question as one governed by the law of the state which granted the decree and to give it the effect it had under that law;[35] or to discern the answer from the text of the Regulation; or to revert

[31] *Schwebel v Ungar* (1963) 42 DLR (2d) 622 (Ont CA) supports the application of the *lex domicilii* over the non-recognition of the *lex fori*.
[32] Regulation (EC) 2201/2003; SI 2001/310, as amended.
[33] SI 2001/310, reg 9, amending the Family Law Act 1986.
[34] Recital 10.
[35] cf Case 145/86 *Hoffmann v Krieg* [1988] ECR 645.

to the common law;[36] or to pretend that the Family Law Act 1986, section 50, had not been made inapplicable to such cases.[37]

Fifth, public policy may intervene at the point when a rule of the *lex causae*, even after making allowance for different cultural and social traditions, offends the English conception of marriage, freedom to marry, and the equality of the sexes. For example, if the personal law of one of the parties denies marital capacity to a person on grounds which are capricious, penal, or discriminatory,[38] such an impediment will, or at any rate should, be ignored. And if the personal laws were to confer marital capacity at the age of five, or allow marriage to a dead person,[39] it is possible that public policy would deny recognition. But English law draws the limits of public policy tightly, with the result that marriages which are considerably different from the English domestic law model may be recognized.

2. CIVIL PARTNERSHIP

English courts did not have to decide whether any special rule applied to marriages celebrated between persons of the same sex. The conflicts issues which might have flowed from the fact that a growing number of countries of the modern enlightenment allow marriage between persons of the same sex could have been fascinating. If private international law could find room for polygamy within the pale of marriage, same-sex monogamous marriages provided for under the laws of liberal secular democracies should not have been too challenging. On the other hand, the states in question have legislated in various ways: while some permit marriage, others provide for unions which in varying degrees resemble marriage; and issues of characterization could certainly have been expected to arise. But before any such thing could happen, and to the regret of private international lawyers everywhere,

---

[36] Giving primacy to the personal law: *Schwebel v Ungar* (1963) 42 DLR (2d) 622 (Ont CA).

[37] Despite the wording of SI 2001/310, reg 9.

[38] *Scott v AG* (1886) 11 PD 128; cf *Sottomayor v De Barros (No 2)* (1879) 5 PD 94.

[39] Not as improbable as it sounds: certain laws may allow a person to marry, *post mortem*, a fiancé(e) who was killed in war service but before the marriage had taken place.

legislation[40] got in first. It provided for the creation of English, and recognition of foreign, civil partnerships on grounds functionally equivalent to those governing marriage, and stipulated that same-sex marriage contracted under laws which provided for it was to be seen, for the purposes of English law, including private international law, as civil partnership. This saved English law from having to deal with arid distinctions between different types of same-sex marriage, according to whether the foreign law under which it was contracted defined it as marriage, quasi-marriage, or anything-but-marriage.[41] For practical purposes, the law on contracting and terminating civil partnership is the same as the law on marriage in England and overseas. It is not yet clear whether the Brussels II Regulation applies of its own force and right to the dissolution of civil partnership: if it does not, English law can produce that effect itself.[42]

3. MATRIMONIAL CAUSES

The private international law of matrimonial causes[43] has to juggle a number of laws which may all be thought to have some interest in the issues which arise; the results cannot avoid being messy. The laws which determine the initial validity of marriage may not be those which apply on its annulment or dissolution; the laws which determine the effectiveness of an annulment or dissolution may not, as has been seen, be the ones which regulate the right to remarry. There are two parties who, by the time matters come to court, may have taken up separate domiciles and residences; there will be laws which had, laws which have, and laws which will have, a connection to the facts and to the parties

---

[40] Civil Partnership Act 2004, Sch 20, as amended, lists the foreign institutions which are deemed to be civil partnerships for the purposes of the Act. If enacted into law, the Marriage (Same Sex Couples) Bill 2013 will enact that overseas same sex marriages take effect as marriages, not as civil partnerships, in English law.

[41] The last, to protect the interests of those with deeply held religious bigotry.

[42] SI 2005/3334.

[43] The rules also cover judicial separation, but the infrequency of this form of decree justifies its omission from a book of this size.

themselves. There may be third parties with personal laws which also have an interest in being taken into account. Decrees of nullity and divorce may be obtained by civil proceedings which may or may not also be fully judicial, but also by reference to religious 'law'. A local policy of being disposed to grant recognition to divorces may clash with a foreign law's policy of not doing so; and all in all there is plenty of scope for a conflict of laws. Perhaps because of this, the *lex fori* features more prominently than one might expect it to be in the field of status; and the rules on jurisdiction and recognition are inevitably complex. Painting the picture by reference to principle is, therefore, rather difficult.

Outside the context of choice of law, the law does not draw a sharp distinction between divorce and annulment, for although the two forms of decree are conceptually distinct, the law is complicated enough without having entirely separate sets of rules for jurisdiction, choice of law, and recognition. Accordingly, they may be considered together as matrimonial causes.

Part of the law is contained in the Brussels II Regulation.[44] The original version[45] was made to govern, if only partially, the jurisdiction of Member States to grant matrimonial decrees, and to deal with the recognition and enforcement of decrees granted in other Member States. The Regulation was amended[46] into the form it currently has. Even though its territorial scope is limited, its rules on jurisdiction to grant decrees are comprehensive, and it is therefore appropriate to regard the Brussels II Regulation as the principal source of English private international law on matrimonial causes. But however it is presented, the law on jurisdiction to grant, and recognition of, matrimonial decrees has become complex.

---

[44] Regulation 2201/2003, [2003] OJ L338/1. Consequential amendments to English statutes are made by SI 2001/310, as itself amended by SI 2005/265. In some books, 'Brussels II' is used to refer to the original Regulation, and 'Brussels IIa' or 'Brussels II*bis*' for the amended Regulation. This distinction seems unnecessary, especially as the europa.eu website simply uses the nomenclature of 'Brussels II': its usage is followed here.

[45] Regulation (EC) 1347/2000, [2000] OJ L160/19.

[46] The amendments are mainly concerned with provisions dealing with parental responsibility for children.

(a) Obtaining decrees from an English court

The jurisdiction of an English court to grant a decree of divorce, legal separation, or annulment is governed in the first instance by the Brussels II Regulation. The point of departure is to ask whether the respondent is habitually resident in a Member State[47] or is a national of a Member State other than the United Kingdom or Ireland, or is domiciled[48] in England, Scotland, Northern Ireland, or Ireland. If he or she is, jurisdiction may be taken only in accordance with Articles 3–6 of the Regulation.[49] According to these, the court has jurisdiction if both spouses are domiciled in England.[50] Alternatively, it has jurisdiction if England is where the spouses are habitually resident; or England is where they were last habitually resident, so long as one of them still resides there; or England is where the respondent is habitually resident or is where (in the event of a joint application) either of the spouses is habitually resident; or England is where the applicant is, and for a year immediately before the application was made was, habitually resident; or England is the country of domicile of the applicant who was also habitually resident there for six months immediately prior to the application.[51] If none of these provisions gives jurisdiction to the court, there is no jurisdictional basis for an application; where they give jurisdiction to the English courts and those of another Member State, Article 19 provides for a first-seised rule to settle any problem of *lis alibi pendens*.[52]

If, but only if, Articles 3–6 fail to confer jurisdiction on the courts of any Member State, Article 7 of the Regulation provides that the 'residual' jurisdiction of the court is a matter for

---

[47] A state of the European Union excluding Denmark: Art 1(3).

[48] As a matter of the law of the United Kingdom: Art 41(b).

[49] Article 7.

[50] Article 2(1)(b). The corresponding rule for the other Member States except Ireland is framed in terms of nationality rather than domicile. 'Domicile' has its common law meaning: Art 4(2); and England is treated as if it were a Member State by reason of Art 41.

[51] Article 2(1)(a).

[52] *Bentinck v Bentinck* [2007] EWCA Civ 175, [2007] ILPr 391; *Prazic v Prazic* [2006] EWCA Civ 497, [2007] ILPr 381.

national law to determine.[53] So far as England is concerned, this is set out in statute, and will require that either party to the marriage was domiciled in England on the date the proceedings were begun.[54] Jurisdiction over proceedings for nullity is substantially the same,[55] save that a decree of nullity may also be granted if one party has died but at death was domiciled, or had for a year been habitually resident, in England.[56] Again, where proceedings are based on Article 7, other proceedings may also be brought in a foreign court. If that court is in another Member State, Article 19 applies a first-seised rule to deny the jurisdiction of the second court, but the Regulation otherwise makes no provision for and takes no account of principles of *forum conveniens* in relation to matrimonial causes. Subject to that overriding rule an English court has a statutory[57] power to stay proceedings. Accordingly, when jurisdiction is taken under Article 7, a stay may be obligatory given prior divorce proceedings in another part of the United Kingdom,[58] and is discretionary in all other cases. Although this statutory power may be distinct from the inherent power to stay on grounds of *forum non conveniens*, any distinction between the two is more technical than substantial. It follows that if the foreign court is clearly and distinctly more appropriate than England for the resolution of the dispute, the fact that

---

[53] Article 8. Even if the respondent was neither resident in nor citizen of a Member State, if a court identified by any of the criteria listed in Arts 3–6 could nevertheless have jurisdiction, Art 7 is inapplicable: Case C-68/07 *Lopez v Lizazo* [2007] ECR I-10403.

[54] Domicile and Matrimonial Proceedings Act 1973, s 5(2) as amended by SI 2001/310, reg 3(4).

[55] Domicile and Matrimonial Proceedings Act 1973, s 5(3) as amended by SI 2001/310, reg 3(5).

[56] ibid.

[57] Domicile and Matrimonial Proceedings Act 1973, Sch 1, para 9, as amended by SI 2001/310, reg 4. Whether a court may stay its proceedings if jurisdiction is founded on Art 2 of the Regulation but the natural forum in a non-Member State may be debatable, but the clear answer given in *JKN v JCN* [2010] EWHC 843 (Fam), [2011] 1 FLR 826 was that a stay was permissible, and that authority derived from the Brussels I Regulation, which would have suggested the contrary, was inapplicable. On any practical view of the matter, the judge must have been correct, especially in the case where there are (as there were in *JCN*) proceedings pending before the other court.

[58] Domicile and Matrimonial Proceedings Act 1973, Sch 1, para 8.

the petitioner will be disadvantaged by having to proceed in the foreign jurisdiction will not ward off a stay if substantial justice may be done there.[59] Given the peculiar pressures in matrimonial cases, there is, and should be, no[60] hard and fast rule that a stay should be granted if the foreign proceedings were begun first, but there will be a rational disinclination to allow later-begun proceedings to continue in a way which simply duplicates earlier ones and which seem to have no proper purpose.

In proceedings for divorce an English court applies English domestic law without exception.[61] There is certainly some sense in this. Whenever proposals are made to alter the grounds upon which a divorce may be obtained as a matter of domestic law, there is public debate and often sharp disagreement, for divorce seems to raise issues of public as well as of private concern. It might be thought to be difficult for some divorces, in cases over which the English court has jurisdiction, to be granted on grounds which would be insufficient in English domestic law or, which would be worse, for a petitioner to be denied a divorce although satisfying the criteria of English law for dissolution of a marriage which has failed. The general application of English domestic law to everyone, equally and indiscriminately, is from this pragmatic vantage-point, just what the equal protection of the laws seems to require.

Yet there is more to be said. The automatic application of English law was established and made sense when the jurisdictional rules which defined when an English court would act at all were very restrictive: if a court could not dissolve a marriage unless both parties were domiciled in England,[62] what else but English law could govern the substance? But as these jurisdictional rules were loosened, first in consequence of the change in the law which meant that a married woman no longer had her

---

[59] *De Dampierre v De Dampierre* [1988] AC 92.

[60] By contrast, the High Court of Australia does appear to have such a view: *Henry v Henry* (1996) 185 CLR 571. It appears to be more European than the Europeans.

[61] It was so assumed in *Zanelli v Zanelli* (1948) 64 TLR 556, and the question was not raised again. Choice of law for annulment is the inverse of the choice of law rule for validity; there is no uniform application of English law.

[62] *Le Mesurier v Le Mesurier* [1895] AC 517.

husband's domicile foisted on her as one of dependency,[63] and then becoming very liberal, the question whether it was still appropriate to apply only English law to the dissolution should have been asked again. If it was asked, it was not done loudly enough for anyone to hear. Yet when the jurisdictional connection to England is relatively weak, some will be tempted to think that the case for applying English law to the substance of the proceedings is less obviously strong; and so long as a sensible structure for alternative choice of law can be devised to deal with the issues raised by the possible termination of a failing marriage, they certainly have a point.

The Brussels II Regulation made no attempt to deal with choice of law, and therefore did not affect the grounds upon which an English court may grant a decree of divorce. A proposal to allow for the limited application of laws other than the *lex fori* for divorce cases failed to secure sufficient support among the Member States for the Brussels II Regulation to be amended to allow for it: the principal objection of some Member States lay in the fear that any departure from the *lex fori* which might provide for the application of a personal law might require a court to apply the divorce (or non-divorce) law of a system characterized by backwardness of the kind which characterizes much religion.[64] However, 14 of the Member States were still prepared to harmonize their rules on choice of law, and Regulation (EU) 1259/2010,[65] known as the Rome III Regulation, is the result. From an English perspective, which means from outside the Rome III Regulation, the main point may be that it does not

---

[63] Domicile and Matrimonial Proceedings Act 1973, which altered the law of domicile and set out jurisdictional rules for the grant of divorces.

[64] Though in the interests of balance, one (Malta) objected that its ultramontane refusal to have anything at all to do with divorce might by threatened by liberal values carried by persons coming in from the northern parts of Europe. It is ironic that this stance was adopted only months before a popular vote overthrew the non-divorce law which the government and church had been so frantic about defending.

[65] [2010] OJ L343/10, adopted pursuant to a mechanism for 'implementing enhanced cooperation': perhaps this status should be reflected by referring to it as the 'Rome iii' Regulation? It is open to Member States which stood aside to subscribe to the Regulation at a later date: TFEU, Art 331(1).

affect the Brussels II Regulation.[66] But in the Member States in which Rome III does apply, the parties will have a limited freedom to choose the law applicable to their divorce, albeit that the menu of choices is limited to their habitual residence or the nationality of either, at the time the agreement on choice of law is concluded, as well as to the *lex fori*.[67] Where no such choice is made, the applicable law will be that of their habitual residence, of or their last habitual residence if one of them still lives there, or of their common nationality, or of the *lex fori*.[68] It is of particular note that where the law chosen or applicable in the absence of choice makes no provision for divorce, or discriminates in this regard between the spouses on grounds of sex, the *lex fori* will apply.[69] If that is not enough to avoid bad outcomes, public policy may direct the non-application of objectionable laws.[70] On one view of the matter, this has the effect of treating the parties as adults in that, if they agree to cooperate, they are allowed to choose the law which will regulate the next stage of their private lives. If they have not so chosen, the court will try to look to laws with which they[71] have established a voluntary connection, always given that no court has to apply laws of the kind which any reasonable person would consider barbaric or otherwise objectionable. It is hard to see how law reform in this area could be better; and if truth is told, it is very hard to find anything wrong with it at all: maybe this is because there actually is nothing at all wrong with it. The fact that it prompts the question whether parties should have some freedom to choose the law by reference to which they will marry is one of the secondary benefits.[72]

Back to the law. For decrees of nullity, the applicable law will be deduced from the grounds of invalidity examined in

---

[66] Article 2.

[67] Article 5.

[68] Article 8.

[69] Article 10.

[70] Article 12.

[71] Only rarely will the connections of one but not the other spouse be material.

[72] It is correct to observe that the cases are not *in pari materia*: in divorce, the existing law, from which the Rome III Regulation departs, was the inveterate application of the *lex fori*. The choice of law rules for marriage are, in the first place, much more complex and subtle than that.

relation to the original validity of marriage: allegations of personal incapacity will be governed by the *lex domicilii*, and so on. If the marriage is plainly void, as distinct from being voidable or dissoluble, there is no need to obtain a decree to this effect, although it will often be prudent to do so. Where the alleged defect relied on is one which is in substance unknown, either precisely or by analogy, to English law, no reported authority exists to confirm that the court may still annul the marriage.[73] Such cases will doubtless be rare, and the chances must be that to grant a decree on such grounds would offend English public policy in any event.

(b) Recognizing decrees from the courts of Member States: the Brussels II Regulation

There are, in fact, three main statutory schemes for the recognition of foreign judgments given in matrimonial causes.[74] There is no natural hierarchy; the principal distinction is the source of the judgment. A decree from Scotland, Northern Ireland, the Channel Islands, or the Isle of Man will be recognized on the same basis as an English decree, that is, that it was granted by a court.[75] A decree from a Member State bound by the Brussels II Regulation will be governed by that regime; beyond that, recognition is governed by the Family Law Act 1986, Part III. But one must start somewhere, so Brussels II is dealt with first.

The law on the recognition of matrimonial decrees from courts in Member States is, pretty much, that such decrees must be recognized. The rules governing recognition are set out in Chapter III of the Regulation, which tracks the corresponding provisions of the Brussels I Regulation,[76] which fact allows the discussion of it here to be abbreviated. The effect is to align judgments in civil, commercial, and matrimonial proceedings from other Member States so far as their recognition is concerned: this

---

[73] cf *Vervaeke v Smith* [1983] 1 AC 145.

[74] By virtue of, and by virtue of regulations made under the authority of, the Civil Partnership Act 2004, the rules relating to the dissolution and annulment of civil partnerships is practically identical to those which apply to the dissolution of marriage.

[75] Family Law Act 1986, s 44.

[76] Regulation (EC) 44/2001.

is a radical departure from the tradition of English law, which had kept them well apart. Recognition under Chapter III will apply to decrees obtained from a court in a Member State given in proceedings which were instituted after 1 March 2001.[77] A divorce, legal separation, or annulment pronounced by a court[78] in a Member State is recognized without any procedure or formality.[79] Non-recognition is permitted[80] where recognition is manifestly contrary to public policy; where the judgment was given in default of appearance and there was no due and timely service, unless the respondent has unequivocally accepted the judgment; where the judgment is irreconcilable with a local judgment in proceedings between the same parties; or where it is irreconcilable with an earlier judgment from a non-Member State in proceedings between the same parties which qualified for recognition. But the jurisdiction of the adjudicating court may not be reviewed or subjected to the test of public policy;[81] recognition may not be withheld on the basis that the recognizing court would not itself have granted the decree;[82] and the substance of the judgment may not be reviewed.[83] Unexpectedly, perhaps, recognition is said not to affect the property consequences of the marriage, maintenance obligations, or other ancillary measures,[84] although it is hard to see how that could be completely observed. As was observed above, the Regulation does not explain whether it is implicit in the obligation to recognize a decree that the parties to the former marriage have restored to them their capacity to marry, even if the personal law of one of them would refuse to acknowledge it. Recital 8 to the Regulation might suggest

---

[77] That it to say, according to the commencement date of the original, and materially identical, Brussels II Regulation.

[78] Which includes all authorities with jurisdiction in these matters, so that non-judicial decrees are treated as if they were judicial decrees: Art 2(1). By way of derogation, it appears from recital 7 that 'purely religious procedures' are excluded from the scope of the Regulation, and decrees granted in such circumstances are therefore recognized, if at all, under the Family Law Act 1986.

[79] Article 21.

[80] Article 22, on which see Art 34 of the Brussels I Regulation.

[81] Article 24.

[82] Article 25.

[83] Article 26.

[84] Recital 8 to the Regulation.

that recognition of the decree extends only to the dissolution of matrimonial ties, but there is English authority, vouched for by common sense, for the proposition that a decree can hardly be said to have been recognized if it does not carry with it the freedom to remarry unencumbered by the previous marriage.[85] The procedure for enforcement, where this is required as a separate legal effect, is set out in Articles 28–30, which corresponds closely to the provisions of the Brussels I Regulation.

(c) Recognizing other foreign decrees: Family Law Act 1986

Whether the Brussels II Regulation applies depends on whether the decree was granted by a court in another Member State, which makes it easy to determine whether the decree is one to which it applies. If it does not apply, the recognition of foreign decrees is a matter for the Family Law Act 1986.[86] The Act also draws a fundamental distinction, but according to where the decree was obtained: they are either divorces obtained in the British islands[87] or are overseas divorces. A distinction framed in this way would be rational if divorces were always obtained in a single country, as will be seen, the untidy reality does not conform to that template.

The point of departure is to deal with decrees obtained in England and the rest of the British islands: they must be obtained by means of judicial proceedings if they are to be of legal effect.[88] There may be a personal problem for a wife who feels the need for a 'religious' divorce when her husband has obtained an English judicial divorce but refuses to cooperate in obtaining a 'religious' divorce, so leaving these unfortunate women to believe that they

---

[85] *Lawrence v Lawrence* [1985] Fam 106 (CA); Family Law Act 1986, s 50. But s 50 does not apply to decrees recognized under the Regulation: Family Law Act 1986, s 45(2) as inserted by SI 2001/310, reg 9.

[86] The legislation draws no distinction between divorces and annulments, and the term 'decrees' is used to encompass both. But for convenience of explanation, 'divorce' is used to include divorce and nullity.

[87] This expression includes England, Scotland, Northern Ireland, the Channel Islands, and the Isle of Man (decrees from the Republic of Ireland fall under the Regulation). Nevertheless, for convenience we will refer to English and overseas divorces.

[88] Family Law Act 1986, s 44.

are 'tied' by the original marriage. This was addressed by legislation allowing the court to stay the husband's judicial divorce proceedings until he behaves himself.[89] 'Overseas divorces', which means divorces obtained in a country outside the British islands, will be recognized, according to section 45(1), only in accordance with sections 46–49; and according to section 46 it is necessary to decide whether they were obtained by means of proceedings (whether judicial or otherwise) or not.[90] The separate treatment of divorces obtained 'without proceedings' requires the drawing of a peculiarly useless line of division, the only effect of which is to require a court to pay more attention than it should to the weird mechanics of some 'religious' divorces. Were any distinction really thought to be necessary, separate treatment of civil-judicial, and religious-non-judicial, divorces would have reflected the rather different procedures and assumptions underpinning each kind of case. But this was not done and, for the recognition of foreign divorces, all now turns on whether the divorce was obtained by 'proceedings'.

It gets worse. The scheme put in place by sections 44 and 45(1) proceeds on the unspoken assumption that every divorce or annulment is obtained in a single country. Problems arise when a decree is obtained by means of proceedings whose component parts touch more countries than one. In relation to decrees presented for recognition as overseas divorces, the leading cases[91] were both ones where part of the procedure leading to the divorce—in each case a divorce obtained outside court and under 'religious law'—had taken place in England. In holding that this precluded recognition of the decree, the court did not limit its reasoning to a case where part of the procedure had taken place in England. Instead, it deduced from the statutory definition of an overseas divorce that to be recognized as such, all the elements required for it to be obtained must be located in one foreign country. It would follow that a Jewish divorce requiring the elaborate writing and delivery of a bill of divorce, or a form of Muslim

---

[89] Divorce (Religious Marriages) Act 2002. see also *Re RAI* [2013] EWHC 100 (fam).

[90] ibid, s 46.

[91] *Berkovits v Grinberg* [1995] Fam 142, applying *R v Secretary of State for the Home Department, ex p Fatima* [1986] AC 527 (a case on earlier legislation).

divorce obtained by the writing of the words of repudiation and sending them both to the wife and to a statutory agency, will be denied recognition if any of the elements—often the sending of notice or service of a document—was geographically separated from the rest; and it appears to be irrelevant that the divorce would be recognized as effective in all of the countries in which a part of it happened. Why English law would wish to deny recognition to a divorce, which is effective under the laws of each and all of the countries which had a factual connection, on the ground that it did not all happen in the one geographical place, is beyond rational explanation.

Daft enough as this is, it goes on to produce three further consequences of hilarious absurdity. The first is that such a trans-national divorce, being excluded from the definition of an overseas divorce, is not one which section 45(1) requires to be recognized under the Family Law Act 1986 or not at all: that dichotomy is applied only to overseas divorces, which means those obtained in *a* country. No provision of the Act specifically proscribes the recognition of divorces which are not, in this particular sense, mono-territorial overseas divorces. As all other statutory schemes for recognition have been repealed, it appears to follow that such decrees fall to be recognized under the rules of the common law thought to have been abolished 40 years ago.[92] The second is that a divorce obtained from, say, a Canadian court could not be recognized as an overseas divorce if any of the procedural elements—such as the service of the petition on the respondent—took place outside Canada: it will no longer be a divorce obtained (only) in Canada and it will no longer fall under section 45. The third is that where service of an English petition is made outside England, the divorce will, by parity of reasoning, not be seen as a divorce obtained in England, with the restrictions which the law places on such divorces. The whole thing is a torrent of nonsense, but follows from the legislative categorization of divorces according to where they were

---

[92] The Recognition of Divorces and Legal Separations Act 1971, which abolished them, was itself repealed by the Family Law Act 1986. The rules recognized a divorce if granted by a court which had a real and substantial connection to the case.

obtained, and the judicial insistence that this requires all elements to be concentrated in the one place. As a cautionary tale against legislation, private international law offers none more startling than this. It makes the case for begging the European Union to come and sort things out almost unanswerable.

If the decree was obtained in a single country outside the British islands, and is not covered by the Brussels II Regulation, the rules governing its recognition depend on whether it was obtained by judicial or other proceedings.[93] Judicial proceedings are not hard to identify as such, but 'other proceedings' require the involvement of an agency of or recognized by the state whose role is more than merely probative.[94] Quite why this was considered to be a line worth drawing is also a mystery,[95] and it requires some intricate analysis of religious and foreign law. For example, a 'religious' divorce conforming to the (Pakistani) Muslim Family Law Ordinance 1961 is obtained by proceedings,[96] because the requirement to notify a statutory agency and the imposition of a statutory timetable may be seen as amounting to proceedings. The same was held, but on rather less convincing grounds, in the case of a Jewish divorce, which was obtained by proceedings because, it seems, of the elaborate or costly ceremonial involved in writing the bill of divorce.[97] But a purely religious Muslim divorce, commenced and completed in three words of repudiation spoken by the husband,[98] is not obtained by means of proceedings.[99]

If the decree was obtained by proceedings and is to be recognized as such, it must be obtained where either[100] party was

---

[93] Family Law Act 1986, s 54(1).

[94] *Chaudhary v Chaudhary* [1985] Fam 19 (CA).

[95] Indeed, it may not have been intended as a line at all: its appearance in the Recognition of Divorces and Legal Separations Act 1971 may have been intended to clarify that *all* divorces, whether judicial or not, were within the Act. Only after it had been held that 'judicial or other proceedings' were not inclusive, but served to exclude some forms of divorce, did the idea take root that there was a line to be drawn, and this understanding, or maybe misunderstanding, was subsequently taken up into the Family Law Act 1986.

[96] *Quazi v Quazi* [1980] AC 744.

[97] *Berkovits v Grinberg* [1995] Fam 142.

[98] 'Talaq, talaq, talaq' ('I divorce you', again and again).

[99] *Chaudhary v Chaudhary* [1985] Fam 19 (CA).

[100] Husband or wife, petitioner or respondent.

domiciled, according either to English law or to the law of the place of the obtaining,[101] or was habitually resident, or was a national. The decree must be effective under that law to dissolve the marriage.[102] Where domicile or habitual residence is relied on as the jurisdictional connection, the decree must be effective in the relevant law district, such as Nevada as distinct from the United States; but in the case of nationality, it must be effective throughout the entire national territory,[103] a fact which may raise issues of constitutional law. Recognition of the decree may be denied[104] on grounds of lack of notice or of the right to be heard, or if the matter is already *res judicata*. It may also be denied on grounds of public policy, and the claim of that policy to be applied may vary according to whether the marriage or the spouses had a significant connection to England.[105] Although the grounds upon which the decree was obtained are not specified as a ground of objection, they will, in an extreme case, be relevant, such as where a marriage is judicially[106] annulled for racial or religious reasons. Some may read the cases dealing with 'religious' divorces and wonder how it can be correct for the law to recognize a form of divorce in which one spouse has no right to be consulted, never mind represented and heard. Perhaps Article 6 of the European Convention on Human Rights will provide the only civilized answer: that recognition of such practice is hardly consistent with the human rights supposed to be secured by the Convention. The proposition that such treatment is warranted by religious belief or other cultural discrimination is manifestly insufficient, and the fact that the law of another country may tolerate it or be in thrall to it is nothing to the rational point.

If the decree was obtained without proceedings, its recognition requires that it be obtained where both parties were domiciled when it was obtained; or obtained where one was domiciled, with the country of domicile of the other party recognizing the

---

[101] Family Law Act 1986, s 46(5).

[102] ibid, s 46(1); though not necessarily to reattribute marital capacity: s 50.

[103] ibid, s 49(3)(a).

[104] ibid, s 51.

[105] cf *Chaudhary v Chaudhary* [1985] Fam 19 (CA).

[106] If a marriage is said to be dissolved by operation of law when one of the parties changes religion, this should not be seen as done by divorce.

decree. But it will be denied recognition in any event if either party had been habitually resident in the United Kingdom throughout the year prior to its being obtained.[107] The statutory grounds of non-recognition include those which may be raised against decrees obtained by proceedings but, in a final spasm of legislative caprice, recognition may also be denied if there is no official document certifying the effectiveness of the decree under the law of the foreign country.[108]

(d) Financial provision and maintenance

The jurisdictional rules governing maintenance application are complex, and several bases for the exercise of jurisdiction need to be dealt with. The complexity reflects two broad facts: the first is that there are many and diverse reasons why, or circumstances in which, an English court ought to be able to make such orders, which in any event would make for an untidy list, the content of which would not be susceptible to an organization which will lay bare the principle which made it rational. Second, the European Union has recently organized the law on maintenance obligations. The Maintenance Regulation deals with jurisdiction, applicable law, recognition and enforcement of decisions, and judicial co-operation in matters relating to maintenance obligations. The Regulation is certainly welcome, though it is not without its quirks. Foremost among these is the fact that Article 2 contains a substantial list of definitions, but the one term which is not so defined is 'maintenance'. According to Article 1(1), the scope of the Regulation is 'maintenance obligations arising from a family relationship, parentage, marriage, or affinity', and apart from the obligation to interpret this autonomously,[109] it is left at that. It will presumably include proprietary legal relations arising directly from the marriage or its dissolution, and exclude those which have no connection with the marriage, if that is any help.[110]

---

[107] Family Law Act 1986, s 46(2).

[108] ibid, s 51(4), a requirement read minimally in *Wicken v Wicken* [1999] Fam 224.

[109] Recital 11.

[110] cf Case 143/78 *De Cavel v De Cavel* [1979] ECR 1055.

According to Article 3 of the Maintenance Regulation,[111] the
English court will have jurisdiction if either the creditor or the
defendant is habitually resident in England, or if the English
court has jurisdiction over proceedings concerning status or
parental responsibility and the matter relating to maintenance
is ancillary to those proceedings: this provides the formal basis
for the English court to continue to be able to make orders for
ancillary financial relief as part of the divorce or annulment proceedings before it.[112] Article 4 confers or recognizes a restricted
right for the parties to choose a court, the choice being required
to be in writing, though there is no power to make a choice of
court if the maintenance obligation is in respect of a child under
18. Jurisdiction may also be based on voluntary appearance.[113]
Where those provisions do not give jurisdiction to the courts
of any Member State, the courts of the Member State of the
parties' common nationality (which in England means common
domicile) have 'subsidiary' jurisdiction.[114] And where none of
these provisions serves to give jurisdiction to the courts of any
Member State, all that remains is an exceptional power to take
jurisdiction as a matter of necessity.[115] It will therefore be seen
that the jurisdictional provisions of the Maintenance Regulation
are exhaustive, and do not provide for any 'residual jurisdiction'
over defendants who have no domicile in a Member State.

So far as concerns choice of law, an English court applies
English law to substantive claims for financial provision.[116] In
exercising its statutory powers a court may give dominant effect
to a pre- or post-nuptial agreement, but no principle of private

---

[111] Regulation (EC) 4/2009, [2009] OJ L7/1; see also SI 2011/1484. Both are in
effect from 18 June 2011.

[112] For the English court's power to grant financial relief after a foreign divorce,
see Matrimonial and Family Proceedings Act 1984; *Agbaje v Agbaje* [2010]
UKSC 13, [2010] 1 AC 628. But the jurisdictional rules of the Maintenance
Regulation will prevail to the extent that they conflict with those of the 1984
Act (eg insofar as the application is for maintenance as opposed to some other
property adjustment order).

[113] Article 5.

[114] Article 2(3) read together with Art 6.

[115] Articles 3–7. *Lis alibi pendens* is regulated by Art 12.

[116] *Sealey v Callan* [1953] P 135 (CA).

international law appears to be involved in calibrating the role which is accorded to the agreement in question.[117]

A foreign divorce, even if recognized in England, does not automatically terminate an English maintenance order.[118] A foreign maintenance order which is final and conclusive[119] may be recognized and enforced in England at common law and under statute,[120] for it is a civil judgment *in personam*. The provisions for recognition are largely reciprocal with the grounds of jurisdiction exercised by English courts. Otherwise, orders from Member States may be enforced under Chapter IV of the Maintenance Regulation; the registration is made in the magistrates' court for the place where the respondent is resident for the purposes of this instrument, or where assets against which enforcement may be made are situated. The permissible objections to registration are few.

4. PERSONAL BANKRUPTCY

The law on corporate insolvency is discussed in the following chapter, as part of the law of corporations. A substantial part of it will also be seen to apply to individual bankruptcy, but something needs to be said of it here.

The Insolvency Regulation[121] applies its regime of jurisdiction, choice of law, and recognition and enforcement of judgments to personal bankruptcy as well as to corporate insolvency. But because it is, in practice, most commonly applicable in corporate insolvency, the summary of its provisions which properly belongs in the following chapter, but which will be equally applicable to personal bankruptcy, will not be pre-repeated here. The account which follows in this section is, therefore, the law as it

---

[117] *Radmacher v Granatino* [2010] UKSC 42, [2011] 1 AC 534.

[118] *Macaulay v Macaulay* [1991] 1 WLR 179.

[119] Though as the court which made the order usually has the power to vary the figures, it may be that its decision is only really final in relation to payments the due date for which has already passed.

[120] Maintenance Orders Act 1950, Part II; Maintenance Orders (Facilities for Enforcement) Act 1920; Maintenance Orders (Reciprocal Enforcement) Act 1972; Civil Jurisdiction and Judgments Act 1982.

[121] Regulation (EC) 1348/2000, [2000] OJ L160/1.

applies to bankruptcies to which the Regulation does not apply, which principally means cases where the centre of the debtor's main interests is outside the territory of the Member States.

The English courts have jurisdiction to declare bankrupt any debtor who is domiciled or present in England on the day of presentation of the petition.[122] They also have jurisdiction if he was ordinarily resident, or had a place of residence, or carried on business (or was a member of a partnership firm which carried on business) in England at any time within the three years prior to the presentation of the petition.[123] A debtor who has subjected himself to a voluntary arrangement submits to the jurisdiction by doing so.[124] In deciding whether to exercise their discretion to make the order, the courts will consider the location of assets, any foreign bankruptcy, and other issues of general convenience.[125] The bankrupt may be examined by order of the court, but the private examination of any other person is probably limited to those who are present within the jurisdiction to be served with the summons requesting their attendance.[126]

As to choice of law, an English court applies English law to the bankruptcy.[127] The making of the order operates as a statutory assignment of the debtor's property, wherever situated, to his trustee;[128] the bankrupt may be ordered to assist the trustee in recovering property outside the control of the court. A creditor who is or who has made himself subject to the personal jurisdiction of the court may be restrained from taking proceedings overseas, in order to safeguard the principle of equal division.[129] Foreign debts must be shown to be good by the law under which they arise, but the court will use its own rules to secure, as best it may, equality between creditors of the same class.[130] The power of the court to set aside an antecedent transaction is not subject

---

[122] Insolvency Act 1986, s 265.

[123] ibid, s 265.

[124] ibid, s 264.

[125] *Re Behrends* (1865) 12 LT 149; *Re Robinson, ex p Robinson* (1883) 22 Ch D 816 (CA).

[126] cf *Re Seagull Manufacturing Co Ltd* [1993] Ch 345 (CA).

[127] *Re Kloebe* (1884) 28 Ch D 175; *Re Doetsch* [1896] 2 Ch 836.

[128] Insolvency Act 1986, ss 283, 306, 436.

[129] *Barclays Bank plc v Homan* [1993] BCLC 680 (CA).

[130] *Re Scheibler* (1874) 9 Ch App 722.

to express limitation, but the defendant against whom reversal of the transaction is sought must be (or by service out with leave of the court, be made) subject to the jurisdiction of the court, and the test is whether it is just and convenient in all the circumstances of the case to make the order.[131]

An English discharge operates in relation to all the debts provable in the bankruptcy, irrespective of the law which governed the debt,[132] and a discharge under the law which governed the debt will be effective in England.[133]

A foreign bankruptcy will be recognized if the debtor was domiciled[134] in or submitted[135] to the jurisdiction of the court; and the bankruptcy will vest English movables (but not land) in the assignee if this is the effect it has under the foreign law.[136] The result may be that the debtor no longer has property in England, and this will tell strongly against making an English order. A discharge from a foreign bankruptcy is effective in England only if it is effective under the law which governed the debt.[137] A court may not question the bankruptcy jurisdiction of a Scottish or Northern Irish court; and the effect of such an order extends to all property in England, not excluding land.[138]

B. CHILDREN

Leaving aside questions of legitimacy, which today seem archaic and offensive, and adoption, which is omitted on grounds of space, the law of children is principally concerned with guardianship and custody. The last of these has given rise to a substantial amount of legislation, local and international, to deal with the distressing problem of child abduction, which is a miserable

---

[131] *Re Paramount Airways Ltd* [1993] Ch 223 (CA).

[132] Insolvency Act 1986, s 281.

[133] *Gibbs and Sons v Soc Industrielle et Commerciale des Métaux* (1890) 25 QBD 399 (CA).

[134] *Re Hayward* [1897] 1 Ch 905.

[135] *Re Anderson* [1911] 1 KB 896.

[136] *Re Craig* (1916) 86 LJ Ch 62.

[137] *Gibbs and Sons v Soc Industrielle et Commerciale des Métaux* (1890) 25 QBD 399 (CA).

[138] Insolvency Act 1986, s 426.

consequence of family unhappiness. Much has been accomplished by international convention, no doubt because the area is too delicate or sensitive to be left to national laws and the willingness of national courts to adopt an approach which other courts would see as being even-handed. It is all very well to start from the premise that the dominant concern is to make orders which are in the best interests of the child, but this is easier said than done, because it needs to be done in such a way that does not, unintentionally, give encouragement to those who abduct children from lawful custody. *Quot homines, tot sententiae* could have been formulated to describe the private international law of children.

1. PARENTAL RESPONSIBILITY, CHILD CUSTODY

The law has become especially complex, but the rational starting point for explaining the law is the Brussels II Regulation. The Regulation applies in civil matters relating to the attribution, exercise, delegation, restriction, or termination of parental responsibility.[139] This covers rights of access, rights of custody, guardianship, fostering, and the protection and preservation of a child's property: in other words, a very substantial chunk of the private international law of children, though as currently enacted, it does not include disputes over parenthood, or adoption and the procedures leading up to it.[140]

(a) Jurisdiction

The basic jurisdictional rule is to give jurisdiction to the courts for the place of the child's habitual residence,[141] but where the child has moved lawfully from one Member State to another

---

[139] It has been held that it also applies where the powers under which actions are taken are public law (police) powers relating to child protection: Case C-435/06 C [2007] ECR I-10141. This stretches terms to their limit, but is justified by the need to avoid avoidable divisions in the overall law of parental responsibility and child protection.

[140] Article 1.

[141] Article 8. But where this cannot be determined, the court will have jurisdiction if the child is present: Art 13.

Member State, the courts of the former retain a short period of exceptional jurisdiction as well.[142] If a court is exercising matrimonial jurisdiction under the Regulation, it may also have consequential jurisdiction over a matter of parental responsibility. It will do so if the child is habitually resident in England, at least one of the spouses has parental responsibility, and the jurisdiction has been accepted by the spouses and is in the best interests of the child.[143] Jurisdiction comes to an end once the matrimonial proceedings have terminated in dismissal or a final decree, or on final judgment in the parental responsibility proceedings. In a development which appears to be a novelty within the framework of European legislation, a court has a statutory power to ask a court in another Member State to assume jurisdiction in its place.[144] This reflects the welcome truth that, no matter how detailed the rules of jurisdiction, there may still be cases which ought, in the interests of justice, to be dealt with by a court in another Member State which has jurisdiction and where that jurisdiction is more appropriate. The jurisdictional rules of the Brussels II Regulation are complex, and do not lend themselves to concise accurate summary. The reason is that there is no real principle at work, rather an attempt to create a set of rules which is detailed and sufficiently balanced for courts to apply them, and to require unquestioning respect orders made by courts in other Member States which they might not have made for themselves.

Where the Regulation does not ascribe jurisdiction to the courts of a Member State, most obviously where the child is not habitually resident in a Member State, a state will exercise what may be described as its 'residual jurisdiction'.[145] So far as the United Kingdom is concerned, this jurisdiction will now be defined in part by the common law, and in part by the Hague Convention on Jurisdiction, Applicable Law, Recognition, Enforcement and Co-operation in respect of Parental Responsibility and Measures for the Protection of Children of 1996, which took effect in the United Kingdom on 1 November 2012.[146] This Convention

---

[142] Article 9.
[143] Article 12.
[144] Article 15.
[145] Article 14.
[146] Implemented by SI 2010/1898.

applies where the child is habitually resident in a state which is a Contracting State to the 1996 Convention but not a Member State of the European Union; its provisions generally resemble those of the Regulation. Where neither the Regulation nor the 1996 Convention applies, then so far as concerns orders for guardianship and custody, the English courts have jurisdiction to make an order otherwise than as regards care, education, and contact where the child is a British national or is present within the jurisdiction of the court.[147] Orders for contact, residence, or specific issues may be made in matrimonial proceedings;[148] also if the child is habitually resident in England or is present in England and not habitually resident in Scotland or Northern Ireland[149] (and on such basis, an order for care, education, or contact may also be made; this is also permitted if the child is present and the immediate exercise of the power is necessary for the protection of the child[150]). But if the matter of the proceedings has already been determined by a foreign court the English court may decline to act;[151] and if proceedings are pending in a foreign court the English court may stay its own if it is appropriate to do so.[152]

(b) Choice of law

Where they have jurisdiction, English courts apply English domestic law.[153] Whatever else may be said, these cases are often so complicated, and require such urgent attention, that the pleading, proof, and application of foreign law would be utterly self-defeating: in this area of the law especially, the best cannot be allowed to be the enemy of the good.

---

[147] *Re P (GE) (An Infant)* [1965] Ch 568 (CA).
[148] Family Law Act 1986, ss 1, 2 (as amended).
[149] ibid s 2(2) (as amended).
[150] ibid s 1(1)(d) (as amended).
[151] ibid s 5 (as amended).
[152] ibid.
[153] *J v C* [1970] AC 668. The Hague Convention 1996 provides, by Art 15, for the application of the *lex fori* in cases to which it applies, though certain issues may also be referred to the law of the habitual residence of the child. The Brussels II Regulation contains no rule to deal with the applicable law, but for tidiness, SI 2010/1898, reg 7, applies the rule in the Hague Convention to proceedings in which the court has jurisdiction under the Brussels II Regulation.

(c) Recognition of foreign orders

So far as concerns the recognition of foreign orders, orders made by the courts of a Member State and required to be recognized under the Brussels II Regulation are dealt with within a structure which closely resembles that in the Brussels I Regulation. So, for example, there is a power to refuse to recognize an order made in another Member State on grounds of public policy, but as the jurisdiction of the foreign court, and the substance of the foreign decision, may not be reviewed, the grounds on which public policy may overturn the obligation to recognize the judgment are, as they are intended to be, decidedly narrow.[154] It is unsurprising that the most hotly-contested questions are those concerning the obligation of a court simply to accept and give effect to orders made in another Member State: where there is a perception that the order made is not one which the recognizing court would itself have made, or that the original court should have made, or would not have made if it had known what the recognizing court knows now, the obligation to swallow hard and recognize it nonetheless may be a demanding one.

So far as orders relating to custody are concerned, it has been held that the obligation to recognize a foreign order under Chapter III of the Regulation does not extend to provisional measures relating to custody taken under Article 20.[155] Likewise, the *lis pendens* provisions of Article 19 have been held to be inapplicable where the proceedings before the court first seised appear to be only for provisional measures and (surely controversially) the court seised second considers that it is unable to ascertain whether the court seised first is also seised of proceedings for substantive relief.[156]

The 1996 Hague Convention requires measures taken by the authorities of a Contracting State to be recognized by operation of law,[157] though subject to a number of defences.[158]

---

[154] *Re L (A Child)* [2012] EWCA Civ 1157. In principle, though, proceedings for a decision that a foreign judgment should not be recognized may be brought even though no attempt has yet been made to have the judgment recognized: Case C-195/08 PPU *Rinau* [2008] ECR I-5271.

[155] Case C-256/09 *Purrucker v Vallés Pérez I* [2010] ECR I-7353.

[156] Case C-296/10 *Purrucker v Vallés Pérez II* [2010] ECR I-11163.

[157] Article 23; SI 2010/1898, reg 8.

[158] Article 24.

(d) Foreign orders from Member States concerning the return of children

At this point in the narrative, we cross into the area which is governed by special rules concerning child abduction and return, which are otherwise examined in the next section. But the recognition of orders made in other Member States, and dealt with under the Brussels II Regulation, should be examined here. Where a court in a Member State has ordered the return of a child in terms of Articles 11(8) or 40, and has issued a certificate in the form required by Article 42(2), the foreign judgment is required to be recognized and enforced without question.[159] Even though there may be good grounds for believing that the facts and matters certified by the original court were incorrect, and even where it is apparent that there may well have been a breach of the child's right to be heard,[160] the foreign judgment must still be recognized and enforced, and any allegation of infringement raised before the court which made the original order.[161] To the same effect, a change in circumstance since the original judgment and certification will not permit the non-enforcement of the certified judgment; again, the matter must be raised before the original court.[162] In this respect the policy of automatic enforcement of certified judgments ordering or requiring return is reinforced by the need to avoid lengthy proceedings, and by the perception that matters relating to the child will be best dealt with if one court has the power of decision, and the others confine themselves to enforcing those decisions.[163] One simply observes that while it may be possible for the court in Luxembourg to take so detached a view of the issues, it asks a lot, and possibly just too

---

[159] Case C-195/08 PPU *Rinau* [2008] ECR I-5271.

[160] Article 42(2)(a).

[161] Case C-491/10 PPU *Aguirre Zarraga v Pelz* [2010] ECR I-14247.

[162] Case C-211/10 PPU *Povse v Alpago* [2010] ECR I-6673.

[163] The conclusiveness of the certificate issued by the original court is at odds with the position adopted in Case C-619/10 *Trade Agency Ltd v Seramico Investments Ltd* [2012] ECR I-(Sept 6). The best available explanation presumably is that in a commercial case, the need for urgent enforcement is less acute, and that under Art 54 of the Brussels I Regulation, the certificate is not essential to the enforcement of the judgment.

much, of the individual national judge to insist that he or she act or refrain from acting in a way which is perceived, and probably on good grounds, to be wrong to the point of being cruel, simply because a foreign court has issued a certificate saying that it has done everything it should have.

(e) Foreign orders made by the courts of non-Member States

Orders made by courts in Contracting States to the 1996 Convention will be recognized according to Article 23 of the Convention. Otherwise, so far as concerns orders made by courts which are neither Member States nor Contracting States to the 1996 Convention, a guardianship order made by a court of a country of which the child was a national or in which it was present will usually be recognized in England;[164] but the power of the guardian will extend no further than the powers of a foreign parent. A foreign custody order does not prevent an English court making such order as it thinks fit in relation to the welfare of the child.[165]

2. ABDUCTION, REMOVAL, AND RETURN

Apart from cases where jurisdiction and the recognition of orders is governed by the Brussels II Regulation, the wider law of child abduction and the circumstances in which there should or should not be a return is otherwise substantially derived from international convention. It is usual to deal with this question as one of private international law, but it is not really obvious that this is where it belongs. As a matter of domestic common law, the power to order the return of a child who has been abducted is a particular example of orders generally made in the interests of the welfare of the child.[166] In practical terms, this was superseded by the Hague Convention on the Civil Aspects of Child Abduction 1980. The point of departure when dealing with this Convention

---

[164] *Re P (GE) (An Infant)* [1965] Ch 568 (CA).
[165] *McKee v McKee* [1951] AC 352 (PC).
[166] *J v C* [1970] AC 668 (PC).

was originally taken to be that a child who has wrongfully[167] been removed, or who is being wrongfully retained, outside the jurisdiction of the court of his or her habitual residence should almost always be restored to custody[168] in the country of its habitual residence,[169] whether or not a prior court order has been made, for it is there that it is most appropriate that decisions about the custody and welfare of the child are made. If a child who was habitually resident in a Contracting State is wrongfully removed from that state to the 1980 Convention, the Convention obliges the authorities of the state to which the child is removed, or in which it is retained, to return the child. The application for a return order is made according to Article 8, transmitted, received, and implemented. If the proceedings are begun within one year of the removal, Article 12 prescribes the return of the child 'forthwith'. Article 13 sets out limited defences to the claim for return.

The inclination of the English courts at one time appeared to be to read these defences as restrictive, only applicable in exceptional cases, and that the duty imposed by Article 12 was pretty uncompromising. What it certainly did not require was a lengthy factual investigation of the circumstances of the individual case, not least because this was likely to mean that, by the time a decision came to be taken and implemented, the speedy return of the child would be liable to involve uprooting him or her instead. However, it is now clear that the objective of swiftly returning the child did not necessarily outweigh the need to give weight to the best interests of the child. Like it or not, there are some pretty challenging places from which children may be removed to England, and if these countries are scary for adults, they may be utterly terrifying for the young and defenceless. If an English court is faced with the reality of returning a child to, say,

---

[167] That is, in breach of custody rights attributed to a person, institution, or other body under the law of the state of habitual residence and which were actually exercised, or would have been exercised but for the removal: Art 3 of the Hague Convention.

[168] Which may be of a person or, in appropriate cases, a court: *Re H (Child Abduction: Rights of Custody)* [2000] 2 AC 291.

[169] *Re J (A Minor)(Abduction: Custody Rights)* [1990] 2 AC 562; *Re F (A Minor) (Abduction: Custody Rights)* [1991] Fam 25 (CA).

Somalia or Zimbabwe,[170] a judge may do well to take a sceptical view of the so-called need to secure a swift, no-questions-asked, return. He or she may observe, as it has been memorably put, that '[t]hese children should not be made to suffer for the sake of general deterrence of the evil of child abduction worldwide'.[171] More recently still it was accepted that the Conventions and the Brussels II Regulation had each been devised with the best interests of the child as a primary consideration, and that 'the whole of the Hague Convention is designed for the benefit of children, not of adults'.[172] If this is now accepted as the new point of departure, the proposition that the Convention aims to secure a swift return of the child to wherever he or she had been taken from must be taken to be subject to considerable qualification.[173] From the perspective of the child, one wonders how it could ever have been thought to have been otherwise. But however that is, the whole matter has little to do with private international law; there is no real issue of jurisdiction; the *lex fori* is applied; and the Hague Convention does not provide for the recognition of foreign judgments as such.

By contrast, in relation to non-Convention countries, the English courts have always given predominant weight to the principle of the welfare of the child, and did not approach its decision as though the principles of the Convention, if they were really different, were applicable.[174] The principle of the welfare of the child gives rise to what are, in one respect, delicate questions where the country to which return is sought is one where a particular religious 'law' is in force. In some cases the court has taken the robust and rational view that, in effect, the threat of damage liable to be done by religion cannot be allowed to prevail over the best interests of child, and a return to a country where

---

[170] Or a Swiss judge with the prospect of returning a child from Geneva to Israel: *Neulinger v Switzerland* [2011] 1 FLR 122 (ECtHR).

[171] *Re M (Children) (Abduction: Rights of Custody)* [2007] UKHL 55, [2008] 1 AC 1288 at [54]. See also *Neulinger v Switzerland* [2011] 1 FLR 122 (ECtHR); *Re E (Children)* [2011] UKSC 27, [2012] AC 144.

[172] *Re E (Children)* [2011] UKSC 27, [2012] AC 144 at [52].

[173] *Re E (Children)* [2011] UKSC 27, [2012] AC 144 at [18].

[174] *Re J (A Child) (Custody Rights: Jurisdiction)* [2005] UKHL 40, [2006] 1 AC 80.

this may result cannot be ordered.[175] Other courts, not surprisingly, have preferred the view that it is not their business to pass judgment on what is, in effect, the cultural structure of a foreign system.[176] It is a distinctly delicate area for judicial assessment and decision. It has to be dealt with as part of the conflict of laws and conflict of jurisdictions, but in truth the conflict operates at a quite different level, and its resolution by the application of rules of law is challenging.

---

[175] *Re JA (Child Abduction: Non-Convention Country)* [1998] 1 FLR 231 (CA), which was generally approved in *Re J (A Child) (Custody Rights: Jurisdiction)*.
[176] *Osman v Elisha* [2000] Fam 62 (CA).

9

CORPORATIONS

Although a corporation is a person—albeit a legal rather than a natural person, a *persona ficta*—it has long been the tradition of English private international law to treat corporations separately from the law of persons, and instead to examine the private international law of corporations alongside corporate insolvency, presumably on the basis that insolvency is a significant fact of corporate life and litigation. That tradition is observed here.

The rules of the common law for choice of law used, and still use, the *lex incorporationis* to govern many of the issues raised under the law of corporations. Insolvency, by contrast, was dominated by the application of *lex fori*. But this ignored a problem which, in recent years, grew to alarming size. The uncoordinated consequences of corporate insolvencies with cross-border components came to be seen as simply intolerable: for a court to insist on applying its own law, and taking jurisdiction whenever there was a sufficient local justification for doing it, was not designed to promote, and did not promote, the orderly resolution of the cross-border issues raised by a huge cross-border insolvency. Even where they were receptive to the idea, which did not always appear to be the case, there was only so much that judges could do to manage the proceedings before them in a way which was sensitive to the fact that other courts were liable to be involved in the same work.[1] Although domestic legislation made modest provision for rendering assistance in relation to foreign insolvency proceedings, the first serious attempt at harmonization took the form of a European Regulation,[2] which applies to corporate insolvency as well as to personal bankruptcy. A Model

---

[1] Even so, for a remarkably bold suggestion of what a court proposed to do under its inherent jurisdiction, see *Cambridge Gas Transportation Corpn v Committee of Unsecured Creditors of Navigator Holdings plc* [2006] UKPC 26, [2007] 1 AC 508 (but regarded as wrongly decided), which is discussed further at p 380 below.

[2] Council Regulation (EC) 1346/2000, [2000] OJ L160/1.

Law[3] on cross-border insolvency was given effect in English law in 2006: it has the aim, and certainly offers the prospect, of further developing the cross-border cooperation and coordination of insolvency procedures. These statutory steps taken to bring order to the administration of cross-border insolvency have been far more successful than anything national parliaments or individual judges could ever have achieved. Although the detail of the law is complex, the field of cross-border insolvency is an excellent example of when legislation to improve the state of the law is the only way ahead.

A. CORPORATIONS

It makes sense to look first at the private international law of corporations, and then at the law of insolvency: as to this latter, what is said about corporate insolvency will apply also to personal bankruptcy which was otherwise mentioned in the previous chapter. The sources of private international law are principally those of the common law, though European law on the freedom of movement and establishment makes an increasing contribution to the private international law of corporations.

1. THE ROLE OF THE *LEX INCORPORATIONIS*

A corporation is an artificial creation, a legal person. The question whether, and with what powers, a body corporate has been created is determined by the law under which its creation took place, which the common law considers to be the *lex incorporationis*. Likewise, the question who is empowered to act on its behalf is a matter for the *lex incorporationis*, even though the consequences in law of an act which an officer or organ was not entitled to perform may also be referred to another law.[4] The question whether an individual is personally liable for the acts of a corporation is also governed by the *lex incorporationis*; and, in

---

[3] UNCITRAL, 30th session, 1997. For the implementing legislation, see Insolvency Act 2000, s 14(4) and SI 2006/1030.
[4] *Janred v ENIT* [1989] 2 All ER 444 (CA).

principle, all issues having to do with the internal government and management of a corporation are reserved to that law.[5] It is hard to deny that this offers an incentive to incorporate under a law which offers advantages to those who may wish to create a corporation with wide powers but restricted liabilities, or to incorporate with no significant risk of allowing liability to affect individual officers or corporators: there are times when one wonders whether onshore[6] or offshore[7] havens of this kind actually have any other purpose.[8] This is, however, little more than a consequence of the doctrine of separate corporate personality and the fact that some laws offer more than others to the careful corporator. Although it is sometimes suggested that the place of incorporation should not be decisive, and that the law of the place of daily or central management and control should assume a more prominent role;[9] or that the doctrine of separate corporate personality really needs to be countered by an analysis based on the economic realities of life and the need to assert effective control over multi-national enterprises,[10] these arguments have tended to be directed at jurisdiction over companies rather than at the hegemony of the *lex incorporationis* as the determinant of legal personality, power, and responsibility.

(a) Recognition of corporations

English law recognizes the creation of corporations, and the acquisition of legal personality by them, by reference to the *lex incorporationis*. The recognition of corporations has been extended to those which are created under the ordinances of a semi-state,

---

[5] *Risdon Iron and Locomotive Works v Furness* [1906] 1 KB 49 (CA); *Bonanza Creek Gold Mining Co v R* [1916] 1 AC 566 (PC); *Lazard Bros v Midland Bank* [1933] AC 289; *National Bank of Greece and Athens SA v Metliss* [1958] AC 509; *Carl Zeiss Stiftung v Rayner & Keeler Ltd (No 2)* [1967] 1 AC 853; *JH Rayner (Mincing Lane) Ltd v Department of Trade and Industry* [1990] 2 AC 418.

[6] Delaware, for example.

[7] The Channel Islands and the Isle of Man are obvious examples, but British possessions in the Caribbean are notorious as well.

[8] Although it is possible that the question whether the corporate veil will always protect whoever is behind it will not necessarily be answered by the *lex incorporationis*. See *VTB Capital plc v Nutritek International Corp* [2013] UKSC 5; Tham [2007] LMCLQ 22.

[9] Drury [1998] CLJ 165.

[10] Muchlinski (2001) 50 ICLQ 1.

such as Taiwan, or the *soi-disant* and otherwise illegal entity styled the 'Turkish Republic of Northern Cyprus'.[11] Moreover, although English law does not recognize the legal personality of an international organization in the absence of domestic legislation to confer such status, where a foreign law has conferred such personality under its law, the resultant legal person may be recognized in England.[12] So the Arab Monetary Fund, an international organization of states of which the United Kingdom is not a member, had been given legal personality under the laws of the United Arab Emirates, and was accordingly recognized as a person under English law. What would have happened if it had been given personality under the laws of more states than one raises questions to which no easy answers exist and which it is therefore convenient not to ask.

(b) Dissolution of corporations

What the law creates the same law can also destroy, so the question whether a corporation has been dissolved is likewise one referred to the *lex incorporationis*[13] alone. The validity of a corporate dissolution may raise difficult questions when the law under which the corporation was created ceases to exist and in its geographical place a new law arises. But corporations created under the law of Tsarist Russia were recognized as having been dissolved under the law of the Soviet Union, and, at the end of the same century, in a satisfying piece of legal and political symmetry, vice versa.[14]

(c) Amalgamation of corporations

A combination of the rules for creation and dissolution means that the amalgamation of corporations, the recognition of the new corporation, and whether it assumes the rights and liabilities of the dissolved corporation(s), are in principle all questions for

[11] Foreign Corporations Act 1991, s 1.

[12] *Arab Monetary Fund v Hashim (No 3)* [1991] 2 AC 114; *Westland Helicopters Ltd v Arab Organisation for Industrialisation* [1995] QB 282.

[13] *Lazard Bros v Midland Bank* [1933] AC 289; *Russian and English Bank v Baring Bros* [1932] 1 Ch 435 (and if there is a branch in England it cannot sue after the corporation has been dissolved; it should be wound up).

[14] *The Kommunar (No 2)* [1997] 1 Lloyd's Rep 8.

the *lex incorporationis*,[15] although the issue whether this process also discharges liabilities incurred by the old corporation is a distinct and contractual one, which will be governed by the law applicable to those obligations.[16] A court will naturally endeavour to give effect to a case of corporate succession, and will do what it can to ensure that it is effective in English private international law.[17] But corporate reconstruction can be untidy, and a court may reach the view in a particular case that the process is not a true succession or amalgamation notwithstanding the language used by the foreign legislator.[18]

(d) Migration of corporations

The fact that a corporation's residence may determine its liability to pay tax provides an incentive to companies, who wish to avoid the taxes which they doubtless expect[19] others to pay instead, to try to migrate from one state to another. National laws variously put obstacles in their way, limiting or removing the power of a corporation established under their laws to remove their residence or central management and control to another country while remaining incorporated under the original law. These restrictions are challenged from time to time for their compatibility with European Union law on freedom of establishment; and the challenges usually fail. It has been held, pretty consistently, that European law does not prevent the *lex incorporationis* itself preventing a company moving its central management and control to another country, or does not impede its requiring governmental consent to do so, if the company intends to

---

[15] *National Bank of Greece and Athens SA v Metliss* [1958] AC 509; if the two corporations are incorporated in different countries the *lex incorporationis* of each must recognize the amalgamation. See also *Adams v National Bank of Greece and Athens SA* [1961] AC 255 for cases where there may not be a true and complete succession to the rights and liabilities of the former companies.

[16] *Adams v National Bank of Greece and Athens SA* [1961] AC 255.

[17] *Toprak Enerji Sanayi SA v Sale Tilney Technology plc* [1994] 1 WLR 840; *Eurosteel v Stinnes* [2000] 1 All ER (Comm) 964; *Astra SA Insurance and Reinsurance Co v Sphere Drake Insurance Ltd* [2000] 2 Lloyd's Rep 550.

[18] *The Kommunar (No 2)* [1997] 1 Lloyd's Rep 8.

[19] And if they are newspapers, stridently insist that everyone else should pay, which is one of the ironies of Case 81/87 *R v HM Treasury and the IRC ex p Daily Mail*.

remain incorporated in the original state.[20] In the same way, the *lex incorporationis* may prevent the transfer of a company's seat to another Member State while retaining its original incorporation.[21] But it will be otherwise if the company migrates and simply converts itself into a company governed by the law of the migrated-to Member State, always assuming that the law of the migrated-to state does not require the incoming company to be wound up in the state from which it is migrating. In essence, unless or until there is greater substantive harmonization in company law in the Member States, the European Court understands that the freedom of establishment provisions of the Treaty cannot be interpreted in such a way as to authorize a corporate stampede to those Member States which look or behave uncomfortably like tax havens.

(e) Domicile of corporations

As a matter of common law, a corporation is domiciled at the place of its incorporation.[22] This, for example, means that the capacities[23] of the corporation are governed by its *lex incorporationis* and the general principle that legal capacity is governed by the law of the domicile is preserved. It also means that, as far as the common law is concerned, a corporation has only one domicile.

In other contexts, however, a 'statutory domicile' may be conferred, which is separate and wholly distinct from the common law determination of domicile.[24] In the context of jurisdiction in civil and commercial matters under the Brussels I Regulation, a corporation is domiciled where[25] it has its statutory seat or has its central administration or has its principal place of business.[26]

---

[20] Case 81/87 *R v HM Treasury and the IRC ex p Daily Mail* [1988] ECR 5505; Case C-208/00 *Überseering BV v NCC* [2002] ECR I-9919.

[21] Case C-210/06 *Cartesio Oktató és Szolgáltató bt* [2008] ECR I-9641.

[22] *Gasque v Inland Revenue Commissioners* [1940] KB 80.

[23] To some extent this will also determine its liability to pay taxes; see above.

[24] *Ministry of Defence and Support of the Armed Services of Iran v FAZ Aviation Ltd* [2007] EWHC 1042 (Comm), [2008] 1 All ER (Comm) 372.

[25] In the sense of 'wherever'.

[26] See Art 60. For the purposes of the United Kingdom, 'statutory seat' means the registered office or, where there is no such office anywhere, the place of incorporation or, where there is no such place anywhere, the place under the law

It is obvious that this cannot be seen as 'the' domicile which determines corporate capacity, for a corporation may, under this slightly inelegant provision, have as many as three domiciles for jurisdictional purposes. It is right that this is possible, for the function and purpose of domicile in the Brussels I Regulation is to define and describe a connection with a Member State sufficient to expose the defendant to the general jurisdiction of the courts of that place; a company or corporation may certainly have more than one of these. It follows that the two varieties of corporate domicile—the common law domicile of the *lex incorporationis*; the Brussels domicile or domiciles for the purpose of jurisdiction in civil and commercial matters—have nothing in common but their unfortunate use of the same word.

2. JURISDICTION OVER CORPORATIONS

Just as is the case for individual defendants, a corporation can be sued in England when process can be served on it. In one respect, service on a corporation is more complex than service on individual defendants, for there can hardly be personal service on an artificial person. But the changes to the methods of service brought in by the Civil Procedure Rules simplified matters considerably, and the statutory changes made by the Companies Act 2006 have made statutory service on companies less complicated.[27]

A company registered under the Companies Acts may be served by leaving the document at, or by posting it to, the company's registered office. An overseas company[28] which has registered statutory particulars with the registrar of companies may be served by leaving the document at, or sending it to, the address of the person authorized to accept service; but if that is not possible it may be left at 'any place of business of the company in

---

of which the formation took place: Art 60(2). The Regulation is at [2001] OJ L12/1.

[27] For the separate nature of the schemes, see *Sea Assets Ltd v PT Garuda International* [2000] 4 All ER 371.

[28] One incorporated outside the United Kingdom: Companies Act 2006, s 1044. The extent of the obligation on such a company to register particulars is governed by ss 1045–48.

the United Kingdom'.[29] In this context a place of business will be taken to mean somewhere fixed and definite and from which the business of the company is carried on. A general guide to whether the company carries on business at such a place is to ask whether it can make contracts there. If there is such a place of business, jurisdictional competence is not limited to the activities of the place of business.[30] Even so, if contracts are not made at the particular place, a court may still find that the activity carried on at the place in question constitutes the carrying on of business, for the statutory rule is not defined in terms of a principal place of business.[31]

As indicated above, in addition to statutory service under the Companies Acts, a company, including an overseas company,[32] may be served in accordance with Part 6 of the Civil Procedure Rules, at any place within the jurisdiction where it carries on its activities, or at any place of business within the jurisdiction. Service is made by leaving the document with a person holding a senior position[33] within the company.

Service is one thing; jurisdiction is another. Where the company is domiciled in a Member State for the purposes of the Brussels I Regulation, Article 22(2) gives exclusive jurisdiction to the courts of the seat[34] of the corporation in proceedings having as their object the validity of the constitution, the nullity or dissolution of companies, or decisions of their organs. This reflects the fact that the birth and death of a company, and the inherent

---

[29] Companies Act 2006, s 1139.

[30] *Okura & Co Ltd v Forsbacka Jernverks AB* [1914] 1 KB 715; cf *Adams v Cape Industries plc* [1990] Ch 433 (CA).

[31] *South India Shipping Corpn Ltd v Export-Import Bank of Korea* [1985] 1 WLR 585 (CA); cf *SSL International plc v TTK LIG Ltd* [2011] EWCA Civ 1170, [2012] 1 WLR 1842 (holding occasional board meeting not enough).

[32] Service under CPR Pt 6 may be made as an alternative to statutory service: CPR r 6.3(2).

[33] CPR r 6.5(3)(b); for the definition of 'senior position', see the Practice Direction 6A. But not if the company does not carry on business within the jurisdiction: *SSL International plc v TTK LIG Ltd* [2011] EWCA Civ 1170, [2012] 1 WLR 1842.

[34] As this seat is specially defined, for the purposes of this rule, by the national law of the court seised, and not as defined by Art 60 of the Regulation: Art 22(2).

validity of acts of its organs, can really only be dealt with in the one place. Of course, the consequences of acts which were based on decisions of corporate organs which were not valid are not comprehended by this rule.[35]

3. CONTRACTS MADE BY CORPORATIONS

The principal issue when dealing with contracts made by corporations is probably one of capacity: of the corporation to make the contract at all and of the organ or officer to bind it. As the private international law of agency is apparently incapable of reform by convention, these questions are still principally left to be resolved by common law rules for choice of law.

If the corporation had capacity under the *lex incorporationis* and the *lex contractus* to enter into the contract, no problems arise. But where it is alleged that it did not, the contract may be *ultra vires* the corporation. Even so, it may in a proper case be estopped by its own conduct from relying on its own incapacity,[36] although it is debatable whether the applicable estoppel principles will be those of the *lex fori* or of the *lex contractus*.[37] Where the corporation had capacity to enter the contract, but the person purporting to act on its behalf did not have authority to so act, the question whether the contract made between the agent and the third party binds or may be relied on by the company is a difficult one, though the better view may be that it is a matter for the *lex contractus* of that contract which was created.[38] The case law is difficult. It seems right that where an agent acts on behalf of a principal, a third party is generally entitled to assume that the agent has such power and authority as he would have under the law which governs the contract which they make. It is true that

---

[35] *Grupo Torras SA v Sheikh Fahad Mohammed Al-Sabah* [1996] 1 Lloyd's Rep 7 (CA); *Speed Investments Ltd v Formula One Holdings Ltd (No 2)* [2004] EWCA Civ 1512, [2005] 1 WLR 1936.

[36] *Janred v ENIT* [1989] 2 All ER 444 (CA).

[37] If there would be estoppel under the one but not the other, there is a conflict of laws; principle suggests that the *lex fori* should defer to the *lex contractus*.

[38] *Chatenay v Brazilian Submarine Telegraph Co* [1891] 1 QB 279; *Maspons v Mildred* (1882) 9 QBD 530 (CA); *Ruby SS Corpn v Commercial Union Assurance Co Ltd* (1933) 150 LT 38 (CA).

where the agent is the representative of a company, a third party will or should be aware that the *lex incorporationis* may place limits upon the extent to which a company can be bound, but this deemed awareness applies more obviously to the legal capacities of the company than to the powers which it has chosen to vest in a particular officer. It follows that there is no reason to make a special rule for contracts made by corporate agents who acted outside their authority: the extent to which the company is bound and entitled should be a matter for the law of the contract made between the agent and the third party. If a corporation has been dissolved and amalgamated with, or to create, another, the question whether dissolution terminates the contract as a source of obligation is a matter for the *lex contractus*. So although the amalgamation may provide for the vesting of all liabilities in the new corporation, it cannot discharge those liabilities, then or later, unless it is also the law applicable to them.[39]

4. WINDING UP OF COMPANIES

The dissolution of companies under the *lex incorporationis* is one thing, but the winding up of companies is more complex. Because of the impact of European legislation, it is necessary to distinguish between solvent and insolvent companies when dealing with winding up.[40] So far as solvent companies are concerned, English courts may wind up a company registered in England.[41] But a solvent company may not be wound up if it has a seat in another Member State and does not have a seat in England.[42]

The regimes which apply to insolvent companies are more complex. The law on the winding up of insolvent companies has been made that way, albeit for good reason, by three principal developments. The first was probably the Insolvency Regulation,[43] which has been in force since May 2002. It applies

---

[39] *Adams v National Bank of Greece and Athens SA* [1961] AC 255.

[40] See Fletcher, *Insolvency in Private International Law* (2nd edn, Oxford University Press, 2005).

[41] Insolvency Act 1986, s 117.

[42] Brussels I Regulation, Art 22(2).

[43] Regulation (EC) 1346/2000, [2000] OJ L160/1. It is not completely clear why the Regulation lies outside the system of 'Brussels' or 'Rome' nomenclature, for

when the centre of main interests of the debtor is in a Member State, and aims to coordinate the insolvency of entities which have their centre of main interests in a Member State. Second, and in approximate parallel to the Regulation, is a statutory scheme made under the auspices of the United Nations, and having the aim to enshrine the policy that insolvency should be concentrated in and organized around procedures at the centre of main interests of the debtor is one which operates in the wider world outside the European Union. Each of these instruments has produced a significant quantity of case law in a rather short time. The third development is that the common law has discovered or rediscovered powers to assist a foreign court exercising insolvency jurisdiction. These appear to have lain dormant for a long time, but have been reawakened to uncertain effect, with the result that they appear to exist in uneasy parallel with statutory powers conferred by Parliament in the form of the Insolvency Act 1986 and the UNCITRAL scheme. All of this makes it difficult to identify a rational point of departure, so we will start with the common law as augmented by the Insolvency Act 1986.

(a) Centre of debtor's main interest not in a Member State: common law and statute

Where the matter is not one governed by the Insolvency Regulation, an English court may wind up a company formed under the Companies Acts.[44] Less expected, perhaps, is the fact that the court may wind up a company not formed under the

---

it is not alone in being concerned with jurisdiction *and* choice of law. The draft EC Convention, on which its text was closely based, was signed by all but one of the Member States at or after meeting in Madrid. The last signature, that of the United Kingdom, was never applied, and it therefore never came into force as a Convention. There appears to be no wish to commemorate the poisonous ancestry of the Regulation by referring to it as the Madrid Regulation, for the reasons which led the United Kingdom to refuse to sign the Convention are a story for our times: a witches' brew of mad cow disease and the consequent ban on the export of toxic meat from the United Kingdom, and hypersensitivity over Gibraltar, of all ridiculous causes. For the story, read Fletcher, *Insolvency in Private International Law* (2nd edn, Oxford University Press, 2005), Ch 7, and weep.

[44] Insolvency Act 1986, s 117.

Companies Acts so long as the company has a 'sufficient connection' with the jurisdiction and is insolvent, and it is not otherwise inappropriate to make the order.[45] A 'sufficient connection' will exist if there are persons in England who could benefit from a winding-up order and there is enough connection with England to justify making the order.[46] Perhaps most unexpected of all is that an insolvent company which has been dissolved under its *lex incorporationis* may be revived for the purpose of being wound up.[47] As Parliament can make any provision it cares to, the creation of what may be seen as a zombie company is not an impossible surprise. But it represents a significant victory for pragmatism over the principle that dissolution is the exclusive concern of the *lex incorporationis.*

Upon making the order, the assets of the company subject to the order are bound by a trust for the benefit of those interested in the winding up. The liquidator is under an obligation to get in all the assets to which the company appears to be entitled, and is obliged to use them to discharge English and foreign liabilities. If there is also a foreign liquidation he is obliged to seek to secure equal treatment for all claimants, not just for English creditors.[48] Many provisions of the Insolvency Act 1986 dealing with orders which may be made in the course of administration or liquidation are unhelpfully silent about what their international scope is intended to be, but they will probably be interpreted as requiring a sufficient connection with England,[49] which may not be very much more helpful, but which probably reflects the common sense of the view that if something cannot be defined well, it is better that it not be defined at all.

So far as concerns a foreign winding up, a liquidator appointed under the *lex incorporationis* is recognized by English private

[45] ibid, ss 220, 221; *Re A Company (No 00359 of 1987)* [1988] Ch 210; *Re Paramount Airways Ltd* [1993] Ch 223 (CA).

[46] *Re A Company (No 00359 of 1987)* [1988] Ch 210; *Re A Company (No 003102 of 1991), ex p Nyckeln Finance Co Ltd* [1991] BCLC 539; *Stocznia Gdanska SA v Latreefers Inc* [2001] BCC 174 (CA).

[47] Insolvency Act 1986, s 225.

[48] *Re Bank of Credit and Commerce International SA* [1992] BCLC 570.

[49] *Re Paramount Airways Ltd* [1993] Ch 223 (CA); cf *Re Seagull Manufacturing Co Ltd (No 2)* [1994] Ch 91 (notice under the Company Directors Disqualification Act 1986).

international law,[50] but there appears to be no authority on the recognition of a liquidator appointed under the law of a third country. The courts of the United Kingdom have a statutory obligation to assist each other in a winding up;[51] in relation to countries outside the United Kingdom the Secretary of State may designate and has designated certain countries whose laws may be applied in an English insolvency, and whose courts (though not liquidators acting on their own authority[52]) may request cooperation from an English court.[53] This means that an Australian court can request cooperation from the English courts, though the critical question will be what form that cooperation may be allowed to take. If, for example, an Australian court requests the remission to Australia of assets in England, to allow these to be distributed in the Australian insolvency which has rules of priority between creditors which are not the same as those which would have been applied in English proceedings, there will be a tension between giving effect to the statutory rules provided for English insolvency and the fact that the main insolvency is in Australia. Though the Insolvency Act would allow the English court to apply Australian law, it does not precisely authorize it to not apply English statutory rules which would govern the case;[54] and in any event, if the assets are remitted to Australia, not everyone will consider this to involve the English court in 'applying Australian law'.[55]

The United States has not been designated under the Insolvency Act, so cooperation with a US insolvency is principally covered by the 2006 Regulations, considered below. But these are incomplete in their coverage, and it remains unclear what a court can do at common law to offer cooperation or assistance which is

---

[50] *Bank of Ethiopia v National Bank of Egypt and Ligouri* [1937] Ch 513.

[51] Insolvency Act 1986, s 426(4).

[52] *Re BCCI SA (No 9)* [1994] 3 All ER 764.

[53] Insolvency Act 1986, s 426(4); and see further below the reference to the Cross-Border Insolvency Regulations 2006.

[54] *Re BCCI SA (No 10)* [1997] Ch 213.

[55] *Re HIH Casualty & General Insurance Ltd, McGrath v Riddell* [2008] UKHL 21, [2008] 1 WLR 852; *New Cap Reinsurance Corpn v Grant* [2011] EWCA Civ 971, [2012] QB 538 (appeal dismissed without reference to this point, *sub nom Rubin v Eurofinance SA* [2012] UKSC 46, [2012] 3 WLR 1019).

not otherwise provided for in legislation. In one case in which a court had been asked to exercise a common law power to cooperate with a US insolvency, the Privy Council had been prepared to make an order requiring a shareholder in a local company to be stripped of its shareholding and this value vested instead in a committee of unsecured creditors, more or less on the say-so of a US court.[56] It was not easy to see where the power to do this came from.

The question recently arose whether an English court could accede to a request from a US court that it assist it by giving effect to an avoidance judgment entered against corporate officers who had not submitted to the jurisdiction of the US court. The Supreme Court held that there was no such power at common law, and that it could not;[57] it considered the earlier Privy Council decision to have been wrong. The enforcement of foreign judgments in insolvency, at least, is governed by the ordinary rules of private international law which were not liable to be circumvented by a request for cooperation. The court may have wondered whether, if such 'cooperation' were ordered today in respect of orders made by US courts, what would happen tomorrow were a Russian court to make similar orders against those said to have siphoned funds out of a Russian company (whose patron-oligarch had been made an outlaw) in administration in Moscow. Cooperation with foreign insolvencies is all very well, but there are times when it should be left to governments to identify those to whom cooperation is and is not to be extended. The common law is not well equipped to conduct a quality audit of foreign insolvency courts; and a common law power to cooperate beyond the terms authorized by a recent statute is a dangerous thing to discover. On the other hand, the rule of the common law that a judgment *in personam* may be recognized if the judgment debtor submitted to the jurisdiction of the foreign court has been held to be satisfied by a creditor submitting a claim in the insolvency to the liquidator, sufficient to allow the English court to enforce a foreign judgment ordering

---

[56] *Cambridge Gas Transport Corpn v Official Committee of Unsecured Creditors of Navigator Holdings plc* [2006] UKPC 26, [2007] 1 AC 508.

[57] *Rubin v Eurofinance SA* [2012] UKSC 46, [2012] 3 WLR 1019.

the return of preferential payments. Not everyone will be persuaded, however, that the simple filling in of a form by a creditor and its posting to a liquidator is the legal equivalent of the issue of a writ by a claimant exposing him, there and then, to the full range of judicial power of the supervising court.[58]

(b) Centre of debtor's main interests in a Member State: Insolvency Regulation

In insolvencies to which the Insolvency Regulation applies, this instrument prescribes and limits the jurisdiction of the courts of Member States in relation to the opening of insolvency proceedings; the choice of law for the insolvency proceedings; and the recognition of judgments from other Member States ordering the opening, conduct, and closure of such proceedings. Its purpose is to bring order to an area which was excluded from the original jurisdictional scheme of what is now the Brussels I Regulation, and for which the coordination of the judicial function had been particularly problematic.

The Regulation applies to debtors wherever they are domiciled, but the critical requirement is that a debtor's main interest is centred in a Member State. In the nature of things, this test is likely to be hardest to use in the cases in which its guidance is the most needed, for the kind of business for which this is a crucial definitional tool is likely to be cross-border in the first place; and there is more than a trace of suspicion that some companies, faced with the prospect of insolvent winding up, may try to perform a kind of forum shopping to a Member State whose insolvency law is more forgiving of bad business and more prepared to allow a fresh start than are some others. Still, the general rule is that for a company the centre of main interests is presumed to be the place of the registered office,[59] although it seems inevitable that scrutiny of the whole of a company's activities may be required where the issue of location is contested.

---

[58] ibid.

[59] Article 3(1). The expression has an autonomous meaning. The presumption applies even though the debtor is a subsidiary of a company incorporated elsewhere, on the broad footing that it is the appearance to those dealing with the debtor which is the principal concern: Case C-341/04 *Re Eurofood IFSC Ltd* [2006] ECR I-3813.

The Regulation applies to collective insolvency proceedings which involve the complete or partial divestment of a debtor and the appointment of a liquidator,[60] whether the debtor is an individual or a corporate body. It excludes insurance undertakings and credit institutions.[61]

The overall aim is to ensure that, within the European Union, the lead role is given to a single court, and to relegate to a subordinate role proceedings in all other courts. Accordingly, 'main proceedings' may be opened only in the Member State in which the centre of a debtor's main interests is situated at the date of the request to open the proceedings, even if it later moved.[62] 'Secondary' or 'territorial' proceedings may be opened in any Member State in which the debtor has an 'establishment';[63] although their effect is confined to assets situated[64] in the Member State in which the secondary or territorial proceedings are opened, they may be opened before main proceedings are.[65] The law which is generally applicable to insolvency proceedings and their effects is the *lex fori*,[66] which governs most issues,[67] but exceptions are made for a list of other matters for which this would not be the appropriate choice of law.[68] An order from a court in a Member State opening insolvency proceedings must be recognized, from the time it becomes effective, in all other Member States, and be given the same effect as it has in the state of origin.[69] Judgments relating to the conduct and closure of insolvency proceedings are recognized in all other Member States,[70] and enforcement of orders takes place under the Brussels I Regulation. A liquidator appointed in the main

---

[60] Including a trustee or an administrative receiver appointed under a floating charge: Art 1(1).

[61] Article 1(2).

[62] Case C-1/04 *Re Staubitz-Schreiber* [2006] ECR I-701.

[63] Any place of operations where the debtor carries out a non-transitory economic activity with human means and goods.

[64] Defined in Art 2(g).

[65] They are then known as territorial proceedings.

[66] Article 4.

[67] Article 4.

[68] Articles 5–15.

[69] Articles 10 and 17.

[70] Article 25.

proceedings is to be recognized in all other Member States[71] and accorded the powers which he has under the law of the state of his appointment. If there are secondary proceedings in another Member State, his powers are limited in relation to those assets; but the various liquidators are under an obligation to share information and to cooperate with each other.[72]

From time to time a court has to determine whether proceedings brought or intended to be brought before a court fall within the material scope of the Brussels I Regulation or under the Insolvency Regulation. The guiding principle is that the right or duty relied on is part of the ordinary civil law, the fact that proceedings are brought against a liquidator does not remove them from the material scope of the Brussels I Regulation; but if they seek to establish rights or obligations which are peculiar to insolvency, then they will fall outside the Brussels I Regulation and may instead fall within the Insolvency Regulation.[73]

(c) Centre of main interests not in a Member State: the 2006 Regulations

In a development reflecting that established by the Insolvency Regulation, the UNCITRAL produced a Model Law on cross-border insolvency which was given effect in the United Kingdom in the form of the Cross-Border Insolvency Regulations 2006.[74] The Model Law, as given effect in England, does not provide a comprehensive scheme to regulate every aspect of cross-border insolvency, but does aim to pave the way for states to enact legislation to provide for the recognition of foreign insolvency procedures (though not the recognition of foreign judgments *in personam*),[75] the right of foreign representatives to have access to courts, requests for cooperation, and judicial coordination of concurrent proceedings. Its guiding principle is that an insolvency being organized at the centre of main interests of

---

[71] Article 18(1).

[72] Article 31.

[73] For example, Case C-111/08 *SCT Industri AB v Alpenblume AB* [2009] ECR I-5655; Case C-292/08 *German Graphics Graphische Maschinen GmbH v van der Schee* [2009] ECR I-8421.

[74] SI 2006/1030.

[75] *Rubin v Eurofinance SA* [2012] UKSC 46, [2012] 3 WLR 1019.

the debtor should be recognized and given priority, and the role of the English courts in such a case is a secondary and supplementary one.[76] It is unsurprising that the extent to which this will require an English court to make orders which it would not have made as part of an English insolvency is yet to be fully mapped.

[76] SI 2006/1030, Sch 1, Art 20.

INDEX